Edited by
David Painting

Foreword by
the Hon Fiamē Naomi Mataʻafa

FRESH FROM THE WORD 2024

**DAILY BIBLE STUDIES
FROM AROUND THE WORLD**
READ · REFLECT · GROW

IBRA
International Bible Reading Association

spck

First published in Great Britain in 2023

Society for Promoting Christian Knowledge
The Record Hall
16-16a Baldwin's Gardens
EC1N 7RJ

International Bible Reading Association
5–6 Imperial Court
12 Sovereign Road
Birmingham B30 3FH
www.ibraglobal.org

British Library Cataloguing-in-Publication Data
A catalogue record for this book is available from the British Library

ISBN 978-0–281–08988–8
eBook ISBN 978-0–281–08989–5
ISSN 2050-6791

1 3 5 7 9 10 8 6 4 2

Typeset by Fakenham Prepress Solutions, Fakenham, Norfolk NR21 8NL
First printed in Great Britain by Clays, Bungay, Suffolk, NR35 1ED

eBook by Fakenham Prepress Solutions, Fakenham, Norfolk NR21 8NL

Produced on paper from sustainable sources

Fresh from The Word aims to build understanding and respect for different Christian perspectives through the provision of a range of biblical interpretations. Views expressed by contributors should not, therefore, be taken to reflect the views or policies of the Editor or the International Bible Reading Association.

The International Bible Reading Association's scheme of readings is listed monthly on the IBRA website at www.ibraglobal.org and the full scheme for 2024 may be downloaded in English, Spanish and French.

Contents

Foreword

Talofa (hello) and warm greetings from Samoa.

The invitation to write the Foreword for *Fresh from The Word 2024* was unexpected and daunting, as by no means do I consider myself an authority on the Bible. Nevertheless, I was compelled to accept if for no other reason than to bear witness to how much *Fresh from The Word* has deepened my faith journey.

My church, the Congregational Christian Church of Samoa, has used the IBRA daily readings for as long as I can recall. The themes and daily readings are translated into a Samoan booklet and distributed annually, Church-wide; not only in Samoa, but to our member congregations in Australia, New Zealand and the USA. It was not until 2020 that I was introduced to *Fresh from The Word*, where the daily reflections explain the readings in the context of the issues of the time, and also through the lives of the weekly contributors; their search for answers and the revelations they have received through reading the Bible and praying to our Living God.

As a small child, reading the Bible had two main purposes: to understand the word of God and to improve one's reading. We played games as to who could find a Bible verse the fastest and who could recite all the books of the Old and New Testament. Many of us had it in our minds that the places in the Bible were in heaven; far away – exotic and unfamiliar. Of course, this changed when we grew older. Nevertheless, the distance of time, place and different cultures presented a challenge to us in connecting with God as depicted in the Bible.

During the Easter period in 2023, a Samoan artist depicted Christ on the cross with a traditional male tattoo covering the body from the waist down to the knees. Many Samoans thought that this was disrespectful of our Lord and Saviour, while others interpreted the artwork as a cultural claiming of Christ for our people.

The contributions of the world Christian community in *Fresh from The Word* brings the good news to all in real time. It bridges the distances referred to above and offers a spiritual path for our individual and collective walk with God. Samoa is a Christian country, enshrined in our constitution: *Fa'avae i le Atua Samoa* ('Samoa is founded on God'). Through the fellowship of the IBRA community, through the sharing of *Fresh from The Word*, I live with the faithful in the kingdom of God.

the Hon Fiamē Naomi Mata'afa
Prime Minister of Samoa

How to use *Fresh from The Word*

How do you approach the idea of regular Bible reading? It may help to see daily Bible reading as spiritual exploration. Here is a suggestion of a pattern to follow that may help you develop the discipline but free up your mind and heart to respond.

- Before you read, take a few moments – the time it takes to say the Lord's Prayer – to imagine God looking at you with love. Feel yourself enfolded in that gaze. Come to scripture with your feet firmly planted.
- Read the passage slowly before you turn to the notes. Be curious. The Bible was written over a period of nearly 1,000 years, over 2,000 years ago. There is always something to learn. Read and reread.
- If you have access to a study Bible, pay attention to any echoes of the passage you are reading in other parts of the biblical book. A word might be used in different ways by different biblical authors. Where in the story of the book are you reading? What will happen next?
- 'Read' yourself as you read the story. Be attentive to your reactions – even trivial ones. What is drawing you into the story? What is repelling you? Observe yourself 'sidelong' as you read as if you were watching a wild animal in the forest; be still, observant and expectant.
- What in scripture or in the notes is drawing you forward in hope? What is closing you down? Notice where the Spirit of Life is present, and where negative spirits are, too. Follow where life is leading. God always leads into life, even if the way feels risky.
- Lift up the world and aspects of your life to God. What would you like to share with God? What is God seeking to share with you?
- Thank God for being present and offer your energy in the day ahead, or in the day coming after a night's rest.
- Finally, the † symbol is an invitation to pray a prayer that has been written for the day's reading. You are invited to say these words aloud or in silence with thousands of other readers around the world who will be reading these notes on the same day in dozens of languages.

Acknowledgements and abbreviations

The use of the letters a or b in a text reference, such as Luke 9:37–43a, indicates that the day's text starts or finishes midway through a verse, usually at a break such as the end of a sentence. Not all Bible versions will indicate such divisions.

We are grateful to the copyright holders for permission to use scriptural quotations from the following Bible versions:

NIVUK   Scripture quotations marked NIVUK are taken from The Holy Bible, New International Version (Anglicized edition). Copyright © 1979, 1984, 2011 by Biblica. Used by permission of Hodder & Stoughton Ltd, an Hachette UK company. All rights reserved. 'NIV' is a registered trademark of Biblica. UK trademark number 1448790.

NKJV   Scripture quotations marked NKJV are taken from the New King James Version. Copyright © 1982 by Thomas Nelson, Inc. Used by permission. All rights reserved.

NLT   Scripture quotations marked NLT are taken from the Holy Bible, New Living Translation, copyright © 1996. Used by permission of Tyndale House Publishers, Inc., Carol Stream, Illinois 60189, USA. All rights reserved.

NRSVA   Scripture quotations marked NRSVA are taken from the New Revised Standard Version of the Bible, Anglicised Edition, copyright © 1989, 1995 by the Division of Christian Education of the National Council of the Churches of Christ in the USA. Used by permission. All rights reserved.

NRSVCE   Scripture quotations marked NRSVCE are taken from the New Revised Standard Version: Catholic Edition, copyright 1989, 1993 the Division of Christian Education of the National Council of the Churches of Christ in the USA. Used by permission. All rights reserved.

Introduction from the Editor

I am writing this early in the new year of 2023, and, having reflected on the past year, I am now wondering what the world will be like in a year's time when we begin to read this new edition. What changes will we have seen and what global events will be fresh in our minds? What highs and lows will we have encountered? What surprises will we have had that brought unexpected joy? And in the midst of all those things, how will we make sense of it all? That's where *Fresh from The Word* comes in!

In this edition we spend three weeks telling the whole story of the Bible so we have a framework in which to better understand each part – just as the picture on the box of a jigsaw puzzle helps us understand where each piece fits. Alongside that, our readings through 1 Chronicles culminate in Solomon building the temple, and those from Mark and Luke show us how the Master Builder came and lived among us. We see how God began to build his church, looking at leaders in the New Testament – and how Paul encouraged one of those leaders as we read his letters to Timothy.

Then, when the building gets broken, we study how to be reconciled. As we walk through Nehemiah we see a worked example of how God uses his people to rebuild. And in our readings from the Song of Solomon we see the aim of it all: an intimate, loving relationship with God himself.

'A God of Surprises' is one of our themes this year. Having just enjoyed Christmas morning with young grandchildren, my mind is filled with images of their happy faces as they tore through the wrapping to see what was underneath. May you be similarly surprised by joy as you encounter God this year through *Fresh from The Word 2024*!

Hope for a new year (1)

Notes by **Andy Heald**

Andy is a professional communications, marketing and fundraising consultant, and has led fruitful young adult and small group ministries. He is an active pilgrim exploring how to introduce a fatherless generation to their heavenly Father. In 2019 he sold his home in Sussex and, with his wife and three young daughters, began travelling Europe in a motorhome, to explore God's principles of faith, freedom and family and to live a different way. Andy has used the NRSVA for these notes.

Monday 1 January
What are you looking for?

Read John 1:35–39

As he watched Jesus walk by, he exclaimed, 'Look, here is the Lamb of God!' The two disciples heard him say this, and they followed Jesus. When Jesus turned and saw them following, he said to them, 'What are you looking for?'

(verses 36–38a)

Aged fourteen, I dreamed of the woman I would marry and her features (albeit in silhouette) were emblazoned on my mind. Seven years later my gaze landed on a beautiful girl during my first week at university. I knew she was the one – rather like those two disciples on seeing Jesus.

John preaches the coming of God's kingdom to his disciples and declares that their long-awaited Saviour, the Lamb of God, is here. Immediately after John points Jesus out, the disciples follow him. Later declaring they had found the Messiah, they see the true light come into the world (John 1:9).

The Romans named January after Janus, the god of doorways, transitions, beginnings and ends. The new year invites us to see things with a fresh perspective. In Europe we see the first signs of spring, a new season come, and the days get lighter and longer.

Are you seeking the end to something or the beginning? Meeting that young woman (my wife of many years now), I stepped through a doorway into a new life. Jesus knows what we are looking for and offers us hope in new life, shining light into our darkness. He is the door (John 10:9), but it's our choice whether we cross his threshold.

† Jesus, in our desire for new life, help us to look for you. Thank you that you are the door to our new beginnings.

Tuesday 2 January
Come and see!

Read John 1:43–46

Philip found Nathanael and said to him, 'We have found him about whom Moses in the law and also the prophets wrote, Jesus son of Joseph from Nazareth.' Nathanael said to him, 'Can anything good come out of Nazareth?' Philip said to him, 'Come and see.'

(verses 45–46)

'Come and see, Daddy!' is a frequent request from my young daughters. Sceptical that their latest find (often random garden objects or household junk) will be a genuine treasure, I'm happy to simply hear about it rather than stop what I'm doing. But that's not enough for them. They need me to see it and share in their excitement, despite my indifference. So it is with Philip.

Philip knows the cultural legends of the Israelites' messianic King and, responding to Jesus' direct invitation to follow him, finds Nathanael to tell him, too. He is excited! Can you imagine that moment for Philip? After hundreds of years of waiting, an oppressed people's promised rescuer turns out to be real. Wouldn't you be bursting to tell others?

The invitation to follow Jesus is infectious, yet it can be dampened by our prejudice. Like me when my girls demand that I look at their latest discovery, Nathanael reveals his doubt, but Philip is persuasive. The invitation to come and see something for yourself is powerful, as those who extend such an invitation stake their own belief and credibility on it. There's something irresistible about it. Is it of little significance or is there something here that's really worth seeing? Do we dare to hope?

I suspect I turn my children's invitations down too often and occasionally miss seeing something new, interesting or beautiful. Have you accepted the invitation to come and see Jesus? Or have you persuasively extended it to someone else? Nathanael is daring enough to step past his doubt and take a look for himself, and so should we.

† Lord Jesus, help us to overcome our prejudices and scepticisms. Help us to see you in people, places and circumstances where our knowledge or experience clouds our perspective. Help us see you for ourselves.

For further thought

Is Jesus is calling out to you? Directly or through a friend? Are you sceptical? Is he what you're looking for? Go and see for yourself.

Wednesday 3 January
Don't worry

Read Matthew 6:25–34

*'Do not worry, saying, "What will we eat?" or "What will we drink?" …
Your heavenly Father knows that you need all these things. But strive
first for the kingdom of God and his righteousness, and all these things
will be given to you…'*

(verses 31a, 32b–33)

The apostle James writes, '…You do not even know what tomorrow
will bring' (James 4:14a). In my career I have spent hours writing
financial forecasts and making recommendations to charity leaders
about investing resources to increase income. Yet the truth is, no
one knows what will happen tomorrow, let alone in one, three or
five years' time.

As I write this, I know that many people are worried about rising
costs, especially in terms of energy, food and housing. How will
they survive? Jesus tells us we don't need to be concerned about
these because God already is. We all need to focus on Jesus'
kingdom. By doing that collectively, God, through us, will meet all
our needs.

Jesus makes a promise about faith, telling us to be humble and
trust him. It can feel more responsible to use our earthly means
to meet our needs – often by striving to be in control and make
things happen ourselves. A few years ago, my wife and I gave up
our jobs, mortgage and the stability of modern life to follow Jesus
on a pilgrimage around Europe in a motorhome. We experienced
lockdowns in several countries, but never lacked a place to stay or
food to eat. It was a formative lesson in trusting God. Truthfully,
it was scary at times, but our faith grew as we allowed God to
evidence those promises and give us comfort and peace.

Jesus tells us not to worry, but to change our focus – placing our
hopes, needs and future lives on him, not on ourselves.

† Father, give us today our daily bread. Help us to focus on the now and not to be
distracted by the tomorrow that never comes. Help us to be free from unbelief and
to humbly trust in you.

For further thought
Write down your needs for today. Then at the end of the day, ask
yourself if God supplied them. Repeat this every day. Is God faithful
to his promises?

Thursday 4 January
God's love never ceases

Read Lamentations 3:22–26

The steadfast love of the LORD never ceases, his mercies never come to an end; they are new every morning; great is your faithfulness ... The LORD is good to those who wait for him, to the soul that seeks him.

(verses 22–23, 25)

Are you filled with new hope each day? As a child I experienced significant trauma and distanced myself from God. I couldn't believe in a God who would allow the things to happen that I had experienced. Years later, God revealed himself to me – though I did not seek him – and his presence became unquestionable to me.

When I responded to the call to follow him, I embarked on a journey to understand God's own experience of trauma. Not only did Jesus experience the pain and suffering of the cross, but our heavenly Father, compelled by his love for us, had to let it happen. This revelation lifted me, helping me to understand that God sees us in this broken world that we have cursed (Genesis 3), and watched his only begotten Son die so that we can be restored to him and to the fullness of eternal life. I learned that, despite my love for God temporarily ceasing, his love for me never had.

The writer of Lamentations also changes his view of God, moving from sorrow about God's wrath upon him to remembering that God's love is steadfast, unceasing and offers never-ending mercy. That gives him hope. A hope we can share in.

I'm not one for new year's resolutions (eating just one chocolate quickly ends a diet for me), so I take great comfort in knowing that, despite my sin and failings, I can receive God's forgiveness every day. New mercies mean a fresh start each day. We can leave our past behind and hold on to our hopes for the future, whichever day of the year it is.

† Father, thank you for your unending love and new mercies every day. Help us to remember your promise every morning and to seek you and your kingdom. Awaken us with fresh hope and help us to leave past hurts behind.

For further thought

Read Lamentations 3. Consider your inheritance (portion) from God. Is it good? What does waiting for God look like for you?

Friday 5 January
I am with you

Read Isaiah 43:1–9

*'Because you are precious in my sight, and honoured, and I love you …
Do not fear, for I am with you … Everyone who is called by my name,
whom I created for my glory, whom I formed and made.'*

(verses 4a, 5a, 7)

My first long-distance flight was to New York. I hadn't flown
much before that and was unsettled by the descent. I became
increasingly scared as the ground quickly approached. Eyes closed,
I reached out and gripped my fiancée's hand. Knowing she was
with me made me less fearful.

Being hopeful is a journey. A journey *of*, and *in*, faith. We can't
always see God or his actions, but of course he knows that. He
knows about our struggles, the overwhelming waters and burning
fires in our lives, and how they can make us feel afraid. So he
reminds us who we are and what we're worth. We don't need to
be fearful because 'I AM', the only God, is our creator and we are
precious to him. And then he comes close. 'I will be with you,' he
promises. He knows that we sometimes need our hands held, too.

But there's more. God raises our gaze to his big picture of our
restoration. He zooms out, opening our eyes as he opens his
hands, gathering everyone who is called by his name together, for
his glory. What a story! Hope can grow.

Do you have any big dreams or audacious hopes? God's promises
are in the large and in the small. I find it easy to be hopeful about
little things, but it can be harder to hope for bigger things: a
career, owning a house, finding a spouse, healing, or that wars will
end and strivings cease. Yet, thanks to Jesus' sacrifice on the cross,
we can be sure of what we hope for (Hebrews 11:1).

† Help us to not be fearful, but to remember that we are yours, Lord. Thank you for
promising to be with us through the struggles and battles of our lives.

For further thought

Write down your hopes and dreams. Pray about them regularly.
Journal your conversations with God. Will your hope grow and
your dreams be realised?

Saturday 6 January
A rainbow of hope

Read Genesis 9:13–17
'When I bring clouds over the earth and the bow is seen in the clouds, I will remember my covenant that is between me and you and every living creature of all flesh; and the waters shall never again become a flood to destroy all flesh.'

(verses 14–15)

Whenever I see the story of Noah with cartoon animals in a wooden boat I wince. The illustration doesn't bother me; the focus does. This story illustrates the deathly consequences of sin and God's life-giving, compassionate love for his children. Cute animals cannot communicate the scale of human depravity that God saw in Noah's time or his sorrow about making human beings (Genesis 6:6). A wooden boat cannot convey God's grace and protection, which held back the waters from devastating the land (Job 12:15), or the grace he extended through the hundred years in which the ark was built. Without this context, the powerful truth of the rainbow remains unseen.

Thankfully, in the midst of the great wickedness and the evil human thoughts (Genesis 6:5), God saw something else: Noah. Noah was a righteous man and walked faithfully with God (Genesis 6:9). He found favour in God's sight, and God promised to preserve his life.

Having kept Noah and his family alive, God gave them a sign of his promise. Light shining through the clouds revealed the beautiful phenomenon we call a rainbow.

Hope isn't always tangible or visible. It is often something we cling to in dark places, sometimes with the fragility of a match flickering in the wind, threatening to be snuffed out. Sin is like a cloud in our lives, blocking out the light and threatening us with death. Like Noah, we, as God's children, need a saviour. Our hope is the light of the world, shining into our darkness. Jesus is our promise, our sign, our rainbow of hope.

† Thank you, Father, that your Son died on the cross, covering our sin. Jesus, thank you that your living water does not drown us, but cleanses and births us into new life.

For further thought
What are the signs of Jesus in your life? How does his light shine into the dark clouds that threaten you?

Hope for a new year (2)

Notes by **Helen Van Koevering**

 After living in Mozambique for twenty-eight years, Helen, raised in England, moved to the USA with her family. She is now Rector of Lexington's St Raphael Episcopal Church. As a parish priest and Director of Ministry in Niassa, she witnessed a move of the Spirit that doubled the size of the church. Seeing this within an economically and environmentally vulnerable country taught Helen a great deal about the hope, thankfulness and joy of nature, the church and community life. Helen has used the NRSVA for these notes.

Sunday 7 January
Nature will awake

Read Joel 2:22–25

'O children of Zion, be glad and rejoice in the Lord your God ... he has poured down for you abundant rain, the early and the later rain, as before. The threshing-floors shall be full of grain, the vats shall overflow with wine and oil. I will repay you for the years that the swarming locust has eaten.'

(verses 23, 25a)

Northern Mozambique has known a generation of war: ten years of war for independence from Portuguese colonial rule, followed by a civil war fuelled from outside in those turbulent last years of apartheid in South Africa. An estimated two million Mozambicans were displaced; more than a million were refugees. The new country was devastated.

But as peace settled, people returned to their land and many brought with them the church that had nurtured them through those years as refugees. For the Anglican Church of northern Mozambique, the growth was like the wildfire that farmers used to clear land for planting. We coined the phrase 'running after the Spirit', while others talked of the change to the 'fabric of the nation'. All were in thankful awe that God's time for the healing of this heartbroken nation had come.

And with the fields cleared, the people waited for the early rains: the sign that the land was ready to be fruitful. Just as they had waited for the land to be restored, they waited again. If those rains were delayed, the tension was palpable. Their arrival brought inexpressible relief, embodied in danced celebration; fullness of life for those who had suffered as they waited on God's promise.

† Loving God, you walk with us through our suffering. Your grace holds us close, like those poured-out rains bringing new life to the earth. Thank you for your grace-filled love!

Monday 8 January
Spring flowers are coming!

Read Isaiah 35:1–2

The wilderness and the dry land shall be glad, the desert shall rejoice and blossom; like the crocus it shall blossom abundantly, and rejoice with joy and singing. The glory of Lebanon shall be given to it, the majesty of Carmel and Sharon.

(verses 1–2a)

When the wilderness blooms, when the desert is fertile, it's as if nature is singing a chorus of 'Alleluia!' It is amazing that harsh conditions over many years seem to pave the way for the stunning explosion of blossoms in the desert.

This passage is addressed to a people in exile: to the people of Israel in literal exile, held captive in other lands, but also in all times and places. It is as if the earth is a visual reminder to our hearts of a rising 'Alleluia!' at work under God's watchful eye. January may be a frosty season or a rainy season, depending on where we find ourselves in this world, but seeds are lying dormant, awaiting the new season of growth.

Isaiah paints a picture of the ransomed returning to Zion, where the road to restoration will be paved with abundance, safety and pools of water. The drought will be over. The journey home will be made with song. A vision of all that is good, true and beautiful will return.

Salvation is a journey of wholeness. God woos a broken people home to himself, to be restored as Zion was, and to establish ways of justice and righteousness in places of dryness. Isaiah vividly and poetically imagines for us the glory of God in all of his creation, like a desert in bloom – a place of surprise, a moment of delight, a sight for sore eyes – so that we can let hope arise and find ourselves singing a new song. Call it joy and sing its tune.

† Creator God, you know us better than we know ourselves. Before we know what we need, you provide the way home. Nature sings your joy. Teach us to do the same. Amen

For further thought

Remind yourself today of moments in your life when you have been surprised by joy, known hope or experienced real peace. Dwell on those memories today.

Tuesday 9 January
Being thankful

Read Colossians 3:12–17

As God's chosen ones, holy and beloved, clothe yourselves with compassion, kindness, humility, meekness, and patience ... Clothe yourselves with love, which binds everything together in perfect harmony. And let the peace of Christ rule in your hearts, to which indeed you were called in the one body. And be thankful.

(verses 12, 14–15)

All the affirmations listed here are rooted in God's character, witnessed in Jesus and placed squarely on the disciples of Jesus. We are to reflect the truth that we are chosen, holy and loved by our creator, our friend and the lover of our souls.

Paul talks a lot about our nature in terms of it clothing us. We are to 'undress' from the negative, divisive and disruptive, and to 'reclothe' ourselves with 'compassion, kindness, meekness, and patience'. Yes, we still have our human natures, and there will be disagreement between us. Forgiveness will be necessary, and we must regularly acknowledge our need for a refilling of the Holy Spirit in order to honour Christ and others in everyday life. All this must be bound together and held by love.

Just as we clothe ourselves daily, we are to reclothe ourselves in love, in honour of Christ and the body of Christ. Just as a community is held together by its common respect for the law, a believing community is bound together by love. All relationships, decisions and plans are to honour the peace of Christ and to seek shalom; a resting place of wholeness and harmony. It takes practice, intention and honesty, and the key to it all is in being thankful.

Opening our eyes to all that is God's gift to and for us, we are to let thankfulness transform our outlook, our inner lives and our desires as we seek to act in the name of Jesus. We are called to be his disciples, together, as his living, incarnate body around the world, in our neighbourhoods and within our families.

† Teach us to be more like you, Lord Jesus. Show us the way, remind us. Remake us to be your disciples and to love as you loved us. Amen

For further thought

What does it mean to you to 'clothe' yourself with these attributes of Christ? How can you be like Christ today?

Wednesday 10 January
Hold on to good

Read 1 Thessalonians 5:16–24

Rejoice always, pray without ceasing, give thanks in all circumstances; for this is the will of God in Christ Jesus for you. Do not quench the Spirit. Do not despise the words of the prophets, but test everything; hold fast to what is good; abstain from every form of evil. May the God of peace himself sanctify you entirely.

(verses 16–23a)

It is winter in the northern hemisphere and summer in the southern hemisphere, but we all are still wishing each other a happy new year. This letter to the Thessalonians is encouraging to read at the beginning of the year, with its comforting reminders that following Jesus is the right path, and that Jesus is with us to the end of time. In the previous chapter, the Thessalonians are admonished not to be afraid or discouraged. Instead, they are to encourage one another with confidence in the vision of Christ's return. Today's verses turn to how we should live our lives in the light of that understanding.

'Rejoice always.' These instructions are brief and general. The verbs are plural. All are to rejoice. Not at a particular time, nor only in good times, but *always*. The Thessalonians are to pray always. They are to give thanks; not just for the good times, but 'in all circumstances'. The Thessalonians suffered and endured, and perhaps they found that it was not easy to follow Christ. But here the call is simple and direct: rejoice, pray and give thanks, regardless of what happens.

They are also told to 'hold fast to what is good'. Seeing fauna and flora joyfully growing on mountainsides during a trip I took to Yosemite National Park, this phrase took on new meaning. The nature of faith is a balance of seeking the freeing truth of the Holy Spirit as he leads us in the way of love, peace and joy, and holding fast to the already heard and known words of the prophets. In these ways, we shall know what is good. If a flower can grow in a hard place, so can faith.

† Lord Jesus, show me what is good, and teach me to rejoice and be thankful always. May I choose the good today in all that I say and do because you are with me. Amen

For further thought

What do you count as good in your life today? Are you grounded and holding fast to what is good, letting the light of your understanding of Jesus encourage you?

Thursday 11 January
Grounded in love

Read Ephesians 3:14–21

I pray that, according to the riches of his glory, he may grant that you may be strengthened in your inner being with power through his Spirit, and that Christ may dwell in your hearts through faith, as you are being rooted and grounded in love. I pray that you may have the power to comprehend, with all the saints, what is the breadth and length and height and depth, and to know the love of Christ that surpasses knowledge, so that you may be filled with all the fullness of God.

(verses 16–19)

What incredible words we are reading today! For those feeling weak, Paul's prayer declares the Spirit's strength to hold us faithfully in the love of Christ. For those feeling alone, he prays for understanding to know that we stand with all the saints. For those who feel purposeless, anxious and afraid, Paul prays we will know that we are rooted and grounded in love. He prays that we will know we are God-filled as we look towards God's reconciling face in Jesus Christ, the One who lived, died and rose again for the world.

God's mission of reconciliation answers all human sin and suffering. Our lives of faith through Christ and with the Holy Spirit are primarily about relationships of trust, and our journey towards God and one another. Calling the journey a 'mission' helps us to see ourselves as pilgrims. With faith and trust, we join in God's mission of reconciling all creation, all things, all people, to God's immeasurable love. Reconciliation is the key to God's mission for the healing of estranged relationships between God and humanity, within the human community and within God's world.

Our individual brokenness and personal relationships need God's healing. Much of what distances us from God is held in our inner being, and these words today are worth repeating, gently and slowly, prayerfully and meditatively. Be reminded of God's love. Know that you have been welcomed into the expansive, ever-present power of God's healing love. And join in God's mission to our neighbours and the world.

† Our Father, holy is your name! Your kingdom come, your will for reconciliation be done. And may it begin in me. Amen

For further thought

Write out today's reading and pin it somewhere you will see it regularly, perhaps a mirror or a fridge door. Pray for God's reconciling love to be known.

Friday 12 January
Strengthen your knees!

Hebrews 12:1–2, 12–13
Lift your drooping hands and strengthen your weak knees, and make straight paths for your feet … Be healed.

(verses 12–13)

Every year on 4 July, the city of Lexington, Kentucky, holds prepared for those who love a run or walk race spanning six miles. It is not a marathon, but neither is it just a jog in the park. Any race takes preparation, the right food and equipment, and the building of stamina, energy and focus to finish the race and receive the prize (even if it is just a cool drink at the finish line!). But as this is a road race, practice runs are also needed to strengthen the knees on such a hard surface.

The book of Hebrews reads like a sermon. Admonishment is followed by encouragement. It was written at a time when large numbers of Jews had confessed faith in Jesus Christ (and were facing persecution), yet the writer of Hebrews sees that they haven't yet got to grips with the unique nature of the Christian faith. They were still clinging to old beliefs, and they needed to move forward to full maturity in Christ – the author and perfecter of their faith, and the One who had suffered the cross with the vision of reconciling joy, offered for all the world.

Hebrews encourages believers to persevere and to reflect their faith in reverent, awe-filled worship. Christian worship is indelibly marked by the cross and the cruciform life of Christian discipleship. Our focus on this in the face of our reconciling God is like 'strengthening our knees' for the race of life set before us, whatever hardship or joy may come, whatever service we are called to, inside or outside our communities of faith.

† Lord, we worship you in spirit and in truth. Strengthen us for your service in your world, as we commit to following you always. Amen

For further thought
Which area of your life of discipleship and service to others needs strengthening? Bible study, contemplative prayer, generosity and discipline are all needed. Committed communal worship is vital for the strength of our witness and mission together.

Saturday 13 January
A new beginning

Read 1 Peter 1:3–9

Blessed be the God and Father of our Lord Jesus Christ! By his great mercy he has given us a new birth into a living hope through the resurrection of Jesus Christ from the dead, and into an inheritance that is imperishable, undefiled, and unfading, kept in heaven for you … You are receiving the outcome of your faith, the salvation of your souls.

(verses 3, 9)

Hope is made real in the circle of life, celebrated with each new season and each newborn child. The birth of a first child is also the birth of a mother. In matrilineal northern Mozambique, a dancing ceremony performed by those who are already mothers blesses new mothers and newborns, welcoming both to new birth and identity. The newborn is handed to each in the circle of mothers, symbolising the circle of life that was completed by birth and yet to be completed by the fullness of life. The new mother would no longer just be called by her first name, but rather *mae* ('mama') of the named child (and later *vovo* or 'grandmother'): Mae John, Mae Suzanna, Mama Helena. The mother could never stop being a mother, whatever happened. She was changed in her very nature and being.

Peter does not use metaphor or simile to explain the spiritual transformation birthed in our lives. He simply writes: 'He has given us new birth.' This is a hope-filled birth into a sure inheritance in heaven and within the shield of God's power for our lives of faith. Grief and suffering may come, faith may be tested, but love will hold us, and belief and joy will bring life and salvation. All those born into this world have a journey to discover and life-long learning ahead. The birth that Peter describes brings us into a life within the landscape of God's grace, love, faith and companionship.

This birth makes all the difference.

† Thank you, Father, for new birth made possible through the resurrection of Jesus. Thank you, also, for those who birthed us, both physically and spiritually: our parents, families, friends, leaders and teachers. Thank you for those who have blessed us so that we can be a blessing to others. Amen

For further thought

Write a list of all those who have blessed your life. Then list the names of lives you have blessed. Consider how blessing changes lives.

The Gospel of Mark (1)

1 Preparing the way

Notes by **Tim Yau**

Tim Yau is a Pioneer Missioner for the Anglican Diocese of Norwich, encouraging missional practice: 'not trying to get people to go to church, but trying to get the church to go to the people'. He's one of the few Chinese heritage priests in the Church of England and wants to see more minority ethnic vocations, believing, 'To be it, you have to see it.' He's frequently found immersed in the latest sci-fi epic, and dreams of being a superhero. Tim has used the NIVUK for these notes.

Sunday 14 January
John's journey to Jesus

Mark 1:1–15

'Prepare the way for the Lord, make straight paths for him.'

(verse 3b)

Wearing a top hat, tailcoat, silk waistcoat and cravat, I looked like I should have been the centre of attention, but I wasn't. All eyes were on the bridegroom and not on me, his best man. Likewise, the Gospel of Mark opens with John the Baptist, a striking figure in the manner of an Old Testament prophet, the like of which hadn't been seen for 500 years. However, this story isn't about John. He is simply there to 'prepare the way for the Lord'.

John is a wild, holy man living an off-grid existence in the wilderness. Some saw him as the prophet that Elijah had promised 'before that great and dreadful day of the LORD comes' (Malachi 4:5).

John preaches repentance to his generation, living under the oppressive occupation of the Roman Empire. John senses the Messiah is coming, a holy, anointed king who will be more powerful than him. He recognises that holy revolution is imminent, but he isn't to be the figurehead.

John baptises Jesus and witnesses him being empowered by the Holy Spirit, then endorsed and affirmed by his Father God. John has prepared the way, but Jesus will lead the world-transforming movement forward.

† Jesus, allow us to prepare the way for you in our world, and help us to step aside so that you might lead your holy revolution. Amen

Monday 15 January
First disciples, first miracles

Read Mark 1:16–34

'Come, follow me,' Jesus said, *'and I will send you out to fish for people.'*

(verse 17)

I am an Instagrammer, Facebooker, Tweeter, WhatsApper and YouTuber. I have social media followers, subscribers and likers. Portuguese footballer Cristiano Ronaldo has 475 million followers on Instagram, whereas I have a paltry 117. In social media terms, followers equate to influence and revenue. Whether you're marketing an online business, giving product endorsements or receiving direct advertising revenue from the platform, followers equal funds.

Today, people follow others on social media in order to be informed, entertained, educated and inspired. Many still want to connect with people who are similar to themselves, so they like a particular brand or personality.

I only know a few of my social media followers personally. I interact with others online, but I wouldn't recognise the vast majority if I met them face to face. I ask very little of my followers, and I doubt they'd do anything if I asked them to. This is not the way of Jesus!

When Jesus invited people to follow him, it came with immediate consequences and purpose. They were to get up, leave what they were doing and go with him at once. Simon, Andrew, James and John hadn't been searching for an aspirational celebrity to emulate, but these hardworking fishermen suddenly left their livelihoods, families and community to follow Jesus.

At the time, the closest people got to influential celebrities were the rabbis, who would choose only the best-of-the-best disciples to teach. However, Jesus – the itinerant, holy, miracle-working rabbi – found these fishermen, saw their potential and believed they could be like him: preaching, healing, exorcising revolutionaries. So when he called them, they followed.

† Jesus, help us to hear your call to follow you, and to see what you see in us. Give us the courage to follow you wherever you might lead us in your holy revolution. Amen

For further thought

What's stopping you from following Jesus' call? What if you focused on the things you might gain over the things you might lose? How would that help?

Tuesday 16 January
Prayer, purpose and preaching

Read Mark 1:35–45

Jesus replied, 'Let us go somewhere else – to the nearby villages – so that I can preach there also. That is why I have come.'

(verse 38)

As a fresh-faced teenager, I was sitting in a circle of trainee nurses during our first day of college when our tutor asked us, 'Why are you here?'

The apprentices began to explain their valid reasons as to why they wanted to pursue the vocation. As one of only two males in the cohort I felt scrutinised, so when the question came to me, I panicked and said: 'I don't really know. I thought it was a good idea at the time.'

There were some embarrassed looks from around the room and an icy glare from my tutor, followed by some heavy scribbling in her notes.

The truth was, I wasn't clear about my career choice as an adolescent. I was just trying nursing out. I didn't yet know who I was supposed to be or what I was supposed to do.

Thankfully, we meet Jesus as a thirty-something; confident and clear about his purpose. We can only imagine the conversations he had with his family, friends and neighbours, nagging him to get married, reprimanding him for not staying in the family business or lecturing him for not approaching a rabbi to follow.

Jesus knew his heavenly Father's will. The solitary place of prayer was a practice that informed his mission and gave him the clarity to know what to pursue. Neither the temptation of physical comforts, the recognition of his people nor the incessant needs of those who were sick in mind, body or spirit would direct his way.

Jesus had come to preach – to make known, publicly and loudly, the good news about the kingdom of God (Mark 1:14-15).

† Jesus, may we hear your voice and follow your lead. May our words and actions announce your heavenly kingdom. May we not be swayed from the task by the distractions of this world. Amen

For further thought

What is God's purpose for you? How can you publicly and loudly make known the good news of the kingdom of God through your role?

Wednesday 17 January
Friendship, faith and forgiveness

Read Mark 2:1–12

When Jesus saw their faith, he said to the paralysed man, 'Son, your sins are forgiven.'

(verse 5)

I was living in the medieval city of Norwich and looking to buy my first home there. With a limited budget, I discovered a housing estate where the house prices were significantly cheaper than elsewhere. When I told friends where I was considering buying, they would exclaim, 'That's a bad area!'

I have to admit that my friends' warnings put me off buying there, and God surprisingly led me to become part of the estate's church. Once I'd befriended local residents and moved beyond the stereotypes, it was obvious that not everyone who lived there was bad. However, any association with this area meant a bad reputation, which was hard to shake off.

In the culture of Jesus' time, reputation was important. A bad reputation meant exclusion. The psalmist wrote: 'Have mercy on me, LORD; heal me, for I have sinned against you' (Psalm 41:4). The common belief was that sin and sickness were interlinked; that if you were sick there was probably some unresolved sin in your life. We don't know what caused the man's paralysis, but to the bystanders it implied a sinful reputation.

So the paralysed man's friends, who saw beyond his sickness, took him to Jesus. They battled with crowds and roofing, but mostly against society's suspicions that if you're in a bad way you must be a bad person. Jesus cut through the situation and pronounced a forgiveness of sins. He knew that the man's supposed sin had led to his estrangement from his community and his God, and that he needed spiritual restoration before physical healing.

Forgiveness restores broken reputations, relationships and communities.

† Jesus, forgive us when we lazily stereotype people and label them as bad. Give us eyes to see people as you see them, then the courage, compassion and companionship to carry them to you. Amen

For further thought

Who is labelled 'bad' in your community? How could you meaningfully connect with those people? What would forgiveness and restoration look like between you and them?

Thursday 18 January
Sinners, sceptics and the Saviour

Read Mark 2:13–17

Jesus said to them, 'It is not the healthy who need a doctor, but those who are ill. I have not come to call the righteous, but sinners.'

(verse 17)

Music boomed through the walls and the muffled sounds of partying seeped in under the door. We sat in a circle and prayed for our friends as the teenage house party erupted around us.

Coming to faith in Christ at fifteen saved me from a lot of adolescent issues, but sadly my church weighed me down with some extra-religious baggage. The Pentecostal church that adopted me was at the fundamentalist end of the Christian spectrum, with a literal interpretation of scripture that advocated strict adherence to the biblical principles they highlighted. Church was a holy people, and anyone outside that was a sinner to be saved or avoided. No pubs, parties, or play; just prayer, praise and preaching.

They encouraged us to read the Bible for ourselves, and we read that Jesus went to parties with 'sinners', so we felt we should do the same. However, our church had moulded us to believe that everything happening at parties was bad, and we didn't have a positive role model for how to behave at a party. The drinking, the music and the anarchic behaviour made some want to leave, fearing they would be polluted by it, while others wanted to denounce the party and the devil's influence altogether. We wanted to be like Jesus, but we were acting like the Pharisees.

Jesus entered into the world, not as a spectator keeping his distance or a police officer taking names and investigating crimes, but as a doctor offering healing and wholeness to those who recognised their brokenness. Jesus' holy revolution broke down barriers.

† Jesus, wherever you are is holy ground. Help us to follow you wherever you go, forgive us when we refuse to acknowledge the people you commune with and transform our attitudes to be like yours. Amen

For further thought

What religious baggage are you carrying? Who do you refuse to commune with? Who are the spiritually ill you can introduce to Doctor Jesus?

Friday 19 January
Method, message and maturity

> **Read Mark 2:18–22**
>
> *'And no one pours new wine into old wineskins. Otherwise, the wine will burst the skins, and both the wine and the wineskins will be ruined.'*
>
> (verse 22a)

The school hall was buzzing with activity as children and adults gathered around tables, playing, eating and talking together. The quiet reflection corner was covered in prayers written on sticky notes and the biblical thought for the day was provoking discussion around the room. It felt like church was really happening. However, one sceptical visitor stood on the sidelines and asked, 'This is all well and good, but when are they coming to *church*?'

This sceptic had been schooled in an expression of church that met on Sundays in a stone building with a bell tower and performed formal liturgical worship with monologue-style sermons and prayers. For the sceptic it couldn't be church unless it was in a church building. The method of worship had been confused with the message of Jesus.

Britain's wartime prime minister, Sir Winston Churchill, requested that Parliament's House of Commons be rebuilt exactly as before, after it was bombed during the London Blitz. In his speech to the House of Lords, he famously said: 'We shape our buildings and afterwards our buildings shape us.'[1]

The same is true of our religious buildings and practices. They end up shaping our faith, but they're not supposed to be the focus of our faith; they're simply signposts to 'Jesus, the pioneer and perfecter of faith' (Hebrews 12:2).

Jesus was confronted about his disciples' decision not to fast. Likewise, I was challenged about a fresh expression of church not being in, or like, the parish church. Thankfully, Jesus declared that new wine needs new wineskins; flexible containers that allow for growth and maturity. New places for new people in new ways.

† Jesus, you call us into your holy revolution. Forgive us when we slip into religiosity. May we flow with the Holy Spirit's creativity, while honouring the traditions of the faith passed on to us. Amen

For further thought

Which devotional acts are sacrosanct to you? How would stopping them affect your faith? What might the Spirit lead you to if you did stop them?

[1] 'Churchill and the Commons Chamber': www.parliament.uk/about/living-heritage/building/palace/architecture/palacestructure/churchill (accessed 28 April 2023).

Saturday 20 January
Pause, perspective and prayer

Read Mark 2:23–28

Then [Jesus] said to them, 'The Sabbath was made for man, not man for the Sabbath. So the Son of Man is LORD even of the Sabbath.'

(verses 27–28)

Returning home after a holiday you notice subtle changes. Usually for me it's how different the neighbour's children look. Stepping away from a place for a while gives a fresh perspective on it.

In today's reading, Jesus responds to detractors about the principle of Sabbath: a holy pause moment, a time to rest and take stock.

I share a house with a teenager, junior and preschooler, all with competing and conflicting wants and needs. At the end of the day, my wife and I are often exhausted, and the idea of a self-reflective moment seems elusive. Pausing can be problematic!

When I was a child, businesses closed on Sundays and churches met. However, it was the most boring day of the week for me. My family didn't do church, country walks or life-affirming family activities; it was just a day with nothing to do.

Unfortunately, due to the busyness of modern life, not all of us get a regular Sabbath to rest and reflect on our personal circumstances. A return to a nationally agreed Sabbath seems unlikely, as keyworkers will always be needed at their posts. However, some form of regular personal Sabbath rhythm of rest from normal activity is a must for our wellbeing.

Sabbath is a space to pause with God in prayer. It gives us a sense of perspective in our lives. Jesus said, 'Come to me ... and I will give you rest' (Matthew 11:28). Often I don't feel like it. I'm too busy, tired or distracted. But when I Sabbath with God, I am restored.

† Jesus, we find our rest in you. Forgive us when we ignore you and the weariness of our minds, bodies and souls. May we be restored by your Spirit and by our heavenly Father's love. Amen

For further thought

How do you find rest? How will you create Sabbath space to pause with God? What can you do to encourage Sabbath in your community?

The Gospel of Mark (1)

2 Sowing the seed

Notes by **Raj Bharat Patta**

Raj Bharat Patta is proud to celebrate his identity in multiple settings: Dalit, Christian, Asian, (im)migrant, India, UK, church, academic, postcolonial, public sphere, husband, father and friend. He currently serves as a minister in the Methodist Church and completed his PhD at the University of Manchester. He is a member of the Inter Faith Theological Advisory Group (IFTAG) of Churches Together in Britain and Ireland (CTBI), and sits on the Cliff College Committee and on the steering group of the Centre for Theology and Justice. Raj has used the NRSVA for these notes.

Sunday 21 January
Law or life?

> **Read Mark 3:1–12**
>
> *Then [Jesus] said to them, 'Is it lawful to do good or to do harm on the sabbath, to save life or to kill?' But they were silent.*
>
> (verse 4)

'Life in all its fullness' is one of the focal aims of Jesus' mission and ministry. No tradition, no ritual, no text, no practice, no empire can stop Jesus from giving life. Celebrating life in all people is what matters for Jesus. In order to affirm and celebrate life, he is willing to risk contravening and trespassing on any man-made rule, because Jesus cares about people's lives no matter who they are.

In the text today, the Pharisees were waiting to see if Jesus would stick to their tradition of keeping the Sabbath holy or if he would heal the person with the withered hand. It was a tricky situation. If he had chosen the former, he would have been celebrated by the Pharisees as one who upheld the law, but Jesus chose the latter and healed the person, conveying that he chooses life over law and love over rules.

There are many today who continue to suffer as a result of tradition, law, caste, race, gender, sexuality or class. 'Is it lawful to do good or to do harm on the Sabbath, to save life or to kill?' remains a pertinent question.

† May the Spirit of God empower us to join with you, Lord, in choosing life, in healing people and in not being limited by tradition, ritual or law. Amen

Monday 22 January
Team Jesus

Read Mark 3:13–19

And he appointed twelve, whom he also named apostles, to be with him, and to be sent out to proclaim the message, and to have authority to cast out demons.

(verses 14–15)

Look at the composition of Team Jesus. They were from different backgrounds. Peter, Andrew, James and John – partners in a fishing business – were probably comfortably off, and Matthew the customs official must have been well-to-do. They were of different political ideologies (Simon the Zealot had extreme nationalist views, while Matthew was a pragmatist, collecting taxes for the Romans). They also had different personalities. Peter was impulsive and passionate, while James and John – called 'the sons of Thunder' by Jesus – were boisterous. Thomas had an intense disposition. Matthew was probably methodical, Philip was rather hesitant and lacked confidence, and Andrew was positive and enterprising.

What we learn from all these variations of disciple in Team Jesus is that Jesus loves diversity. He chooses people with different opinions, perspectives, backgrounds, identities, personalities and characters, then forms them into a community of disciples. Team Jesus is a diverse, inclusive, multicultural and pluralistic community. It is not a monocultural, homogenous, uniform group. The purpose Jesus called his disciples for was to be with him and to proclaim that same message of love and inclusivity, and to have the authority to cast out the demons of society.

It is the same call that he has for us as the church: to be an inclusive, multicultural, diverse community that demonstrates the love of God. And to take the love of Jesus to those on the margins, to proclaim the gospel of love to the unloved and to cast off the demons of injustice.

† Help us, O God, to be a community of disciples that celebrates diversity and inclusivity. Help us to be a rainbow community of disciples, relevant for you today. Amen

For further thought

Take an audit of your local congregation. Are we diverse, pluralistic and inclusive enough? What are our mission priorities?

Tuesday 23 January
A willingness to be misunderstood

Read Mark 3:20–34

When his family heard it, they went out to restrain him, for people were saying, 'He has gone out of his mind.'

(verse 21)

Jesus was declared insane for the way he spoke, the things he claimed, the people he met with and the things he did. He radically altered the doctrine and practice of the law, cutting across the religious authorities, who considered themselves to be custodians of the law. If Jesus had upheld the religious laws and practices, these Pharisees, Sadducees, Scribes from Jerusalem and Herodians wouldn't have had such a problem with Jesus. But Jesus disrupted the status quo, broke down the walls of division, resisted empire, befriended people who were considered outcasts, embraced the excluded, and built a just and inclusive community.

This is not a rational approach designed to keep the peace or to remain personally safe. On the contrary, he was misbranded as a person who had 'gone out of his mind'; a person who had Beelzebul, the ruler of the demons, inside him; a person with unclean spirits.

I wonder how people view us as Christians and as the church. Are we known by our love or by our doctrine? By those we include or those we exclude? By giving up our rights or by insisting on our traditions? Perhaps this passage is a call for us to be known in our communities by our love.

Like Jesus, we may be misbranded, yet it is worth it for the cause of love. May the Spirit of God be with us in contesting the demons of our times and in striving for the kingdom of God here on earth. Amen.

† Lead us, Spirit of God, so that we will be known as followers of Jesus Christ by our love and only by our love. Help us to be prepared to be misbranded and to strive for love to thrive. Amen

For further thought

How are we, as the local church, branded in our communities? Are we known by our radical and reckless love for others?

Wednesday 24 January
Choking

Read Mark 4:1–20

'And others are those sown among the thorns: these are the ones who hear the word, but the cares of the world, and the lure of wealth, and the desire for other things come in and choke the word, and it yields nothing.'

(verses 18–19)

Serious cases of choking – when a piece of food or an object blocks the top of the trachea and causes difficulty with breathing – are terrifying. Without emergency medical treatment, the patient will die. In the parable of the sower, Jesus describes how thorns in the ground cause a growing seedling to be choked, with the same tragic result.

He explains that the blockage to life and growth, the thorns, are the cares of the world, the lure of wealth or desires for other things, and that this choking prevents the word from transforming our lives. And this, of course, has an impact beyond our own experiences of God. Instead of bringing 'good news to the poor', we become like the rest of the world; so focused on our own comfort and security that we become instrumental in maintaining and even causing poverty.

Jesus invited us to take up our cross and follow him. The consumeristic world today attracts us with the lure of wealth, calling it prosperity. But when we seek that, when money becomes our goal and directs our choices, we choke out the possibility of something so much better: life in all its fullness – for us and for those we are called to serve.

There are many in the world who do not have the choice to pursue. The poor are not only materially poor; they are also poor in terms of life choices. Those of us who have the luxury of choosing to pursue the allure of wealth must learn to do as Jesus did when he laid aside his rights, his comfort and his security. Otherwise we will continue to choke the poor.

† O Lord, where we are choking, help us to clear our ground. Give us your compassion for the poor as a sign of our yielding the fruit of the word. Amen

For further thought

Work out some remedies to help with the type of choking caused by the allure of wealth. How could these be used as a means of alleviating poverty in your context?

Thursday 25 January
The parable of the lamp

Read Mark 4:21–25

[Jesus] said to them, 'Is a lamp brought in to be put under the bushel basket, or under the bed, and not on the lampstand?'

(verse 21)

During our childhood in India, we held cottage prayer meetings at different congregation members' houses in the evenings for forty days during the season of Lent. Those were the times of power cuts, so we had no electricity at peak times in the evenings. We had to carry a big kerosene lantern to every house, place it on a wall and hold our prayer meetings in that light. If the lantern was placed on the ground, many people didn't benefit from its light, but when it was placed on a wall or an elevated place it reached out to more people.

If the word is a lamp, where have we put that lamp? Keeping the word under a basket or bed does no one any good. The purpose of the word is to show light to many people, up on its lampstand. If the word is not impacting the lives of people in our communities, it is evidently under a basket or bed.

Likewise, if life is a lamp, where have we put that life? Self-seeking in order to meet our own needs is not the purpose of life. Life has to be up on a lampstand, showing love and light to many people around us. That is what makes life purposeful and meaningful. Life is like a lamp, designed to illuminate the path for others. It is to offer people warmth and to accompany them in their difficulties and vulnerabilities.

† Dear God, help me to see that the word is a lamp unto my feet and a path of transformation for many. Help me to acknowledge that life is a lamp to lighten and enlighten others in our neighbourhoods. Amen

For further thought

Try worshipping God with a lamp today. Make a checklist of how you are making the word and your life like a lampstand in your community.

Friday 26 January
Like a mustard seed

Read Mark 4:26–34

'It is like a mustard seed, which, when sown upon the ground, is the smallest of all the seeds on earth; yet when it is sown it grows up and becomes the greatest of all shrubs, and puts forth large branches, so that the birds of the air can make nests in its shade.'

(verses 31–32)

What is the purpose of an apple tree? To be fruitful and yield a great harvest of apples. Similarly, what is the purpose of a mustard tree? To grow mustard seeds and yield a great harvest of mustard seeds. This is a very human-centred view of the tree's purpose, where we selfishly think that trees grow fruit or seed for the benefit of humankind.

But when Jesus narrated this parable, he said that the mustard seed would grow to be the greatest tree, never mentioning harvesting the mustard seeds. He said it was 'so that the birds of the air can make nests in its shade'. The purpose of the tree is not simply to produce seed-containing fruit that will go on to produce more trees. Nor is its purpose just to provide fruit for people to eat. Of course, perpetuating the species and feeding people are important functions, but these must never displace the bigger purpose: to provide shelter for creatures that would otherwise have no protection.

Perhaps we view the church as a tree designed to produce seeds so that it can replicate itself, or as a tree that grows fruit to nourish us. We should certainly be involved in evangelism, promoting growth and continuity. And of course the church needs to nourish believers with the good fruit of teaching, discipleship and pastoral care. But perhaps we have become so focused on these aspects that we have missed another dimension: that the church, like the tree, is not just for our benefit. It is there to provide a place of safety and protection for those who are completely unlike us.

† O Lord, thank you for the church and all that we receive from it. Help us to see beyond that and to embrace those who need a place to shelter.

For further thought

How can we become places of welcome and safety to those who have nowhere else to go?

Saturday 27 January
Jesus calms the storm

Read Mark 4:35–41

*He woke up and rebuked the wind, and said to the sea, 'Peace! Be still!'
Then the wind ceased, and there was a dead calm.*

(verse 39)

It had been an exhausting day; the crowds ever-present and demanding. The disciples were probably glad to get back to something many were familiar with – sailing – and to take a break from the people. In reality, they were heading across the lake to free a man distressed by demons – and even though they were now in a boat, many from the crowd simply got into other boats and followed. As with today's celebrities, there was no escape!

And then a huge storm hit the boats on the sea; a supernatural storm that was beyond their fisherman skills. Jesus was asleep in the stern of the boat and the disciples warned him of their peril, crying out for help. Jesus rebuked the storm (or perhaps the demons causing it) and said, 'Peace! Be still!' The wind ceased and there was 'dead calm'.

Jesus didn't just protect his disciples and the boat they were travelling in. By stilling the storm, he saved the entire fleet and the crowds in the other boats. Jesus stilled the storm rather than just saving his own boat.

This is the gospel of Jesus Christ we are called to. We are not to be self-centred, only thinking about ourselves and our own boats; we are called to join with Jesus in stilling the storm, saving all the boats and the creation around us. Jesus' peace is a peace for the entire creation, not just for a select few. The salvation offered by Jesus is ever-widening and all-inclusive. The peace offered by Jesus is available to the whole of creation.

† Dear God, help us to celebrate the all-inclusive saving grace of Jesus for your entire creation. Help us to join with Jesus in offering your peace to all around us. Amen

For further thought

Reflect the all-inclusive nature of Jesus' saving grace and list the ways you have offered this saving grace to the community around you.

Calling

1 Biblical figures are called

Notes by **Paul Nicholson SJ**

Paul Nicholson is a Roman Catholic priest belonging to the Society of Jesus, a religious order popularly known as the Jesuits. He works in London as Socius (assistant) to the Jesuit Provincial. He edited *The Way*, a journal of Christian spirituality, and is author of *An Advent Pilgrimage* (2013) and *Pathways to God* (2017). Since his ordination in 1988, he has worked principally in ministries of spirituality and social justice, and was novice master between 2008 and 2014. Paul has used the NRSVA for these notes.

Sunday 28 January
Abraham, the first of many

Read Isaiah 51:1–3

Look to Abraham your father
and to Sarah who bore you;
for he was but one when I called him,
but I blessed him and made him many.

(verse 2)

Each passage we'll be praying through this week speaks of someone being called by God, and of that individual's response. In one of the central prayers of the Roman Catholic liturgy, Abraham is called 'our father in faith'. He stands as the foundation for all who believe in the God who called himself 'the God of Abraham, the God of Isaac, and the God of Jacob'.

Abraham's call is a call into uncertainty, supported only by his trust in a promise. He has to leave behind all that is familiar and travel into an unknown land. He is already an old man, and his wife Sarah has borne him no children. It would have been easier to stay where he was and enjoy his comfortable lot. But he responds to God's call by setting out, and by repeatedly committing himself to the promises God makes to him, even when it seems impossible that they can be fulfilled.

Isaiah invites us to recall Abraham's example and to learn from it. Maybe it's Abraham's trust in God that strikes you most, or his persistence, or his readiness to tread a hard road. As you think of him, what echoes do you hear of your own journey of faith?

† Lord, help me to remember your call to me. Give me the gifts I need to keep responding in trust, as Abraham did.

Monday 29 January
Samuel, called as a child

Read 1 Samuel 3:1–10

Eli said to Samuel, 'Go, lie down; and if he calls you, you shall say,
"Speak, LORD, for your servant is listening."' So Samuel went and lay
down in his place. Now the LORD came and stood there, calling as
before, 'Samuel! Samuel!' And Samuel said, 'Speak, for your servant is
listening.'

(verses 9–10)

At the time when Samuel was growing up, we are told that 'the word of the Lord was rare'. People, even good people, went about their daily lives with little expectation of being called by God. It's no surprise, then, that Samuel is slow to recognise who is calling him. It takes help from someone else for him to identify what is going on.

Christians sometimes speak of having received a 'vocation'; a technical term for the experience of being called by God. This can sound mysterious … frightening, even. After all, many cultures are rightly wary of those who claim to hear disembodied voices. Yet Eli's advice to the boy is simply to indicate his willingness to listen further. He believes that this type of patient and open listening will be enough to reveal the true source of all that Samuel hears, and to enable him to know how best to respond.

As you read this passage, take time to reflect in that same patient and open way, on whatever sense you have of God calling you. This could range from a dramatic conversion that changed the course of your life ever after, to a word or phrase of scripture that has struck you in the past and has continued to mean something to you since then. You might recall those who have taken the role of Eli in your life, helping you to recognise the voice of God amid all the competing voices in the world around you. Or maybe you have been able to help others in this way.

† Lord God, make me ready to hear your call today – wherever and whenever it comes, and whomever you send to help me to recognise it.

For further thought

Is there anything in your own life that is making it more difficult to hear and recognise the ways in which God is calling you?

Tuesday 30 January
Noah, called to serve

Read Genesis 7:1–5

Then the LORD said to Noah, 'Go into the ark, you and all your household, for I have seen that you alone are righteous before me in this generation' … And Noah did all that the LORD had commanded him.

(verses 1, 5)

According to this story from the book of Genesis, God's call to Noah involves very precise instructions. He is not simply to follow, preach or trust; rather, he is given a building project with detailed and exact specifications, to the bemusement of his neighbours. He has already been singled out by God for his 'righteousness', and now he further demonstrates this by doing all that is asked of him.

The stakes are high here. God's plan is nothing less than to preserve all life on earth, human and animal, by the work Noah is to carry out. There were, presumably, other ways this could have been done. Perhaps a representative sample of humanity and the world's fauna could have been led to a high mountain, a peak spared the general deluge. But the story of Noah points to something we see repeatedly in scripture; something that continues to this day. In each generation God seeks out those who will hear him and work alongside him to carry out his plans on earth.

You are unlikely to be called by God to build a huge wooden vessel to save all humankind from a worldwide deluge. But there may well be specific, concrete tasks that God is entrusting to you, and to you alone. Even today, animal species are threatened with extinction and people fleeing danger entrust themselves to fragile crafts to cross oceans. Is there a call to you from God to help those facing situations like that? Or is there some other role God is calling you to play?

† God, help me to see, in the concrete details of my everyday tasks, the ways in which you are calling me to serve those around me.

For further thought

The Noah's ark story appeals to children. What spoke to you when you first heard it? What makes it attractive to children today?

Wednesday 31 January
Amos, a humble shepherd

Read Amos 7:14–17

*Then Amos answered Amaziah, 'I am no prophet, nor a prophet's son;
but I am a herdsman, and a dresser of sycamore trees, and the Lord took
me from following the flock, and the Lord said to me, "Go, prophesy to
my people Israel."'*

(verses 14–15)

Amaziah is the priest of Bethel, the royal sanctuary at this time
in Israel's history. Amos appears out of nowhere, prophesying
the kingdom's downfall. Unsurprisingly, Amaziah opposes him
and tries to get him sent away, but Amos will neither depart, nor
modify, his message. He's not a 'professional' prophet, praising the
king in God's name; he's a simple herdsman. But he is a herdsman,
conscious of responding to what he hears from God and faithful
to the mission he has been given.

This passage invites you to reflect on your own response to
God's call to spread the gospel message to your family, neighbours
and friends. Every Christian receives this call. You don't have to be
a minister, a 'professional', to share the good news. Perhaps this is
not too difficult (although you may find it difficult enough!) when
the message is one of love, joy, God's care for every person and
an ultimate promise of salvation. But it's much more challenging
when you have to point out situations where those around you,
or society as a whole, is failing to live in the way that God wants.

Not everyone is called by God to proclaim this kind of message to
those in political power, as Amos was. But each of us will, at times,
encounter others – even those near to us – who are living by values
that are contrary to those of the gospel. Strength is needed here,
certainly; the strength to bear Christian witness. But discernment is
also required, to know when and how to speak out. You may wish
to pray for these gifts today.

† Lord, give me the strength to speak out in your name, and the discernment to
know when and how best to do so.

For further thought

As you hear or read the news today, take note of events or
situations that are at least in part contrary to the values of the
gospel.

Thursday 1 February
Called and called again

Read Jonah 3:1–6

The word of the LORD came to Jonah a second time, saying, 'Get up, go to Nineveh, that great city, and proclaim to it the message that I tell you.' So Jonah set out and went to Nineveh, according to the word of the LORD.

(verses 1–3)

Jonah is clearly someone who is reluctant to respond to the call of God. As this passage makes clear, this is the second time God has asked him to act. It has taken Jonah being trapped for three days inside a whale to convince him to speak God's word to the people of Nineveh!

But why is it that Jonah is so slow to answer God's call? The text doesn't spell this out in detail. It isn't that he doubts that he is called, or that he is too lazy to respond or that he doesn't know what to do. Maybe he just wants to see the evildoers of Nineveh punished. Perhaps what is deterring him is that his prophetic word might be successful. He knows that God is merciful, so when he threatens the people of Nineveh with God's retribution, they will – if they repent – be forgiven and receive God's love instead. Maybe Jonah fears that he will look foolish for predicting a destruction that will never come about. And that is exactly what happens.

In many cultures and societies today there is little overt opposition to the Christian message. But the Christian faith, and by implication those of us who hold to it, are regarded as irrelevant at best. Sometimes we are even considered ridiculous for believing in incredible events and trying to live by seemingly impossible ideals. It's no wonder that a call to bear Christian witness will not always be received with enthusiasm. I am no more enthusiastic about looking foolish in the eyes of those around me than Jonah was.

† Give me courage, Lord, to answer your call to live by your word, even if I look foolish in the eyes of others as a result.

For further thought

How might you try to answer those who regard the Christian message as both incredible and foolish?

Friday 2 February
Jeremiah, called and empowered

Calling – 1 Biblical figures are called

> **Read Jeremiah 1:4–10**
>
> *Then I said, 'Ah, Lord God! Truly I do not know how to speak, for I am only a boy.' But the Lord said to me, 'Do not say, "I am only a boy"; for you shall go to all to whom I send you, and you shall speak whatever I command you.'*
>
> (verses 6–7)

The Jesuit religious order to which I belong is known for its long training. At a prayer service to mark the end of this period – sixteen years after we had set out on this road – two of us chose the passage above as one of the readings. For us, it captured something important about the call that we felt we were answering. The priest leading the service saw it a little differently, however. He remarked, with a smile, to those gathered: 'Sixteen years of preparation and they still think of themselves as too young to preach the gospel!'

Anyone who hears a call to bear witness to Christ is likely to think of him or herself as ill-equipped for the task. I'm too young or too old; not virtuous enough or insufficiently well-read; I have too many other commitments or need more time to prepare. It's not difficult to find good excuses as to why our response to God should be put off until a later date or passed on to someone else who will make a better job of it.

What unites all these excuses is that they focus on *me* and *my* abilities: my gifts and talents, the time I have (or don't have) available. The truth is that God has been hearing these excuses since long before the time of Jeremiah, and he has an answer ready. God always promises to remain with those he calls, equipping them with everything they need. All we have to do is trust and act accordingly.

† Lord, when I feel ill-equipped to answer your call, remind me of your constant presence and all the gifts you have given me.

For further thought
Which of the many gifts you have received from God has best enabled you to bear witness to him?

Saturday 3 February
The disciples, called by Jesus

Read Matthew 4:18–22

As he walked by the Sea of Galilee, he saw two brothers, Simon, who is called Peter, and Andrew his brother, casting a net into the lake – for they were fishermen. And he said to them, 'Follow me, and I will make you fish for people.' Immediately they left their nets and followed him.

(verses 18–20)

Some years ago, I watched a famous actor reciting, from memory, St Mark's Gospel. He paced the stage as he spoke, giving a dramatic force to the various scenes. He was using the King James version of the Gospel; its seventeenth-century English just different enough from present-day speech to give a different emphasis to phrases or passages at times. One that stood out for me was a single word that Mark uses a lot in the King James Bible: 'straightway'.

Hearing the Gospel proclaimed in its entirety – rather than in the separate scenes offered as standard in our church services – left me with a powerful impression of Jesus on the move. He never stopped! Over and over again he would tell a story, perform a miracle or offer some teaching. Then 'straightway' he'd be off, carrying his message to the next town or village until he reached Jerusalem. There was an urgency about his mission. And an urgency in calling people to share it.

That urgency is reflected in the passage we're considering today. Simon, Andrew, James and John, leave what they're doing straightaway to follow Jesus; to catch others and engage them in the task of hearing God's call in their own lives. Those people, in turn, want to pass the message on, and so it continues through the centuries until it reaches us. But it mustn't, and won't, stop here. If you're reading this book, the call has already reached you. How are you going to respond, straightaway?

† Jesus, when I hear your call, as Peter and John heard it by the Sea of Galilee, help me to respond quickly, as they did.

For further thought

If you have the time, either today or tomorrow, try reading the whole of St Mark's Gospel in one go. Note the impression it leaves on you.

Calling

2 God calls us

Notes by **Catrin Harland-Davies**

Catrin is a Methodist minister and currently works as a tutor at The Queen's Foundation for Ecumenical Theological Education in Birmingham, UK. She teaches biblical studies and directs the foundation's Centre for Continuing Ministerial Development. She is passionate about helping people to discern, be equipped for and live out their vocations, whether that be lay or ordained – a passion she developed during ten years of chaplaincy among university students, where her role was often that of a companion in discipleship. Catrin has provided notes for ten days using the NRSVA version.

Sunday 4 February
Set apart for the gospel

Read Romans 1:1–6

Paul, a servant of Jesus Christ, called to be an apostle, set apart for the gospel of God ... the gospel concerning his Son ... through whom we have received grace and apostleship to bring about the obedience of faith among all the Gentiles for the sake of his name.

(verses 1, 3a, 5)

Imagine you, or your local community or church, have a dream – one that will cost a lot. It may be your perfect holiday, a church roof or a new school. If you are lucky enough to have a little disposable income, you might set aside a small amount each month, gradually saving up. There's nothing inherently special about that money; it's the same currency you spend on food. But you have chosen and dedicated it for a special purpose.

Paul believes he is called as an apostle. He describes himself as 'set apart for the gospel of God'. But he never tells us from whom he is set apart. Is it from those who do, or those who do not, share his Christian faith? Perhaps it is both. He has been set aside for the gospel, which can surely be said of all followers of Christ; but he has also been given a specific mission: to Gentile communities.

Like Paul, we all have a calling that we hold in common with all Christians – to follow Christ. But also like Paul, we must each work out our distinctive way of living out this discipleship, using our unique gifts in God's service.

† God of grace, you have created me as my unique self and called me to join all who walk with you. Give me the grace to follow.

35

Monday 5 February
Sent by the Spirit and the church

Read Acts 13:1–5

While they were worshipping the LORD and fasting, the Holy Spirit said, 'Set apart for me Barnabas and Saul for the work to which I have called them.' Then after fasting and praying they laid their hands on them and sent them off.

(verses 2–3)

The church in Antioch, near the modern-day Syria–Turkey border, was founded by refugee Christians who had fled there from persecution. So it should probably come as no surprise that we find there a diverse group, including people from as far away as present-day Libya and members of the Judean social and political elite – among them a number of recognised prophets and teachers, who may have been most at risk.

Among these leaders is Barnabas, who is already well respected across the wider church, and who has been sent to Antioch specifically to build up and encourage the church there (Acts 11:22). There is also Barnabas's protégé, Saul, whom Barnabas has invited to join him (11:25).

It is important to note that the beginning of Saul's missionary journeys is not the result of his own sense of vocation alone. The Holy Spirit speaks to the whole community of prophets and teachers, and the two missionaries are commissioned and sent by the church. Luke is keen to emphasise that the initiative is the Spirit's. It is God who calls, and it is God's mission in which we are engaged. But the discernment of that call, and of the mission, is the task not of individuals but of the whole community of faith.

Along the way, Saul and Barnabas have to work out the details of that mission for themselves, following the prompting of the Spirit. But they are always accountable to the church, as the church is accountable to God. And in turn, the church has a responsibility to support, encourage and pray for them.

† Thank you that you call us to follow you, send us to do your will and walk with us along the way. Amen

For further thought

Think about the ways you follow God. How much does your church community know about these? How much do you know about the discipleship of other Christians or congregations? Do you pray for them?

Tuesday 6 February
In step with the Holy Spirit

Read Galatians 5:22–26

By contrast, the fruit of the Spirit is love, joy, peace, patience, kindness, generosity, faithfulness, gentleness, and self-control … If we live by the Spirit, let us also be guided by the Spirit. Let us not become conceited, competing against one another, envying one another.

(verses 22–23a, 25–26)

According to a popular song my children used to sing, a pineapple does not count as a fruit of the Spirit! I love pineapples, but they are not universally appreciated. The same, sadly, can be said of the fruit of the Spirit. We can feel threatened by other people's self-control, envious of their joy, frustrated by their gentleness or challenged by their generosity.

Fruit is not a plant, but the *produce* of a healthy plant, which may provide pleasure and nutrition for us or other creatures created by God. It contains within it the seed of new life – the next generation of plants – enabling the cycle of life to continue.

So it is with the fruit of the Spirit. These virtues are not the means by which we become holy, but rather the produce of a life lived in tune with the Spirit. They are measures by which we can know that we are in step with the Spirit of God.

Discipleship is not, or shouldn't be, a competitive sport! If, like me, you look at that list and feel somewhat inadequate, don't be discouraged. We all have much progress to make, and we don't always produce a fruitful harvest. But we should delight in one another's virtues, learn from one another, encourage one another and recognise that we are on a shared journey together.

When we bear spiritual fruit, we sow the seeds of faith in those we meet: the seeds of hope in a world full of despair and the seeds of love in the midst of hate and division. That is fruit worth bearing and sharing!

† Holy Spirit, guide me in all I think, say and do, so that I may bear fruit for the kingdom and grow in faith. Help me to value the fruit you produce through the lives of others.

For further thought

Which fruit of the Spirit do you struggle with the most? What could you change to bear more of that fruit?

Wednesday 7 February
Easy discipleship or learning from play?

Read Matthew 11:25–30

At that time Jesus said, 'I thank you, Father, Lord of heaven and earth, because you have hidden these things from the wise and the intelligent and have revealed them to infants ... Take my yoke upon you, and learn from me; for I am gentle and humble in heart, and you will find rest for your souls. For my yoke is easy, and my burden is light.'

(verses 25, 29–30)

Have you ever applied for a job, only to find that the reality doesn't match the description? I wonder what you make of these words of Jesus, as a description of the work of the kingdom.

Jesus proclaims a topsy-turvy kingdom in which small children become the bearers of wisdom, while the burdens of labour bring rest and relief. Elsewhere he warns us that the work of the kingdom can be hard, so what can he possibly mean here?

Perhaps the clue is in the nature of small children. One beautiful aspect is their capacity to find enjoyment in the mundane: the endless pretend cups of tea served; the fun of 'helping' with household chores; the thrill of re-enacting shopping trips with a toy till and basket.

Perhaps if we can engage in the work of the kingdom with the wisdom of a child, we might find the labour brings rest. If we can engage our imaginations to catch a vision of what the world could be like, we might not be ground down by what we actually see around us. If we can take huge delight in tiny achievements and small progress, maybe we will feel less overwhelmed by the task ahead. If we can draw others in, offering them the privilege of participating in our discipleship, we might find that companionship makes the journey more manageable.

In other words, if we can see the world through God's eyes, as a child might do, perhaps the yoke will be easy and the burden light, even where the obstacles are many.

† Help me to learn the wisdom of childhood; to find excitement in each task, the wonder in each day, refreshment in each new experience and an eagerness to share each new discovery.

For further thought

Children are not perfect angels. Which childish ways might be less helpful to imitate, and who else might we learn from in those areas?

Thursday 8 February
Moving in, moving out

Read Isaiah 45:22–25

'Turn to me and be saved, all the ends of the earth! For I am God, and there is no other. By myself I have sworn, from my mouth has gone forth in righteousness a word that shall not return: "To me every knee shall bow, every tongue shall swear."'

(verses 22–23)

When God calls, is it an invitation to come or to go? The Bible offers us both ideas. Jesus calls disciples to follow him, then sends them out on a mission. God calls Moses to approach the burning bush, then sends him to Pharaoh. Isaiah's call, in chapter 6, includes the offer, 'Send me!'

In our passage today, Isaiah offers us an image of movement – of people coming from 'the ends of the earth', turning to God and kneeling; those who have previously rejected God coming in penitence. But at the same time, out from God goes 'a word that shall not return'; God's creative, saving power being sent forth.

Perhaps our own calling is like that. At the same time, we are called to turn towards God in penitence, humility, praise and gratitude, and sent out to bear God's message in our lives, words and deeds. We are invited into God's embrace and sent out to do God's work.

But in this constant cycle of movement we see another dimension at work. God's word cannot leave God behind, but it is the bearer of God's loving power itself. Wherever God's word is heard, God's self is surely present. After all, when Moses was sent back to Egypt and then across the Red Sea into the wilderness, God was there, leading, guiding and accompanying him. Likewise, having been sent out to deliver God's message, Isaiah does not go alone, but with God.

We, too, are invited to be part of that energy of movement that is God's mission; always inwards towards God, and always outwards with God.

† God of mission, draw me closer into your love and send me out to proclaim your love, knowing that you go before me, beside me and behind me. Amen

For further thought

Where is God sending you today, and what is the message that you will proclaim in the things you say and do?

Friday 9 February
Revolution or survival?

Read 1 Peter 2:18–21

If you endure when you do right and suffer for it, you have God's approval. For to this you have been called, because Christ also suffered for you, leaving you an example, so that you should follow in his steps.

(verses 20b–21)

Few passages of the New Testament have been as controversial as this one, or have been so misused to justify one of humanity's greatest evils. Many people have, entirely understandably, rejected the passage as conservative, oppressive and abusive – a product of a patriarchal society built on the blood and labour of enslaved peoples.

The first letter of Peter is written, almost certainly, to a marginalised and perhaps persecuted people. Those who made up the churches that received it seem to have been those with little power – women, slaves and those of low social status. To accept Christ as Lord was to put yourself outside a society built around the worship of the Graeco-Roman gods, inviting suspicion, hatred and maybe even violence upon yourself.

Perhaps the writer should have been more radical – calling on slaves to resist, and to call for revolution and uprising. Or perhaps he is being pragmatic in a context where a small group of powerless individuals could not change much in practice, and was suggesting ways of simply surviving.

Or maybe this is a different kind of radical. To overthrow the structures of society was probably impossible, but to live in a way that undermined the usual play of power and aggression was an act of resistance that was not only available, but revolutionary. This is how Jesus modelled true, powerful humanity, and it enables his followers to challenge oppression implicitly, by refusing to accept that they are less than human, or less than beloved children of Christ.

Our calling is to know that we are loved and to imitate Christ – nothing less.

† God of grace and freedom, I pray for all who are suffering, all who are enslaved, all victims of injustice. Give us strength to resist injustice and to work for a just peace. Amen

For further thought

If you have more political or social power than those early Christians, how might you use it to reduce the suffering of others?

Saturday 10 February
The hope to which we are called

Read Ephesians 1:15–23

I pray that the God of our Lord Jesus Christ, the Father of glory, may give you a spirit of wisdom and revelation as you come to know him, so that, with the eyes of your heart enlightened, you may know what is the hope to which he has called you, what are the riches of his glorious inheritance among the saints, and what is the immeasurable greatness of his power for us who believe, according to the working of his great power.

(verses 17–19)

Later this year, many of us will be cheering for our national sportspeople in the Olympic and Paralympic Games, and, from our armchairs, basking in the reflected glory of any medals won.

It's a natural and normal human reaction to feel implicated in the glory of those with whom we share a badge of identity, but this becomes more problematic when such pride turns into an exclusive, narrow form of nationalism – when we want to reserve privileges for those who are 'like us'. Similarly, it is natural to want our country to be governed by those who share our values, but it is more problematic when we believe that people 'like us' have the right to rule.

The promised reign of Christ has shaped Christian hope in different ways. For some it is to be exercised vicariously in this world by Christians and imposed by might. It is seen when a candidate secures votes by professing a Christian faith that is not reflected in their actions, or when those fighting 'for God' embark on a crusade against a particular nation, tribe or religious group.

But the teaching and life of Jesus show a very different understanding of reign. Jesus' power came through love, service and humility. The privilege of being part of Jesus' reign – of basking in his reflected glory – is the privilege of sharing in his service. Jesus' rule offers a vision of a world in which power is not an end in itself, but something to use for the good of all.

This is the hope to which we are called and the kingdom to which we belong.

† Christ the King, rule in our hearts and in our world through the power and authority of your self-giving love. Make us ambassadors for your kingdom, living out its values and speaking out its truth. Amen.

For further thought

'Hope' in the New Testament is not vague optimism, but a confidence that things can be different. How is that hope seen in your life?

Sunday 11 February
Stones and sacrifices: what makes a church?

Read 1 Peter 2:4–5

Come to him, a living stone, though rejected by mortals yet chosen and precious in God's sight, and like living stones, let yourselves be built into a spiritual house, to be a holy priesthood, to offer spiritual sacrifices acceptable to God through Jesus Christ.

(verses 4–5)

The church is not the building, but the people. When we become preoccupied with our premises – whether we're bowed down with the pressure of maintaining a leaky roof or excited about refurbishing the worship area – we would do well to remember that the building is there to *serve* the church, not to *be* the church.

But despite that, a church building can be a striking symbol of the presence of Christ within the local community and a visible reminder that God is being worshipped. This makes it a natural metaphor for the real church – the assembly of Jesus followers. As with other such metaphors (such as Paul's image of the body), it begins with, and centres around Christ, bringing us into community with him and one another. Christ is the foundation stone on which the church is built, and we are called to imitate him.

It goes without saying that a single stone can't make a building, but equally, removing one stone from a building makes the whole structure unstable – or at least draughty! So it is with us. I cannot be the church alone, and neither can one worshipping congregation. But we each have a crucially important part to play in maintaining the whole.

The metaphor is made richer as we learn that we're not only the temple building, but also its priesthood – just as a church building is not just a structure, but a place of worship. Together, in communion with one another and with Christ, we become a powerful sign of the presence of Christ within our communities, and a reassurance that God is being worshipped. We become the church.

† Christ Jesus, you invite us into community with you and with one another. Help us to hold together in faithful worship, with you at our centre, in a structure that no storm can destroy.

For further thought

A priesthood offers worship on behalf of the community and communicates God's word to that community. How can you be a part of this?

Monday 12 February
Holy partners in a heavenly calling

Read Hebrews 3:1–6

Therefore, brothers and sisters, holy partners in a heavenly calling, consider that Jesus, the apostle and high priest of our confession, was faithful to the one who appointed him, just as Moses also 'was faithful in all God's house' … Christ, however, was faithful over God's house as a son, and we are his house if we hold firm the confidence and the pride that belong to hope.

(verses 1–2, 6)

'Tell me about your call.' That's an invitation that has opened up many times in my life. Sometimes I'm asked about why I am a Christian, sometimes why I'm in ordained ministry, and occasionally why I am exercising that ministry through theological education. But the focus is on me and my particular response to God's call.

And therein lies a simple, but often overlooked, truth. While a call will invite a response – to follow Christ, and perhaps a particular outworking of our discipleship – the call is not ours, but God's. The initiative is God's, and it is an act of his grace reaching out to us in our human frailty and inadequacy, and inviting us to be part of something far greater than us.

When I remember this, it radically changes my answer whenever I'm asked to tell the story of my call. It's not, first and foremost, a story of my giftings or challenges, my response or commitment. Before all else, it's a story of how much I am loved by God, and how gracious God has been to invite me to join in the work of loving the world with a radical, transforming love. It is a story not of how much God needs me, but of how willingly God makes space for me and chooses to make use of me. And it's a story of salvation; of all that God has done for me in Christ, of what God could achieve without me and yet chooses, with extraordinary grace, to achieve with me.

† Gracious God, thank you that you have given us your Son, Jesus Christ, to be faithful over your house, and that you have invited me to be a part of both your house and your work. Amen.

For further thought

Do you have a story to tell of God's call on your life? How does it go? What might the next chapter say?

Tuesday 13 February
A life worthy of the calling

Read Ephesians 4:1–6

I ... beg you to lead a life worthy of the calling to which you have been called, with all humility and gentleness, with patience, bearing with one another in love, making every effort to maintain the unity of the Spirit in the bond of peace. There is one body and one Spirit, just as you were called to the one hope of your calling, one Lord, one faith, one baptism, one God and Father of all, who is above all and through all and in all.

(verses 1b–6)

God's call is an act of grace, not a reward for our achievements. That, for Paul, is the heart of the gospel message, but not the end of the story. A call invites a response, and grace invites gratitude. So the Christians in Ephesus, and Christians today, are challenged to 'lead a life worthy of the calling to which you have been called'.

In our world today, we often focus on the rights and responsibilities of the individual, and that's certainly a good place to start – ensuring that our actions, words and choices are as Christ-like as possible. But this passage goes further than that. It reminds us that we always live in relationship to others, and that our lives should be worthy; not just as individual Christians, but as a Christian community. And our individual discipleship should be orientated towards others with patience, gentleness and humility.

We often speak of the virtues of tolerance or inclusion, but this only takes us so far. Tolerance allows others to live their lives but doesn't necessarily welcome them. Inclusion can become about allowing 'others' to join *our* lives, while we remain in control. It makes space for others, but doesn't commit to allowing our lives to be changed or transformed by their presence.

What the letter to the Ephesians offers is deeper and fuller. It recognises that it's not *our* community, but *God's*. All of us are here only by grace, and God's love is most fully seen when there is no 'us and them', but one glorious, diverse unity. One body, one Spirit and a bond of peace.

† God, ever three and ever one, help me to value the difference others bring into my life, and to seek the unity that comes through our shared faith, in your grace and love. Amen

For further thought

Who in your church community (or which other local congregations) do you find particularly hard to value? Why is that?

The big story: Bible framework

The following readings are by **David Painting**. *You can read his biography on Sunday 18 February. David has used the NRSVA for these notes.*

Wednesday 14 February (Ash Wednesday)
God is love

Read Genesis 2:1–17

The LORD God took the man and put him in the garden of Eden to till it and keep it. And the LORD God commanded the man, 'You may freely eat of every tree of the garden; but of the tree of the knowledge of good and evil you shall not eat, for in the day that you eat of it you shall die.'

(verses 15–17)

I'm not a fan of jigsaw puzzles, but I often have to do them with our grandchildren. As they get older, the puzzles are becoming harder with more pieces! Sometimes the children will take a piece and become frustrated, trying to fit it where it doesn't go. They are so focused on the piece that they can't see the big picture it is part of. When they finally look at the picture on the box and see where it goes, we all breathe a sigh of relief!

I think we sometimes treat pieces of the Bible in the same way. We read something and can't work out how it fits with the rest. Over the next two weeks, we're going to paint a big picture of the Bible so we see where the pieces fit without forcing them.

And where better to start than the beginning! God creates the universe, creates the world, creates all kinds of life and declares it good. And finally, he creates humankind and gives them a mandate to fill the earth and have dominion over it. And crucially, he also gives them the choice of how to do that: in relationship with God or independently from him.

Today is Ash Wednesday, the beginning of a season where we reflect on how our choices led Jesus to a cross. It is also St Valentine's Day, when people tell each other how much they are loved. How appropriate, then, that this is the foundation of the biggest picture of all: of God's love for us.

† Loving God, help us to see the big picture of who you are, so that we might understand your word more fully.

For further thought
If you had to describe the big picture of the Bible story, what would you say? Try to write down your thoughts in a couple of sentences.

Thursday 15 February
Love gives us a choice

Read 1 Corinthians 13:1–7

Love is patient; love is kind; love is not envious or boastful or arrogant or rude. It does not insist on its own way; it is not irritable or resentful; it does not rejoice in wrongdoing, but rejoices in the truth. It bears all things, believes all things, hopes all things, endures all things.

(verses 4–7)

This extraordinary passage from Paul is perhaps the best definition of love ever composed. Often used at weddings to describe the relationship to which the newly married couple should aspire, it points of course to the love we see revealed in Jesus.

Because if God is love, then whatever love is like, God is like that too. If love is patient and kind, then so is God. If love endures all things, then God endures all things. If love does not insist on its own way, then neither does God.

And that is the heart of today's part of the big picture: a God who is all-powerful; who could insist on his own way but chooses not to enforce it by might, accomplishing it instead through the freely made choices of those he lovingly created. 'Not by might, nor by power, but by my spirit, says the LORD' in Zechariah 4:6.

Why do it that way? Because otherwise we would be relegated to mere puppets; actors on a cosmic stage, repeating the prescribed lines with no more opportunity to love than a train has to choose whether or not to leave its tracks.

Of course, there are consequences to the choices we make, and God has made those known from the beginning, as we saw yesterday. A little later, Moses famously sets before the people a choice between 'life and death', and challenges them to 'choose life' (Deuteronomy 30:19). But although there are consequences to our decisions – from Eden to today – God gives us the dignity of choosing, because he longs for us to love and be loved.

And without choice, there can be no love.

† O Lord, you taught us to pray 'your will be done'. Help us today to make choices that line up with your will.

For further thought

Ultimately, Jesus has paid the price for our wrong choices. Reflect on the love he must feel for us to make the choice to create humankind, knowing the cost.

Friday 16 February

Wrong choices have consequences

Read Genesis 3:1–13

Now the serpent was more crafty than any other wild animal that the LORD God had made. He said to the woman, 'Did God say, "You shall not eat from any tree in the garden"?' The woman said to the serpent, 'We may eat of the fruit of the trees in the garden; but God said, "You shall not eat of the fruit of the tree that is in the middle of the garden, nor shall you touch it, or you shall die."'

(verses 1–3)

How important it is for us to know what God's word says rather than what we think it says or what others have told us it says. 'Did God say … ' asks the enemy. Eve recites the injunction not to eat, but then adds, 'nor shall you touch it'. Good advice, no doubt, but confusing godly advice with what God has said gives space for the enemy to do what he always does: deceive.

'You will be[come] like God,' he says, and it sounds like godly advice. What could be wrong with becoming godlier? Except that God had already made humanity in his image. Adam and Eve were already like God in every way necessary for them to partake and respond to his love. The enemy first sows doubt about God's word, and then he denies God's word, saying, 'You will not die.'

God wasn't stopping Adam and Eve knowing the difference between good and evil, he was ensuring that their understanding was founded on their relationship with him. Just as children learn from their parents, so they would have learned what he knew to be good. But the enemy distorts God's character by implying that he has withheld something good from them out of jealousy.

From that place of deceit they eat the fruit, and when God comes to spend time with them they are gone. Adam blames Eve and, by implication, God himself: 'The woman whom you gave to be with me …' Eve blames the serpent, and no one owns their responsibility. The disintegration of creation begins.

† O merciful God, you dignified us with such a precious gift and we discarded it, misunderstanding its worth. As we continue to do so today in our everyday choices, show us again the value of Jesus, grant us the courage to own our sin and be gracious to us.

For further thought

How can you encourage others to use *Fresh from The Word* as a means of ensuring that we really know what God has said?

Saturday 17 February
Separation and distortion

Read Genesis 3:14–24

The LORD God said to the serpent, 'Because you have done this, cursed are you among all animals and among all wild creatures; upon your belly you shall go, and dust you shall eat all the days of your life. I will put enmity between you and the woman, and between your offspring and hers; he will strike your head, and you will strike his heel.'

(verses 14–15)

Eating fruit from the tree of the knowledge of good and evil can be seen as humanity deciding to make moral choices based on their own understanding rather than outworked from a relationship with God. Like a father with a child, humankind was intended to learn right and wrong by observing, by asking, by practically seeing. But now Adam and Eve have to make up their own minds as to what is good and bad outside that broken relationship.

Having eaten, they look at each other and decide for themselves that nakedness must be bad. It obviously wasn't just moments ago, because if it had been God would have covered them from the moment they were created. But now the enemy heaps on shame, and they seek human ways of covering it. The leaves sewn together are inadequate, to say the least – as our efforts always are when we try to deal with spiritual issues ourselves.

How does God respond? As we saw in the first of these readings, love is patient and kind. It doesn't insist on its own way, but endures all things. And wonderfully, having outlined the consequences of their choices, God now accommodates them. Adam and Eve have decided that nakedness is bad, so God lovingly responds by clothing them. He covers what they now believe to be shameful.

And we also read that love hopes all things, so he guards against them eating the fruit of the tree of life; not as a punishment, but as a protection against them living forever in this broken state. Because God knows that one day the brokenness will be healed, the relationship restored, and sin and all its consequences dealt with forever. Only then we can safely eat of that fruit.

† Father, help us to align our understanding of right and wrong based on who you are rather than on our own made-up rules.

For further thought

Where else do we see God accommodating people's wrong view of him? (Consider him giving them the law or a king, for example, or the very act of him becoming incarnate.)

Notes by **David Painting**

David's passion is to see people encounter God more profoundly. A science graduate, he has held senior roles in industry and commerce, alongside a pastoral ministry in UK Baptist churches. Having spent time with YWAM, leading and teaching at its Discipleship Training Schools in the UK and overseas, he currently divides his time between software development, co-leading a house church, teaching and writing. Most recently he was a theological advisor and data contributor for The Infographic Bible. David enjoys being a grandfather and all things related to space. He is excited to be Editor of *Fresh from The Word* and has used the NRSVA for these notes.

Sunday 18 February
God could have destroyed humanity

Read Genesis 7:17–24

The flood continued forty days on the earth; and the waters increased, and bore up the ark, and it rose high above the earth.

(verse 17)

God's plan to create a world in which humankind could enjoy an unhindered, loving relationship with him and one another has been disastrously derailed. The pace of destruction and evil has accelerated, and hatred and selfishness have replaced love. Within one generation of the fall, the first murder has occurred. What will God do in response?

The next major event is of course the flood. But how should we view it? Is it a demonstration that a just, all-powerful God has the right and the might to punish and destroy? Or is it a picture of cleansing, of renewal, of a new beginning – of salvation for all who will receive?

In Genesis 1, God holds back the waters and pushes back the seas to form dry land. We should remember that, throughout the Bible, people considered water to be inhabited by evil. In their minds, God holding back the waters was the same as him holding back evil, mitigating the just impact of our sin. The flood, then, is seen as us experiencing the full consequence of our sinful choices.

But wonderfully, even there within the story, is a glimpse of hope: a righteous man, lifted high above the earth on something made of wood, through which any who believed could be saved.

† Lord Jesus, thank you for becoming sin for me, so I might be cleansed and saved from the ultimate consequences of my sin.

49

Monday 19 February
God could not ignore their sin

Read Genesis 11:1–8

The LORD came down to see the city and the tower, which mortals had built. And the LORD said, 'Look, they are one people, and they have all one language; and this is only the beginning of what they will do; nothing that they propose to do will now be impossible for them.'

(verses 5–6)

As we saw in the face of our rejection of his love, God could have exercised his omnipotence and destroyed creation. It would have been a just response; yet because of his love, God used the flood as a reboot rather than an end.

In the story of Babel we see another choice that God could have made. If the flood hinted at a 'destroy' option, Babel implies a 'withdraw' option. It begins with a conversation within the Trinity: 'Let us go down and see … ' (Genesis 11:7). And what does God find when he re-engages with the world? A different type of flood. A tide of unchecked evil and arrogance. A people, missing the presence of God and deciding they could reach him through their own efforts. A people who, instead of receiving a name from God, believed they could make a name for themselves.

God had removed his hand of protection during the flood, resulting in a reset. Here, for a season, he had removed himself completely, allowing an unrestrained rush towards hell on earth. It is a picture intended to show all generations the true consequences of our sin – and of a God who refuses to turn his back on us. He says that unless they act to slow down evil, to mitigate the effects of sinful choices, 'there is no limit to the evil they will conceive'.

So God confuses their languages ('Babel' means 'confuse'), hindering their ability to communicate and execute their plans. It is an act born out of love, creating space for repentance, for different choices, for the redemption of all that was lost.

† O Lord, thank you that your love means you never withdraw from us, even when we offend you.

For further thought

God could have destroyed us or left us to face the consequences of our sin and ignored us, but instead he promises to be with us. Spend time reflecting on the enormity of his great love.

Tuesday 20 February
God will redeem

Read 1 Corinthians 13:8–13

When I was a child, I spoke like a child, I thought like a child, I reasoned like a child; when I became an adult, I put an end to childish ways. For now we see in a mirror, dimly, but then we will see face to face. Now I know only in part; then I will know fully, even as I have been fully known. And now faith, hope, and love abide, these three; and the greatest of these is love.

(verses 11–13)

Here's the story so far … God created humanity with the capacity to love and be loved. But that requires real choice with real consequences. We chose (and still choose) to exist outside the loving relationships we were created for. We rejected God, who could have wiped us out or withdrawn and left us to suffer the consequence of our rebellion. But although he demonstrated his ability to do both, he sowed the seeds of something else in each story.

He would have been right to judge and punish, right to walk away. But he didn't, because that isn't what love does. As Paul tells us, and as the cross confirms, love endures all things. It bears all things, and outlasts them.

When we look at the stories in Genesis through this lens, they come into new focus. What comes to the fore is not a wrathful God punishing wayward children, but a loving father carrying the pain of our sin, refusing to be embittered by it, refusing to lash out and hurt in response. Instead, he bends down to cover our shame, protecting us from permanent harm and holding back the flood of evil we have unleashed. And at unthinkable cost, he prepares a way to redeem and win us back.

Everything else may come and go, but this rock is solid ground. God loves us unshakeably, and that love – along with the hope it brings and the faith it inspires – stretches into an eternal future.

† Father, we are overwhelmed by your great and unfailing love. May it inspire us to love others in the same way.

For further thought

If love led Jesus to step down into our world, how should our love for others lead us? How can we step out of our world to genuinely be with others?

Wednesday 21 February
A people in a place (1)

Read Genesis 11:27–32

Terah took his son Abram and his grandson Lot son of Haran, and his daughter-in-law Sarai, his son Abram's wife, and they went out together from Ur of the Chaldeans to go into the land of Canaan; but when they came to Haran, they settled there.

(verse 31)

God won't destroy or withdraw. He will lovingly endure the consequences of our sin in order to redeem. A literal translation of Revelation 13:8 tells us that Jesus was 'the lamb that was slaughtered' before the foundation of the world. God himself was destined to step down into our world. But how would people recognise him? He couldn't come in majesty and splendour. He couldn't use his deity to impose his will because love does not insist on its own way. Indeed, if he was to reverse the impact of Adam's choice he would have to come, as Paul describes him in 1 Corinthians 15:45, as 'the last Adam'; like us in every way, only without sin.

But if Jesus were to come looking just like anyone else, how would people recognise him as God? The plan starts in today's passage. God would bring together a people in a place to love one another and love God, and this would be seen by the whole world, so that at the right time, when the one who *is* love came in person, everyone would recognise him.

And it begins with Terah, who starts the journey towards Canaan, but grief stops him. His eldest son Haran dies, and Terah cannot bear to leave him far behind. So he settles in a land close to the start of the journey – a land that became known as Haran. The name 'Terah' means 'delay', because the plan is on hold until the next generation can respond.

Graciously, the Bible never criticises Terah for stopping. God patiently accommodates the understandable grief of a bereaved father, puts his arms around Terah and then waits for Abram.

† Lord, thank you that your love sits with the brokenhearted, and lays aside its own agenda and comforts. In my pain and loss, please will you gently sit with me too?

For further thought

What plans do we need to put on hold in order to give time to those who need our presence right now?

Thursday 22 February
The law

Read Exodus 24:9–18

The glory of the LORD settled on Mount Sinai, and the cloud covered it for six days; on the seventh day he called to Moses out of the cloud. Now the appearance of the glory of the LORD was like a devouring fire on the top of the mountain in the sight of the people of Israel. Moses entered the cloud, and went up on the mountain. Moses was on the mountain for forty days and forty nights.

(verses 16–18)

God is trying to get a people in a place so they can represent him to the world, in order that, when he comes in person, people will receive him. But the people have become slaves in Egypt. Enter Moses. Brought up in both the Hebrew and Egyptian worlds, he is surrounded by power, majesty and splendour. He observes the most powerful man on earth, commanding and receiving. And he assumes that God must be the same, and be looking for the same, in a leader. So when he sees injustice, Moses uses his power to kill the oppressor. But God does not join in, and he has to flee.

Years later, God speaks to Moses through a bush that is on fire but isn't burnt. Something powerful (fire) doesn't do what is expected. Just as God, who is all-powerful, doesn't use his power to insist on his own way. Moses is confused and asks God to define himself by giving his name. God replies, 'I AM WHO I AM' (Exodus 3:14). In other words, get to know me. Yet in today's passage, God gives Moses what he wants, etched in stone: a description of the ways of God.

Relationships are hard work! How much easier to follow rules and tick boxes rather than having the pain of getting to know someone. How much more convenient to recite creeds rather than have the difficulties that arise from a dynamic, interactive relationship with God. But when faith reduces us to a legalistic adherence to rules, we miss out on the joy, the love and the life God longs for us to have.

† Thank you, Lord, that you have so much more for us than rules. Thank you for life in all its fullness.

For further thought

Look at the ten commandments (Exodus 20) and see how they are all underpinned by the love of God.

Friday 23 February
The plan rejected

Read 1 Samuel 8:4–20

Then all the elders of Israel gathered together and came to Samuel at Ramah, and said to him, 'You are old and your sons do not follow in your ways; appoint for us, then, a king to govern us, like other nations.'

(verses 4–5)

Remember, God's plan was to have a people in a place who would be distinctively different from the other nations; a people who would live in such a way as to visibly represent who he was, so that everyone would recognise him when he came in person.

It's a plan that has been delayed, derailed and almost destroyed, but finally here they are. Moses had led them to the edge of the land and Joshua has led them into it. And under the judges, there is a people in a place at last. The plan about to bear fruit.

Yet at this key moment, disaster! Instead of embracing the plan to be holy (different, distinctive), the people cry out that they want to be the same as the other nations. They demand a king like everyone else has. What a rejection of God! He has been impossibly patient and indescribably gracious, but now they are looking to throw it all away.

When we read the story of the fall and read passages like today's, we are rightly appalled, shocked at such obvious rejections of the love and grace God has poured out on us. And yet, when I look at my life and some of the choices I have made, or at some of my character weaknesses, I see glimpses of the same. I, too, have rejected God's love, abused his grace and demanded to be king of my life.

We, too, are called to be holy – not for the sake of piety alone, but for the sake of those who don't yet know God and need us to represent his loving ways to them.

† Holy God, help us to become different in the same way that you are different – loving, kind, generous and patient – so that others might see you reflected in us.

For further thought

In which ways are we different, like God? Think about this question in terms of our personal and our collective lives as the church?

Saturday 24 February
The plan works ... briefly

Read 1 Kings 10:1–13

'Blessed be the LORD your God, who has delighted in you and set you on the throne of Israel! Because the LORD loved Israel for ever, he has made you king to execute justice and righteousness.'

(verse 9)

It works! Despite everything; every delay, every setback, every wrong or wicked choice – when we finally live together in accord with who God is, the plan works. Others are attracted to what they see. They begin to recognise something of God in our midst. They see love reflected in our relationships.

And they come to find out more, just as the Queen of Sheba does. She comes with her questions and Solomon answers them with the wisdom God has given him. She starts out being impressed by his power, with the splendour and wealth of Israel. She returns focused on the love of God.

Jesus said: 'When I am lifted up from the earth, [I] will draw all people to myself' (John 12:32). And he did. The tax collectors and sinners came, the fishermen left their nets. The sick and the dying, the rich and the poor, the educated and the uneducated, the powerful and the oppressed – they all came. From Nicodemus to the Samaritan woman, they came to find out more and returned knowing more of the love of God.

And if we lift Jesus high, making his love visible, then we, too, will see the rich, the poor, the powerful, the dispossessed all come to discover more. As God promised Abraham, all people will be blessed through the revelation of who God is. As Jesus put it: 'For where two or three are gathered in my name, I am there among them.' Where people interact together in the way a loving God interacts, God is made visible.

In Solomon's day, the plan worked. It still can.

† Thank you, Lord, that your purposes never fail to bear fruit. Help us to be more like you, individually and collectively, that the world might see and receive you.

For further thought

The root word for 'church' simply means 'group come together with a common purpose'. To what extent can we say that nobody *goes* to church but that rather we *are* church when we represent Christ together?

Sunday 25 February
The kingdom divided

Read 2 Chronicles 36:11–20

The LORD, the God of their ancestors, sent persistently to them by his messengers, because he had compassion on his people and on his dwelling-place, but they kept mocking the messengers of God, despising his words, and scoffing at his prophets, until the wrath of the LORD against his people became so great that there was no remedy.

(verses 15–16)

The Bible reveals the Father, Son and Holy Spirit as being so united by love that they are one God. It is the same picture used to describe love in marriage: two becoming one. This love that makes one from many is the true representation of God, and is why shalom (wholeness, unity, peace) is such a key theme in the Bible. If there is no love, if there is division rather than unity, there is no witness to who God is, and the blessing to the nations we are called to be cannot be poured out (Psalm 133).

As we saw yesterday, 600 years after Terah had taken those first steps there was finally a united nation and the plan began to bear fruit. But almost as soon as it had begun, the kingdom divided. The unity that represented God was fractured. The books of Chronicles graphically describe the unfolding tragedy: king after evil king, each outdoing the other in leading the people astray. Reading these books in one sitting is relentless. The pattern of bad king, worse king and prophetic call back to God, followed by bad king and worse king is repeated, generation after generation.

Finally, the people sinned until there was 'no remedy'. How dreadful to live at a time when grace ends and judgement has to come. 'We want to be like the other nations' had been the cry. Ten of the twelve tribes finally have what they wanted – to be so like the other nations that they become indistinguishable from them and are lost to history. The remaining two tribes are taken from their rightful place into captivity.

† O holy God, we thank you for your amazing grace, but we come humbly, not taking it for granted. Rather, we ask that we might live lives worthy of it.

For further thought

Justice demands that there be consequences for the choices we make. Grace gives space between the choice and the outcome. Reflect today: are there areas where God has graciously given you time to respond, where you haven't yet?

Monday 26 February
Children of the dream

Read Psalm 126:1–6

When the LORD restored the fortunes of Zion, we were like those who dream. Then our mouth was filled with laughter, and our tongue with shouts of joy; then it was said among the nations, 'The LORD has done great things for them.' The LORD has done great things for us, and we rejoiced.

(verses 1–3)

What of God's plan now? Ten of the twelve tribes are gone, and those who are left have been taken into exile. Jerusalem (city of shalom) lies in ruins. Yet the prophets pointed to something better; a God who is love, and whose love endures all things and never fails. And miraculously after seventy years, a foreign king turns to God and calls on the Hebrews to return and rebuild.

What joy to have been in that generation, to have heard the news – whispered at first, then shouted from the rooftops – that God is moving again, and once again there will be peace in the city of peace. Even though it appeared to be dead, the plan is still alive.

You can read in Daniel, Esther, Ezra and Nehemiah the story of the exile and of the return. Far from easy, it was won at great cost, requiring wholehearted commitment from the people and extraordinarily courageous leadership.

But pause for a moment and ask: how did this foreign king know about God? Well, we don't have the details, but we have hints. We see in Esther that the king spent a lot of time reading through the annals of the kingdom, and we know that the exploits of Daniel and his friends were part of these records. Their unity, their love, their distinctiveness gave credibility to their prophetic words. The king read and believed, and God's plan was fulfilled.

† Lord, give me the courage to believe that, as I come together in unity with my 'two or three', we will make Jesus visible in ways we cannot imagine.

For further thought

In what ways can you be distinctive from the world around you without being separate from it?

Tuesday 27 February
God comes, but isn't recognised

Read John 1:1–14

And the Word became flesh and lived among us, and we have seen his glory, the glory as of a father's only son, full of grace and truth.

(verse 14)

God's heart has always been to walk with us, to have a loving relationship with us and to inspire us to do the same with each other. We have seen that, despite having rejected this love, it was always his plan to come in person to restore the possibility of it. And we have seen how he planned to have a people in a place to represent him so that when he came everyone might recognise and receive him.

And we've seen how that plan was delayed, derailed and almost destroyed – but also how God's patient grace used the few who responded to reveal who he really is to those who would see.

And now, silently, humbly, the unthinkable happens. God comes and lives among us, 'full of grace and truth'.

But instead of the joyful recognition he should have received, the people argued with him, denied him, accused him, abused him and killed him. 'He was in the world, and the world came into being through him; yet the world did not know him. He came to what was his own, and his own people did not accept him' (John 1:10–11).

But why? Because those who had gone before him had failed to represent him, had failed to live like him, had failed to paint a true picture of what he was like.

Nevertheless, the light shone in the darkness and the darkness was sent fleeing. The dawn was gathering pace, the night would never return. Immanuel is forever.

† Lord Jesus, we are so grateful that we have recognised you and so thankful to all those who made you visible to us. Help us to be the light of the world.

For further thought

The question is unavoidable: are there those who will misunderstand who God is, who will miss recognising him when he comes to them because of our inaction; because of our lack of love?

Wednesday 28 February
Two gardens

Read John 20:11–18

*When she had said this, she turned round and saw Jesus standing there,
but she did not know that it was Jesus. Jesus said to her, 'Woman, why
are you weeping? For whom are you looking?' Supposing him to be
the gardener, she said to him, 'Sir, if you have carried him away, tell
me where you have laid him, and I will take him away.' Jesus said to
her, 'Mary!' She turned and said to him in Hebrew, 'Rabbouni!' (which
means Teacher).*

(verses 14–16)

The pivotal moment in history is upon us. In that first garden
(Eden), Adam chose his own will – independence from God –
rejecting his love. Now Jesus comes as 'the last Adam' to another
garden (Gethsemane) and prays 'not my will but yours be done'
(Luke 22:42). In making this choice, in inviting upon himself all the
fatal consequences of Adam's choice, Jesus undoes the fall and
reopens the possibility of a loving relationship with God.

In today's passage we see the fulfilment of this, in another
garden. It is early on Sunday morning, the third day. The whole of
history is paused, holding its breath, waiting for the risen Jesus to
make himself known. The two women come first, and although
they see an empty tomb and hear the words of the angels, Jesus
does not reveal himself. Then the two men who will be pillars in
the church come and go, still without seeing Jesus.

Finally, Mary Magdalene returns to the garden alone, and now
Jesus reveals himself. The universe can wait. He needs this moment
alone with Mary to complete her healing and to see the joy in her
eyes as she learns for sure that she is loved.

'Mary!' Jesus says and the world changes.

This is the extraordinary mystery about God's love. He holds the
big picture and the minute detail as equally important. He redeems
creation and heals this woman. This is our God and this is his plan;
not just for the universe, but for you.

† Dear Jesus, we cannot comprehend the cross. We cannot imagine the pain, the
cost. But we can understand the love in your voice as you call our names, and
see the joy in your eyes as we turn to you and feel the warmth of your embrace.

For further thought

Reflect on the idea of a first and last Adam. What contrasts and
comparisons can you find?

Thursday 29 February
A people in a place (2)

Read Acts 2:14–21

'In the last days it will be, God declares, that I will pour out my Spirit upon all flesh, and your sons and your daughters shall prophesy, and your young men shall see visions, and your old men shall dream dreams.'

(verse 17)

The disciples know that Jesus is risen. Surely he will now use his power to demonstrate who he is, kick the Romans out and begin his reign on earth. No! After a few days, he takes them to the mountain and renews the mandate given in Eden. Then it was described as filling the earth and having dominion. Now it is framed as going out into the world and making disciples of all nations. Then it was a rippling out from the garden into Eden, and from there to the whole world. Now it will ripple out from being witnesses in Jerusalem, Judea and Samaria to the ends of the earth.

God's plan has never wavered. He recommissions us to the same role: to be a people united by love, to demonstrate who he is. And now he sends the Spirit to empower all those, Jews and Gentiles alike who choose him, to become like Jesus. A Spirit who is holy – distinctively different from other powers, precisely because of his love. A Spirit who empowers our godly choices, convicts us of our ungodly ones and refines us in the fire of circumstances. A Spirit who produces the fruit of love in our lives and who enables his people to bear that fruit in the most challenging of places.

'For where two or three are gathered in my name, I am there among them.' This is our high calling: to be like Jesus as his Spirit leads, that all might see him and be drawn to him.

† Come, Holy Spirit, to convict me of sin, to strengthen my resolve, and to comfort and encourage me in all circumstances to be like Jesus.

For further thought
How do our interactions with others – with those we like, those we dislike, those we fear, our enemies – make Jesus visible?

Friday 1 March
The Bride of Christ

March

The big story: Bible framework

Read Revelation 19:6–9

Let us rejoice and exult and give him the glory, for the marriage of the Lamb has come, and his bride has made herself ready; to her it has been granted to be clothed with fine linen, bright and pure.

(verses 7–8)

Throughout the Bible, God uses the imagery of marriage to signify the level of loving intimacy he desires with all humankind. In Song of Songs, we journey with a man and woman through the wonders of love and joy of marriage. In John, the first miracle recorded is the wedding at Cana, and Jesus himself tells many parables using weddings as the message carrier.

And here John speaks of a bride, resplendent in wonderful clothing that is pure and unspoiled in any way. She has come to meet the one longed for, in order to be joined with him forever. It is an extraordinary picture, speaking as it does of oneness, mutuality, intimacy and joy. This is the joy that the writer of Hebrews spoke of when he said that 'for the joy that was set before Him, [Jesus] endured the cross'. We are that joy. *You* are that joy.

Yet how tragic it is for those who don't recognise the bridegroom or who are unprepared when he comes. That is why the plan is as it has ever been; not to help people recognise God when he first came, but for when he returns. This is a plan for those who already constitute the bride to ensure that everyone else will recognise the Groom when he comes.

Just as any human bride looking forward to her wedding day cannot help but speak about the groom, and cannot help but do everything she can to enhance his reputation and demonstrate by every means possible her love – so we as the bride of Christ must surely do the same.

† O Lord, how we long for that wedding day! To the fulfilment of all our hopes; to see you face to face; to know the depths of your love and approval. Come, Lord Jesus, come.

For further thought
Think about the best aspects of human marriage. What does that communicate to you about God, and about the relationship he longs to have with you and all people?

Saturday 2 March
The plan complete

Read Revelation 21:1–7

And I heard a loud voice from the throne saying, 'See, the home of God is among mortals. He will dwell with them; they will be his peoples, and God himself will be with them.'

(verse 3)

Unsurprisingly, we began our whirlwind overview of the Bible with creation. We end it today with a re-creation; with all things being made new; with the tree of life available to all people and nations once again; with a new city of peace, a renewed wholeness, a revitalised shalom at the centre.

What wonderful imagery: lions and lambs united; vulnerable babies safe with serpents. A place without fear; a place without suffering; a place where all tears are kindly wiped away, along with the need for them to be healed. A place where people and God can walk together, learn from one another, enjoy one other and do extraordinary things together.

And we are called to make this kingdom as real on earth as it will be on the recreated earth. Of course, we know that won't really be possible, but in hoping for the future earth we should at least be inspired to try to give it our all to make it so now. We are to care for those who weep; to heal those who are sick; to give ourselves as Jesus gave himself, that others might live. To be generous and openhanded with what we have been given. As lambs to sit down with lions; as children to engage with serpents. To bring the light of the new into the old, so everyone can glimpse what will be and welcome it into their hearts.

This is an extraordinary story. The thread throughout it is simple: God loves you, and you have a significant part to play in it.

† Father, thank you for the Bible and the love story it proclaims. Help me to be a part of that story.

For further thought

What scary lions do you know, what deceptive serpents? How can you sit down with them and reveal the love of Christ?

Rebuilding in Nehemiah (1)

Notes by **John Birch**

Based in South Wales, John is a Methodist Local Preacher, writes prayers and Bible studies for faithandworship.com, and is amazed at where these are being used and how God has blessed lives through them. Some prayers have been adapted for use within choral and more contemporary worship settings. John has published several books, and in his spare time sings folk songs. With his wife Margaret, he has an allotment, walks and explores the country in a campervan called Lola. John has used the NIVUK for these notes.

Sunday 3 March
A broken city

Read Nehemiah 1:1 – 2:10

The king said to me, 'What is it you want?' Then I prayed to the God of heaven, and I answered the king, 'If it pleases the king and if your servant has found favour in his sight, let him send me to the city in Judah where my ancestors are buried so that I can rebuild it.'

(verses 2:4–5)

Think of the cities destroyed or damaged by conflict in your lifetime, of populations forced to flee or taken into exile. In the fifth century BC, we find Jerusalem's walls in ruins and just a remnant of its original population living there, with many having settled in Persia and reluctant to return.

Restoration had begun, with the city temple rebuilt, but then everything stalled, leaving the population vulnerable. They needed someone to reignite the fire of pride and faith in this city and complete the work. Step forward Nehemiah, a Jewish official in the Persian court.

How many church congregations can empathise with those people living in Jerusalem? I have sat in many a meeting trying hard not to be noticed until someone says, 'OK, I'll take that job on!' And often that's all it takes for others to chip in with, 'If you need help, I'm available!'

In my local town, individuals have stood up, talked about, begun and, with the help of others, seen through to completion projects such as a lovely sensory garden and play area for children. Nehemiah is about to find out that the help and skills he needs to rebuild the city walls are not far away.

† We give thanks for those willing to stand up and take a lead in the building up and restoration of our local communities and churches. May their courage inspire others to offer what they can.

Monday 4 March
Making Plans

Read Nehemiah 2:11 – 3:5

Then I said to them, 'You see the trouble we are in: Jerusalem lies in ruins, and its gates have been burned with fire. Come, let us rebuild the wall of Jerusalem, and we will no longer be in disgrace.' I also told them about the gracious hand of my God on me and what the king had said to me. They replied, 'Let us start rebuilding.' So they began this good work.

(verses 2:17–18)

Over the years, I have engaged in several 'home improvement' projects. I now understand my limitations, and beyond those I bring in the professionals! My son, however – aided by an array of fancy tools and YouTube videos – has developed skills way beyond my own, and I can only admire his perseverance, and the end results.

I'm not good at making plans, preferring to simply get on with things, which is maybe why some of my projects never quite fulfil their original intention. My son is less scatty, more focused like Nehemiah – making sure he has the skills and the tools to complete a task.

Nehemiah didn't just turn up at Jerusalem and attempt to put together a working party. He spent three days assessing the scale of the problem; scrambling around broken walls, rubble-strewn roads and crumbling gates destroyed by fire many years previously. Only then did he share his plan with local officials and those with influence. Nehemiah knew what his strengths were, and that he had the backing of both the king and God in this matter. What he needed now were the people and the skills to see this through to completion.

This would be a team effort – 'Come, let *us* rebuild the wall of Jerusalem' (italics mine) – and it is Eliashib, the high priest, who sets an example for all those who will subsequently offer their help. The required skills had been lying there unused for generations, locked away until revealed and inspired into action by God through Nehemiah's words.

† We give thanks for those whose skills and talents make a real difference, both to individuals and to the communities in which they live and work.

For further thought

Consider your own hidden talents, and how, despite your uncertainty, they might prove useful locally.

Tuesday 5 March
Working together

Read Nehemiah 3:6–21

*Uzziel son of Harhaiah, one of the goldsmiths, repaired the next section;
and Hananiah, one of the perfume-makers, made repairs next to that.
They restored Jerusalem as far as the Broad Wall. Rephaiah son of Hur,
ruler of a half-district of Jerusalem, repaired the next section. Adjoining
this, Jedaiah son of Harumaph made repairs opposite his house, and
Hattush son of Hashabneiah made repairs next to him.*

(verses 8–10)

Having walked around the city walls, Nehemiah knew where his
priorities lay – and these were the ten city gates vulnerable to
attack. Help came from an unlikely range of backgrounds and even
from surrounding towns. We see goldsmiths and perfume-makers
doing what they can; family members working on sections of wall
near their homes; and stonemasons and carpenters concentrating
on the gateways and doors. They needed large stones for the city
walls – a challenge for those more used to working with gold or
herbs and spices – but together they worked, with Nehemiah at
the helm, and progress was made.

It is wonderful when churches and community groups work
together to get things done, whether in organising food banks to
help those struggling to feed their families; raising money to fund
playgrounds for local children; or hosting support groups, art-and-
craft sessions or other activities that encourage engagement.
These and similar projects make a real difference to the way people
view the places where they live, encourage further interaction
and improve wellbeing. I've seen this locally, when incomers have
posted on social media about how friendly this little town is,
and what a brilliant move it has been for them as a family. And I
sense something of this in Nehemiah's story, in a groundswell of
enthusiasm in its population to get the city looking beautiful once
again; somewhere that its lost people would be happy to return to.

† Inspire us, Lord, as churches and individuals, to become good neighbours who
reach out and help wherever there is a need.

For further thought

Are there ongoing projects in your local community, set up to help
others, that you and your church fellowship could engage with?

Wednesday 6 March
Opposition surfaces

Read Nehemiah 4:1–18

When Sanballat heard that we were rebuilding the wall, he became angry and was greatly incensed. He ridiculed the Jews, and in the presence of his associates and the army of Samaria, he said, 'What are those feeble Jews doing? Will they restore their wall? Will they offer sacrifices? Will they finish in a day? Can they bring the stones back to life from those heaps of rubble – burned as they are?' Tobiah the Ammonite, who was at his side, said, 'What they are building – even a fox climbing up on it would break down their wall of stones!'

(verses 1–3)

Not everyone likes change, and that's often the way within the church. Sometimes we find our comfort levels threatened by proposed changes ... or maybe it just seems wrong, too expensive or unnecessary. But when groups of any kind split into opposing views, it can damage the wellbeing and stability of a community that has previously seemed strong.

In today's reading, it's the outsiders who get upset; perhaps because they see the rebuilding of Jerusalem's walls and gates as a threat to the status quo. In Nehemiah's telling, it seems more of a verbal than a military challenge, if we pay attention to Tobiah's words. Archaeology reveals that Nehemiah's walls were 2.7 metres thick, so it would have taken more than a few foxes to knock them down!

Perhaps the verbal insults found their way to those on the ground, who were already growing tired. Their enthusiasm was certainly waning and fear was creeping in. But Nehemiah could see what was happening and prayerfully came up with a solution that worked, crediting God with the result: a visible defence for the workers, which proved enough to deter those who wanted to disrupt the work or who threatened to attack.

When the plans we make meet opposition, it is important not to ignore but to engage with the issues raised to avoid disruption. If this is done prayerfully, and with sensitivity, solutions can often be found. The way we do church in our local settings has developed over the years in a similar way, and will hopefully continue to do so in the future.

† Help us, Lord, to be aware of those whose views differ from ours, and to embrace rather than dismiss them, so that barriers which are difficult to resolve and overcome do not build up.

For further thought

How quick are you to build walls when faced with change?

66

Thursday 7 March
Helping those in need

Read Nehemiah 5:1–19

Furthermore, a hundred and fifty Jews and officials ate at my table, as well as those who came to us from the surrounding nations. Each day one ox, six choice sheep and some poultry were prepared for me, and every ten days an abundant supply of wine of all kinds. In spite of all this, I never demanded the food allotted to the governor, because the demands were heavy on these people. Remember me with favour, my God, for all I have done for these people.

(verses 17–19)

It is a sad fact of life that within families, churches, communities and larger populations, problems can remain almost invisible until they reach breaking point or until someone speaks out on behalf of those affected. This does not necessarily occur through neglect or design. The issues may simply have gone unnoticed within the day-to-day busyness of life, however connected we might feel to those around us.

Today's chapter embraces a larger timeframe than the fifty-two days spent on wall-building, but the issues raised would have become more acute during that period. Hard workers need feeding well, and economic pressures would have made that difficult. The landless were short of grain, while landowners were mortgaging their properties or having to sell their children into slavery to pay exorbitant taxes. And it wasn't foreigners who were being blamed for this crisis, but fellow Jews. The rich were getting richer and the poor were becoming poorer. An issue for every generation, it would seem.

This is very much a cry to God for justice. But those in power often ignore the voice of the poor. Fortunately, Nehemiah heard them and, after giving the issue some thought (one of his greater qualities!), came up with a solution that all could embrace. He could also point to his own example, for as a governor he had never taken the bonuses that went with the post, but had devoted himself to the task at hand and shared what he had with others.

† Forgive us, loving God, when we ignore the injustice that has become, over generations, ingrained within our culture. Help us to fight it as best we can.

For further thought

How important is it for individual Christians and the wider church to be a voice and an accessible presence for those in need?

Friday 8 March
Opposition and false rumours

Read Nehemiah 6:1–19

'It is reported among the nations – and Geshem says it is true – that you and the Jews are plotting to revolt, and therefore you are building the wall. Moreover, according to these reports you are about to become their king and have even appointed prophets to make this proclamation about you in Jerusalem: "There is a king in Judah!" Now this report will get back to the king; so come, let us meet together.' I sent him this reply: 'Nothing like what you are saying is happening; you are just making it up out of your head.'

(verses 6–8)

Propaganda and rumour have ignited many conflicts over the centuries. More recently, with the expansion of social media usage, we have seen the genuine power of fake news and conspiracy theories in influencing political opinions; not only in favour of or against individuals and nations, but in relation to major issues such as climate change and fossil fuels.

Misinformation is a powerful tool, with potentially life-threatening consequences. And in our reading today we can see how this weapon could have undermined everything Nehemiah had worked for, even before the project was completed.

The letter delivered to Nehemiah came unsealed, so anyone interested could, and probably had, already seen its contents. This suggests he had plans to lead a Jewish rebellion and declare himself a king in Judah – something no Persian king would tolerate.

Making this statement public might have encouraged the Jews within the city to believe it and encourage such a rebellion to take place. Nehemiah had no such thoughts and fully appreciated the danger such news might create. He turns to God in prayer once more before returning to the task at hand. Opposition did not end, but Nehemiah was closer to finishing the task God had called him to, which was his absolute priority.

Being aware of the dangers involved in believing all that we see and hear on social media or elsewhere is important. Checking 'facts' before we repeat them can help to avoid misunderstandings, arguments or even worse consequences.

† God of justice, we pray for the truth to triumph whenever people attempt to undermine it for their own benefit.

For further thought

Do you fact-check social media posts before 'liking' or sharing them with your online friends?

Saturday 9 March
A gathering

Read Nehemiah 7:1–7, 70–73

Now the city was large and spacious, but there were few people in it, and the houses had not yet been rebuilt. So my God put it into my heart to assemble the nobles, the officials and the common people for registration by families. I found the genealogical record of those who had been the first to return.

(verses 4–5)

Through the story of Nehemiah we have an insight into the way God works, in this case to bring about the promised restoration of the people of Israel to their land. It does not simply happen through the vision, prayer and organisational skills of Nehemiah; but through a Persian king who allows it to proceed, and with enough skilled workers and volunteers who – empowered to overcome opposition from their enemies, and despite the exhaustion caused by their labours – complete this epic task.

We are naturally impatient and want our prayers and plans to come to fruition instantly, and although this wall went up relatively quickly, it needed the right people in place. I look back at my own life and can see that I am here, writing these words, because of the many people whose faith, experience, words, joys and struggles connected with and helped me in my personal journey of faith.

Nehemiah lists many thousands of people – returnees from Babylon to Jerusalem some ninety-three years previously – whose family connections form the basis of his repopulation plan. We may think this is rather exclusive, or even uninteresting, but it is far better to see them as the names of real people. There are several genealogies found in scripture, and they all act as a reminder of the love of God for all people, known by name. Those who influenced my faith may not know that I still remember and give thanks for their lives, but God knows them and does not forget.

† Loving God, we give thanks for the many people who have been a part of our individual faith journeys.

For further thought

How important is it for people to see our faith reflected in the interactions we have with others through our words and deeds?

Rebuilding in Nehemiah (2)

Notes by **Bola Iduoze**

Bola is an author, conference speaker and mentor. She began her career as an accountant more than thirty years ago and her entrepreneurial journey in 2000. Bola co-pastors Gateway Chapel, a multicultural church in Kent, UK. She has a passion to encourage, equip and empower people to live their best lives ever. Bola and husband Eddie Iduoze have two children, Asher and Bethel. She has used the NLT version for these notes.

Sunday 10 March
Ezra reads the law

Read Nehemiah 8:1–18

He faced the square just inside the Water Gate from early morning until noon and read aloud to everyone who could understand. All the people listened closely to the Book of the Law.

(verse 3)

I grew up attending a Baptist church in Ibadan, Nigeria, where I was exposed to public Bible reading as well as Bible quizzes from the reading sessions. These sessions made it easy to not only get acquainted with the Bible, but also to memorise, meditate on and start loving the instructions of the Lord. This great experience does not seem to be seen so regularly in today's fast-paced life. The busy schedule of the modern day makes it tougher for many to enjoy the same blessings I did growing up.

The giving of time and attention to listening to the word of God was a remarkable occurrence in Ezra's days, when he read aloud the word of God from daybreak to noon. The Bible said that everyone, including children, listened to the reading for hours.

It is noteworthy that everyone who could understand engaged with the word of God. Getting the whole family to listen to the word is the beginning of change, both in the family and in society. The scripture today encourages us all to listen as well as to share the word of God to all who understand around us, so let's make this a priority.

† Lord, please give us the grace to listen to and take in your word consistently, in Jesus' name.

Monday 11 March
A time of repentance

> **Read Nehemiah 9:1–8, 32–38**
>
> *They remained standing in place for three hours while the Book of the Law of the Lord their God was read aloud to them. Then for three more hours they confessed their sins and worshiped the Lord their God.*
>
> (verse 3)

The gathering of Israel to listen to the Book of the Law continued in Nehemiah, and this gathering led to the repentance of the nation, so that they start realigning their ways and minds to the word of God.

Repentance is a product of looking into the word. As the people stood to read the word of God aloud, their understanding of it was kindled, and this led to the realisation of their inadequacies, which resulted in the confession of sins. The whole congregation then started to worship the Lord.

Reading and listening to the word of God is a great investment of time into our spiritual growth and development. As the Israelites heard the word they were able to see why they were experiencing hardship, and the fact that they – as well as their leaders – were not following God's word or paying attention to the statute of the law.

It is easy to take our attention away from the Lord and not even know that we have deviated from his plans and his will if we do not continue to align our ways to the word. There is no better way to stay in line than by giving attention to the word of God.

Following on from reading it, the word begins moving hearts to repentance. As it happened to the people of Israel, so it can be in our lives today.

† Lord, open my eyes to your word and my heart to your will, so I can realign my ways to yours in all things, in Jesus' name.

For further thought
Looking into the law of the Lord shows us areas where we need repentance. Therefore, we need to give more time to the word of God – Nehemiah 8:1–18, for example.

Tuesday 12 March
An agreement reached

Read Nehemiah 10:28–39

The people and the Levites must bring these offerings of grain, new wine, and olive oil to the storerooms and place them in the sacred containers near the ministering priests, the gatekeepers, and the singers. 'We promise together not to neglect the Temple of our God.'

(verse 39)

The people of God had a unique response to the law of the Lord. They agreed to give themselves to the work of the Lord and live their lives in such a way that God and his work were given priority when it came to their earnings.

It was once said that genuine repentance can be seen in our ability to commit our totality to God. This is inclusive of our wallets. Our commitment to God where income is concerned is still as essential today as it was in biblical days.

As a young lady in a Baptist church, I understood the principle of tithing more as a law. This is what we do as genuine Baptists; we pay our tithes, alongside a few other rules. So I started out paying my tithe in agreement with what I had been taught.

As time went on, I grew to know the Lord for myself and started looking into his word to see what he says, I started following that. I developed a better understanding of what and why I gave. I totally agreed with giving my tithe to the Lord as part of my Christian responsibility to the house of God I am a part of. Not because it is a law I have to obey in order to be a part of the house of God, but because it is the responsible thing to do as part of a house and to show my understanding of God as my source and priority.

† Lord, grant me a heart that is responsive to your word, and put to good use my consistent giving to your house in Jesus' name.

For further thought

The people chose to respond to the word of God through their giving. Everyone took responsibility for the upkeep of the house of the Lord. We, too, can show our maturity and responsibility by deciding to contribute to the house of God consistently.

Wednesday 13 March
The settlers

> **Read Nehemiah 11:1–4, 20–36**
>
> *The chief officer of the Levites in Jerusalem was Uzzi son of Bani, son of Hashabiah, son of Mattaniah, son of Mica, a descendant of Asaph, whose family served as singers at God's Temple. Their daily responsibilities were carried out according to the terms of a royal command.*
>
> (verses 22–23)

God is intentional about the way he settles his people and the community he designed for us to grow in. As the Israelites settled, the Levites were expected to settle among the other tribes to help them in their understanding and their worship.

In today's reading, some men were moved into the city, whereas others were expected to settle outside the city. However, everyone was expected to be in a community, and everyone's strengths were to be of use in the kingdom of God.

One of the most remarkable people we read about is Uzzi, a leader of the Levites in Jerusalem. He was not just a leader of one of the groups; he also stood out as a singer in the service of the Lord's house.

Diligently serving in God's house, or overseeing the worship team in church, made this gentleman stand out. He was not just referred to as a settler, but was specifically mentioned because of the additional service he brought into the community.

What will you add in value terms to the community God has settled you in, which will make you stand out? You and I were designed to be part of our communities, and we should embrace our task in contributing to the communities we are settled in.

† Lord, open my eyes to see the community you want me to settle in as well as the task you have gifted me to carry out, in Jesus' name.

For further thought

Serving the church and the wider community was key to Uzzi. How are you serving both?

Thursday 14 March
A service of dedication

Read Nehemiah 12:27–47

Many sacrifices were offered on that joyous day, for God had given the people cause for great joy. The women and children also participated in the celebration, and the joy of the people of Jerusalem could be heard far away.

(verse 43)

Nehemiah led the people of God in the huge project of building the wall, then rounded it off with reading the word and worship. The worship session was a session of genuine gratitude, joy, thanksgiving and celebration. There was so much celebration in the house during this time of worship that the shout of joy was heard from far away.

This reminded me of my time growing up, when our Baptist church went on a weekly outreach to a nearby village for a few months. After that it was decided by the committee of leaders that our church would plant a church in this remote village.

Over the next few years, the church diligently built this outreach centre. The day of the commissioning of the building was phenomenal. We had a dedication service, at which thanksgiving songs were sung throughout the whole village. It was such a joyful and attractive time that the noise of it went round the village and brought even the non-Christians to come and see. The dedication service became an outreach opportunity.

This little incident helps me to see how the dedication service in the reading for today must have been a time of joy for the Israelites, a tool of evangelism for the neighbours and a joyful moment in heaven.

As we sacrifice joyfully in our dedication and service to the Lord, we will attract others to Christ and bring all the glory to God.

† Lord, help me to come joyfully to the place of worship and thanksgiving, that my service might please you and draw people to you continually, in Jesus' name.

For further thought
The more we dedicate our lives and service to God, the more he can use us to bring joy to many and change lives around us.

Friday 15 March
Nehemiah's reforms

Read Nehemiah 13:1–14

I immediately confronted the leaders and demanded, 'Why has the Temple of God been neglected?' Then I called all the Levites back again and restored them to their proper duties.

(verse 11)

Despite the people's excitement about building the wall, they neglected the service of the Lord at their first opportunity when their leader wasn't there. This disappointing practice reflected the hearts of the people and their need for a leader who would bring restoration and transformation to the community.

Nehemiah was surprised that everyone, including the Levites, left their duties when there was no strong leader to keep them in service.

Personal motivation to serve the Lord seems to be a challenge for every generation. While spiritual growth and personal disciplines should dictate our ability to keep some spiritual practices going, we still fall prey to slacking if there are no strong leaders.

In many cases there has been a need for leaders in the house of the Lord to arise and show people why we cannot afford to neglect the temple of God, and to come back to our posts of service in the temple. Nehemiah brought a reform, putting in a new structure to help the people return to the service of the Lord.

† Lord, help me to stay faithful in my service to you, irrespective of who else remains faithful. Please use me as your agent of reformation today.

For further thought

What measures have you put in place in your life to enable you to continue growing spiritually, even if your leaders are not around to motivate you?

Saturday 16 March
In those days

Read Nehemiah 13:15–30

I immediately confronted the leaders and demanded, 'Why has the Temple of God been neglected?' Then I called all the Levites back again and restored them to their proper duties.

(verse 11)

On Nehemiah's return, he saw that a huge amount of decadence had permeated the Israelites' culture during his time away. The people of God totally forgot all the structure that had been put in place to help them live in line with God's commands. They started to buy and sell on the sabbath day, kept the wrong company and intermarried with people of other cultures. They even married people from cultures that God had clearly warned them against. The result of such actions is always a separation from God's plan and command.

Every time the children of God allow themselves to be unequally yoked, they dilute what distinguishes them as God's own children. We are called to be separate, so we can be true examples of what God desires his own to be. This can be difficult to achieve, but as we stay close to God and his word, we are able to follow in his footsteps and live our lives in a way that showcases him to our world.

Solomon thought mixed marriage was harmless, but his wives led to his fellowship with God being damaged. God doesn't want us to be diluted, but separated to him, so we can be the example he delights in and the world can see what God is able to do with his own.

Nehemiah achieved the hard task of driving away the mixed-married and the strangers, and also introduced sanctification as well as various other rules. Although they were hard, these measures brought the people back into fellowship with the Lord and reformation occurred in the land.

† Lord, help me to stay focused on your word. May I not be subtly led away from you by making wrong choices, in Jesus' name.

For further thought

God does not want us to be unequally yoked or to take on the culture of the world and influences around us, lest we are led away from him.

The Gospel of Mark (2)

1 Authority over evil

Notes by **Kristina Andréasson**

Kristina was ordained as a priest in the Church of Sweden in 2007 before moving to the Swedish Church in London in 2014. In 2019 she started serving the Church of England as Associate Vicar of St John's Wood Church in London. She believes that God is there for everyone, no matter who we are or where we're from. She reflects on how, and in what way, God is there for us when life is difficult. Kristina has used the NRSVA for these notes.

Sunday 17 March
Jesus calls us by name in times of struggle

Read Mark 5:1–20

A man out of the tombs with an unclean spirit met him. ... Jesus asked him, 'What is your name?' He replied, 'My name is Legion; for we are many' ... The unclean spirits came out and entered the swine ... And he ... began to proclaim in the Decapolis how much Jesus had done for him; and everyone was amazed.

(verses 2b, 9, 13b, 20)

Tombs, demons and swine leave us with a dramatic and unpleasant impression. But, as Elijah discovered, God is not always in the drama. Sometimes he is found in the peaceful background; in a gentle, loving touch.

Jesus quietly asks the man's name. As well as 'many', 'Legion' means 'military army'. This could refer to demons, but it might also relate to a traumatic memory about the Roman legions' oppression. Whatever might be troubling him, Jesus is trying to reach this troubled man.

There is something very caring about letting the swine catch the people's attention, because I'm sure the man knew all too well about people staring and pointing fingers. The swine also gives people closure in their worries about demons. But in the background, in such a gentle way, Jesus meets the man. Jesus believes in him. He tells him to go home and preach. Was he a bit nervous? I wonder what he preached. Whatever it was, everyone was amazed!

Today, the man tells us about the God who gently seeks us, lovingly sees us for who we are and believes in us, even in times when we struggle to believe in ourselves.

† God of life, thank you for calling us by name and for believing in us, even in times when we feel lost in our struggles. Amen

Monday 18 March
When we feel like we don't belong

Read Mark 5:21–43

Now there was a woman who had been suffering from haemorrhages for twelve years. She had endured much under many physicians, and had spent all that she had; and she was no better, but rather grew worse. She had heard about Jesus, and came up behind him in the crowd and touched his cloak, for she said, 'If I but touch his clothes, I will be made well.' Immediately her haemorrhages stopped ... He said to her, 'Daughter, your faith has made you well; go in peace ...'

(verses 25–29a, 34)

What courage this woman has. Or did she approach Jesus out of complete despair, as she had nothing left to lose? With her illness at that time, she would have been seen and treated as unclean; as someone who was not allowed to come close to others; someone who had to warn the people around her that she was unclean so they wouldn't approach her.

This woman had spent all she had on physicians. That tells us she is poor, but that there had been a time when she wasn't. She had once been a part of society, with some kind of financial security. Now she has nothing left and no one to turn to. I wonder what the hardest part for her was: the physical pain, losing all she had owned or no longer being part of someone else's life and being someone other people backed away from. Was it out of courage that she touched his cloak, or was it out of despair, knowing that things couldn't possibly get worse?

We read that she was healed. Jesus mentions her faith, but also calls her 'daughter' – and maybe this is what should be emphasised. Because this is actually the only time Jesus refers to someone as his daughter. For the first time in many years she finds herself in relationship with someone else.

She is healed, but I think she knew as well as we all do that difficult times might come again. However, she wasn't just physically healed; she belonged again. *'Daughter,'* he said. Imagine the healing peace it must have given her lonely heart. She finally belonged.

† God of life, thank you for your love, which tells us every day how we belong with you. In times of desperation, let us feel your comfort – even just in a small, loving touch. Amen

For further thought

Have you ever felt left out and then experienced someone making you feel more included? What did they say?

Changes: sometimes difficult, yet needed

> **Read Mark 6:1–6**
>
> *He left that place and came to his home town … [They said] 'Is not this the carpenter, the son of Mary and brother of James and Joses and Judas and Simon, and are not his sisters here with us?' And they took offence at him. Then Jesus said to them, 'Prophets are not without honour, except in their home town, and among their own kin, and in their own house.'*
>
> (verses 1a, 3–4)

'You don't get to be a prophet in your hometown.' This is, in some parts of the world, an expression to use when you're not being listened to or taken seriously by those closest to you, especially when you have something new to share.

I think most of us feel the need to take a new breath every now and then, whether we've stayed in the same village our entire lives or lived in different parts of the world. We might pause and feel that something within us has changed, even though the world around us is carrying on like it did before. The change to our perspectives and feelings might come from a specific and sudden source or grow slowly within us.

As with Jesus, however, the people around us might still see the same person. Even those we love the most might need time to understand that there is something new. To the people in his hometown, Jesus was still that little boy they saw growing up next to his brothers and sisters. I can imagine it saddened Jesus not to be listened to or taken seriously, just as it does us.

What does this story tell us? Maybe it says something about the changes needed in order to be true to ourselves. That change is not always easy, and is not always understood, but it is still needed.

'You don't get to be a prophet in your hometown.' Maybe that's just how it is. But the safety of the bud can't keep the flower from bursting out into bloom. In the same way, we grow and bloom.

† God of life, be close to us in times of change. Help us take the right steps and make wise choices when we find ourselves standing at the crossroads. Amen

For further thought

Like flowers we change, even though we remain the same. But might it also feel good that some people remember who we once were?

Wednesday 20 March
He sent them two by two

Read Mark 6:7–13

He called the twelve and began to send them out two by two, and gave them authority over the unclean spirits.

(verse 7)

In Salvador Dalí's paintings you can sometimes find crutches. I've been told that these symbolise how none of us can manage in life completely on our own. We all need help and support. Maybe this is why Jesus sent his disciples out two by two. Yet loneliness is something I think most of us have experienced, more or less. In our journeys through life, we don't always walk two by two.

I remember once, when travelling on my own, I got stuck at Dublin Airport overnight due to bad weather conditions. It was late evening. I sat down on the floor and another woman of my age did the same. We looked at each other, both tired and on our own. We started chatting. The restaurants were closed, but we went to the small supermarket to buy some food to share. With the help of a few tissues my suitcase became a dinner table, and laughter and thoughts about life turned our cheese, bread and juice into a little feast. Our life journeys crossed, but we never spoke again.

Could it be that God sends strangers our way sometimes, as supporting crutches? Two by two. Maybe the one next to us isn't always someone we know very well. Maybe it's someone who just briefly crosses our path. Other times we can feel utterly alone, without even a stranger to be found.

Then I think of another feast: simple bread and a drop of wine. A feast where I sense a love that, like a crutch, is there to support us, even in times of loneliness.

† God of life, be close to us in times of loneliness. When it hurts not to have someone next to us, send a friend our way. Let us know that you are there. Amen

For further thought

Can you remember a brief meeting with a stranger that meant a lot to you? Could you have been that stranger to someone else?

Thursday 21 March
The brutal death of John the Baptist

Read Mark 6:14–29

Immediately she rushed back to the king and requested, 'I want you to give me at once the head of John the Baptist on a platter.' The king was deeply grieved; yet out of regard for his oaths and for the guests, he did not want to refuse her. Immediately the king sent a soldier of the guard with orders to bring John's head. He went and beheaded him in the prison, brought his head on a platter, and gave it to the girl.

(verses 25–28a)

John the Baptist is patron saint of the church I currently serve. You can find a statue of him just outside, next to a beautiful red rosebush. He stands strong, firmly pointing forward with one hand. Pointing at the church, Christ, the future. If you look closely, you will spot tiny bees on silver candle holders, reminding us of the wild honey he ate. We make sure to always celebrate our patron saint on his birthday.

But rarely do we speak about his death. I like the fact we don't, because his death is so brutal and says something about the awful things humankind is capable of. I'm afraid that by talking about it too much we get used to it and it doesn't upset us as much. It is one thing to know what happened. That can be important. But it is another thing to open up space to something so brutal.

We don't know what thoughts and feelings John the Baptist had at the very end of his life. He had dedicated his life to preparing the way for Christ, but his death speaks of the evil and extreme brutality we meet in this world. God didn't save him from that. A life with God doesn't save us from hurt and pain. Maybe he doubted, just as we do sometimes.

But I see the statue of him next to those red roses. Red roses remind us of thorns and the blood shed on the cross; a silent promise from a God who never leaves our side, even in times of brutal pain.

† God of life, when the world appears brutal and evil, help us not to lose faith in the strength of love. Don't let evil harden our hearts. Amen

For further thought

How can we stay aware of what is happening in the world without becoming numb to cruelty and evil?

Friday 22 March
Our world needs small, loving actions

Read Mark 6:30–44

So they sat down in groups of hundreds and of fifties. Taking the five loaves and the two fish, he looked up to heaven, and blessed and broke the loaves, and gave them to his disciples to set before the people; and he divided the two fish among them all. And all ate and were filled; and they took up twelve baskets full of broken pieces and of the fish.

(verses 40–43)

In one of her songs, Swedish hymn writer Lina Sandell wrote something that I would translate along the lines of: 'Do the little that you can, and never look upon it, thinking it is too small or unimportant. Because how would you then be able to joyfully walk where your Lord sent you?'[1] These words often come to my mind when I think of a tiny amount of bread and fish feeding thousands. There is so much power in the smallest action of love. This should never be underestimated.

In many places of the world, spring is on its way. We see power and beauty in one little flowerbud. Spring can be a time when God's creation becomes very present to us. Maybe we also start to feel worry. Climate change and extreme weather conditions are a fact. How do we take care of God's creation so it will still be there for future generations?

Maybe that's when we really need to hear about this miracle; about this tiny action that fed so many. We should do the little we can for our world and its future, and trust in the power of small, loving actions. Lina Sandell wrote in the same song: 'Do the little that you can, willingly and happily. Soon the precious opportunities might be gone.' The feeding of the 5,000 might sound implausible, and so might any good news for our future earth at times. But in a tiny morsel of fish and bread there is a rebellious hope. We need this hope, and so does our world.

† God of life, give us the imagination and the courage to work for a better future. Help us to see power in the smallest of actions, so that we never give up. Amen

For further thought

Imagine the many small actions of love and care for our world that would stop if we lost our faith in a new tomorrow.

[1] English version of L. Sandell's 'Gör det lilla du kan' (https://hymnary.org/text/goer_det_lilla_du_kan), translated by Kristina.

Saturday 23 March
Take heart; God is there

Read Mark 6:45–56

*He came towards them early in the morning, walking on the lake …
'Take heart, it is I; do not be afraid.' Then he got into the boat with
them and the wind ceased. And they were utterly astounded, for they
did not understand about the loaves, but their hearts were hardened …
And wherever he went, into villages or cities or farms, they laid the sick
in the market-places, and begged him that they might touch even the
fringe of his cloak; and all who touched it were healed.*

(verses 48b, 50b–52, 56)

We have walked together through Mark this week, and we have
walked through many emotions. We have been reminded about
times of struggles and feelings of not belonging. We have reflected
on changes in life and the experience of loneliness. Mark has
shown us the brutality of the evil world we live in. We have looked
at our own lives and actions in relation to the world's future.

We end today with Jesus walking on water. And as he walks,
I imagine the water surface reflecting everything around him:
the disciples in the boat and the shore filled with all the people
who are about to meet him. There on the water surface it's like
everything is summed up; what has been and what is to come.
The feeding of the thousands is still so alive within the disciples.
The wind captures something about the change that is coming.
The scary deep of the water acknowledges something of our
world's brutality. The people on the shore speak of loneliness and
struggles. The woman's desperate action echoes, knowing that the
fringe of his cloak will be touched again. Everything seems to be
mirrored on the surface as he walks on the water.

Danish author Hans Christian Andersen is quoted as saying (my
translation): 'In human life … there is an invisible thread that
shows how we belong to God. I live *with* this conviction and I live
in it; it is pierced through my entire life.'

Maybe that's what Jesus shows us as he walks on water.
Whatever we're going through, let us take heart. God is there.

† God of life, just as you once walked peacefully on the water, be close to us when
the waves are high. Calm our storms, bringing peace to our lives. Amen

For further thought
Think of an invisible thread that goes through us all, stating that
we belong to God. Will this affect your interaction with the next
person you meet?

Gospel of Mark (2)

2 Holy Week with Mark

Notes by **Revd Dr Ash Barker**

Ash is a leadership developer, shalom activist, communicator and pioneer minister. He has lived on the front line of urban poverty for more than thirty years, beginning in Melbourne before spending twelve years in Bangkok's largest slum. He and wife Anji now live in community at Newbigin House in Winson Green. Ash has authored eight books and leads postgraduate courses at Nazarene Theological College. He is minister at Lodge Road URC and leads Seedbeds to help grow community leaders. Ash has used the NRSVA for these notes.

Sunday 24 March
Jesus defies public expectations

Read Mark 11:1–11

Then he entered Jerusalem and went into the temple; and when he had looked around at everything, as it was already late, he went out to Bethany with the twelve.

(verse 11)

This a critical moment. Jesus had invested in a handful of leaders and a broader community movement of disciples. However, when addressing crowds he only told parables, so his intentions were not yet public. Jerusalem, under the iron rule of Rome, was a powder-keg, ready to explode. Expectations of a violent revolution to free God's people had been building. Could Jesus be the Messianic answer to Jewish prayers and prophecies about their desired freedom?

As Jesus prepared to enter Jerusalem he sought to downplay those expectations. He came on a donkey, not a war horse. The crowd pressed in with their hopes about Jesus anyway, claiming him as their liberating Saviour with palms and raised voices.

How would Jesus respond? Like the spies of old, he undertakes a reconnaissance mission. The next day, assessment clear, he would intentionally clear the temple of money-changers and others.

There are times to quietly work below the surface without worrying about what others think of us or our intentions. Other times require us to go public and leave people in no doubt.

Like Jesus, we must pick our moments, plan intentionally and be prepared to pay the price.

† Risen Lord, please give us the courage and conviction to go public, no matter the cost.

Jesus clears barriers to the temple

Read Mark 11:15–25

Then they came to Jerusalem. And he entered the temple and began to drive out those who were selling and those who were buying in the temple, and he overturned the tables of the money-changers and the seats of those who sold doves.

(verse 15)

As we saw yesterday, Jesus carefully assessed and planned for the events that are unfolding in today's passage. This is no spur-of-the-moment release of pent-up frustration. He intentionally went to the Court of Gentiles in the temple and flipped over tables, creating havoc for the money-changers and dove sellers. This seems unbecoming for any leader, never mind the Son of God! Could you imagine an equivalent scenario in a Christian church, or at a conference or festival? Why such extreme behaviour?

Jesus explained that this prophetic action was about inclusion and access. He quoted Isaiah 56:7, stating that the temple was to be 'a house of prayer for all nations'. While the courts for priests and Jews were free from these traders – and therefore available for their proper use – the only place available to Gentiles to use had been taken over. Access for 'all nations' included overcoming barriers of race, class, gender and disability. However, the leaders here had created serious barriers; barriers they profited from. Jesus wasn't having any of it from these 'thieves'. He stood up to their racket and hit them hard, where it hurt the most: financially.

Vested interests that create barriers don't move easily. Vested interests protected and enjoyed by religious powers are especially stubborn when they are linked to livelihoods and income streams. Christian faith, however, is not a business or an industry, but a movement of the people of God for change; God's reign on earth, as in heaven. Where our income security comes from, and the ways in which we fail to address inequality, exclusion and disparities, are often linked.

† Lord, where are the tables we need to turn over to include others in our shared lives?

For further thought

Who are we excluding because of our own self-interests?

Tuesday 26 March
Jesus anointed at Bethany

Read Mark 14:1–9

'Why was the ointment wasted in this way? For this ointment could have been sold for more than three hundred denarii, and the money given to the poor.'

(verses 4b–5)

Jesus retreated to Bethany to the home of Simon the leper. Bethany was a place of peace for him, where he received support and renewal. A woman in that house used her precious oil to anoint Jesus for what she could see was about to happen. The disciples can't see what she does and complain that it's a waste of much-needed resources.

Perhaps they took the view that many still take: 'There's nothing you can do about poverty, so let's all worship Jesus! After all, didn't Jesus say, "You'll always have the poor with you"?' Yet the location of the event (Simon the leper's home), the event itself (a woman ministering to Jesus in a priestly way) and Jesus' response in verse 7 ('you can show kindness to [the poor] whenever you wish') affirms his concern that the social location of God's people is always in solidarity with the poor.

Jesus genuinely received ministry from Mary. Jesus commends her because she saw what was about to happen in a way that the men in that room, and the power elite in Jerusalem, couldn't. She surrendered to the moment and will always be remembered because she anointed Jesus for burial.

I am often surprised by the generosity, insights and creative actions of people who have experienced marginalisation. Kindness and freedom can unleash pent-up emotion, and out rush truthful actions. Those close to power so often miss what God is doing and requiring in a unique situation. Our traditions, controls and politeness can blind us to what is needed in any given moment.

† Lord, open our eyes to what you are doing and need from us. Help us to be generous, insightful and spontaneous like Mary of Bethany.

For further thought
Just like Mary, we can bless God and minister to him.

86

Wednesday 27 March
The Last Supper and its promises

Read Mark 14:10–26

While they were eating, he took a loaf of bread, and after blessing it he broke it, gave it to them, and said, 'Take; this is my body.' Then he took a cup, and after giving thanks he gave it to them, and all of them drank from it. He said to them, 'This is my blood of the covenant, which is poured out for many.'

(verses 22–24)

Jesus' community is hidden away in secrecy for what will be their final meal together. They are back in Jerusalem, but it had taken some clandestine planning to find a room where they could all meet, safe from the authorities. Jesus knew betrayal was at hand and needed to prepare the apostles for what was about to happen.

In so many ways, this meal is an experience of the good news of the kingdom that Jesus had preached so much about. One loaf was blessed, broken up and then eaten by the community. Jesus was that one loaf, and his body would be broken. They were one community but would soon be scattered. In eating the bread, the disciples were accepting Jesus' role: to be his hands, feet, heart and voice in the world.

The cup was offered with thanks, and wine was drunk by all as a further act of identifying with their Lord. His blood would soon flow down as he was tortured and executed, and within a few years most of those present would be martyred. Yet there is life within the blood, and in Jesus there is new life – resurrection life. By identifying with him, the disciples would receive it. New life would flow there, too. In Jesus' own words: 'Those who believe in me, even though they die, will live' (John 11:25).

Jesus' plan to put all things right would be inaugurated in such a way: bread, wine, hope. In so many ways these elements are central to the Christian faith, along with unity, diversity, forgiveness and grace. Whenever we receive Communion, may we experience anew these life-transforming meanings.

† Lord, let us never take for granted your costly, sacrificial life. May we join your life in overcoming death in all its forms, so fullness of life can come for all.

For further thought

Research areas of the world where Christians are persecuted and killed. How can we support them and advocate on their behalf?

Thursday 28 March
Jesus distressed in Gethsemane

Read Mark 14:32–52

They went to a place called Gethsemane; and he said to his disciples, 'Sit here while I pray.' He took with him Peter and James and John, and began to be distressed and agitated. And he said to them, 'I am deeply grieved, even to death; remain here, and keep awake.'

(verses 32–34)

Jesus' humanity included real vulnerabilities: anxiety, severe distress, agitation and frustration. Many of us have felt these kinds of emotion. Too often our society wants us to just numb them or avoid them altogether. Jesus turned to prayer and meditation.

Jesus went to pray alone, but he also tried to encourage the community to 'keep awake' for him. This request was about far more than simply being on guard or on the lookout for approaching enemies. It was also about staying alert and paying attention to what God was doing in those moments. In so many ways, prayer is all about staying awake.

In these moments, Jesus had intimacy with his 'Daddy God'. He expressed deep and personal feelings. *'Abba, Father, for you all things are possible; remove this cup from me ...'* (verse 36). Jesus knew where this was all heading and the pain it would cause him and others. Could drinking from this cup be avoided? Was there another way?

This wrestling with God is an important part of prayer. Yet a kind of surrender emerges from Jesus: *'... Yet, not what I want but what you want.'* These elements – paying attention, honest intimacy, wrestling and surrender to God – are some of the greatest disciplines of the spiritual life. They were key in preparing Jesus for what was to come.

The disciples, however, were unprepared. They weren't awake to the situation, didn't have those moments of intimacy and had no opportunity to wrestle through the issues with God. In the end, Judas betrayed Jesus and Peter used violence when the mob came.

Let's seek to stay awake and bring all that we are to our loving Father God.

† Lord, help us to pay attention to you, to be honest, to wrestle and to surrender to your will.

For further thought

How can we resist numbing, violence and betrayal as a way out of our stresses and anxieties?

Friday 29 March
The death of Jesus

Read Mark 15:21–41

It was nine o'clock in the morning when they crucified him. The inscription of the charge against him read, 'The King of the Jews.' And with him they crucified two bandits, one on his right and one on his left.

(verses 25–27)

I met Ko Jimmy in Melbourne in 2016, and he immediately reminded me of Martin Luther King Jnr. Both were passionate, articulate and had dreams of a better life for their countries. Ko Jimmy was destined to be a voice for Myanmar, I was sure of it.

The next time I heard of Ko Jimmy was in July 2022. I was in Mae Sot, on the Thai–Burma border, supporting some remarkable civil disobedience movement workers when news started to filter through of the Junta's execution of Ko Jimmy and others. When it was confirmed we all sat there, stunned and devastated. We all wept and got angry. How could such evil happen to such good people?

There was an idea in MLK's famous 'I have a dream' speech that kept returning to me: that 'unearned suffering' can be 'redemptive'. This idea was emphasised by Jesus: 'No one has greater love than this, to lay down one's life for one's friends' (John 15:13). Such sacrifice is never in vain. Ko Jimmy's love for his friends and country will be the seeds of new life that Myanmar so desperately needs.

In the Christian imagination, death is not the end. Jesus' resurrection is the first fruit of a new creation (1 Corinthians 15:12-23). I look forward to the day when I see Ko Jimmy again. It will be a day when all the earth, including Myanmar, is fully free from all evil, injustice, suffering and death. A day when the Lord's Prayer is fully answered and heaven is on earth.

Let us keep loving one another with the sacrificial love that comes from God.

† Join with some others and pray the Lord's Prayer together.

For further thought

The others who died with Ko Jimmy were Phyo Zeya Thaw, Hla Myo Aung and Aung Thura Zaw. Imagine they are your friends. How would you react? How can you respond now?

Saturday 30 March
Jesus is buried

Read Mark 15:42–47

Then Joseph bought a linen cloth, and taking down the body, wrapped it in the linen cloth, and laid it in a tomb that had been hewn out of the rock. He then rolled a stone against the door of the tomb. Mary Magdalene and Mary the mother of Joses saw where the body was laid.

(verses 46–47)

The death of Jesus came as a shock to the disciples and its suddenness added disappointment and anger to the grief that loss always brings. I remember three losses we suffered in quick succession a few summers ago, and what they meant for me.

The first was Rich, one of our neighbours who, with his wife Juls (who worked with Anji), were real local characters and leaders. They were holidaying on a remote island when Rich had a heart attack and never recovered. He was just forty-seven years old.

The second was Gogh, who played on the Saturday with our under-sixteens at the Klong Toey community centre football tournament in Bangkok and died suddenly (still wearing his tournament shirt) the next Friday.

The third was Joy, our much-loved, six-month-old Alpaca at Newbigin House. The unusually stifling summer heat messed with all kinds of plant and animal ecosystems, and baby Joy was one of its victims.

As waves of grief washed over me, I was reminded of these three realities about life:

1 How fragile we are. We can't insulate ourselves from suffering or death in a fallen world. Acceptance of the fragility of life can help us fight to make the most of it with others.
2 Time is short. We don't have control over how long we have left to see our hopes and dreams realised. Appreciating that life could be gone in a split second can help us focus.
3 Compassion matters most. The things that last are those we have completed in faith, hope and love.

† I read these words at Rich's funeral: 'Faced with the mystery of life, we affirm that love is unconfined. Faced with the mystery of death, we affirm that love is stronger than the grave.'

For further thought

Believing that love defeats death gives us hope that what we invest in now is worth it.

Reconciliation

1 Stories of reconciliation

Notes by **Delroy Hall**

Dr Delroy Hall is a trained psychodynamic psychotherapist with more than thirty years' experience as a pastor and bishop. He is CEO of Delwes Consultancy, which specialises in helping those facing loss, depression, anxiety, clergy stress, black male suicide and cultural competence. Delroy is committed to dealing with human pain while developing trust, so people can recover and thrive. As a former 400-metre hurdler, he is now training to compete in various aqua bike events. He is married with twin daughters. Delroy has used the NKJV for these notes.

Sunday 31 March
Out of the darkness

Read John 20:1–10

Then Simon Peter came, following him, and went into the tomb; and he saw the linen cloths lying there.

(verse 6)

What an intriguing verse. For decades I have read this verse and missed something important. While the others did not enter the cave, Peter did.

I can hear the comments already: 'Here we go. Peter, jumping in without thinking again.' But hold on a minute. Peter shows us how to deal with difficulties and uncertainties. How? By facing them!

On entering the darkness, he saw the linen and handkerchief of Jesus neatly folded. It was possibly a cultural practice for women not to enter a tomb, but Peter did, paving the way for another disciple to do so.

How often have we refrained from entering the darkness of our lives? Spiritual teacher Kyle Cease, says: 'Fear shows us what we will lose, but does not show us what we will gain.'[1] Many self-help gurus talk about how fear has much to teach us ... but not if we run away from it. When we run away from fear it will always control us. We need not run away from our darkness because God remains with us, and maybe, like Peter, when we muster the courage to enter the difficult times in our lives, we might be surprised by what we find.

† Lord, help me to understand and believe that when we enter life's darkness, though we often fear, you are there with us.

[1] K. Cease, 'Why You Need to Stop Saying What People Want to Hear' (https://www. youtube.com/watch?v=Vc1hCpbkRz4).

Examples of reconciliation: the lost son and the Father

Read Luke 15:11–32

'But as soon as this son of yours came, who has devoured your livelihood with harlots, you killed the fatted calf for him.'

(verse 30)

These words from the elder son are striking as he refers to his brother as 'this son of yours'. You can almost feel the vitriolic tone as you read the scripture. One can only imagine the feelings the eldest brother harboured towards his younger brother over the years due to the disruptive heartache he had caused the family.

Some elements of this story remain perplexing. The mother is never mentioned; she remains a silent witness in this drama. In addition, the elder brother is rarely spoken highly of by preachers, but I am left wondering if some of us secretly identify with him. Perhaps we are overlooked for a promotion at work while someone else, who does little, gets it. Or maybe we have cared tenderly for a sick family member who eventually dies, but when the will is read we are left with hardly anything, while the one who did little gets the bigger share of the deceased's estate.

The story ends well for the son who is reconciled with his father, but the elder brother is left dealing with unresolved emotions. The story does not a happy ending for him. Maybe his response is one of relief for the return of his brother, yet he is still filled with anger towards him and his father. Does this ending sound familiar to you? Reconciliation is not easy, but if it is to succeed it must include all who were hurt by the perpetrator's actions.

† Lord, help us to be reconciled to all those we may have hurt by our ill-thought-out actions; even those who remain silent but have felt the bad effects of my behaviour.

For further thought

Do you identify with the elder brother? If so, seek help. Sometimes we need extra support in dealing with some of life's toughest issues.

Examples of reconciliation: Jacob and Esau

> **Genesis 33:1–17**
>
> *But Esau ran to meet him, and embraced him, and fell on his neck and kissed him, and they wept.*
>
> (verse 4)

Such a display of emotion and love between these twin brothers is seen in these twenty words. Today's reading elicits an array of questions, especially if you do not know the backdrop of the story. What is clear is that they were more than delighted to see each other after such a long time.

The story begins in Genesis 25. It tells the story of twins Jacob and Esau who struggled with each other in their mother's womb, signifying the difficult relationship they would always have. Through dishonesty and deception, the birthright, a link in the line of descent through which the Promised Messiah was to come (Numbers 24:17–19), which was rightfully Esau's as the firstborn, ended up falling to Jacob. On hearing what had happened, Esau was furious and went to kill his brother, but Jacob ran for his life.

The biblical story focuses on the life of Jacob, who becomes an important continuation in God's plan for his people. Esau is pretty much silent, but we are left wondering what happened in the heart of these men as a result of their early encounter.

Let's be honest. Painful experiences embitter some people, and they live and die wrapped in bitterness from an event that may have happened years earlier. Others, with the passing of time, are able to learn, mellow and become more philosophical. Life, time and reflection on personal experiences nurtures and matures them.

If you have had a broken relationship, could time and reflection on personal experiences nurture and mature you?

† Father, I have experienced painful and broken relationships, and I am still holding on to the feelings of hurt and betrayal. These feelings are doing me more harm than good. I need your deliverance.

For further thought

We all experience difficult and broken relationships. As tough as they are, would you be willing to learn something about yourself as you reflect on these difficult moments in your life?

Examples of reconciliation: Joseph and his brothers

Read Genesis 45:1–15

Then he fell on his brother Benjamin's neck and wept, and Benjamin wept on his neck. Moreover he kissed all his brothers and wept over them, and after that his brothers talked with him.

(verses 14–15)

Reading this, the psalms and other portions of scripture, we are left asking where this idea that men are not emotional and do not talk about their feelings has come from. Yes, it may be cultural, but here we find grown brothers being vulnerable with each other.

You may recall the story of Joseph being sold into slavery, yet despite his ordeal, God remained with him and blessed his life abundantly. The time came, through a series of events, including a national famine, when the brothers met again. However, Joseph had changed significantly, to the point where his brothers didn't initially recognise him.

When they finally did, they immediately became fearful. Joseph assured them they would come to no harm but emphasised that there was a much bigger picture surrounding his and their lives, and how he had found himself in Egypt.

The story of Joseph is laden with difficulty – especially for descendants of the transatlantic slave trade – surrounding the notion of slavery being the will of God. What is clear is this: Joseph was able to find the hand of God in his life, despite his circumstances, and was later able to reconnect with his brothers.

We are unable to grasp the inner wrestlings and groanings of Joseph. He had such awesome dreams as a young man, then found himself sold into slavery, before facing a number of adventures in life and with God. We can only surmise that introspection and time was needed for him to understand God. That is a process we can never rush.

† Loving Father and friend, I have no idea what Joseph went through to become such a gracious person. Help me, especially where I am innocent and badly treated, not to allow bitterness or hatred to become my companions.

For further thought

Human transformation is an amazing journey, but there are no short cuts. Prayer, introspection and a commitment to becoming more Christ-like are the prerequisites.

Examples of reconciliation: Paul and John Mark

Read Acts 15:36–41; Colossians 4:10

Aristarchus my fellow prisoner greets you, with Mark the cousin of Barnabas (about whom you received instructions: if he comes to you, welcome him).

(Colossians 4:10).

When I was a pastor, preaching regularly, I loved taking two portions of scripture, and braiding (plaiting) and bifurcating (dividing) them. Not twisting scriptures out of context, but seeing how they compared with each other and what new insights could be gained.

What a situation we find in our reading today. Paul and Barnabas were once friends, then not, due to a bitter conflict over John Mark, and then reconciliation followed. We are not told what took place in the lives of these men, but whatever the rift they once had, it was no more.

As I reread this scripture, I was ushered back to a time in my life, forty years ago, when my cousin and I were unable to get on. I couldn't even tell you why if you asked me. I remember seeing him, literally weeks after becoming a Christian and, oh my goodness, my heart sank. I could no longer use the insults we had once thrown at each other. It took courage to tell him I had become a Christian, and then he blurted out that he was too, having had a dynamic experience with Christ. We don't know what took place in our hearts, but something had suddenly changed.

When he was alive, my father would often say, 'Time will tell.' These two scriptures, in conversation with each other, show how 'the contention became so sharp' between these men, but in time changed to 'if he comes to you, welcome him'.

† God, grant me the serenity to accept the things I cannot change, the courage to change the things I can, and the wisdom to know the difference.

For further thought

There are times we must be in conversation to restore relationships, but there are other times it is best if we leave well alone. What do you think?

April

Reconciliation – 1 Stories of reconciliation

Examples of reconciliation: Peter and Paul

> **Read Galatians 2:11–14; 2 Peter 3:14–18**
>
> ... *Consider* that *the longsuffering of our LORD is salvation – as also our beloved brother Paul, according to the wisdom given to him, has written to you.*
>
> (2 Peter 3:15)

Today we are confronted by another set of scriptures in conversation with each other. Paul stood up to Peter and called him out for his racial bigotry. Reading the scripture, it is clear that Paul did not have a quiet word with Peter in the privacy of his office or behind closed doors. No: 'I said to Peter before *them* all.' Paul was not messing. He gave Peter a real telling off in front of his friends.

In some cultures, public rebuke still happens today. Not only had Peter acted in an ungodly manner, but his behaviour had affected the rest of the Jews, including Barnabas. This was not Paul rebuking Peter as a matter of social conscience or morality. No, it was a matter of holiness and the gospel of Jesus Christ.

In the UK, one might be faced with a lawsuit for defamation of character if there were a public haranguing like this. However, we read of the public humiliation of Peter, but the author does not record any response. We can assume that he was firmly put in his place.

We do not know how Peter felt after this public dressing down. He was probably used to being embarrassed in public due to his impulsive nature. But later we see a Peter who is transformed. In the tone of the letter, he bears no malice towards Paul. Indeed, he is actively supportive of Paul's ministry, patience and wisdom. He freely shares the various letters Paul wrote to encourage the Christian believers and protect them from the false teachers of the day.

† Lord, help us to handle difficult situations with your grace and compassion, especially when people are wrong. For those of us who have been publicly humiliated, heal us by your grace, so we can be made whole.

For further thought

Is there a difficult matter you must address? How might you speak the truth in such a way that what you say will be heard and received?

Saturday 6 April

Examples of reconciliation: peace with our neighbours

Read Hebrews 12:14–17

Pursue peace with all people, and holiness ...

(verse 14a)

I can hear folks already. What is being asked is impossible. Never! Do you know what 'them folks' are like? Negative and derogatory words have been expressed by people towards so-called 'lesser people' for eons.

Today is the thirtieth anniversary of the Rwandan Genocide. Those of us who were alive and witnessed the graphic scenes of dead bodies in the streets on various news outlets were deeply shocked. Neighbours who had lived in peace for years became violent enemies overnight. Rwanda has a long and complex history, much of which can be found online.

The story of reconciliation was a long and painful one. The important thing was that the perpetrators were made to confront the surviving victims, hear their stories and then seek forgiveness. This method of reconciliation was a traditional dispute resolution forum well acquainted with the Rwandans, which gave victims the space and time to speak their truth.

In one sense, this returns us to our first reading of the week, where Peter entered the darkness of the tomb. How do we deal with fear? We face it. We do not run away. When we run away from fear it continues to run the show.

Pursuing peace is not for the faint-hearted. It's scary, but it is possible. Just as God was with Peter when he stepped inside the tomb, he remains with us as we attempt to restore peace and order in our lives and with others.

A guiding vision as we try to make reconciliation a lived reality is to continually ask: 'What might the future look like?'

† Master and friend, you ask us to pursue peace with all people. Do you know how hard that is? Yes, you do. You reconciled humanity back to yourself through Jesus. Thank you.

For further thought

Do you need to be reconciled? Are you ready to step into the darkness like Peter? When you do, what you find may surprise you.

Reconciliation

2 Taking steps to reconciliation

Notes by **Catherine Sarjeant**

Catherine describes herself as living in a messy place, in which she is being treated for complex PTSD. She lives in this messy place with Jesus, and has a passion for helping others meet him in the reality of life. She co-leads a small house church, the members of which are learning together that God is with them in the midst of struggle, bringing order out of chaos. Catherine is married with two teenage children. She has used the NRSVA for these notes.

Sunday 7 April
A ministry of reconciliation

Read 2 Corinthians 5:11–21

All this is from God, who reconciled us to himself through Christ, and has given us the ministry of reconciliation.

(verse 18)

Why do we need a ministry of reconciliation? I've often heard it said that if there is a problem between two people or groups of people, all that is needed is for forgiveness to flow. Problem solved! But as I've discovered, reconciliation is nothing like as simple as that.

Perhaps the start of the process comes in verse 21. Jesus, who did not know sin, stepped down to earth – a place of sin. We see it in action in Luke 8, when Jesus is on his way to heal the daughter of Jairus, the leader of the synagogue. His progress is interrupted when a woman who has been bleeding for twelve years touches him. She shouldn't be out, risking making others unclean, and she certainly shouldn't be touching a man. Yet Jesus stops and listens to her whole story, reconciling her to her own body, to her own people and to God.

My question is this: for the sake of reconciliation, are we prepared to step down and sit with; prepared to lose status? Are we, like Jesus, willing to be touched by those we would rather avoid, to speak truth to power and ask them to put their agendas on hold?

† Thank you, Lord, that you stepped down to sit with us. Open our eyes when we need to step down like Jesus.

Monday 8 April
Steps to Reconciliation: Confession

Read 1 John 1:5–10

If we say that we have no sin, we deceive ourselves, and the truth is not in us. If we confess our sins, he who is faithful and just will forgive us our sins and cleanse us from all unrighteousness.

(verses 8–9)

A friend once sat with me and listened as I told him about some of the harm he had caused. He said later that he had wanted to get cross and argue how he was right ... but he didn't. He sat with the hurt and asked the Holy Spirit to show him his sin. A couple of weeks later he came back and confessed the harm his actions had caused. It was a profound moment that broke open doors with me and with God.

Confession (*homologeo* – 'to say the same as') is the process of coming into agreement with God and others about what we have done or failed to do. It requires us to step down, to step into the world of the other and to see it from their perspective. This is challenging! Here are three responses I find myself veering towards:

1 I minimise things by avoiding sitting with God or the other person, and keeping my view as number one.
2 I refuse to own all that is mine for fear that the weight will break me.
3 I own everything, even if it's not mine, because I default to assuming that everything is my fault.

But owning harm is a natural process. We all get stuff wrong. We all cause harm to people. Owning what we have done is a sign of maturity. The Holy Spirit is well able to show us where we have turned away from what God longed for, and he is safe to do that with. Confession and owning stuff isn't bad! It doesn't mean we are degraded in God's eyes. It is a natural, normal process, without which relationships flounder.

† Lord, reveal to me the times when I haven't loved as you do. Help me to change.

For further thought

Do I confess in order to be excused or in order to own what I have done?

Tuesday 9 April
Steps to reconciliation: repentance

Read Jeremiah 34:8–16

You yourselves recently repented and did what was right in my sight by proclaiming liberty to one another, and you made a covenant before me in the house that is called by my name; but then you turned about and profaned my name when each of you took back your male and female slaves, whom you had set free according to their desire, and you brought them again into subjection to be your slaves.

(verses 15–16)

Confession is the process of seeing something from another perspective. Repentance means to change your mind (and therefore what you do) as a result. Confession that doesn't lead to repentance isn't truly confession. Repentance without a change of behaviour isn't really repentance. We see an example of this in today's reading.

People in biblical times sometimes sold themselves as servants (slaves) if they were in dire poverty. The law said that slaves should be offered their freedom every seven years, but setting them 'free' without providing a means for them to live independently was no freedom.

In the passage, the people had 'confessed' to keeping slaves longer than allowed, and had seemingly repented by letting them go. But they hadn't given them any way of keeping their freedom. What they owed wasn't just the lip service involved in keeping the law, but also the heart behind it. They needed to step into the world of their slaves; to experience their walk, their hardship, their struggles, and to hear the cry of a God who loves and redeems all.

We are all too familiar with today's vague confessions: the ones that don't own the true harm; the exonerating confessions, where the person 'confesses' but then expects forgiveness with no consequences; the excusing confession that minimises the change needed. All these avoid repentance and stop the reconciliation process. True repentance comes from reckoning with the harm, confessing it and then changing as a result of grasping God's heart in the situation. It may cost us reputation, status or wealth. But this is true repentance, and it is good!

† O Lord, help me to understand the safety that comes from knowing you, so I might be secure enough to truly repent.

For further thought
To what extent do we see true repentance as losing, and to what extent do we see it as a natural process of mutually flourishing?

Steps to reconciliation: restitution

Read Luke 19:1–10

Zacchaeus stood there and said to the Lord, 'Look, half of my possessions, Lord, I will give to the poor, and if I have defrauded anyone of anything, I will pay back four times as much.'

(verse 8)

We don't talk about this much, as there is an assumption that forgiveness means there is nothing to be paid, but the story of Zacchaeus tells a different story. Forgiveness relates to that which cannot or will not be paid, but Zacchaeus is both able and willing to repay, whatever the personal cost. He stepped out of his world, felt the harm he had done and demonstrated a change of mind by being open-handed rather than grasping.

Confession is an acknowledgement of harm done. It defines what is owed. It isn't a legalistic accounting; it should spring from a generous spirit, reflecting God's compassion, just as it did with Zacchaeus.

Restitution is the act of paying back what you can of what you now acknowledge you owe. The aim is to reverse the harm done as much as possible. It might not be financial restitution; it could be about restoring someone's reputation or dignity.

Zacchaeus understood that defrauding people might have had a greater impact than just the immediate financial loss. They might have lost out on opportunities for themselves and others – they might have been in debt as a result of the defrauding and had to pay back more than just the principal amount. Part of the confession process is about agreeing the full scope of what is owed. Restitution seeks to address the whole, not just the tip of the iceberg.

Of course, there are aspects of what we owe – to God and to others – that cannot be repaid, and we should be honest with everyone about this. It allows those we have hurt the opportunity to forgive the part of the debt that cannot be repaid.

† Lord, show me where I have done harm, and what I can do to repair and repay.

For further thought

What part do we have to play in repairing and repaying the harm caused by previous generations?

Thursday 11 April
Steps to reconciliation: forgiveness

Read Matthew 18:23–35

When he began the reckoning, one who owed him ten thousand talents was brought to him; and, as he could not pay, his lord ordered him to be sold, together with his wife and children and all his possessions, and payment to be made.

(verses 24–25)

The servant never disputes the amount owed. He agrees the debt, so the confession stage is complete! But there's no change of mind, no repentance. He believes he can just pay it back if he's given time, like the gambler who believes he can pay his debts with a winning bet. This isn't an offer of open-handed restitution; it's an unwillingness to accept the reason for the debt and an unwillingness to change.

The king could demand payment, requiring the servant to sell everything – including his wife and children into slavery – but instead, out of compassion, the king forgoes his right to be paid and the servant is forgiven. But even in the light of this generosity, the servant refuses to change. He demands the full repayment of a small debt from a fellow servant, throwing him into jail when he pleads for time to pay. At this point the king reimposes his right to be paid. The debt still exists; what had been forgiven was the need to pay the debt.

As we have seen, forgiveness relates to that which cannot be paid (verse 25). That which can be repaid, should be. This gives dignity and healing transformation to the offender, and brings healing and restoration to the victim. But where payment is neither possible nor offered, the forgiveness we have received from God – the knowledge that Jesus has bound the 'strongman' and plundered all that he stole, and in the fulness of time will restore it to us – empowers us to forgive.

Forgiveness is a process, not a switch. We may need time to lament what we have lost, presenting it as an offering to God. Forgiveness does not mean living as if it didn't happen.

† Father, forgive us as we forgive those who trespass against us.

For further thought

We read in 1 John 8–9 that if we confess, God is faithful and just to forgive. Can there be forgiveness without confession?

Friday 12 April
Rebuilding: safety

Read Deuteronomy 19:7–14

But if someone at enmity with another lies in wait and attacks and takes the life of that person, and flees into one of these cities, then the elders of the killer's city shall send to have the culprit taken from there and handed over to the avenger of blood to be put to death.

(verses 11–12)

Cities of refuge provided a place for those who had killed without intent to stay until a proper investigation could take place. They were not places where the perpetrators of violence could 'get away with it'. These cities of refuge were there to protect the offender from vengeance, not to prevent justice. I wonder if we have created false cities of refuge that actually work against true reconciliation?

Here are some examples of how we sometimes protect an offender from feeling the full weight of the damage they have caused:

- We know that forgiveness is biblical, but forgiving without confession unfairly protects offenders from the consequences of their actions, further harming the one who is hurt!
- When confronted with an offence, we say 'I didn't mean it' and excuse ourselves from the consequences. But the fact that the harm was not malicious does not make the injury any smaller. Indeed, knowing that carelessness was involved might increase the pain. We should still own the harm done and respond accordingly.
- As the person hurt, we might subconsciously seek to justify the offender's actions to minimise our pain by saying, 'They didn't really mean it.'
- Another natural defence mechanism is to blame ourselves in some way: 'I shouldn't have walked home alone.'

One last thought: the person who has been hurt might also need a place of safety where they can heal. They might also need the help of others to work through the harm done and to ensure that responsibility for the harm is owned by the offender.

The process of reconciliation takes time, and the pace needs to be set by the person who has been harmed.

† Lord, help me to be a place of safety for those who need protection.

For further thought

Might there be times when it is unsafe to pursue reconciliation, even when there has been forgiveness?

Saturday 13 April
Rebuilding: relationship

Read John 21:15–19

He said to him the third time, 'Simon son of John, do you love me?'
Peter felt hurt because he said to him the third time, 'Do you love me?'
And he said to him, 'LORD, you know everything; you know that I love
you.' Jesus said to him, 'Feed my sheep.'

(verse 17)

When we misunderstand who God is, and are not honest about who we are, we end up relating to distorted images of one another. This leads to disappointment or disillusion when we discover the truth.

Peter had an unrealistic view of himself and a wrong view of God, amounting to: 'The Messiah can't die, I'll never let that happen... Even if all the others run away, I'll stick with you.' Both misconceptions were eventually exposed. We have seen how confession helps us to line up with a realistic view of who we are and how repentance is the process of changing our minds about ourselves and God.

Jesus asks Peter if he really loves him the way Peter had claimed (*agapē*). And Peter confesses that actually, all he can claim is friendship (*phileo*). Finally, Jesus asks Peter if he is even his friend, and Peter has to look even deeper before replying in the affirmative. It is a progressive confession; a progressive restoration of relationship as honesty allowed trust to be rebuilt. Now the relationship is based on reality and can grow into what Peter always claimed it was.

Allowing the Spirit to convince us of sin and lead us into all truth about ourselves and about him means we can be free to be who we actually are. It means others can relate to us, rather than to the false images we often seek to project.

We began the week with a focus on the fact that God's ministry in coming to the earth was to reconcile. Jesus' life demonstrates reconciliation at every level. It wasn't a one-off event at Christmas, but a lifelong process. It should be a natural and normal part of our Christian experience.

† Lord, thank you that I don't have to pretend to be more than I am. Thank you that you love me as I am.

For further thought

Given what we have explored this week, are there people with whom you need to reconcile?

Arts in the Bible (1)

1 The power of song

Notes by **Liz Clutterbuck**

 Liz is a Church of England priest who combines parish ministry with a ministry training role for the Stepney area of the Diocese of London. She also has a research interest in exploring how church impact can be better measured, so we can learn how and where missional initiatives work best. Liz is passionate about social media, film, baking and travel. She loves it when she manages to combine as many of her passions as possible! Liz has used the NRSVA for these notes.

Sunday 14 April
Triumphant and thankful

Read Exodus 15:1–18

The LORD is my strength and my might, and he has become my salvation; this is my God, and I will praise him, my father's God, and I will exalt him.

(verse 2)

Singing to the Lord is a common theme throughout scripture, and something that is still an essential element of our worship today. Over the next two weeks, our readings will explore songs that have appeared through the Bible: from Moses all the way to Revelation.

Many of the songs mention the ways God has looked upon people with favour. Today's reading follows the dramatic escape of the Israelites from Pharaoh's troops, thanks to the miraculous separation of the Red Sea. It is a song of praise to the God in whom they had faith to lead them to safety. It is a moment when the Israelites look back at what they have experienced, and recognise the role God has played in it – and they give God the credit for saving them.

It serves as a reminder for us to give thanks when we are blessed by God. It might not be as dramatic as a sea dividing to provide a route to safety, but even giving thanks to God for the dawn of a new day is important. We can easily become complacent, only thanking him at times when we have really needed divine intervention. Let us sing our thanks to God every day!

† What are you thankful for today? Write a list and lift up your prayers of gratitude to God, perhaps even in song.

Song of warning

Read Deuteronomy 31:19–22

'And when many terrible troubles come upon them, this song will confront them as a witness, because it will not be lost from the mouths of their descendants.'

(verse 21a)

Moses' song is one that praises God, while also warning Israel of the consequences it will face if it forgets the promise their Lord fulfilled. It comes immediately after Moses has given instructions about keeping the law in the ark of the covenant for safekeeping. In contrast, his song was to be taught to all Israel, so that it was known in their hearts and minds.

A curious thing about songs is how long they stay in our memories. It's one of the reasons why it's a technique used to teach children useful, but long, information – like the order of the monarchs of England. Research has shown that songs are one of the longest-lasting elements of memory for dementia patients.

By giving Israel his final words in song, Moses was ensuring that it would be learned by all; not just those alive to hear them for the first time, but for future generations, too. Writing the song down would have limited its audience to the very few who could read. A song, however, could be passed on by anyone, enshrining it in the oral tradition of the community.

Chapter 32 contains the whole song, all forty-three verses of it. It tells the story of God's favour towards Israel and the times when Israel turned away from God. It serves as a reminder of God's gifts, but also his wrath. The Bible tells us that Israel did not heed Moses' warning and that Israel turned away from God once again. But the song of Moses is still remembered today.

† God of Israel, thank you for this reminder of your faithfulness to your chosen people. We bring to you the times when we have turned away from you. Forgive us our sins and strengthen our confidence in you.

For further thought

Challenge yourself to learn at least some of the verses of Moses' song in Deuteronomy 32. Could you sing them?

Tuesday 16 April
Singing God's victory

Read Judges 5:1–9

'When locks are long in Israel, when the people offer themselves willingly – bless the LORD!
'Hear, O kings; give ear, O princes; to the LORD I will sing, I will make melody to the LORD, the God of Israel.'

(verses 2–3)

This is a song of victory. It tells the tale of Israel's defeat of the Canaanites, ending two decades of oppression. It's a ballad, in the sense that it tells the story of how the enemies were overcome; and it is also an example of speaking truth to power. Deborah calls out to the kings and princes to listen to the words she is singing to the Lord.

The song of Deborah is unique, as it is the only victory hymn in the Old Testament that celebrates the victory of women: Deborah and the warrior Jael. Deborah is no longer engaged in battle; she has returned to her 'ordinary' life of being a prophet and judge. However, it is a song in which she recounts her own role in the battle, centred on her praise to God for securing victory. Later in the chapter Deborah urges herself to awake and sing this song; to share the story of triumph and the part the Lord God of Israel played in it.

Many hymns and worship songs are inspired by experiences the writers have had in their journeys with God; praises of joy as well as seasons of lament. These songs provide ways for those singing them to connect with their own experiences of following Christ. We may not be victorious in physical battles, but there is always a song we can sing of how God has been at work in our lives.

† Victorious God, may we know your presence alongside us as we fight the battles of life. May we give you praise for your victory over the grave.

For further thought

Which song do you want to sing to God today? It could be one that someone else has written or you could even write your own!

April

Arts in the Bible (1) – 1 The power of song

Wednesday 17 April
Responding to songs of emotion

Read 1 Samuel 18:1–7

The women came out of all the towns of Israel, singing and dancing, to meet King Saul, with tambourines, with songs of joy, and with musical instruments. And the women sang to one another as they made merry, 'Saul has killed his thousands, and David his tens of thousands.'

(verses 6b–7)

This song of victory comes after one of the most famous events of the Old Testament: the killing of Goliath by David. It is a surprise victory that sets the stage for David to become King of Israel. Saul immediately sends David into battle, and David is victorious wherever he goes.

The song the women sing to King Saul is not about the surprise of David's victory over Goliath, but about what might be possible with this new young warrior. Saul may have killed thousands, but David may kill tens of thousands. It is prophetic as well as victorious. It is a song that feeds into Saul's feeling of insecurity, which results in his rage against David in the next chapter of 1 Samuel.

Songs are powerful and emotive. There is something about expressing a hope or desire through song that increases its impact. This is one of the reasons why love songs are so popular. They express an emotion we can relate to and experience something of when we join in with singing the song.

The Israelite women were singing in a way that would have encouraged others to join in. The dancing and tambourine playing would have made for an infectious fiesta of joy. This is why their words about David hurt Saul and planted seeds of rage in his soul. Why was this youngster distracting the women from solely praising their king? Why were so many others joining in with them? It was a powerful song sung by members of society whose voices often went unheard.

† God of power and might, help us to check whether our emotional reactions are in line with your will for our lives. Keep us on your path.

For further thought
Make space to listen to a powerful song or piece of music, and pay attention to the reactions it stirs up in you.

Songs of refuge

> **Read 2 Samuel 22:1–4**
>
> *He said: The Lord is my rock, my fortress, and my deliverer, my God, my rock, in whom I take refuge, my shield and the horn of my salvation, my stronghold and my refuge, my saviour; you save me from violence.*
>
> (verses 2–3)

Songs give us the words to express the deepest feelings of our hearts. We may not have written them ourselves, but we can still use the words of others to share how we feel.

I once had an elderly parishioner who was drawing near to the end of her life. She had been a Christian all her life and her faith shone through in all that she did. She was a prayer warrior, always praying for others before herself, and whenever I visited her we would pray together. At the end of these times of prayer she would begin singing a classic hymn, taking the hymnwriter's words to lift her praises to God and express her faith.

David's song is a statement of faith. He praises God following a time of significant trial, as the Lord had delivered David from his enemies. David took refuge in the Lord and was protected by him. This song is the basis for so many of David's psalms. Psalm 19 contains the same imagery of the Lord as a rock and a redeemer. Psalm 23 features powerful images of taking refuge in the Lord.

The songs of David give us the words we need when we don't have our own. They paint pictures of what it means to be a child of God, passed down through generation after generation of those who seek to praise the Lord.

† God of David, give us David's faith. May we build our lives on the One who keeps us safe, and is our rock and our redeemer.

For further thought

Choose one of the psalms of David and meditate on it. Which words meet you where you are today?

April

Arts in the Bible (1) – 1 The power of song

Friday 19 April
The freedom to sing

> **Read 2 Chronicles 5:1–14**
>
> *It was the duty of the trumpeters and singers to make themselves heard in unison in praise and thanksgiving to the LORD, and when the song was raised, with trumpets and cymbals and other musical instruments, in praise to the LORD, 'For he is good, for his steadfast love endures for ever.'*
>
> (verse 13a)

This passage is a beautiful description of worship in the Holy of Holies within Solomon's temple. When the singers sang their praises, accompanied by instruments, the cloud of God's presence would descend and the glory of the Lord would fill the temple.

God's people have praised the Lord with music throughout history, and it has often caused stirrings of the Holy Spirit in the hearts of those lifting their voices to God and in those listening to them.

During the Covid-19 pandemic, one of the hardest rules to keep when we were able to return to having services inside our church buildings was not singing. It just didn't feel right to worship God without lifting our voices in praise. I was not surprised to hear murmurs of singing through face masks as members of the congregation fought their inner urge to join in with the hymns we were listening to.

In the UK, we were allowed to sing – outdoors – in church services from Easter 2021. On that Easter morning, tears ran down my cheeks as I sang not just with the joy of the resurrection, but with the joy of being able to praise God in community with others for the first time in more than a year.

We should not underestimate the power of singing in worship to God. No longer is it just the select few who are allowed into the temple; all are welcome to worship God in church services or wherever else they choose. We raise our voices because God is good and because his love lasts forever.

† God of eternity we worship you with our bodies and souls. May our praises rise up to greet you, unhindered by human concerns. May our voices be as one as we sing of your goodness.

For further thought

What is your favourite hymn/song? Sing it aloud today or find a recording of it to listen to.

Coming to sing

Read Psalm 95:1–7

O come, let us sing to the Lord; let us make a joyful noise to the rock of our salvation! Let us come into his presence with thanksgiving; let us make a joyful noise to him with songs of praise!

(verses 1–2)

In the Anglican tradition we have a pattern of daily prayer in which Psalm 95 has had a significant role. When The Book of Common Prayer (BCP) was published in 1662, Psalm 95 was the opening psalm, known as the *venite* – the Latin for 'come'. Day after day, Christians would greet the sun with the words of the psalm, calling one another to make a joyful noise unto God.

This psalm is an invitation. In fact, it is a double invitation!

The opening verses invite those reading the psalm to join in with their worship of the Lord; to share in making a joyful noise, singing songs of praise. But it is also a broader invitation. When we sing our praises we are also inviting those around us – who might not yet know the Lord – to hear our song and join in with us, too.

The psalm goes on to explain who God is; that he is a great king and above all other gods; the God who created the world. It succinctly summarises God's identity, as understood by the people of Israel. God is ours, but he can be yours, too.

Think about your favourite hymns and worship songs. What do they say about the gospel? Are there any songs you can think of that not only praise God, but also invite others to know Jesus as their Saviour? Are we singing in an echo chamber or are there people outside the church who might hear our voices?

† Creator God, please help us to share our praise of you with others so that more may know how mighty you are and receive your salvation.

For further thought

Read through Psalm 95 a number of times. Listen to what God is saying to you with each reading.

Arts in the Bible (1)

2 The power of song

Notes by **Jane Gonzalez**

Jane is a Roman Catholic laywoman. Retirement has offered her the opportunity to spend more time in Spain, where she and her husband have a home, but also to indulge her creative side. She is currently writing haikus (seventeen-syllable poems) and illustrating them with her own photos. Projects for the future include weaving and collage. Between all this, she remains an active member of her local parish, particularly in the Justice and Peace Group. Jane has used the NRSVCE for these notes.

Sunday 21 April
The songs of silence

Read Psalm 98:1–9

Make a joyful noise to the Lord, all the earth; break forth into joyous song and sing praises. Sing praises to the Lord with the lyre, with the lyre and the sound of melody.

(verses 4–5)

One of the most delightful films I have in my collection of DVDs is *Into Great Silence* (Zeitgeist Films, 2005), a documentary about the life of Carthusian monks at the Grande Chartreuse monastery. The hermit monks are completely silent, except for the hours when they gather to sing and pray the liturgical Divine Office and enjoy the weekly hour's recreation, when they are allowed to talk and laugh together. It's a long film with no commentary, as such. But in the silence it is possible to hear a range of joyful noises: icicles melting and dripping; birdsong and cats mewing; the squeak and creak of the lay brother's trolley as he brings the monks their midday meals. Within the silence we become aware of how creation itself adds to the voice of praise.

We live in an ever-moving, noisy world. Entering into stillness and silence can be almost impossible. But as we ponder 'song' this week, can we create a few moments in which to add our songs – be they of joy, lament, praise or questioning – to the song that creation itself is singing? Can we find space to listen to the song of the Spirit, directing, conducting and blessing us?

† Father, you are my song, my strength, my salvation. Give me the grace to listen to you and the courage to do your will.

Tell out, my soul

> ### Read Isaiah 12:1–6
> *With joy you will draw water from the wells of salvation. And you will say on that day:*
> *Give thanks to the LORD*
>   *call on his name;*
> *make known his deeds among the nations.*
>
> (verses 3–4a)

This year I celebrate a significant birthday, and my family have bought me tickets to see James Taylor in concert. Taylor is an American singer-songwriter, and I have loved his voice and music since I was in my teens. As a student I saved up to buy his albums and spent many a night, with wine and friends, listening and singing along. He managed to capture and express all our experiences and hopes, in songs of good times and bad, celebration and sorrow.

Taylor stands within a tradition that is as old as humankind. Through the centuries, human beings have told their stories through song. Bards, troubadours and psalmists have told the story of the human family, and every emotion and facet of relationship has been the subject of songs, poems and hymns. These singers put into words what less talented mortals cannot articulate. Somehow they can tell us all about our pain, our joy and our longing. They can voice our anger, bewilderment and shame. They can also tell of our God and all his works.

The prophets and psalmists tell of salvation history with honesty and openness as they react to the deeds of the Creator. Nothing is out of bounds. We, therefore, also have permission to sing whatever song is within our hearts to God; be it a song of pain, anger, love or joy. It is all right to bare our souls before the Lord, to be honest with him about how our lives are, to make known our deeds to him so we can proclaim his deeds to our needy world.

† Father, help me to be honest in my conversations with you. You know me and love me, and I can be sure of your grace and mercy whatever and wherever I am.

For further thought

Which is your favourite psalm? Reflect on it and write your own psalm in response. What do you want to say to the Lord today?

Tuesday 23 April
Singing the blues

Read Lamentations 1:1–16

The roads to Zion mourn, for no one comes to the festivals; all her gates are desolate, her priests groan … For these things I weep; my eyes flow with tears; for a comforter is far from me, one to revive my courage.

(verses 4, 16)

When I was five years old, I was chased away – along with some friends – from the front door of a neighbour. We had decided to go 'carol singing' in the summer and had bawled out the latest hit, 'Singing the Blues', at his door. It was a childish prank. We had no understanding of what the blues were or why people should sing about them. Only when I was older did I appreciate the blues as music of pain. Originating in the Deep South of the USA after the emancipation of slaves, and rooted in gospel and spirituals, the blues express heartfelt responses to life's troubles in songs of melancholy and sadness.

The author of Lamentations is a blues singer. He laments the destruction of Jerusalem; the affliction of his fellow citizens; the seeming absence of God. His song is one of mourning, helplessness and despair. Faced with the news that is present to us 24-7, we can often feel the same way. The news seems to be one long catalogue of conflict, pain and suffering; something that hasn't changed through the centuries. It is no wonder that we often doubt and ask, 'Where is our God?'

At these moments we need to grieve or mourn. We need to sing our blues in whichever way suits us best. We need to express the negative as well as the positive, so that each day we can find the faith to see that God never abandons us. We need to find him every day – in the rubble, with the broken-hearted, with the poor.

† Father, I feel helpless in the face of so much horror and suffering in our world. Give me the grace to see where you are at work and the courage to work with you.

For further thought

They are not afraid of evil tidings; their hearts are firm, secure in the LORD (Psalm 112:7). Look for good news today and give thanks.

April

Arts in the Bible (1) – 2 The power of song

114

Wednesday 24 April
In heart and conscience free

> **Read Acts 16:16–30**
>
> *Following these instructions, he put them in the innermost cell and fastened their feet in the stocks. About midnight Paul and Silas were praying and singing hymns to God, and the prisoners were listening to them.*
>
> (verses 24–25)

When I was a student I spent an academic year in Barcelona, immersing myself in the life and culture of the city. I lived with a Catalan family and made Catalan friends. After a year I was a fluent speaker and a forever fan of my adopted city.

My time in Barcelona came as the Francoist dictatorship was entering its last years and society was opening up. There was still censorship and repression, however. While people were no longer publicly chastised for speaking Catalan in the streets, there was little encouragement or education in the language of the people. Rights we now take for granted were severely curtailed. One of the ways our friends and their contemporaries voiced their frustration with the situation, along with their hopes for the future, was through music – in particular what they called *Nova Cançó* – new song – songs of resistance and protest sung in their own language.

Song has always been a potent vehicle for resistance, and a means of binding oppressed people together in hope and solidarity. The words of the old hymn say, 'Our fathers chained in prisons dark, were still in heart and conscience free' (F. W. Faber, 1949, public domain). Paul and Silas found solace in singing and praise – most likely in the psalms – and voiced, even as things looked grim, their faith and trust in the providence and presence of God. Singing may not bring physical freedom for us, and for our enslaved sisters and brothers, but it can affirm the spiritual freedom and hope that our souls need. The hope that one day, we shall overcome.

† Father, give me strength and courage to overcome the doubts and fears that imprison me. I believe – help me to overcome my unbelief.

For further thought

What can you, or your faith community, do to support those who have been imprisoned for their beliefs? Aid to the Church in Need (www.acnuk.org) and the Barnabas Fund (www.barnabasfund.org) are two organisations working to help persecuted Christians.

Thursday 25 April
Let go and let God

Read Ephesians 5:15–20

Do not get drunk with wine, for that is debauchery; but be filled with the Spirit, as you sing psalms and hymns and spiritual songs among yourselves, singing and making melody to the LORD in your hearts.

(verses 18–19)

I was at the theatre recently when we were invited to join in with the singing. Even allowing for our surprise at the invitation, the response was timid! With the encouragement of the professional singer, however, we eventually gathered enough courage to sing with confidence. It just took a while to overcome our inhibitions. They were popular songs, well within most people's capabilities, yet there was a reluctance to sing. Perhaps the writer of Ephesians has hit the nail on the head. Many of us seem to need some kind of exterior stimulus to overcome our insecurities and timidity.

Our responses can also be inhibited in our spiritual lives. Enthusiasm may be frowned upon or misinterpreted. Do you remember the reaction to Peter at Pentecost (Acts 2:13–15)? Some of us are bound by cultural responses that are deeply ingrained: the idea that we shouldn't show off or put ourselves forward; that overt signs of joy or 'happy-clappy' responses are somehow not 'done'; that restraint is always the order of the day. As the old adage goes, 'moderation in all things'.

No one would disagree with the author of Ephesians (or anyone else) in advocating restraint, but for Christians there should be no room for moderation when it comes to expressing our faith. No moderation, either, in our love – for God, ourselves and our neighbour. There should be no boundaries or inhibitions when it comes to proclaiming the gospel or in condemning injustice. No excuse for refusing to let go and letting the Spirit work through us, in us or with us, however we choose to express ourselves.

† Father, your love for me knows no bounds. Help me to embrace others with a similarly overwhelming love and acceptance.

For further thought

Reflect on 2 Corinthians 9:6–7. Are you miserly with your love, time or money? Where could you be more generous?

The tracks of my tears

Read James 5:13–15

Are any among you suffering? They should pray. Are any cheerful? They should sing songs of praise…

(verse 13)

One of the longest-running radio programmes in the UK is *Desert Island Discs*. On it, a celebrated person is invited to discuss their lives and choose eight pieces of music from any genre or era that are meaningful to them. They are, in effect, sharing the soundtracks of their lives with the audience.

I have a particular fondness for soundtracks. As a fan of cinema, I love to know who composed, played or orchestrated the music. For me, the score or soundtrack is not just something that forms a pleasant but forgettable accompaniment to the action. A good musical score illuminates and illustrates the story. If it's really memorable I will buy it, so that by listening I can revisit the film in a different way.

As Christians we are encouraged to reflect upon our lives – to revisit our stories and listen to the soundtrack of the years. There will be songs of sorrow and songs of joy. There will be regrets that sometimes I did it *my way* rather than God's way. There may be snatches of a tune, long-forgotten, that flags up a sense of shame that needs facing and forgiving. There could be a melody that brings back buried or ignored hurts that need reconciliation.

Running alongside that soundtrack is another one. It is the one the Holy Spirit composes to accompany our story. It is music of love, forgiveness and joy, which we sometimes cease to hear. The noise of our own soundtracks and worldly concerns often drowns it out. Is it time to pay more attention to the song of the Spirit?

† Father, many times I have not heeded your call, especially when you call me to conversion. Make my heart more willing to follow and learn from you.

For further thought

Reflect on these words of the Lord's Prayer: *'thy will be done'*. Where is the Holy Spirit urging you to change your tune?

Saturday 27 April
Singing a new song

Read Revelation 14:1–3

I heard a voice from heaven like the sound of many waters and like the sound of loud thunder; the voice I heard was like the sound of harpists playing on their harps, and they sing a new song before the throne.

(verses 2–3a)

I was privileged to have an inspiring musical education at my primary school. The driving force was a religious sister who formed a choir, a music society and an orchestra. The choir performed to a very high standard because Sister weeded out those whose voices were deemed to detract from the 'joyful noise'. They were fully involved in every other aspect of the school's musical life, but being classed as a 'non-singer' hurt people, and has continued to do so. A friend told me how difficult it has been for her to join in the hymns at church because she 'can't sing'. Sister took the joy out of singing in her quest for perfection.

Fortunately, things have changed, and many people in the UK are experiencing the joy of choral singing. There has been an enormous increase in community choirs with an open door policy. No voice is deemed unsuitable or untrainable. All singers contribute. Television programmes that chart the progress of reluctant singers as they develop and grow in confidence have encouraged many more to join local choirs. These programmes highlight the joy and solidarity that singing together brings to people of diverse backgrounds and abilities, and the cohesion and inclusion choirs can foster in broken or fractured communities.

These choirs sing a new song with a different concept of harmony, like the 'sound of many waters'. The author of Revelation is speaking of the world to come, but can we, as Christians today, do more to bring heavenly harmony and inclusivity into our churches and society?

† Father, forgive me for the times when I disturb the harmony of my home and sow discord and upset. Help me to walk in the ways of peace.

For further thought

'Blessed are the peacemakers.' Are there situations at home or church where you can bring people together? Is exclusion or factionalism hurting your community?

Letters to Timothy (1)

Notes by **Revd Mandy Briggs**

Mandy Briggs is a Methodist minister who lives in Bristol. She is Education Officer at John Wesley's New Room, the oldest Methodist building in the world (www.newroombristol.org.uk). She works with schools and other groups to tell the story of John Wesley and Methodism, making it relevant to today. Mandy recently developed a passion for houseplants and is learning how to keep them (mostly) thriving. She has used the NIVUK for these notes.

Sunday 28 April
Ephesus

Read 1 Timothy 1:1–17

I thank Christ Jesus our Lord, who has given me strength, that he considered me trustworthy, appointing me to his service.

(verse 12)

Welcome to the first day of a two-week exploration of Paul's letters to Timothy, a young leader based in the city of Ephesus.

What was Ephesus like? Today the ancient ruins of the town can be found in Turkey. When Paul's letter was written it was an important and thriving city. Under Roman rule it had been proclaimed the capital of the Roman province of Asia. It was a centre of commerce, culture and learning – and at its core was the Temple of Artemis, one of the so-called seven wonders of the ancient world. The temple, dedicated to the Greek goddess of hunting, Artemis (Roman name Diana), attracted many pilgrims, but was also controversial.

Ephesus was a major base for Paul and the spread of Christianity, but there was confusion and false teaching in the early church community. This may be in part due to the city hosting multiple other religions that worshipped various other gods and goddesses.

As we reflect on Paul's first letter to Timothy this week, there may be parts we find uncomfortable, and language and attitudes we find outdated. My prayer is that learning more about Ephesus and the trials of its Christian church will enable us to learn more about the background of the letter and to see it through a new lens of understanding.

† God of exploration and understanding, we pray for new thoughts and understanding as we begin this study of Paul's first letter to Timothy.

Monday 29 April
A local difficulty

> **Read 1 Timothy 1:18 – 2:15**
>
> *I urge, then, first of all, that petitions, prayers, intercession and thanksgiving be made for all people – for kings and all those in authority, that we may live peaceful and quiet lives in all godliness and holiness.*
>
> (2:1–2)

It is important to acknowledge the hurt and pain that the misuse of 1 Timothy 2:11–15 has caused in the church down the centuries. These are difficult verses, and provide a classic example of the need to understand the context in which they were written rather than setting them in stone to last for centuries.

One of Paul's main reasons for writing to Timothy was to counter the work of false teachers in the church at Ephesus. He is really worried about this and wants them stopped. In chapter 2, the whole church is being called back to prayer. This is so important for Paul that he names different kinds of prayer that he particularly wants the church to engage in.

The men and women of Ephesus are all being called to return to prayer, and here *both* sexes are challenged about outward behaviour. For the men it's anger and argument, for the women it's an obsession with vanity and outward appearance instead of prayer and good deeds.

And so to those difficult verses. In the context of all Paul's letters, this is the only time he gives instructions like this, so there is an argument that he is addressing a specific local situation – possibly trying to cope with a false female teacher or trying to provide an alternative to the Temple of Artemis, which was apparently run by female priests and eunuchs.

Different theories abound, but my suggestion is that, overall, Paul did not discourage women from taking leadership roles in the early church or in households (see Phoebe the deacon and Junia the apostle in Romans, and Lydia in Acts). The overall context is a serious call to prayer, which is often hidden behind those more controversial verses.

† God, we are sorry for the times when the Bible has been, and still is, used to hurt others. We pray for restoration for all people whose gifts have been rejected or suppressed by the church.

For further thought
Who was the last female preacher or teacher who inspired you?

Tuesday 30 April
A high calling

Read 1 Timothy 3

If I am delayed, you will know how people ought to conduct themselves in God's household, which is the church of the living God, the pillar and foundation of the truth.

(verse 15)

It is worth bearing in mind that for all the good Christian leaders in the world, there are also regular news reports of pastors and teachers who have had to leave their posts because of personal indiscretion, misconduct or even breaking the law. Sadly, there are also ungodly leaders who have remained in their posts, supported by other leaders more concerned about maintaining their power and the status quo.

In this section of his letter to Timothy, Paul is clear that leadership in the church is a high calling, and that there is no room for overseers or deacons to let their standards slip. Paul is trying very hard here to challenge the church to do better; to ensure that its leaders are seen as exemplary in a world of false teaching and multiple religions. Good leadership, for him, is a witness to the community and the world.

The 'job descriptions' given for this role seem like a tall order, but reading between the lines, and patriarchal language aside, I think Paul is simply trying to ensure that the church does not fall apart. Timothy, who Paul rates as a committed leader, is also encouraged work in partnership with other mature, authentic, committed Christians. Godliness springs from Christ, who is at the centre of everything.

Maybe Paul's standards are too high for us mere mortals. But maybe authenticity is the key again here. We are to aim high, but also to be open to correction. We are to be accountable and admit our mistakes.

† God, we are only human, but in our humanity, help us to put you at the centre of our lives and to work hard to be the best possible version of ourselves.

For further thought
What styles of leadership have you observed? What would you say makes a good leader?

121

Wednesday 1 May
Train yourself to be godly

Read 1 Timothy 4

Have nothing to do with godless myths and old wives' tales; rather, train yourself to be godly.

(verse 7)

An advert popped up on my social media feed the other day for a 'habit tracker journal'. This notebook-style stationery was designed to encourage the user to focus on building new habits and reaching new goals and achievements.

For example, say you want to make sure you drink more water every day. The tracker helps you record and plot your daily consumption. Or if you want to walk every day, you can also record the days you get some exercise – and the days you don't. It's all about forming good habits.

In this part of his letter, Paul continues to advise Timothy on dealing with the corrosive problem of false teaching, and false teachers, in the Ephesian church. He tells the young leader: 'Physical training is of some value, but godliness has value for all things.'

While it is good to train our bodies and stretch our minds, it is just as important to maintain our spiritual health and build godly habits into our days. I would suggest some of these habits should include prayer, praise, service and study.

Discipline and training can be seen in many spheres of life, from Olympic athletes to celebrities competing on dancing shows. Paul is clear, however. Training oneself to be godly is not for personal glory – it is all rooted and grounded in the hope that is offered through the living God.

† Loving God, teach me your ways and help me to be rooted and grounded in your love and compassion.

For further thought

Which 'spiritual habits' would you like to develop? Would a habit tracker journal help with that?

A community of care

Read 1 Timothy 5:1–16

Treat younger men as brothers, older women as mothers, and younger women as sisters, with absolute purity.

(verses 1b–2)

Widows – what do we do with them? Are these words from Paul outrageous or simply practical? Are they sexist or rooted in community?

This part of the letter to Timothy recognises the Christian church as a place of social concern and care, but also as a group with limited resources. If you are reading this and are linked to a church, you may be all too aware of the pastoral needs in your church community. A lot of churches have a good network of 'pastoral visitors' who look after the needs of others.

A system of pastoral care was just as important in Paul and Timothy's age, because there was no system of state help. There were no pensions or housing benefits. The expectation was that widows would be cared for by their children and extended family. If they didn't have that, then what?

Paul encourages Timothy to see the church community as a family, caring for those in particular need but also encouraging families to do their bit. I think it's the paragraph about the younger widows that I find most controversial – judgemental, even – but again, this may just be blunt practicality in a society that was wholly centred around the family unit. It reads as if there may have been particular issues, too.

For me this very specific set of instructions raises questions for us today. Who do we care for as a church community? Which groups do we prioritise? Are they the right ones? And which boundaries do we consciously (or unconsciously) set?

† Compassionate God, be alongside all those who are living with the shock and grief of bereavement today.

For further thought

Find out about the work of Cruse Bereavement Support in the UK (www.cruse.org.uk) or Mental Health America (mhanational.org).

May

Letters to Timothy (1)

Friday 3 May
The challenge of leadership

Read 1 Timothy 5:17–25

I charge you, in the sight of God and Christ Jesus and the elect angels, to keep these instructions without partiality, and to do nothing out of favouritism.

(verse 21)

As a young female Methodist probationer minister, I was initially given pastoral charge of five village churches. When chairing meetings, especially church councils, I was acutely aware of my age. Everyone in those meetings was older than I was, with more life experience, and more time spent in those churches and communities. Sometimes it felt quite intimidating, although overall the churches were very supportive of a new, green minister.

In Timothy's situation, the elders of the church in Ephesus were under his authority, working as a team with him to, as Paul says, 'direct the affairs of the church'. This is a calling and an honour, but a position that is open to abuse – whether it is others complaining about the elder or the elder bringing the role into disrepute.

Again, Paul provides very specific instruction and encouragement to Timothy. At this point in the letter I find myself wondering how Timothy is responding to Paul's micro-management! Has he asked for help and instruction? Or does he feel as if he has his own ideas as well as listening to Paul's?

Leadership is difficult and challenging, so it is good to know that, as seen in the last part of today's reading, Paul is concerned for Timothy's health and gives him some specific advice. Therefore, the question for me today is: how do we effectively train our new church leaders and continue to care for them while they are in post? Do they receive adequate support, especially when things go wrong?

† We pray for good training, support and encouragement for young leaders in the church.

For further thought

Who do you know in leadership? How can you encourage them today?

Saturday 4 May
Challenge and contentment

Read 1 Timothy 6:1–10

But godliness with contentment is great gain. For we brought nothing into the world, and we can take nothing out of it.

(verses 6–7)

We are coming to the end of our first week looking at Paul's encouragement and instructions to Timothy. There have been some difficult issues to tackle in the church at Ephesus, and today's reading is no different.

In Paul and Timothy's world, enslaved persons were 'kept' by their masters to serve them in their homes. Paul is not challenging the system of enslavement here, which may seem strange to us. Instead, he encourages a good relationship between master and enslaved person – which may be as far as his understanding takes him at this time.

False teaching has been a constant theme this week, and Paul is still concerned that Timothy should take urgent action to counter these people who are causing unrest and trouble, especially those who are trying to make money out of it. The oft-misquoted phrase 'the love of money is a root of all kinds of evil' (1 Timothy 6:10) does not just confine itself to Ephesus, but is still extremely pertinent today.

Paul suggests that a life in which we focus on God is much more likely to bring peace and contentment, since we are not striving for things that will not last. While not challenging the norms of slavery, he is starting to question what a healthy society looks like. What do we chase and run after, and does it bring happiness? Where, in the end, do we find fulfilment? According to Paul, true fulfilment comes from following Jesus.

† Loving God, may my focus be on you, putting everything else in perspective.

For further thought

Think about the films and books you have watched and read recently. What is their outlook on money?

Letters to Timothy (2)

Notes by **the Honourable Fiamē Naomi Mata'afa and Lemau Pala'amo**

Fiame and Lemau met when they attended Malua Bible School in Samoa and formed a friendship based on their shared faith in God. Fiame is a deacon of the Congregational Church of Samoa in the village of Lotofaga. She has been an MP since 1985 and became Prime Minister of Samoa in July 2021. Lemau is a lecturer's wife at Malua Theological College and the mother of three boys. She co-founded Soul Talk Samoa Trust with her husband. Fiame and Lemau have used the NRSVA for their notes.

Sunday 5 May
Discipleship (Fiamē)

Read 1 Timothy 6:11–21

Timothy, guard what has been entrusted to you. Avoid the profane chatter and contradictions of what is falsely called knowledge.

(verse 20)

I left Samoa to attend boarding school in New Zealand when I was eleven years old in 1969. My mother had also left home at a young age to attend school in New Zealand in 1945. Her father wrote to her and her siblings every week, as she did for me when I went away to school. These letters came by sea in the earlier years and then latterly by air. These days when I write or receive letters or messages electronically, it is instantaneous.

My mother wrote of happenings at home and gave advice on issues I had asked about, but always reminded me of the values I had been raised by and reaffirmed that we were a family grounded in the Christian faith. Paul's letters to Timothy were designed to convey correct Christian doctrine and practice, and to authorise Timothy as his apostolic messenger.

Reading the daily messages from *Fresh from The Word* and writing this contribution is like the receiving and sending of letters; reaffirming our faith, as manifested in the way we profess, in words and in action, that we live in a renewed world as people who are saved through the ultimate sacrifice of Jesus, our Saviour and Redeemer.

† Lord God, teach us to know your will in our daily lives, and give us the courage to allow your will to be done. Amen

Monday 6 May
Faith nurturers (Lemau)

> **Read 2 Timothy 1:1–14**
>
> *Guard the good treasure entrusted to you, with the help of the Holy Spirit living in us.*
>
> (verse 14)

Grandmothers, mothers and aunts are often the first to come to mind when we refer to 'faith nurturers', as these are usually our first teachers of life, education and, most importantly, our faith.

Every second Sunday of October, churches in Samoa celebrate 'White Sunday', where the children wear white and preach to the congregation through plays and dramas based on Bible stories, and through hymns, songs and creative dance. It is the one Sunday of the year that the children take centre stage. Grandmothers, mothers and aunts have everything shining, from new white shoes to new white clothes, to help their children prepare to preach the word of God in various ways.

Paul's letter was to encourage Timothy and remind him to keep going and to hold firmly to the faith that his grandmother Lois and mother Eunice had taught him from the beginning.

In the world we live in today, we are reminded of our own faith journey and where it all began. Who started us on our own individual journeys of faith? Faith nurturers are vital, as one of the keys to a successful journey of faith. We need to hold strong to and uphold the teachings we have been taught from the beginning of our lives.

Faith in God is taught from an early age here in Samoa. It is important that our faith journeys continue as we develop and grow. We must continue to study the Bible, reflect on daily devotions and fellowship with believers. We must guard and protect our faith with the help of God.

† Lord, give us the strength and guidance to stand strong in our faith in you alone. Teach us to teach others, especially our children. Amen

For further thought

Are we following in the footsteps of our faith nurturers? Are we constantly evaluating and ensuring the continuation of our faith?

May

Letters to Timothy (2)

Families of Faith (Fiamē)

> **Read 2 Timothy 1:15 – 2:13**
>
> *And what you have heard from me through many witnesses entrust to faithful people who will able to teach others as well.*
>
> (2:2)

Earlier this year the extended family on my mother's side celebrated the 130th anniversary of our annual family gathering to worship. The progenitor of our family was a pastor, and he had seven sons and two daughters. I am the fourth generation of my line. We had more than a thousand attendees, and each branch had a different coloured T-shirt for ease of identification, with the picture of the family tree printed on the back. Our family also has chapters outside Samoa – in New Zealand, Australia and the United States.

As with many other families, members are present in all walks of life, with many notable achievers. The family especially honours and celebrates those who have followed in the steps of our progenitor in the calling to do God's work and in the practice of service to others through other life paths.

The event always starts with worship, led by family clergy, as well as readings from the Bible, an accompanying message, prayers, praise and a recommittal as a family to God's work. We remember those who have passed on and welcome new members of the family; all gifts from God.

I am writing this at sixty-five years of age, reflecting on all those years we have gathered to worship together as a family – starting from childhood – to hear, share and learn about God, his faithfulness and our salvation through Jesus Christ. From the laps of grandparents and parents to the community of our extended families, this has been a major foundation of my learning, engaging and advocacy as a woman of faith.

† Lord, we pray for your continued blessings on our families, from the nuclear to the extended. We pray for those with no earthly family, that they may know they are your beloved children. Amen

For further thought

In many families there are estrangements and those who remove themselves from contact. How do we bring resolution where there have been differences, and how can we reconnect with lost family members?

Calling to serve God (Lemau)

> **Read 2 Timothy 2:14–26**
>
> *Do your best to present yourself to God as one approved by him, a worker who has no need to be ashamed, rightly explaining the word of truth.*
>
> (verse 15)

As a minister's wife I had no intention of living permanently in Samoa. However, through my love for my husband and our passion to serve others, we are still living in Samoa, going on twenty years.

Individual calling is imperative so we can then congregate with families, churches, communities and villages. Our own intentions and plans for the future are not necessarily God's destiny for us. To be able to move out of our comfort zones to an unknown environment gives us a sense of uncertainty and even fear of the new journey we are about to embark upon in being called to serve the Lord.

Samoa's national motto is *Fa'avae i Le Atua Samoa* ('Samoa is founded on God'). This resonates with today's passage from the Bible, which suggests that the more people who work together for the purpose of fulfilling God's work, the stronger our individual faith will be.

As Christians, we need to stand strong in the work God has called us to do for him. We are to serve God wholeheartedly. We are to be wary of false teachings and, rather than steering in the wrong direction, we are to stand firm.

Leading by example is very important, though not always easy. Paul encourages Timothy to serve people with compassion, courage and patience. Viewing ourselves and our surroundings is just as important. Paul warns Timothy to view himself as a servant seeking to please God. We need to work and serve our Lord with honesty in the duties and responsibilities we have been called to, if we are to please him.

† Lord, please help us to recognise our calling in whatever capacity. We seek your help and guidance, and ask you to stand by us in all that we do. Amen

For further thought

In what capacity are you called to serve God wholeheartedly?

May

Letters to Timothy (2)

Community of all believers (Lemau)

> ### **Read 2 Timothy 3**
> *So that everyone who belongs to God may be proficient, equipped for every good work.*
>
> (verse 17)

An important question can be asked here: what do we need to do to become proficient and equipped for every good work? Reflecting on this passage, in order to be skilled and competent to do something, we must have a close relationship with God.

As in previous passages, our faith starts from the moment we enter this world as a baby through our faith nurturers' teachings. As we develop and grow in faith, we find that God equips us for every task or duty we are involved in. Having the right pathway from the beginning is significant.

For a Samoan child, this begins in Sunday school, and youth group activities then build on the child's faith. Samoans are known to wake up in the morning to a devotion or prayer (*Lotu taeao*). Likewise, once the work and duties of the day are completed, family members return home and conduct a devotion at the end of the day (*Lotu afiafi*). Clergy are invited to start work conferences, meetings and workshops with a devotion. Samoa's communities, workplaces and schools start their day with prayer and end with prayer. In saying so, it is just as important to connect with God through reflection and prayer at any time of the day.

Paul confirms that learning from and reading the Bible blesses our lives. This is a confirmation that the way we were taught by our parents, grandparents, families and communities we must continue for the generations to come. All good work and love for Christ Jesus will show through individuals and through the community of all believers.

† Our Father, we are thankful that you guide us each and every day of our lives. We pray for all communities and that you would continue to equip us for every good work. Amen

For further thought

Is there anything you are missing to be proficient and equipped to do God's work?

Passing the mantle (Fiamē)

Read 2 Timothy 4:1–8

Proclaim the message; be persistent whether the time is favourable or unfavourable; convince, rebuke, and encourage, with the utmost patience in teaching.

(verse 2)

Samoans love to sing, and many are blessed with natural talent. Church choirs are a significant element in our music scene and much time is taken for practice. Our congregation, however, had only one organist, and when he was unavailable there would be no instrumental accompaniment for the singing.

Our church minister organised for a music teacher to come and teach interested students. Two young men and one girl from our church took advantage of this programme. Within a relatively short time, these young people began accompanying the choir and taking turns to conduct the singing. Their confidence grew, not only with the music and the choir, but in their general demeanour. They stood straighter, spoke more clearly, and were more purposeful in their interactions with our congregation.

The Sunday school teachers began collaborating with our new musicians for their events and programmes. Our church minister worked with them to choose and practise appropriate hymns for the worship services. They formed a support group with young people from our neighbouring churches who were in their music class, and encouraged other young people to learn music.

These young people have gained knowledge, developed skills and gained a practised discipline, and can see a clear purpose in their new endeavour. As an older member of our congregation, I feel excited and pray that they will continue to grow in their walk of faith and in the service of our Lord.

In his last days, Paul encouraged Timothy to carry on the work of spreading and defending the faith. He was passing on the mantle. As a community of believers, we look to our youth to carry the mantle to the generations that follow.

† Lord, we pray for your continued blessing and guidance for our church youth, that they may be worthy instruments to do your will wherever they are placed. Amen

For further thought

Do you engage with the young people in your church community? If not, how can you do so?

May

Letters to Timothy (2)

Saturday 11 May
Farewell blessings (Lemau)

Read 2 Timothy 4:9–22

The LORD be with your spirit. Grace be with you.

(verse 22)

In Samoa we have many traditional stories that speak of farewell blessings between loved ones or departing parties. The families or church families gather together over a meal to bid farewell to those who will be departing, either for a short or long journey.

At the end of 2016, when we were preparing to return to Samoa from my husband's studies in Auckland, we were invited by good friends to a farewell lunch. The lunch was attended by our good friends as well as their eighty-five-year-old father, who was a retired Methodist minister. It was the first time we had met him.

After lunch we exchanged words of thanks and best wishes in farewell to one another. The elderly father became emotional as he stood up to have the last say, giving us encouragement, support and farewell blessings for our family. I felt the wisdom and experience, the love and genuine care, through the words the elderly father spoke, which gave us a sense of strength and God's presence that we needed to continue our journey back to Samoa.

To end this week's reading we have Paul's farewell blessings to his young disciple Timothy. Paul lists all those who can support Timothy in continuing the mission. Paul draws Timothy back to remind him that the Lord will always be with his spirit. Paul's words of wisdom and experience give Timothy the strength to continue God's work.

When we depart from our loved ones, we remember God's grace to comfort and protect us all as we live our lives in faith.

† Lord, we pray for all our family members and friends who are apart from us. Guard and help them live their lives in faith. Amen

For further thought

Who is supporting you in your journey of faith?

Camels are useful for ...

Notes by **Ian Fosten**

Ian Fosten has ministered within the United Reformed Church in Norfolk, Suffolk and on Holy Island (Lindisfarne). He is Director of a community theatre in Lowestoft, where he lives with his wife and two youngest children. He runs open-mic poetry readings, edits book reviews, and has a particular interest in landscape and spiritualty. Ian has used the NIVUK for these notes.

Sunday 12 May
... winning a bride

Read Genesis 24:15–27

Before he had finished praying, Rebekah came out with her jar on her shoulder ... The servant hurried to meet her and said, 'Please give me a little water from your jar.' ... After she had given him a drink, she said, 'I'll draw water for your camels too, until they have had enough to drink.' So she quickly emptied her jar into the trough, ran back to the well to draw more water, and drew enough for all his camels.

(verses 15a, 17, 19–20)

I remember my younger brother learning his alphabet with the help of an illustrated Dr Seuss book. The letter 'C' was decorated with a picture of an elderly lady and a camel. The caption that accompanied the picture of Aunt Ada calling to her camel, as if to a pet cat, amused us no end.[1] Nearly six decades later we still laugh at our shared memory.

In the UK, camels are often seen as comedic with their lumps and bumps and spindly legs. Elsewhere in the world, as in biblical times, camels are far from a joke. Rather, they are a valuable means of transport, food and clothing; a visible, portable sign of wealth and even a prized sporting accessory.

In today's story of Abraham seeking a suitable wife for his son Isaac, camels serve as an indicator of potential candidates. To offer water to a thirsty traveller is one thing. To look after the welfare of his camels points to a generous spirit and a sound grasp of life's practicalities. That Rebekah was also very attractive and available was a real bonus – but as far as this future wife selection task was concerned, it was the camels that clinched it!

Enjoy this week's journey in the company of these marvellous beasts.

† Today, dear Lord, may I know you and delight in you; not least in the lumpy, bumpy, spindly parts of life. Amen

[1] P. D. Eastman and Dr. Seuss, *The Cat in the Hat Beginner Book Dictionary* (New York: Random House USA Children's Books, 1964).

... winning a brother

Read Genesis 32:9–21

In great fear and distress Jacob divided the people who were with him into two groups, and the flocks and herds and camels as well ... For he thought, 'I will pacify him with these gifts I am sending on ahead; later, when I see him, perhaps he will receive me.'

(verses 7, 20b)

Today's reading is emotionally evocative. At the very least, Jacob is extremely anxious as he prepares to meet the brother whom he cheated out of their father's inheritance many years previously. How will he be received, and what are the chances that Esau will view his visit favourably? Pretty slim on both counts, he assumes.

Jacob has every reason to suspect that the outcome may be the slaughter of his people and livestock, and he takes damage-limiting precautions. To discover what happens next you really need to read the next chapter, but (spoiler alert!) I'll fill you in anyway.

When confronted with this huge display of four-legged wealth, Esau's response is neither violent nor particularly grateful. He is already comfortably placed, and just how many camels does a person need? Not to mention sheep, cattle and all the rest. It turns out that all the brothers need is to give and receive genuine brotherly love.

I once visited a woman in hospital following fairly major surgery. I went in armed with my best bedside manner, wisest words and carefully crafted prayer. Some while later, at home and fully recovered, she reflected back to me on her experience of my hospital visit. 'When you came to see me,' she said, 'I appreciated your being there and your kind words, but all I really needed was a hug!'

† Dear God, you know me and love me simply as I am. Help me to bring the same readiness to welcome and accept into all the relationships you lead me into. Amen

For further thought

A genuine offer of friendship is more valuable than a whole herd of camels!

Tuesday 14 May
... winning a war

Read Judges 7:9–14

The Midianites, the Amalekites and all the other eastern peoples had settled in the valley, thick as locusts. Their camels could no more be counted than the sand on the seashore. Gideon arrived just as a man was telling a friend his dream ... 'A round loaf of barley bread came tumbling into the Midianite camp. It struck the tent with such force that the tent overturned and collapsed.' His friend responded, 'This can be nothing other than the sword of Gideon ... God has given the Midianites and the whole camp into his hands.'

(verses 12–14)

Gideon faced an army of enormous strength, not least in the immeasurable number of camels that could have been used, both as rapid transport and as cavalry mounts. Gideon's fighting force had already been pared down, at God's command, to just 300 men. The outcome of any battle fought with such massively unequal numbers ought to have been beyond doubt, and yet the wholly improbable happened. Not with any weaponry, but on the strength of an alarming dream, the confidence of Gideon's opponents evaporated and they took flight.

While the plausibility of some elements of this story may not withstand close scrutiny, the underlying purpose of it is robust. Many centuries later, in a letter to the church in Corinth, Paul expressed the same purpose in these words: 'Three times I pleaded with the Lord to take [a major impediment] away from me. But he said to me, "My grace is sufficient for you, for my power is made perfect in weakness"' (2 Corinthians 12:8–9a).

In building the kingdom, God does not call people to be superheroes or passive bystanders. He calls us to be partners. We bring the gifts we have, but we also bring our frailty and incompleteness. Often it is when our strength is depleted and we fall back on these latter attributes that the grace of God works sufficiently to resolve whatever it was we were facing. If, by way of a scary dream, God was able to outflank a host of cavalry camels, maybe the trials we are facing today are not as insurmountable as they seem.

† Today, dear God, I pray not so much for strength to win my battles as the ability to discern where you are already at work – and not get in your way! Amen

For further thought

The world faces overwhelming challenges. What dreams might you pursue in order to win even a few small victories today?

May

Camels are useful for ...

... making money

Read Isaiah 60:1–6

Then you will look and be radiant, your heart will throb and swell with joy; the wealth on the seas will be brought to you, to you the riches of the nations will come. Herds of camels will cover your land, young camels of Midian and Ephah. And all from Sheba will come, bearing gold and incense and proclaiming the praise of the LORD.

(verses 5–6)

I live near the clifftop of the most easterly part of England. Out to sea, one of the largest container ships ever built lies at anchor, as it has done for several weeks, awaiting an opportunity to sail to Hamburg, Germany, to unload. It carries approximately 3,400 containers, and the variety of goods within them is almost unimaginable.

The writer of Isaiah 60 is struck by a similar thought as he searches for an image that adequately reflects the scale of the restoration of fortune that will follow Israel's years of devastation and exile. For him, it is not ships but caravans of camels carrying untold wealth that are poised to 'cover [the] land' with super abundance and prosperity.

Yet even as I read Isaiah and look out to sea, a balancing thought strikes me. I have read about and seen an immense assemblage of wealth, but in neither instance is the value of that wealth yet realised. Until the ship is able to dock and have its containers distributed, its cargo is worthless. Until God's people make living God's way their top priority, the marvellous promise in this reading will remain undeserved and unfulfilled.

In our insatiable pursuit of material goods, humanity has failed to notice that justice, peace and obedience to God are the hallmarks of true wealth. Instead of scanning the horizon for camels or container ships today, we might choose better, living simply and obediently, and find that we are rich indeed.

† Loving God, help me to live more simply, tread more gently and love more openly, that the fragment of the world you have placed in my care may prosper as you wish it to. Amen

For further thought

How might you live more simply, tread more gently and love more openly today?

136

Thursday 16 May
... making a coat

Read Matthew 3:1–10

In those days John the Baptist came, preaching in the wilderness of Judea and saying, 'Repent, for the kingdom of heaven has come near.' ... John's clothes were made of camel's hair, and he had a leather belt round his waist. His food was locusts and wild honey. People went out to him from Jerusalem and all Judea and the whole region of the Jordan. Confessing their sins, they were baptised by him in the River Jordan.

(verses 1–2, 4–6)

I was familiar with this reading and with John the Baptist's camel hair clothes long before I encountered a real live camel. When I finally met one of these robust beasts and came close enough to stroke its side, I was surprised to discover that it was not as I had imagined. Instead of coarse bristle, my hand sank into deep-pile softness.

Until then I had assumed that John's garments were aids to an ascetic lifestyle. The 'wearing of a hairshirt' is a well-known expression based on that practice in some strands of Christianity – though usually, as it turns out, the donor of the hair in question is a goat and not a camel. Much more likely, it seems, John is dressed practically and comfortably for an outdoor lifestyle, but with more than a passing reference to the 'prophet uniform' of Elijah.

By contrast, and with the exception of four highly symbolic moments (birth, transfiguration, death and the empty tomb), the Gospels make very little mention of how Jesus dressed. I assume this is because nothing Jesus wore distinguished him particularly from the people among whom he lived, travelled and taught. This deliberate, inconspicuous immersion into the lives and culture of ordinary people put Jesus at odds with the Pharisees and others who prized their separate aloofness from the common herd. They, like so many of us today, used clothes to signal their identity and worldly status. Jesus, it seems, preferred to let the inescapable integrity of his words and actions be his identifying feature. That strikes me as a 'dress style' worth copying.

† Today, dear God, may I not hide behind the projected message of the clothes I wear, but be simply, confidently and open-heartedly the me you have made. Amen

For further thought

Do you dress to project an image of how you want others to see you?

... making a point (1)

Read Matthew 19:16–26

Jesus answered, 'If you want to be perfect, go, sell your possessions and give to the poor, and you will have treasure in heaven. Then come, follow me.' ... Then Jesus said to his disciples, '... Again I tell you, it is easier for a camel to go through the eye of a needle than for someone who is rich to enter the kingdom of God.'

(verses 21, 23–24)

Jesus' trade was that of a carpenter like his father, Joseph, right? However, there are few allusions to carpentry in the Jesus stories. More frequently he refers to horticulture, animal husbandry and keen observations of the natural world.

In today's reading, Jesus adds 'cartoonist' to this list of trades as he creates a picture that only the insight and wit of a life-observing humourist could conjure. Commentators (who may themselves lack a sense of humour) have sought to rationalise this absurd image and suggest the 'the needle' is a small gate in Jerusalem's city wall. But I think the story works best at face value because, like a gifted cartoonist, Jesus is skilled in the art of hyperbole – an exaggerated presentation used to make a serious point.

The man in the story (and the rationalising commentator) displays our very human tendency to justify tolerance of what is plainly wrong. We say that all people are created equal in God's eyes, and yet through history, not least within the church, we have justified discrimination, oppression and persecution of the poor, the weak and the 'different'.

The punchline of this story is unequivocal: camels cannot pass through a needle's eye. And, while the impediment in this story is one man's attachment to his wealth, the principle applies more widely. Despising others because of our attitude towards their race, gender, orientation, economic standing or understanding of God is incompatible with any claim we might make to love God and desire his kingdom to come on earth.

† Today, dear God, may I avoid saying 'Yes, but ...' when choosing between what you are asking and the way I feel. Instead, help me to follow wholeheartedly, as and where you lead. Amen

For further thought

'Jesus is more of a cartoonist than a carpenter.' What do you make of that statement?

Saturday 18 May
... making a point (2)

Read Matthew 23:13–24

'Woe to you, teachers of the law and Pharisees, you hypocrites! You give a tenth of your spices – mint, dill and cumin. But you have neglected the more important matters of the law – justice, mercy and faithfulness. You should have practised the latter, without neglecting the former. You blind guides! You strain out a gnat but swallow a camel.'

(verses 23–24)

Here we have more of yesterday's cartoonist hyperbole. You can picture, along with Jesus' hearers, the Pharisees and others straining a tiny insect from their drinks without noticing the enormous camel they have accidentally swallowed. You can almost hear the crowd's laughter rising from the page.

But as the laughter subsides, we might start to feel implicated in this absurd cartoon ourselves. Do we ever get so hung up on a tiny detail that we fail to see the bigger picture? Of course we do; again and again and again.

In valuing other people fairly, in our care for the earth, in our seeking out the kingdom of God rather than worrying over our small chunk of the church, it is so easy to get sidetracked by the minutiae and lose our grip on God's bigger intention. We get upset over trifles and consequently miss the significance of larger injustices.

This reading invites us to recalibrate our response to God and to our world. Never mind if it is raining today or the preacher spoke for ten minutes too long last Sunday, Jesus redirects us to the most important components of our faith: justice, mercy and faithfulness. If we set those as the starting point of our journey, we shall, by God's grace, avoid swallowing any camels. And if the odd gnat choses to take a swim in our drinks, is that really such a big deal?

† Dear God, you know that I am bugged by small inconveniences and often let really important issues pass me by. Help me to discern the difference between a gnat and a camel! Amen

For further thought

The nuts and bolts of life are important. The purpose of the whole machine is even more so.

May

Camels are useful for ...

139

Bringing good news and building the church (1)

Notes by **Alesana Fosi Pala'amo**

Alesana is Head of Department for Practical Theology at Malua Theological College in Samoa. An ordained minister of the Congregational Christian Church of Samoa, his research interests include social ministries, Pacific research methodologies, theology and pastoral counselling. Alesana's PhD research through Massey University New Zealand explored the pastoral counselling practices of Samoans. Alesana and his wife Lemau co-founded a pastoral counselling agency called Soul Talk Samoa Trust, and their sons, Norman, Alex and Jayden, attend college and primary school in Samoa. Alesana has used the NRSVA for these notes.

Sunday 19 May
All were together

Read Acts 1:12–26

Then they prayed and said, 'Lord, you know everyone's heart. Show us which one of these two you have chosen to take the place in this ministry and apostleship from which Judas turned aside to go to his own place.'

(verses 24–25)

For any building activity there needs to be a plan. Whether you are building a wooden bookshelf, a coffee table, a house, or a team of colleagues, there is always a plan. There is also a master builder; the one who comes up with a plan and determines the best possible way of working. The size of the intended build determines how many workers are needed to complete the task. The team of workers recruited to fulfil a specific job is at the discretion and selection of the master builder.

Today's reading sees the gap left after Judas' exit (due to his betrayal of Jesus) being filled. Gathered in Jerusalem following Jesus' ascension to heaven, his crowd of Jesus' followers had sought to select a replacement, and Matthias was chosen.

Our readings this week include some of the key people highlighted in the Bible who were called together to help build the church from its very beginning. The Master Builder is the one who fills the gap. Our part as team players is to allow our Lord to use us in building the church and in bringing the gospel to the masses.

† Lord God, may you use me in my daily living to share the good news of the gospel to people of all nations. Amen

Monday 20 May
Knowing Jesus

Read Matthew 16:13–20

And I tell you, you are Peter, and on this rock I will build my church, and the gates of Hades will not prevail against it.

(verse 18)

In child development, it is amazing how a child associates meanings with symbols that are important to their parents and significant others around them. For example, when one of my sons was four, he was able to link the symbolism of the Latin cross, or the plain Christian cross, with Jesus.

Living on campus with my family at Malua Theological College in Samoa, where I teach, there are several notable images and symbols of Christian significance onsite. Passing by the glass-bricked cross of the main hall, my son pointed to the cross and said, 'I know Jesus.' Then he began to sing the popular Samoan hymn ninety-two, titled *Fa'afetai I Le Atua*, which translates as 'Thanksgiving to God'. It was most likely from our family evening devotions and his Sunday school classes – common practices for Samoan children from a young age, that my son made the connection between the cross and Jesus.

It is in today's reading that Jesus first explicitly discusses the beginnings of the Christian church. Peter knew Jesus and identified our Lord as the Messiah, the Son of the living God. In doing so, Peter was entrusted with the task of beginning the church. Whether Jesus meant that Peter (*Petros* in Greek) or a rock (*petra* in Greek) to build his church upon is uncertain, as the play on words when translated gives significance to either interpretation. Knowing Jesus is foundational for us to continue building the church of today and to bring the gospel of Christ in a relevant way for everyone, including our children.

† Our all-knowing God, forgive me if seeking to understand you pushes me further away from the way you have taught. Help me, Lord, to know you and to build my life around you. Amen.

For further thought

Knowing Jesus means thinking, acting and having an attitude like Jesus. Do your actions show that you know Jesus or not?

May

Bringing good news and building the church (1)

Stephen

Read Acts 6:1–8

The word of God continued to spread; the number of the disciples increased greatly in Jerusalem, and a great many of the priests became obedient to the faith. Stephen, full of grace and power, did great wonders and signs among the people.

(verses 7–8)

More people became believers in Christ as the work of Peter and the other apostles gathered momentum throughout Jerusalem. The masses were converting to the Way of Christ, and it became evident that reinforcements were needed to assist in building the early church. To meet the demand, seven spirit-filled believers were chosen by the people to be deacons, serving the poor. Often linked to God creating all things in six days and resting on the seventh, seven is a significant number, representing completion, perfection and wholeness.

Stephen, a loyal and faithful follower of Christ, was among the selected seven. Alongside the practical work, he preached about the history of Israel and the gospel of Christ. The religious leaders took offence at the applications of such teachings, leading to Stephen being stoned to death and becoming the first Christian martyr.

Samoa is predominantly a Christian nation today, having first received the gospel of Christ through the efforts of the London Missionary Society, followed by other Christian missions. People who, like those early deacons, preached the good news and lived it out in practical ways.

In a world with a growing number of disciples of Christ, with the figures rising into the billions, the need for those who will serve him in building his church is greater than ever before. As the passage reminds us, serving practically requires just as much devotion and faithfulness as being a martyr. The challenge now is for us to engage in similar efforts in order to continue leading others to Christ.

† Our Creator God, may you use me as a disciple of Christ to bring the gospel to others and build your church in a modern world filled with change and challenges. Amen.

For further thought

Allow yourself to be recruited by God as a disciple of Christ, and to lead others to follow him as well.

May

Bringing good news and building the church (1)

Wednesday 22 May
Baptism on the move

Read Acts 8:26–40

He commanded the chariot to stop, and both of them, Philip and the eunuch, went down into the water, and Philip baptized him.

(verse 38)

After completing my high-school years in Sydney during the late 1980s, I worked for a printing company in the inner-city suburb of Alexandria. This suburb was an industrial area at the time, with factories that produced goods and services for various trades. Every lunchtime, a fleet of utility cars converted into mobile tuckshops would drive around the factories and sell food to the workers. Drivers of these utility cars would sound their distinctive horns so that interested factory workers would know they had arrived.

Today's reading speaks of a baptism on the move. Philip brought the gospel message to a lone believer returning from Jerusalem, just as those mobile tuckshops brought lunch to where we worked! He explained the book of Isaiah and preached Christ, and the result was that the Ethiopian's hunger was satisfied – and he requested to be baptised. Philip's response fulfils the Great Commission to go out and make disciples of all nations, baptising in the name of the Father, of the Son and of the Holy Spirit.

As with Stephen, Philip was appointed as a deacon to serve the church in practical ways. But while structures are important in facilitating the work, the Spirit isn't constrained by them – and Philip, filled with the Spirit, wasn't either. This baptism on the move demonstrates a willingness to change his plans, with the underlying purpose of spreading Christianity to the world.

Instituted by Christ, baptism continues today as one of the sacraments observed by Christians from both the Roman Catholic and Protestant traditions. Although practices today mostly involve official church ceremonies inside church buildings, today's reading demonstrates that, while traditions are important, we need to be responsive to the Spirit's leading.

† O God, thank you for baptising me with your Holy Spirit, that I might become a new creation through my faith in Jesus Christ as my Lord and Saviour. Amen.

For further thought

A willingness to be flexible in how and where we serve God is important. Are we set in our ways or flexible when it comes to serving God?

Bringing good news and building the church (1)

Thursday 23 May
Used as an instrument of God

Read Acts 9:10–18

But the Lord said to him, 'Go, for he is an instrument whom I have chosen to bring my name before Gentiles and kings and before the people of Israel; I myself will show him how much he must suffer for the sake of my name.'

(verses 15–16)

It is important to use the most suitable tools for any building task. In building a house, for example, the right instruments are needed for different sections of the house to align with the plans. The speed and pace of the build also depends on the most efficient instruments being used. The finished product demonstrates whether all components of the build have worked well, with the most suitable instruments used at each stage of the process.

Today's reading refers not so much to the instruments used to build a physical structure, but rather to the use of human resources as instruments needed to bring the gospel of Christ and build the church. Take, for example Ananias – a disciple used as an instrument by God to take the gospel to Saul, relieve Saul of his blindness and, most importantly, baptise Saul into the Christian faith.

After Saul's conversion from persecuting Christians to becoming one himself – when he met the risen Lord on the road to Damascus – God chose him as an instrument to bring the gospel of Christ to many.

Rather than using his Jewish name by blood relation and religion, Saul became known as Paul shortly after this, choosing instead to use his Roman name by birth and citizenship. Paul, who often called himself the apostle to the Gentiles, was effective in both communities because he was from both worlds. Paul's Jewish heritage and Roman citizenship enabled him to reach a larger collective audience and, consequently, assisted in bringing the gospel to many and building the church.

† Lord God, thank you for our Lord and Saviour, Jesus Christ, who has demonstrated how I, too, can become an instrument of your love and an agent for your grace. Amen.

For further thought

Let us all become instruments of God's peace and channel the love of God in all that we do.

Friday 24 May
God gives life and breath

Read Acts 17:22-34

The God who made the world and everything in it, he who is LORD of heaven and earth, does not live in shrines made by human hands, nor is he served by human hands, as though he needed anything, since he himself gives to all mortals life and breath and all things.

(verses 24–25)

As Paul continued his work to build Christ's church, Paul noticed that the city of Athens was full of idols. He debated with the locals, explaining that Jesus was alive and brings life, unlike their dead idols. Through his words and the work of the Holy Spirit, some hearers turned from their old ways to follow Christ. One such convert is Dionysius who eventually became the first bishop of Athens and later died by fire as a martyr. Another is Damaris, believed to be the wife of Dionysius.

As the Master Builder, God gives life and breath to any build he is involved in. This means that God is the source, provider, and sustainer of all created beings, great and small; of all that he has built through the efforts and work of his servants. The statues and idols Paul observed in the city of Athens represented the gods of the city. The reminder for us today is to take a hard look at our own lives to see what we can identify as idols that we worship and value. In essence, items that are lifeless that we allow to control our lives.

Paul teaches us here that God is a living God, who gives breath and life to all creation. This is the good news for all: that God is alive and, through Christ, we can live a vibrant, full and abundant life in the service and honour of our living God.

† O God, I thank you, for you are a living God; the source and sustainer of my being in this world, who gives me breath and life. Amen.

For further thought
Do we serve things that have no life, yet control all that we do? Let us serve our Lord, who gives us life every day.

May

Bringing good news and building the church (1)

Saturday 25 May
Priscilla and Aquila

Read Acts 18:1–4, 18

After staying there for a considerable time, Paul said farewell to the believers and sailed for Syria, accompanied by Priscilla and Aquila. At Cenchreae he had his hair cut, for he was under a vow.

(verse 18)

Paul faced resistance in bringing the gospel to the Greek city of Corinth. Nevertheless, Aquila and his wife Priscilla – Jewish refugees from Italy – had become believers. These converts helped in building the church and accompanied Paul in his mission. Then we read this strange comment about Paul cutting his hair!

To some, haircuts may not be a big deal, but for others this practice marks the end of something or the beginning of something new. In some Pacific families, boys grow their hair until they begin primary school. A haircutting celebration is then held, with family and friends invited to the public event to eat, dance and share in the young boys' rite of passage into their formal education. My parents let my hair grow long until I turned five, when my father cut it for the first time.

For Jews, not cutting their hair denoted being set apart for a period. One example of this is seen in the Nazirite vow described in Numbers 6. Paul had not allowed a razor to touch his head as a visible sign of setting himself apart for a particular task. Cutting his hair signalled the end of one season of service and the beginning of another.

We are not told why Paul took the vow or why it ended, but we can speculate. Some of the resistance he encountered among the Jews came because they felt he no longer valued Jewish traditions. By taking this visible vow, he demonstrated that he did value them. And it worked. Priscilla and Aquila received him and his message – at which point he could express his freedom in Christ by shaving!

† Christ, my Saviour, I am blessed because you have made me a new person through your grace and sacrifice on the cross. Thank you. May my life be devoted to serving you always. Amen

For further thought

Do we sometimes make promises we cannot keep? Let's be honest and return God's love by keeping our promises to him and to others.

May

Bringing good news and building the church (1)

Bringing good news and building the church (2)

Notes by **Stella Wiseman**

Stella Wiseman is a priest in the Church of England, where one of her passions is the intersection of faith and creativity. Having spent many years in journalism, she now writes fiction for children and young adults, and also runs an annual poetry competition and a regular craft market, seeking to build a community of creative people linked with the church. She has three adult children, a husband and nine cats. Stella has used the NRSVA for these notes.

Sunday 26 May
Titus: a loyal child in the faith

Read Titus 1:1–5

I left you behind in Crete for this reason, that you should put in order what remained to be done, and should appoint elders in every town, as I directed you.

(verse 5)

Perhaps, like me, you have heard such phrases as: 'We need to do things the way they did in the early church' or, 'That's not what happened in the early Church'. I used to think the early Christians knew exactly how to live. True, they had a few bits of doctrine to sort out, but they were so close to the time of Jesus, and so full of the Holy Spirit, that surely they didn't get themselves in a mess and a muddle the way we tend to today.

This week's readings, however, give insight into just how similar those early Christians were to us. They were a mix of faithful, loving, compassionate, argumentative, enthusiastic and strong-willed people, just like today's Christians. And they made mistakes, just as we do.

People like Titus, one of Paul's loyal and faith-filled companions, were needed to help give the church structure and oversight, so that the message of Jesus Christ could be spread effectively and everyone could play their part. Today's readings show a church working out how best to operate in order to keep Christ at the centre and to work together in love.

† Loving God, may we always seek to keep you at the centre of everything we do.

Monday 27 May
Phoebe – A woman of importance

Read Romans 16:1–2

I commend to you our sister Phoebe, a deacon of the church at Cenchreae, so that you may welcome her in the Lord as is fitting for the saints, and help her in whatever she may require from you, for she has been a benefactor of many and of myself as well.

(verses 1–2)

As we come to the last chapter of Paul's powerful letter to the Christians in Rome, we find him sending greetings to people he must have held in great esteem or with particular affection. It is fascinating to imagine who these people were and how they played a part in spreading God's good news.

The first mentioned, Phoebe, was a deacon and clearly a woman of wealth and influence. There have been arguments over what the word 'deacon' meant here, with some people suggesting it meant a helper and others that it meant some sort of leader. Certainly, the Greek words used for her – *diakonos* (deacon) and *prostatis* (patroness) – suggest leadership and influence at her home church in Cenchreae – a port in the city of Corinth, which Paul had visited on his missionary journeys. It may be that the Christians met in her home because many churches gathered in the homes of individuals in those days. It seems that she might even have been bringing Paul's letter to the Roman Christians. Imagine how different our faith might be if she hadn't done so!

Phoebe is the only woman specifically referred to as a deacon in the Bible. Whoever she was, Paul expresses his great gratitude and care for her as someone who had helped him and others, and who must be given help in whatever way she needed. She had an important part to play in the church and in sharing the word of God.

† Loving God, may we always seek to discover and then play our part in your mission on this earth.

For further thought

Throughout history, people have faithfully followed God and shared the gospel so that we can know God today. Let's always be grateful for their witness over the years.

A diverse church

Read Romans 16:3–15

Greet Prisca and Aquila, who work with me in Christ Jesus, and who risked their necks for my life, to whom not only I give thanks, but also all the churches of the Gentiles. Greet also the church in their house. Greet my beloved Epaenetus, who was the first convert in Asia for Christ. Greet Mary, who has worked very hard among you.

(verses 3–6)

Here we have a long list of people in the Roman church … and what a mixed list it is! Among them Jewish and Gentile names, and male and female names, are called out for special mention.

The first are Prisca and Aquila whom we met before in Acts. They had been banished from Rome, along with their fellow Jews, by Emperor Claudius. Like Paul, they were tentmakers, and they all worked together in Corinth, where Paul led them to Christ. They travelled with him and had returned to Rome, where they hosted a church in their house. What did they bring to their fellow Christians of their experiences in Corinth and on the road with Paul? We can only imagine, but they were obviously important in the growing early church.

Then there is Mary, a hard-working Jewish woman, and Paul's relatives, Andronicus and Junia, also Jewish, who were in prison with him and actually became Christians before him. Did they influence the young Saul of Tarsus? Did they pray for him? What stories did they have to tell?

What part did Epaenetus – who heard Paul speak in Ephesus and turned to Christ – have to play? And what of the two Roman women, Tryphaena and Tryphosa? There are many more. The church in Rome was a diverse and exciting place. Imagine the way people learned from one another and discovered the ways God was working in them all.

† Loving God, may we always be willing to learn from one another so we can learn more about you.

For further thought

It's well known that organisations grow when they embrace diversity and inclusion, because they find new perspectives. The early church was radically diverse and inclusive, and it grew and grew. That's a lesson for us today.

May

Bringing good news and building the church (2)

Trouble and strife

May

Bringing good news and building the church (2)

Read 1 Corinthians 1:11–17

For it has been reported to me by Chloe's people that there are quarrels among you, my brothers and sisters. What I mean is that each of you says, 'I belong to Paul', or 'I belong to Apollos', or 'I belong to Cephas', or 'I belong to Christ.' Has Christ been divided? Was Paul crucified for you? Or were you baptized in the name of Paul?

(verses 11–13)

In the other readings so far this week, we have seen praise for the hardworking, loyal Christians who were spreading the word of God. There has been a sense of unity and excitement. The church is thriving. Today, though, we read about divisions in a very young church. The Corinthian church had been established for just a few years and, as you will see if you read the whole letter, it was rife with problems; among them, arguments about whose teaching was best. The people they were claiming allegiance to were big names in the church: Paul, Apollos and Cephas, as well as Christ.

We don't know who Chloe was – this is the only time she is mentioned – but she was probably one of the leaders of the Corinthian church. She, or at least those who met in her house, could see that the arguments about which leader's teaching to follow were causing harm to the central message of church teaching: Christ crucified and risen.

Paul is having none of it. For him, it is only Christ's gospel that matters. This is something that it is easy for us to forget as we declare our allegiances to one or other church family within the Christian church. It is fine to have preferences for a particular style, and to have different interpretations of passages in the Bible, but we are often in danger of losing sight of the central figure: Jesus Christ. That way lies problems and decline.

† Loving God, we thank you that, despite our differences, you love us all. Help us to show that love to those with whom we disagree.

For further thought

Jesus reminds us to 'first take the log out of your own eye, and then you will see clearly to take the speck out of your neighbour's eye' (Matthew 7:5).

Of one mind

> ## Read Philippians 4:1–3
>
> *Therefore, my brothers and sisters, whom I love and long for, my joy and crown, stand firm in the Lord in this way, my beloved. I urge Euodia and I urge Syntyche to be of the same mind in the Lord. Yes, and I ask you also, my loyal companion, help these women, for they have struggled beside me in the work of the gospel, together with Clement and the rest of my co-workers, whose names are in the book of life.*
>
> (verses 1–3)

Another disagreement, and more people we know almost nothing about! This time it is two women, Euodia and Syntyche, both members of the church in Philippi. They had worked hard with Paul to spread the news of Jesus Christ, but must have fallen out, though we have no idea what their disagreement was about. It must have been serious, though, as Paul is at pains to nip it in the bud. He knew from experience, as we know from Acts and his letter to the Galatians, how dangerous divisions can be, and how they can spread through the church.

Perhaps they were church leaders, and such conflict might have risked splitting the church. The history of the church is full of such conflicts. At one point there were three popes all vying for supremacy, and today we have many denominations with multiple divisions.

As we grow together in love, and as we seek to move beyond superficial relationships into genuine love, conflict is inevitable. That, in itself, isn't the issue. Allowing the conflict to divide rather than working through the issues to find a loving resolution is the real problem.

For Paul, and for us today – given that many churches are very divided – the important thing is to focus on the message of salvation through the Christ who is for all. As he says in Galatians 3:28: 'There is no longer Jew or Greek, there is no longer slave or free, there is no longer male and female; for all of you are one in Christ Jesus.' This is something for all of us to remember.

† Loving God, please forgive us when we let conflict interrupt our focus on you and your message of unity and love.

For further thought

Resolving conflict isn't about being nice to each other while letting anger fester inside. It may involve being tough and setting boundaries, but focusing on God can help us see how best to do this.

May

Bringing good news and building the church (2)

Radical love

Read Philemon 1–7

When I remember you in my prayers, I always thank my God because I hear of your love for all the saints and your faith towards the Lord Jesus. I pray that the sharing of your faith may become effective when you perceive all the good that we may do for Christ. I have indeed received much joy and encouragement from your love, because the hearts of the saints have been refreshed through you, my brother.

(verses 4–7)

This letter to Philemon, which Paul wrote with Timothy while they were in prison, is very short. We know almost nothing about the recipients, or even if their real names were given. In ancient Greek, the name Philemon means 'kindly' or 'affectionate', and this letter is addressed to someone of that name and two others: Apphia and Archippus (who appears briefly in Colossians 4:17 as someone who has a task to do for Christ). It is also addressed to the church that meets in Philemon's house, which suggests he was a wealthy man, It is generally assumed that he lived in Colossae, an ancient city in what is now Turkey.

What is clear is the love Philemon has demonstrated in his service to others. It isn't his wealth or position, his large house or his fashionable clothes that are praised by Paul, but his love. Being remembered as a person of love is truly something to aspire to.

But this love that Paul praises Philemon for goes so much further than the 'kindnesses' of his name. It is a radical love that turns the world upside down. Take back this absconding slave – not to have him executed or even to reinstate him as a slave – but as a lost brother, returned. Echoing the parable of the lost son, Paul and Timothy call on the love they know is present in Philemon's life and encourage him to stretch to this new depth of 'agape'.

Christ is at the centre, and from there everything else flows.

† Loving God, may we take our discipleship seriously by putting Christ at the centre of our lives.

For further thought

This is a rather more private letter than Paul's other ones, and its presence here reminds us that whether what we are doing is private or public, we should be focused on Christ.

Saturday 1 June
Love is the answer

Read 2 John:1–6

But now, dear lady, I ask you, not as though I were writing you a new commandment, but one we have had from the beginning, let us love one another. And this is love, that we walk according to his commandments; this is the commandment just as you have heard it from the beginning – you must walk in it.

(verses 5–6).

Who is this 'dear lady'? If only we knew. We are not even sure exactly who wrote the letter, other than that it was an elder, or leader, of what was known as the Johannine community. There have been plenty of ideas over the years about who the recipient was, including Mary the mother of Jesus; members of the writer's family; a church leader; and a whole local church. It's fun to speculate, but whomever the letter was addressed to, the message of this passage remains the same, and is timeless: 'Let us love one another.'

This is a commandment that reverberates through the New Testament. 'This is my commandment, that you love one another as I have loved you.,' says Jesus in John 15:12, while Paul writes in 1 Corinthians 13:2–3 that without love we are nothing.

This love is not just a nice word or a feeling about other people; it is an action. It reminds readers that love is to 'walk according to his commandments', following what Jesus taught, and what has been handed down in church teachings for centuries. The letter probably dates from around 100 AD, when there was a schism in the church over understandings of the nature of Christ and salvation. It's not surprising that new ideas had arisen over the years, but the writer wants to go back to Christian basics: love Christ and obey his commandments. A church that does so will surely be doing the will of God.

† Loving God, thank you for your boundless love. Forgive us when we fail to love, and help us to show our love in action.

For further thought
The Greek word for love here is *agape*. This is the all-giving love demonstrated by Jesus, who promised us his Holy Spirit to empower us to the same.

Bringing good news and building the church (2)

The Gospel of Mark (3)

1 Who is this miracle worker?

Notes by **Terry Lester**

Terry Lester serves as an Anglican priest in Constantia, Diocese of Cape Town, South Africa. His family experienced first hand their removal under apartheid during his formative years, leading him to focus his ministry efforts on justice and reconciliation. The non-governmental organisation (NGO) he started records and archives stories of those affected by the Group Areas Act from Constantia, referencing their triumphs and sorrows as people of colour. His three adult children and his four grandchildren live nearby. Terry has used the NRSVA for these notes.

Sunday 2 June
Inner purity

Read Mark 7:1–23

Then [Jesus] called the crowd again and said to them, 'Listen to me, all of you, and understand: there is nothing outside a person that by going in can defile, but the things that come out are what defile.'

(verses 14–15)

In the popular sci-fi television series of the 1960s, *Star Trek*, outer space is referred to as the 'final frontier' when viewers are taken on voyages of the starship *Enterprise*. Many of us will remember the iconic opening sequence in *Star Trek* that defined its ongoing mission. In the same way, we are called to go boldly.

In our readings this week Jesus is presented as someone who is boldly going where his fellow Jewish Galileans would not have dared to venture, let alone engage with anyone. Jesus ventures into these far-flung regions of coastal and inland Galilee with its mostly Gentile inhabitants. The Pharisees, who epitomise religious purity and observance, repeatedly fail to do likewise, and therefore fail to see and hear the remarkable faith of those Jesus encounters. Their elaborate rituals of hand washing, cleaning utensils and food preparation prevent them from encountering other forms of faith.

The journey towards inner purity may not be as exciting as an intergalactic one, but it will take you to a place of greater reliance on God's grace than your own efforts at outer purity ever could.

† Lord Jesus, help me to find peace and comfort in simply being present with myself and with others I feel uncomfortable around. Amen

Monday 3 June
The faith of a Gentile woman

Read Mark 7:24–30

But she answered [Jesus], 'Sir, even the dogs under the table eat the children's crumbs.'

(verse 28)

Venturing into unknown territory can create a wonderful and exciting buzz! It can also be frightening when you realise you have no control over the strangers you may encounter, nor their reactions; especially those you have been warned to avoid throughout your life. It takes courage to confront those fears or to stop and engage with them. In societies in which men and women do not freely engage in public, or in communities with a history of animosity, it can be downright dangerous.

In June 1976 I was stopped by security policemen when I was out riding my bicycle one early winter evening in Zeekoevlei, South Africa. The area is adjacent to ours, with a buffer strip separating us from them, and it was racially demarcated as 'white'. Two burly white men alighted their parked vehicle as dusk settled in, approached me and asked what business I had being there. It was a mere few days after the Soweto uprisings, so the powers that be were on high alert. They needed to reassure their white counterparts who were living close to coloured areas that they were still in charge.

The binary of white–black, perpetrator–victim, Jew–Gentile – so dominant in many parts of our world – exacerbates already tense situations and heightens distrust. Breaking these cycles takes faith and courage; a fact that is not lost on Jesus in this encounter.

† God of our Lord Jesus, help me to break the cycle that keeps people apart. For Jesus' sake. Amen

For further thought

Are you looking for ways to break out of the binaries that keep you and others trapped?

The Gospel of Mark (3) – 1 Who is this miracle worker?

Tuesday 4 June
The healing of the deaf and mute man

Read Mark 7:31–37

They brought to [Jesus] a deaf man . . . He took him aside in private, away from the crowd . . . Then looking up to heaven, he sighed and said to him, 'Ephphatha', that is, 'Be opened.'

(verses 32–34)

A little while ago a friend shared with me about her son who, from his early years, battled in mainstream schooling. He couldn't sit still! He constantly fidgeted with his hands, and bounced or rocked from side to side while sitting. As a result, he was constantly called out as being disruptive and found himself being increasingly pushed aside.

After eventually being diagnosed with autism spectrum disorder, he was placed in a school that specialised in helping children with special educational needs. On his first day there he was given a little rubber squash ball to play with as long and often as he chose, and his fidgeting stopped! Instead of a chair he was given a gym ball to sit on, and he rocked and rolled to his heart's content.

My friend was over the moon. Not only was her son much happier, but she also felt they really 'got' her boy and understood where he was coming from. He lost the need to be constantly distracted and was encouraged to engage in actions that helped him channel the excess energy his body was generating. And there was no more labelling. It was as if he had been taken aside, listened to intently and then action had been taken to help make sitting in a classroom bearable for him.

† Dear Lord Jesus, I am ready to be taken aside by you. Please make me ready to do as you ask. Amen

For further thought
List the ways in which you can assist others and meet them on their terms to show, even in small ways, that they matter.

The feeding of the 4,000

Read Mark 8:1–13

And [Jesus] sighed deeply in his spirit and said, 'Why does this generation ask for a sign? Truly I tell you, no sign will be given to this generation.'

(verse 12)

Food is such an everyday, universal need. In communities all over the world, part of our daily routine centres around the gathering or acquiring of ingredients to prepare the day's meals. In communities where conflicts are rife and historical intertribal animosities loom large, food has often been used as a weapon of war. Food gifted by donor nations for distribution is often withheld or disproportionately distributed; sometimes just to rile others, but also to weaken their resolve or to shame and humiliate a perceived enemy.

The daily reality of hunger can drive people to do things they would never have done if their stomachs were sated and the members of their household were fed. Imagine a world where food is provided to meet the needs of all, even our enemies; where the hunger cries of children are never heard again; where enough is given, so that there is some left over to share out, even with our enemy's enemy!

In most communities, coded words or numbers are used to refer to those who are uninitiated into our way of knowing and dealing. Jews understood the numbers mentioned in today's reading, 4,000 and seven, as numbers that referred to the Gentile world. This is a salutary lesson from Jesus to both Jew and Gentile that God not only provides for all, but that his care and compassion knows no bounds.

† Dear Lord Jesus, I am often tempted to set out conditions in my caring for and being generous to others. Help me to care without bounds. Amen

For further thought

Find out about food banks, a community kitchen serving meals or a school providing sandwiches and offer your assistance.

Thursday 6 June
Yeast of the Pharisees

Read Mark 8:14–21

'Why are you talking about having no bread? Do you still not perceive or understand? Are your hearts hardened?'

(verse 17)

It is astounding how much information lands on our devices daily, most of it unsolicited. I often find myself innocently searching the web for something, and then later that same day, dozens more items relating to something vaguely similar to my search criteria will land on my screen. I have grown accustomed to swiping right to clear these unwanted bombardments, but occasionally something grabs me and before long I am sitting back reading all about it! It can be a veritable minefield as we seek to distinguish between the items we need to pay heed to and the ones we don't.

I have learned that not everything which tugs at the heartstrings in social media posts is necessarily true, even if a 'personal source' is quoted. But equally, some minor detail mentioned in passing could hint at a deeply disturbing truth that needs further exploration. It is a constant challenge to know what to harden our hearts to and dismiss as mere sensation and what to remain openhearted to, so that we discover a truth that might be there. Not everything that is up for consumption, literally or figuratively, is necessarily good, but that does not mean all of it should be dismissed as bad either.

† God our Father, keep my eyes and ears open to hearing you and my heart tender with compassion. Amen

For further thought

Set aside time in your day to research some of the stories and people you come across online, so that you are better informed.

Friday 7 June
Jesus heals the blind man

Read Mark 8:22–26

They came to Bethsaida. Some people brought a blind man to [Jesus] and begged him to touch him.

(verse 22)

In my country of birth – South Africa – race was often the first, and sometimes the only thing, we were taught to see. Signs written in the crudest racial language, announced where each race could sit and which train carriages we could ride in. Signs were visible at the hospital entrance each could use. Segregation was enforced along racial lines in the schools we could attend, the residential areas in which we lived and even marked the section of the cemetery in which we should be buried. Laws prescribed our racially separate existence from the cradle to the grave.

It was not surprising, therefore, that in the struggle for liberation the narrative of good and evil, right and wrong, villain and victim was portrayed in these 'black' and 'white' terms with a tiny smidgen of grey in between. Things seemed simple when described in these categories. But we have since learned that seeing through these racially tinted lenses is inadequate and sets grave limitations when it comes to seeing people for who they truly are. Racial 'seeing' limits possibilities. It restricts relationships and prevents a fuller and deeper encounter with one another. But it does more than that; it boxes people in rather than setting them free to be who they choose to be.

† Lord Jesus Christ, help me see as you see, without the limitations of my own prejudices and fears. Amen

For further thought
Blindness and partial sight are real impediments for many. Visual impairment also takes many forms figuratively. What are yours?

The Gospel of Mark (3) – 1 Who is this miracle worker?

Saturday 8 June
Peter's declaration

Read Mark 8:27–30

[Jesus] asked them, 'But who do you say that I am?' Peter answered him, 'You are the Messiah.'

(verse 29)

When Peter blurts out this response to Jesus' question, it often feels like a stone cast into a quiet lake, the ripples of which go on and on. In the late 1980s I served in a rural area two hours north of Cape Town. The local Dutch Reformed Church, which served most of the town and white farming families, had a quote from Revelation emblazoned above its main entrance: 'Let everyone who is thirsty come to the water.'

At a time when interracial fraternising was prohibited and many churches served racially exclusive groupings, this seemed to be a blatant hypocrisy. No attempts were made to bring in or welcome those of other races. It seemed as though this didn't even raise an eyebrow, something I questioned. One wizened soul took me aside to say that sometimes our words don't fully match our actions, and that our actions often take a while to catch up with our words! That doesn't make us hypocrites – we are just slow to catch up with the God who goes ahead of us.

Growing up in a racially divided South Africa, we all celebrated 'Communion' week by week, yet we remained in our racial, class and social silos. 'The Chorister's Prayer' entreats: 'Grant that what we sing with our lips we may believe in our hearts, and what we believe in our hearts we may show forth in our lives.'[1] May its ripples reach into every corner of our lives.

† Dear Lord Jesus, help me to not only watch what I say, but to live out what I speak. Amen

For further thought
Make a list of anything that easily and glibly slips out of your mouth and write down, as fully as you are able, what it really means.

[1] *The Voice for Life Chorister's Companion* (Croydon: Royal School of Church Music, 2009), p. 90.

The Gospel of Mark (3)

2 Getting the message

Notes by **Orion Johnson**

Orion's Christian faith was nurtured at the Anglican church where she grew up in the suburbs of London. She now lives in Warwickshire, England, where she and her husband raised their two sons. Enjoying drama in her leisure time, she has performed Shakespearean plays in the church where the bard is buried and acted for murder mystery weekends. Orion's career has been in publishing and marketing. She now works in the publications department of IBRA and RE Today. Orion has used the NIVUK for these notes.

Sunday 9 June
Ways of God, ways of man

Read Mark 8:31–38

'What good is it for someone to gain the whole world, yet forfeit their soul?'

(verse 36)

Is losing your soul a terrifying thought? What Jesus says in many of this week's passages in Mark comes into conflict with human inclination. Today's reading challenges two common human characteristics: personal ambition and fear of death.

Peter's response to the prediction of Jesus' death is understandable. It is hard to conceive why Jesus had to die. But Christ has his eyes on the resurrection. In three days he will rise again – and that will bring humans and God together again. It will enable Peter and us to enter God's kingdom.

Sacrifice is not only required on Christ's part. We must also be prepared to suffer – to take up our cross, denying our own desires and ambitions, to follow him. Humanity cherishes wealth, power and privilege. We consider it admirable to have or to strive for those things. But they are not the things of God, and ultimately they are worthless.

Are our souls the only thing we truly own? Earthly life can be granted or ended by God, and property cannot be taken further than the grave. So when we betray God or our principles in the pursuit of worldly advantage, we put that one lasting possession at risk.

† Lord, guide me to cherish you and my soul above all else. Sustain and help me when that is difficult to do.

Son of Man, Son of God

Read Mark 9:1–13

'Let us put up three shelters – one for you, one for Moses and one for Elijah.'

(verse 5b)

Peter always feels the need to say something, whether it is helpful or not; maybe to cover the silence or to sound intelligent. Here it seems he was plucking something out of the air because he and the others were frightened.

But perhaps he is not so daft. Is he thinking of the shelters constructed for the Jewish festival of Sukkot, the Festival of Tabernacles? At Sukkot, many echoes from Jewish history are represented by those temporary cabins. The feast was instituted when the Israelites were at Mount Sinai during their exodus from Egypt, so maybe it made sense to Peter that – confronted by the sight of Moses and Elijah – he should construct 'shelters' for these important Old Testament figures.

The transfiguration of Christ – when his clothing becomes shining white, he meets with the long-dead Elijah and Moses, and the voice of God declares 'This is my Son' – takes place on a high mountain. This echoes the delivery of the ten commandments to Moses on Mount Sinai and numerous other important moments in the Bible when humans encounter the divine. The parallels are many. In Exodus 34:29, Moses' face was radiant – like Christ's clothing – when he returned from an encounter with God. And just as Moses met with God on Mount Sinai, so now he meets with the dazzling Son of God, witnessed by three disciples.

Perhaps we can forgive Peter for bumbling at the sight.

† Thank you for the signs you speak through, whether at an astonishing event like the one Peter, James and John experienced or in whispers that quietly enter our hearts. Help me to remain alert to your voice and to understand your revelations.

For further thought

Look up information about Sukkot. A possible starting point might be www.reonline.org.uk/festival_event/sukkot-feast-of-tabernacles-or-booths, or you could read about the Festival of Tabernacles in Leviticus 23:40–44.

Tuesday 11 June
Jesus commands a demon

Read Mark 9:14–29

'Everything is possible for one who believes.'

(verse 23b)

Today we move from the breathtaking, supernatural scene of the transfiguration to a very human one indeed. Jesus, Peter, James and John return to the other disciples, who are embroiled in a quarrel with the teachers of the law. An afflicted boy is still suffering, after the disciples have tried to help him and failed. Then they have ended up in an argument with the scribes with a crowd watching. Fortunately, the child's father speaks up and brings attention back to the boy in need of healing.

The description of the boy's condition suggests epilepsy or something similar. This condition has characteristics that inexperienced onlookers find strange and frightening even today. An affliction with such effects has at times been regarded with fear and suspicion, and explained in terms of demonic possession.

This brings to my mind how my mother, working as a carer, was taught to help sufferers during an epileptic seizure. She has witnessed other bystanders thrown into an unhelpful panic when a calm approach was most needed. I see in Mark's narrative a composed Jesus ministering to the patient while the disciples, scribes and others curious to watch have been distracted in argument and fuss. Like my mother he gives a confident, calm and reassuring response.

Faith and prayer are instrumental in the boy's recovery, with Jesus offering the encouraging words: 'Everything is possible for one who believes.' The father acknowledges his desire to have greater faith, which in itself suggests that he already has some belief – and he has clearly approached Jesus in hope. It is hard for all of us to have total belief, especially when we do not always receive the 'healing' we are hoping for.

† Lord Jesus, help me to overcome my unbelief.

For further thought

Have you ever felt frightened by or powerless about something that seemed beyond your control? Pray that you will be able to summon strength and reassurance from God next time you are in such a position.

June

The Gospel of Mark (3) – 2 Getting the message

Wednesday 12 June
The first must be last

Read Mark 9:33–37

'Anyone who wants to be first must be the very last, and the servant of all.'

(verse 35b)

Have you ever seen or read a debate about who the greatest sportsperson might be? Often a top footballer or boxer is compared with one from a different era, despite the fact they never competed against each other, to ponder which was really the greatest of all time. The debaters may need to fill airtime or pages in a magazine, but the only conclusion I have ever drawn is that I do not wish to waste my time on such utterly pointless arguments.

The disciples clearly realised their argument was unlikely to meet with Jesus' approval or interest, because as soon as he questioned what they had been talking about they clammed up in embarrassment. This was a wise move on their part, and useful for us, too, because rather than a debate that is going nowhere we instead receive two important ideas about the true nature of greatness and about our protection of the vulnerable.

We see that the first shall be last, the servant of all. The most effective leaders understand who is most important: not themselves, but those they lead. They grasp that their role and duty is to serve. How we would prosper if more leaders granted the privilege of power followed Christ's advice!

Jesus brings a small child into this group to demonstrate who should really come first. In welcoming the little child, the most powerless and vulnerable, the most often overlooked, we welcome Christ himself. How greatly the church, which has not always protected children as it should, would benefit from following Christ's instruction!

† Lord, where you have granted power and influence, I pray that you would also plant humility, and a desire to serve all and protect those with the least power.

For further thought

How does your church or community welcome the most vulnerable?

Thursday 13 June
Be at peace

Read Mark 9:38–51

'For whoever is not against us is for us.'

(verse 40)

The statement above is often considered to mean: 'Whoever is not with me is against me' (Matthew 12:30). But the inversion of 'with' and 'against' makes a big difference.

I have heard the quote 'Whoever is not for us is against us' used – or abused – by leaders of various political causes to stir up resentment against individuals or groups who are different from them. They imply that anyone who does not agree with their views or actions must be 'against' them personally. That removes the possibility of reasonable difference of opinion (to which we are all entitled) and instead suggests that such a person wishes them ill, encouraging fear and hostility. Those emotions can be exploited to divide people from one another. Not seeing eye to eye with someone on a particular matter does not mean we hate each other.

'Whoever is not against us is for us' is far more positive and optimistic. It allows for the fact that anyone who is not actively trying to do you down is on your side. This fits with the more generous attitude Jesus takes with the man described at the start of this passage: in essence, don't worry that he is not 'one of our gang' of disciples. If the man is achieving miraculous results and doing so in Jesus' name, then it is to Jesus' glory.

Jesus ends this passage with the instruction to 'be at peace with each other'. That might feel like a distant hope while disputes over territory, resources, ideology or religion seem increasingly dangerous; but it is an instruction from Christ that we must aspire to with urgency.

† Give peace in our time, Lord. And grant me saltiness, that I might be like flavouring that enhances or preserves, working for the good of my community.

For further thought

Consider the difference between saying that someone is against you and saying that they have a different view.

Marriage and remarriage

This is an uncompromising and challenging passage – especially in light of the old law, which made provision for divorce. The Pharisees may simply have been trying to trip Jesus up on the matter, but even the disciples question what Jesus says here.

Yet elsewhere we read time and again of Jesus' grace and understanding towards people who suffered under society's strict rules and traditional demands, including those who had not adhered to a path of lifelong monogamy. In John's Gospel, Jesus breaks taboos to speak with a Samaritan woman who has had a series of husbands and is now living with yet another man, to whom she is not married. He offers her the water of life, and she – unlike the rule-keeping Pharisees and teachers – is immediately receptive. Jesus also saves an adulterous woman from stoning, stating that he does not condemn her – but he gives her the instruction to 'go and sin no more'. His respect for the sanctity of marriage is tempered with compassion.

To an observing world, Christians tend to be judged not by piety or a super-pure lifestyle, which can seem cold and self-righteousness, but by our empathy and care towards others: our humanity. As Paul urges in 1 Corinthians, if we do not have love, our other virtues are as nothing.

Although we are sinners, we can hold tight to the wonderful reassurance that each of us remains as loved and important to God as his other children, regardless of our deeds or circumstances.

† Lord Jesus, teach me to understand your words and to follow your example. Like you, may I always act with compassion.

For further thought

Is it possible to uphold a particular code of behaviour without judging ourselves or others in a harmful way?

Saturday 15 June
All the little children

Read Mark 10:13–16

'Let the little children come to me, and do not hinder them, for the kingdom of God belongs to such as these.'

(verse 14b)

The disciples find the parents clamouring for a blessing for their children an irritating demand on their busy teacher. They are being practical and protective, but Christ sees the spiritual significance of the parents' requests. He again brings forward those so often overlooked (or those who annoy us when they are noisy in church). Here he reinforces Wednesday's passage: children are important.

Children show us how to approach the message and kingdom of God. My Sunday school teachers defined this as coming to God with unquestioning trust; but although children do have innocent trust, they certainly ask plenty of questions! And that is important. Through questions, we learn and explore. Children often go through a phase of asking 'Why?' about everything. It can be exhausting and may seem irrelevant, but in attempting to answer we are not only teaching them; we are also forced to reason things out for ourselves – or at least to see why something we take for granted seems so different or even inexplicable through another person's eyes.

At Communion during a family baptism service, a friend's child whispered: 'Why do only the grown-ups get food and drink?' That made me question why we treat children and adults differently in church. It also made me think of the wafer and wine as sustenance, 'food and drink'. Another friend was recently questioned by her son about prayer. He observed that we take to God the troubles and illnesses of ourselves or others, 'But why don't we ever ask how God is?' That bedtime, he started his prayer with, 'Dear God, how are you?'

Let's learn from our children's spirituality and keep asking questions!

† Father God, how are you? Thank you that you love and care for me as your child.

For further thought

What was your favourite Bible story as a child? Can you remember why? If you didn't know any Bible stories back then, ask a friend or your own children.

Readings in 1 Chronicles

Notes by **Paul Cavill and Tom Hartman**

Paul and Tom are friends who meet for fellowship and lunch as often as their timetables permit, which is quite infrequent and wasn't made any easier by the pandemic. Paul is an author and specialist on English place names and the faith of ancient peoples. Tom is a zoologist who has specialised in evolutionary genetics and firmly believes that dinosaurs are the key to teaching children about anything. Paul and Tom have used the NIVUK for these notes.

Sunday 16 June
Names, names, names

Read 1 Chronicles 1:1–27

Two sons were born to Eber: one was named Peleg, because in his time the earth was divided; his brother was named Joktan … Shem, Arphaxad, Shelah, Eber, Peleg, Reu, Serug, Nahor, Terah and Abram (that is, Abraham).

(verses 19, 24–27)

The books of Chronicles are short histories of the world and of the Jewish people from the creation to the fall of Jerusalem in the seventh century BC. Here we start with the names of the earliest people, from Adam onwards. The names of ancestors were a kind of identity card for early people, and Jesus' human genealogy is given at the beginning of Matthew's Gospel to remind us that he was a real man.

It's easy to forget names. We know very little about some of the people listed in this passage, but their names meant a great deal to them, and their lives shaped the history of their descendants. Peleg was remembered at a time of division because his name means 'division', and of course Abram's name ('exalted father') was changed when God miraculously renamed him Abraham ('father of many').

The world changed for Mary Magdalen when she heard the risen Jesus say one word at the empty tomb: her name, 'Mary' (John 20:16). God knows us by name, and he doesn't forget. He calls us by name, and each person has a role to play in his purposes for the world.

† Give thanks for those who introduced you to Jesus. Thank him that he knows and values you as an individual.

Monday 17 June
Last but not least

Read 1 Chronicles 2:1–17

Boaz [was] the father of Obed and Obed the father of Jesse. Jesse was the father of Eliab his firstborn; the second son was Abinadab, the third Shimea, the fourth Nethanel, the fifth Raddai, the sixth Ozem and the seventh David.

(verses 12–15)

It's hard to be last in a queue, or the youngest or least significant in a group. As a boy I played in a football league every week for a full season, but I was made a substitute for the cup final. It hurt.

Boaz was a kindly local landowner who took a returned refugee, Naomi, under his wing, and married her widowed daughter, Ruth. Ruth was a Moabite; a foreigner in desperate need, the lowest of the low. Boaz's grandson Jesse, David's father, evidently thought his seventh son wasn't really up to much when Samuel came to visit (1 Samuel 16). As a shepherd, David was not considered important enough to invite to the feast or present to the prophet.

But God honoured the faith of Ruth and the goodness of Boaz. And he chose Jesse's last son to be king of Israel. Boaz, Ruth and David could never have imagined how God would transform their smallness, their insignificance, into the greatness of royalty. Even less could they have imagined that the Saviour of the world would be born through Mary from their line.

Sometimes it is impossible to imagine how God will use us. But we can be sure that he values our faithfulness and trust, even when it seems that nobody else does. 'The Lord looks at the heart' (1 Samuel 16:7) and 'many who are last will be first' (Matthew 19:30). With God, *last* does not mean *least*.

† Thank God that he cares for you and for those who are not valued by society. Pray for those you know who are in need, or who might feel insignificant for whatever reason.

For further thought
Kindness and goodness are fruits of the Holy Spirit. They are never wasted, though they may sometimes be disregarded by others. Think of some areas that you need to persevere in.

Tuesday 18 June
Is this the right way to prosper?

> **Read 1 Chronicles 4:1–10**
>
> *Jabez was more honourable than his brothers … Jabez cried out to the God of Israel, 'Oh, that you would bless me and enlarge my territory! Let your hand be with me, and keep me from harm so that I will be free from pain.' And God granted his request.*
>
> (verses 9–10)

There are times when we read the Bible and suddenly know that the passage is directed at us personally, and that we should take note. The Holy Spirit inspires, challenges and corrects us. In passages like this it is tempting to read such an amazing story and claim it for ourselves, as if it were a universal constant that would bring each person the same benefits as the one written about in the scriptures.

Here we read about Jabez who, being more honourable than his brothers, asks God for a blessing of wealth, territory and safety from harm. The prayer is granted. Jabez, again, is honourable, but in the middle of his prayer we see a request that the Lord's hand should be with him. A hand that guides, a hand that protects, but also a hand that restrains and directs.

How nice it would be if this were a formula to follow, but Jabez is one name among many, and the scriptures point to many figures whose honour and submission to God did not end in an easy life, free from harm and pain. We only have to look at our Lord Jesus to see that God's purposes work out differently for different people.

† Come, Holy Spirit, and guide our prayers in righteousness and honesty, that we might reflect your power and light. Align our wills and desires to your holy way.

For further thought

Do you come before God expecting to be humble before your creator or to ask for wishes from a genie?

June

Readings in 1 Chronicles

Wednesday 19 June
A crisis of loyalty

Read 1 Chronicles 10:1–14

Saul said to his armour-bearer, 'Draw your sword and run me through, or these uncircumcised fellows will come and abuse me.' But his armour-bearer was terrified and would not do it; so Saul took his own sword and fell on it.

(verse 4)

This passage is the story of Saul's last battle against the Philistines. He knew that the battle was lost and he was going to die, and his fear that the Philistines would horribly abuse him seems to be borne out by their treatment of his body. He asked his armour-bearer to kill him, but the man could not, so he died by his own hand. The armour-bearer then killed himself in the same fashion, by falling on his sword.

The terrible details here perhaps obscure the honourable behaviour of these two men, but particularly that of the armour-bearer. His loyalty to the king makes it impossible for him to raise a weapon against Saul, but he is prepared to die for, and with, his king. It is an unresolvable dilemma. He can obey Saul and commit the ultimate treason, or refuse to obey and dishonour his vow to serve the king.

Dilemmas are part of the messiness of life. We are unlikely to face any as difficult as this, but it is almost certain that we will face situations where conflicting demands are made on us, when we won't know which way to turn. Some dilemmas have no right answer and, like this one, won't necessarily end well in human terms.

Jesus didn't want to die on the cross (Matthew 26:39), so he understands how difficult it can be. He respects our choices, he forgives our mistakes, he honours our loyalty and he promises to make all things new.

† Pray for yourself and/or anyone you know facing difficult choices.

For further thought

Where do your loyalties and priorities lie? Write them down in order of importance, then ask God for understanding of what he wants from you.

Thursday 20 June
Unfair and unreasonable?

Read 1 Chronicles 13:1–14

When they came to the threshing-floor of Kidon, Uzzah reached out his hand to steady the ark, because the oxen stumbled. The LORD's anger burned against Uzzah, and he struck him down because he had put his hand on the ark. So he died there before God.

(verses 9–10)

This shocking and upsetting piece of scripture shakes our very understanding of God. We might remember the letter to the Colossians, where Paul proclaims that Jesus is the image of the invisible God, and then look again at the story of Uzzah in horror. How can the two stories reflect the same God?

The tragedy and unfairness of Uzzah's death comes after a period when the ark of the covenant – and the presence of God it represented – was being taken for granted. For some time, King David had been accruing warriors and weapons, and he was head of a mighty army. The previous night there had been a massive celebration, and now everything had changed because one man, trying to steady the ark, had touched it and died. God had changed the picture.

The presence of the ark was no talisman to ensure victory, and there were rules for transporting it (as we see in Exodus 25 and Numbers 5). It should have been carried on the shoulders of Levites using particular poles and not on an ox cart. It should never have been considered mundane or familiar, but held in high regard and the rules governing its movements had to be observed. This was a lesson that David, observing this action, learned and never forgot.

† Lord, may we never take you for granted or see you as just another facet of our lives, but may we, in all humility, obey you.

For further thought

Jesus is the final revelation of God. Let us remind ourselves that he is the lens through which the glory and majesty of God can be witnessed.

The cost of celebrations in messy lives

Read 1 Chronicles 15:11–29

As the ark of the covenant of the LORD was entering the City of David, Michal daughter of Saul watched from a window. And when she saw King David dancing and celebrating, she despised him in her heart.

(verse 29)

David did not have an easy life. His relationship with Saul – the first king of the united kingdom of Israel – was complex and never easy. And neither was his relationship with Michal, Saul's daughter, who was given in marriage to David in exchange for the foreskins of 100 Philistines (David actually gave Saul 200).

Michal seems to have been a pawn in the tribal and national politics of the day, yet when Saul turned against David she protected him. When David was a refugee, on the run from her father, Saul gave her to another man as his wife. Then, when David became king, she returned to being his wife again (among many others).

Just prior to this passage we read about the celebration after bringing home the ark of the covenant. The party was in full swing, and David's power and might were evident. What a heady mix of emotions. It can't have been easy to celebrate the victories of the man who supplanted your father, but it was only at this point that Michal's attitude changed. David was caught up in celebration and his perceived lack of dignity offended her. How complex the relations of human beings can be.

Despite all the problems that ensued, and in all the messiness of their lives, God brought about his final purpose of reconciliation through the line of humans that eventually led to Jesus Christ. Nothing could deflect from that.

† In our complex and messy lives, Lord, reassure us that your holy purposes are at work and that the love you have for us can never be deflected.

For further thought

Some passages of scripture are there to reassure us that despite our complex relationships and difficult lives God can still speak to us and bring his purpose forward.

June

Readings in 1 Chronicles

Read 1 Chronicles 18:9–17

King David dedicated these articles to the LORD, as he had done with the silver and gold he had taken from all these nations … David reigned over all Israel, doing what was just and right for all his people.

(verses 11, 14)

There is reportedly a Chinese curse that says: 'May you live in interesting times.' In recent years we have had 'interesting times', with Covid-19 and various international crises. Sometimes in this kind of turmoil we just want to 'pass our time in rest and quietness', as the Anglican Book of Common Prayer puts it.

By this point in Chronicles, God has established David's kingdom and there is an intermission in the long tale of his wars, during which David plans to build God's temple. This desire is denied him, but God is at the centre of David's life and rule nevertheless. By dedicating the spoils and tributes he has gained to God, David is seeking to honour God and acknowledge his sovereignty in the affairs of the kingdom. David appoints officials and leaders to run the important business of the state, and surrounds himself with effective priests and administrators. Sadly, this state of affairs doesn't last long, and Israel is again plunged into war. (This story is told in more detail in 2 Samuel.)

The writer of Chronicles sees David's wish to honour God as the foundation of the kingdom's peace and security. It brings order and justice. This is still the case, and perhaps when we wish for peace we need above all to pray that God might be at the centre of our politics, our laws, our society, our institutions and our own individual lives. God is a God of order.

† Pray for anybody you know who is in a position of power. If you are on a committee, pray for God to be at the centre, no matter what kind of business it deals with.

For further thought

We often criticise our politicians and leaders. Do we pray for them as much as we should?

Changing Seasons: 1 Chronicles 19–29

Notes by **Dr Ruth Perrin**

Ruth has twenty-five years of experience in ministry and missions, and is associate staff at King's Church Durham. She has a PhD in theology and a passion for scripture, and she enjoys preaching and coaching people in their faith journeys. She has published two books based on her research into faith development and has two websites – one of research findings (www.discipleshipresearch.com) and one containing studies about little-known Bible characters (www.cloudofwitnesses.org. uk). Ruth enjoys gardening, cooking for friends and travelling to new countries. Ruth has used the NIVUK for these notes.

Sunday 23 June
Responding to hostility

> **Read 1 Chronicles 19:1–15**
>
> *'Be strong and let us fight bravely for our people and the cities of our God. The LORD will do what is good in his sight.'*
>
> (verse 13)

The Chronicles were written for the Israelites who were returning from Babylonian exile. In these insecure times, they affirmed the nation's foundations and God's faithfulness.

Chapter 19 describes how, after establishing a good relationship with the king of the Ammonites, David sends a message of sympathy to his son in the hope of continuing peaceful relations. However, Hanun humiliates the messengers, shaving their beards and exposing their genitals. It is an antagonistic act of defiance and disrespect. The chronicler reports David's compassion to the humiliated messengers, and the subsequent battle as the Ammonites and hired Arameans flee before Joab's army. David is vindicated and peace is re-established, but at a great cost to Hanun.

We should note that David didn't lash out and instigate battle, despite the provocation, and that Joab trusted God for the outcome, despite being outnumbered. This is evidence that even if our friends turn against us or our enemies plot our downfall, God will ultimately vindicate the faithful.

Jesus taught us to pray for our enemies and bless those who curse us. It is God's business to judge, not ours. Even when we feel humiliated or angry, it is good to remember the promises that 'in all things God works for the good of those who love him' (Romans 8:28).

† Oh Lord, help me to be gracious when I'm treated badly. I bring you my difficult relationships, asking for wisdom to know how you would have me respond.

Relying on human power: David's census

Read 1 Chronicles 21:1–13

Then David said to God, 'I have sinned greatly by doing this. Now, I beg you, take away the guilt of your servant. I have done a very foolish thing.'

(verse 8)

David was a mighty king in uniting Israel and defeating kingdoms. When an accuser incites him to prove himself, he sends Joab to count the fighting men and to show that he is strong enough to win any battle.

The census was an act of ego. David believed his nation was thriving because he was a great king rather than by God's grace. Others knew this was a sin. God's punishment was to strike the nation, to show where power really lay. Ultimately, David threw himself on God's mercy, but there were consequences for his arrogance. He might have been mighty, but he wasn't perfect. Once again, he was humbled for his sin.

Like David, it is tempting when we do well to believe it is the result of our own skill, and we often relegate God when we experience wealth or success. But just as there were consequences for David, so there are for us when we start to believe that we no longer need the Lord. As individuals, communities and nations, we see the impact when we turn away from God and believe in our own strength.

Jesus says 'Remain in me, as I also remain in you. No branch can bear fruit by itself; it must remain in the vine. Neither can you bear fruit unless you remain in me' (John 15:4). God's enemy always tempts us to go it alone. Chronicles shows us how serious the consequences of this can be, but also that God always offers forgiveness and a way to be restored if we repent and return to him.

† Lord, help me to stay close to you, and to remain grateful for blessings and obedient to direction. Forgive me when I go astray, and in your mercy restore me once again.

For further thought

David was tempted (and warned), but was still responsible for his sin. We often excuse our actions. How might you grow in humility in order to repent and receive forgiveness and freedom?

Tuesday 25 June
Preparing to build the temple

> **Read 1 Chronicles 22:1–10**
>
> *David said, 'My son Solomon is young and inexperienced, and the house to be built for the LORD should be of great magnificence and fame and splendour in the sight of all the nations. Therefore, I will make preparations for it.' So, David made extensive preparations before his death.*
>
> (verse 5)

As David ages, he wants to replace the tabernacle with a permanent temple for God. As a final act in establishing the nation, he wants to situate it where his sacrifice of repentance turns back God's wrath for his sin. However, God does not want his temple to be built by a warrior. He wants a house of peace, built by a man of peace ('Solomon' comes from 'shalom', meaning 'peace' or 'wholeness'). The task and glory will fall to his son, but David generously prepares the materials and workforce to enable Solomon to succeed. It is a multigenerational project.

We live in a time when generations often clash. Youngsters blame their elders for their own failings and the elders criticise the young. Here is a beautiful picture of generations working together. David knows it is more important for the temple to be built than it is for him to build it. Solomon is famed for the temple, but we see that it was David's dream, and that his encouragement and finances were poured into it. Sometimes we need to remember that it doesn't matter who completes the task or gets the glory, but just that the task is completed.

God desires every generation to know him and to be involved in his kingdom plans. Perhaps the challenge for us is to realise that it is not about us, as individuals, but about our partnership with God. How we can equip and support other generations to succeed in that?

† O Lord, show me your Spirit at work in other generations. Help me to become a generous encourager as they serve you.

For further thought

Who blessed you when you were a young Christian, and how? Who do you know that you might support through prayer, friendship or encouragement?

Changing Seasons: 1 Chronicles 19–29

Wednesday 26 June
Establishing worship

Read 1 Chronicles 25:1–8

Asaph, Jeduthun and Heman were under the supervision of the king. Along with their relatives – all of them trained and skilled in music for the LORD – they numbered 288.

(verses 6b–7)

King David was a musician who wrote many psalms. Here we see him prioritising worship in the new temple. Music was at the heart of the nation's expression of itself to God, and these men were agents of divine–human conversation, drawing close to God as they sang and brought prophesy (messages from God). This was ordered and carried out under supervision to make sure it did not become the chaotic frenzy of pagan worship.

In explaining this hundreds of years later, the chronicler hoped the returned exiles would realise that in rebuilding the temple and restarting worship they stood among a long line of faithful people who, for hundreds of years, had drawn close to God on that very spot. Their circumstances in Babylon had been hard, but God had not changed.

We, too, stand among a long line of those who have drawn close to God in worship. Hebrews 12:1 describes a 'great cloud of witnesses' – millions of believers from every continent and generation. When the temple curtain ripped at the time of Jesus' death, God's presence burst out from the Holy of Holies, and at Pentecost filled the disciples. This means that all those who are in Christ can worship in spirit and truth, and that God draws close to us wherever and whenever we do.

Perhaps, like the returning exiles, we had trouble in the last season, but let's be encouraged that we are the latest generation of worshippers, standing on the shoulders of the faithful. We are called to exhort the Lord and encourage each other in that. God is still faithful.

† O Lord, cause praise and gratitude to rise up in my soul as I consider all that you have done for me. Help me lead others to worship you in response.

For further thought

Why do you think some people are self-conscious in worship? Psalm 100:1 (NRSVA) encourages us to 'make a joyful noise to the LORD'. Even if you are not very musical, what might that look like for you?

Thursday 27 June
Commissioning Solomon to build

Read 1 Chronicles 28:8–20

'Acknowledge the God of your father, and serve him with wholehearted devotion and with a willing mind, for the LORD searches every heart and understands every desire and every thought. If you seek him, he will be found by you; but if you forsake him, he will reject you for ever. Consider now, for the LORD has chosen you to build a house as the sanctuary. Be strong and do the work.'

(verses 9–10)

David speaks here as he prepares to pass his throne to his tenth-born son, Solomon. First he affirms the choice of successor, which we know from Samuel's account had been contested. David explains that God has chosen Solomon, just as God chose him.

David was the youngest and least significant of his brothers, yet he was chosen by the Lord. Now he asserts the same thing about this son. Solomon is not the most impressive, the eldest or the wisest, but he is God's choice … so support him.

To Solomon he gives two instructions:

1   Stay faithful to God and he will be with you.
2   Do the work and do not be afraid. (Clearly the prospect of ruling and of building the temple were overwhelming, so David encourages him as Moses had done with Joshua.)

We are all faced with responsibilities that feel overwhelming at times. We can feel burdened and anxious when we look to the future or consider something God has asked of us. David's words are still an encouragement today. God does not always pick the obvious choice, but he understands us. He knows our hearts, our fears and hopes, our challenges and responsibilities. We may not carry the weight of Solomon, but David is right; acknowledging God and serving him with wholehearted devotion and a willing mind is still the best advice we can receive. The Lord is with us, by his Spirit. He will equip us with everything we need. Do not be afraid or discouraged, for God is with you.

† O Lord, help me to stay obedient to your will as I carry out my responsibilities. Give me the strength to serve you in all that I do.

For further thought

How do you react when people doubt you? How can you remain wise and humble; confident in God's power but also open to correction?

June

Changing Seasons: 1 Chronicles 19–29

Friday 28 June
A community effort

> **Read 1 Chronicles 29:1–9**
>
> *Then the leaders of families, the officers of the tribes of Israel, the commanders of thousands and commanders of hundreds, and the officials in charge of the king's work gave willingly.*
>
> (verse 6)

David had collected vast amounts of wealth and supplies for the building of the Lord's temple, and he also led by example in giving personal wealth towards its construction. The amount of gold, silver and precious jewels used was staggering. But David was also wise and knew that support from the community was needed. It would be an epic task that would take many years and much sacrifice. Rather than this being a 'project of kings', he invited the whole community to contribute – and they did, willingly and generously. David was humbled and delighted at their response and their commitment to the Lord's house.

The New Testament makes it clear that the building of God's church and kingdom are also a community affair. The early church was praised for its generosity when individuals sold and shared their possessions. Paul teaches in 1 Corinthians, Romans 12 and other places that *all* believers receive spiritual gifts to share in God's service and to build up his body. The temple might have been David's dream, but it was a place for all God's people to worship.

The vision for a church, ministry or Christian project may be given to a leader, but none of us can fulfil God's plans alone. We need each other. Good leaders set a generous example, as David did, but then invite others to participate. Rather than manipulate or demand allegiance and sacrifice, godly leaders share the vision, then celebrate when others see the Lord's hand in it and want to participate.

† O Lord, help me to be generous with my gifts, time and material possessions. Show me how to use them to build your kingdom and bring praise to your name.

For further thought

Which qualities does a trustworthy leader demonstrate? How can you discern whether a vision is from God or devised by humans?

Saturday 29 June
Solomon is anointed king

Read 1 Chronicles 29:21–25
The LORD highly exalted Solomon in the sight of all Israel and bestowed on him royal splendour such as no king over Israel ever had before.

(verse 25)

What an extraordinary celebration! Almost countless sacrifices are given to the LORD and enjoyed by the people. There is a breathtaking act of worship and the greatest feast witnessed in Israel's history. The people were celebrating several things: a new king – now undoubtedly David's successor – and the intention to build a permanent temple for the LORD. The event also signified peace. The wars were over; Israel was united and secure. And they were home, permanently, with their God. God's promise to Abraham was complete, and countless descendants had settled in his presence, in a land flowing with milk and honey. All those years of struggle in slavery, in the wilderness and in battle were done. Now it was time to flourish.

David's reign ends with glory and honour, which Solomon inherits through no effort of his own. This is a foreshadowing of gospel grace. Jesus – a descendant of David – defeated sin and death to give us an astonishing inheritance, royal status, honour and blessing through no effort of our own. So often we strive to gain God's favour, but grace means that all we to need do – like Solomon – is accept what has been offered. Salvation comes through faith, before we have achieved anything.

Our current circumstances may not look like a feast, but Luke 15 says that angels rejoice, Zephaniah 3:17 says that God sings over us and Paul promises that no one has seen or imagined what God has prepared for those who love him (1 Corinthians 2:9). This coronation is a mere shadow of the time when Jesus returns to claim his bride! Let's rejoice in our hope of that, and take Solomon's celebration as a taster of what is to come.

† O Lord, help us to fix our hearts on the hope of our salvation and the celebration that awaits us when we finally come home to you.

For further thought
Eventually, Solomon's power and wealth led him astray. What do you need to do to be faithful to Jesus today, and then each day onwards?

June

Changing Seasons: 1 Chronicles 19–29

Civil rights

1 Rights and responsibilities

Notes by **Revd Dr Peter Langerman**

Peter is a pastor at a Presbyterian Church in Durbanville, Cape Town. From 2018 to 2021, he was Moderator of the General Assembly of the Uniting Presbyterian Church in Southern Africa (UPCSA). He is married to Sally, and the couple have four daughters. Peter is passionate about the dynamic rule and reign of God. He believes God invites all to be part of his transformative mission through love, and that the most potent and powerful agent for the transformation of local communities is the local church, living in faithfulness to God. Peter has used the NIVUK for these notes.

Sunday 30 June
What choice will you make?

Read Deuteronomy 30:11–20

This day I call the heavens and the earth as witnesses against you that I have set before you life and death, blessings and curses. Now choose life, so that you and your children may live and that you may love the Lᴏʀᴅ your God, listen to his voice, and hold fast to him.

(verses 19–20a)

Every day we are called on to make choices: what to wear, what to eat, what route to take to work and so on. Some decisions are easily made, require little thought and carry minimal consequences. Others, however, demand that we take time, expend energy, consult widely and think carefully before making them. What to study, the person we wish to marry, which house to buy, when to have children and which career to follow are just some of these.

Moses addresses the people of Israel on the east side of the Jordan just as they are about to enter the promised land after forty years of wandering in the desert. This wandering was the result of a poor decision taken many years earlier to respond with fear rather than faith when they had their first opportunity to enter the promised land. Now they are gifted a second chance. Moses hopes they will make better choices the second time around.

The choice is deceptively simple: a life of love for, and obedience to, God that brings blessing – for them and the generations that follow – or death. Like them, we must often make the same choice … so let's choose wisely.

† Gracious God, give me the wisdom this week to make wise, life-affirming choices.

Choices and consequences

Read Ezekiel 33:1–7

*Since they heard the sound of the trumpet but did not heed the
warning, their blood will be on their own head. If they had heeded the
warning, they would have saved themselves.*

(verse 5)

Many of us remember the classic Meryl Streep movie *Sophie's
Choice*, based on the novel by William Styron. Sophie hides a dark
secret deep within her: on the night she arrived at Auschwitz, a
camp doctor made her choose which of her two children would
die immediately by gassing and which would continue to live in
the camp. Sophie chose to sacrifice her eight-year-old daughter,
Eva, in a decision that has left her in mourning and filled with a
guilt she cannot overcome. Unable to live with it, Sophie commits
suicide.

A multitude of choices are made in this passage. The Lord
chooses a person as a watchman. The enemy chooses to launch
an attack. The watchman chooses to sound the alarm, and when
to do so. The people who hear the warning must choose what to
do about it: whether to take evasive action or simply ignore the
warning and go about their business, hoping for the best.

Each choice has consequences, and while we are always free
to make choices, we have to accept the consequences that come
with them. If a friend or a colleague is involved in some form of
destructive behaviour, we have to choose whether to get involved
or not. Each option has consequences, and we must be prepared
to accept them.

† Loving God, give me the courage to make difficult choices and to accept the
consequences of those choices.

For further thought
Think carefully about a choice you need to make and what the
consequences of that choice might be.

Tuesday 2 July
The good news

Read Romans 10:5–13

For there is no difference between Jew and Gentile – the same Lord is Lord of all and richly blesses all who call on him, for, 'Everyone who calls on the name of the Lord will be saved.'

(verses 12–13)

What does it mean to be 'saved'? Many people who self-identify as having no faith or Christian affiliation would baulk at the idea of a need to be saved. In our politically correct society, few people talk of sin any more. Rather, we label things as 'mistakes', 'errors' or 'misunderstandings'.

Identifying people as sinners seems very judgemental and extreme. Yet for those of us who are Christ followers, we know that the journey of following Christ is a daily acknowledgement that, although we should know better, we let ourselves down, let others down and disappoint the God we purport to love and serve. This is the nature of sin: a failure to love God and others as we have been loved and as we love ourselves. Perhaps sin is less than missing the mark or failing to live up to some external moral code, and better understood as a failure to love.

Perhaps this is a better way to think about sin and salvation. Our natural selfishness leads us to look out for number one, but Christ challenges us to live for others, to sacrifice and to be prepared to give up what we want for the good of others without expecting anything in return. This doesn't come naturally to any of us. Therefore, we must call on the Lord to help us. When we ask for help, we will receive the strength we need.

† Holy Spirit, fill me with your strength and give me the ability to love others as I have been loved.

For further thought

Reflect on occasions in the recent past when you have failed to love. Reflect on why that happened.

Wednesday 3 July
Justice or vengeance?

> **Read Numbers 35:9–15**
>
> Then the LORD said to Moses: 'Speak to the Israelites and say to them:
> "When you cross the Jordan into Canaan, select some towns to be your
> cities of refuge, to which a person who has killed someone accidentally
> may flee."'
>
> (verses 9–11)

Among some of the most disturbing and distressing accounts
of the Rwandan genocide – when the majority Hutus killed the
minority Tutsis during a killing spree in 1994 – are those of people
being murdered in the churches where they sought refuge.
Sometimes the very priests and pastors whose help they sought
turned on them and were complicit in the killings. How shocking
it is that a place of refuge can become a killing field; when people
who flee to a place they trust to keep them safe either turns on
them or betrays them into the hands of their attackers.

The tradition of the cities of refuge in the Hebrew Bible was an
acknowledgement that the desire for justice should not devolve
into a thirst for vengeance. In entering the promised land,
provision is made for six cities of refuge to which a person who
accidentally kills another might flee for refuge, presumably as the
legal process unfolds. This is a remarkably progressive innovation
in this ancient culture.

For us, living in a human rights-dominated world, the idea that
people should be protected and granted refuge pending the
outcome of their case is nothing unusual, but for the world of the
Hebrew Bible this is quite startling. The cities of refuge remind us
that every human being is created in the image of God and, as
such, deserves respect and blessing.

† God of justice, help me not to seek revenge in my quest for justice.

For further thought

Think about how someone may have wronged you, and how you
can desire justice without wanting to take vengeance.

Thursday 4 July
What do I have to give to God?

Read Micah 6:1–16

*With what shall I come before the L*ORD *and bow down before the exalted God? Shall I come before him with burnt offerings, with calves a year old? Will the L*ORD *be pleased with thousands of rams, with ten thousand rivers of olive oil? Shall I offer my firstborn for my transgression, the fruit of my body for the sin of my soul?*

(verses 6–7)

In our contemporary society we have people making all sorts of bargains with God. A statement we hear all too often is that: 'There are no atheists on a cancer ward.' For those of us in ministry, it is heartbreaking to sit with a mother whose child is close to death, or with a husband watching his wife slip away, and to hear the pleading in their voice as they try to bargain with God for the life of their loved one. On the other hand, there are moments of good fortune – an engagement, a marriage or the birth of a child – when people of faith want to offer God some token of their gratitude.

If asked, the verse most Christians would associate with the book of Micah is Micah 6:8, but what is the context of that well-known and often-quoted verse? Micah sits with a problem that is common to people of faith: what can we offer God that he needs, requires or wants from us? What can we give God to demonstrate our devotion, love and loyalty to God?

In the world of the Hebrew Bible, the answer consisted of offerings of one sort or another. However, in contrast to that, the prophet answers in this famous verse that what is required to show our loyalty to, love for and obedience to God is not some elaborate bargain or multiple burnt offerings, but a commitment to justice, mercy and humility.

† Gracious God, enable to me to pursue justice, to love mercy and to walk in humility in my daily walk.

For further thought
We are encouraged by James to make our 'Yes' a yes and our 'No' a no. Reflect on the times when you have made commitments to God. Did you follow through or were they quickly forgotten?

Friday 5 July
Facing our failings

Read 2 Samuel 12:1–15

Then Nathan said to David, 'You are the man!'

(verse 7a)

During the days of President Richard Nixon, the break-in at the Democratic Party headquarters in the Watergate building made little sense. Nixon was way ahead in the polls and looked certain to win a second term in office. Why, then, would he knowingly support a violation of his political opponents that carried such a terrible risk, both to him personally and to his chances of re-election? It is probably fair to say that the cover-up brought down the Nixon White House and led to his resignation.

David's sin with Bathsheba is a well-known story, but, as with the Watergate crisis, the cover-up was arguably worse than the original transgression. David commits adultery with Bathsheba, causing her to become pregnant. Then he lures Bathsheba's husband, Uriah, back from the front lines in an attempt to get him to sleep with his wife, but Uriah is more honourable than David, instead sleeping at the king's door with the other servants. Eventually, David commands his general, Joab, to ensure that Uriah is killed in battle.

With Uriah dead, David takes Bathsheba as his wife and believes he has got away with his subterfuge. However, God tells Nathan the prophet what has happened. Rather than confront David directly, Nathan tells David a parable about a wealthy man who steals a poor man's prized possession. David is outraged and demands that the rich man face judgement, only for Nathan to identify David as the guilty one.

All in all, the incident shows the extent to which God observes the actions of human beings and takes the side of justice when the poor and innocent are exploited by the rich and powerful.

† Holy God, please forgive me for my unloving acts and for the times I have used excuses to avoid taking responsibility.

For further thought

How does it feel to be caught out, to have your sins and faults exposed, possibly even publicly? How did you respond?

Saturday 6 July
Scandalous grace

Read John 8:1–11

Jesus straightened up and asked her, 'Woman, where are they? Has no one condemned you?' 'No one, sir,' she said. 'Then neither do I condemn you,' Jesus declared. 'Go now and leave your life of sin.'

(verses 10–11)

In most contemporary versions of the Bible, this incident is printed in italics, or with a textual note to say that the incident is not recorded in most of the original manuscripts. That could be because it was a later addition to the Gospel, but it may also be because Jesus' actions were considered so controversial and provocative that it was not spoken about publicly until it was safer for the Christian faith to do so.

The whole incident is fraught with tension right up to the end. The woman has been caught in the very act of adultery, which presupposes that the people who brought her to Jesus had been watching her or had even set a trap for her.

Whichever way, the woman did not matter to them; she was only a means by which to trip Jesus up. If he applied the law of Moses and agreed to her stoning he was heartless and cruel, no better than the Pharisees. But if he refused to apply the law he was a blasphemer and could be brought up on charges himself. What was he to do?

Jesus reminds the accusers that only the sinless can claim the moral high ground and sit in judgement against the sinful. In that context, Jesus, the sinless one, is the only one qualified to judge, but he refuses to do so. The accusers, recognising their own sinfulness, are shamed into silence, leaving Jesus and the woman alone. Jesus refuses to condemn, extends grace and gives her the opportunity to start afresh.

† Loving God, thank you that, no matter how often I mess up, you give me the opportunity to start over.

For further thought

Who do you identify with in this passage? The woman, the accusers or a bystander watching it all unfold? How does it make you feel?

Civil rights

2 Justice

Notes by **Deseta Davis**

Deseta is Assistant Pastor of a Pentecostal church in Birmingham, UK. Her main vocation is as a prison chaplain, helping to bring hope to those who are incarcerated. Having obtained an MA in Theological Studies, she previously worked as a tutor in Black Theology, bringing the study of theology to a range of people who had not considered such study. Deseta is married to Charles, and they have two grown-up children and a granddaughter. Deseta has used the NIVUK for these notes.

Sunday 7 July
Prison reform

Read 2 Chronicles 16:7–10

Asa was angry with the seer because of this; he was so enraged that he put [Hanani] in prison. At the same time Asa brutally oppressed some of the people.

(verse 10)

This week we continue the civil rights and social justice theme. In today's text we see the prophet Hanani, who spoke truth to power and suffered for it. In those days the king had sovereign power, and he put Hanani in prison even though Hanani had committed no crime.

This fits well with our first theme of prison reform. In the nineteenth century, people were sent to prison for the pettiest crimes or minor offences. They were left in dark, dirty and dangerous places. Males and females were imprisoned together, with children sleeping on cold floors without any bedding. Washing and cooking also occurred in the same place. All this without sentencing!

On visiting Newgate Prison, Elizabeth Fry was so moved at the terrible conditions that she founded the Association for the Improvement of Female Prisoners. She attended to the needs of the prisoners and taught them skills. She also ensured that males and females were separated. Today in the UK, through the work of Elizabeth Fry, people cannot be left to languish in prison without access to trial. By law they have to be treated with dignity, no matter their crime. I'm sure Hanani would have welcomed this!

Reflect on your thoughts about prisoners today. How would they fit with Jesus' philosophy?

† Pray for the rehabilitation of prisoners. Ask God to help those who work with prisoners to treat them with care and respect.

The abolition of slavery

Read Philemon 1:8–17

Perhaps the reason he was separated from you for a little while was that you might have him back for ever – no longer as a slave, but better than a slave, as a dear brother. He is very dear... both as a fellow man and as a brother in the Lord. So if you consider me a partner, welcome him as you would welcome me.

(verses 15–17)

There are parts of the Bible that are very difficult to read; especially the parts that include slavery. Today's text does not make these deliberations any easier, as Paul sends Onesimus – a runaway slave – back to his owner. However, Paul encourages Philemon to receive him as a brother rather than as a slave.

Paul spoke up for the freedom of Onesimus, just as some politicians in the eighteenth and nineteenth centuries advocated for the freedom of enslaved Africans who had been brought to the UK, the Americas and the Caribbean on transatlantic trade ships. Although it is well documented that William Wilberforce led the campaign for an end to slavery, the Slave Trade Act did little for the thousands of people still enslaved across the British Empire. Furthermore, little was written about the resistance of the enslaved people, which played a significant part in their emancipation. Around 60,000 enslaved people rose up across 200 plantations. Many of the enslaved Africans were subsequently executed, which shook the British Empire and eventually led to abolition.

One prime teaching from the Old Testament was that, during the fiftieth year of Jubilee, slave owners were to free their slaves. This freedom was the Bible's abolition policy; any debt was written off. However, when the enslaved Africans were freed, Britain did not 'write off' the debt. In fact, it paid thousands of pounds to slave owners, yet the enslaved Africans received nothing but poverty.

† Merciful God, help us to learn from the history of slavery so that it might be eradicated in all its forms.

For further thought

Biblical law on slavery involved the poorest people working off their debt. Consider how a law designed to provide for the poorest in that society was corrupted into an abhorrent type of slavery?

Tuesday 9 July
Go and do likewise

Read Luke 10:30–37

'Which of these three do you think was a neighbour to the man who fell into the hands of robbers?' The expert in the law replied, 'The one who had mercy on him.' Jesus told him, 'Go and do likewise.'

(verses 36–37)

I have watched the film *Cry Freedom* many times. It depicts the life of a Black man, Steve Biko, who suffered greatly under South African apartheid, and the life of the journalist Donald Woods, who eventually left the country and campaigned for the freedom of Black people in South Africa.

The hatred Black people suffered can take us back to the Jewish–Samaritan divide. The hatred between these two nations was very deep, mainly due to the intermarriage between Samaritans and foreigners, and the adoption of the foreigners' 'idolatrous' religions. The Jews despised the Samaritans to the extent that they had more respect for 'upper class' Gentiles. They had sayings such as: 'He who eats bread from a Samaritan is like one who eats the flesh of swine.' This is similar to the many sayings regarding Black people throughout history.

In today's story, Jesus tells of a Samaritan showing kindness to a Jew and going way beyond the necessary. Many white people were killed for fighting against apartheid. They stood for what was right, knowing how dangerous it was. Steve Biko was eventually killed, but his story lives on. Nelson Mandela was imprisoned for thirty-seven years and classed as a terrorist, yet he bore no grudges; only fighting for freedom until apartheid was dead and buried in a new South Africa.

In his many deeds and actions, Jesus showed us how to love the Samaritans and Nelson Mandela showed us how to love our enemies. This may be something for us to take note of today. As Jesus said, go and do likewise!

† Pray for divisions across the world, racial or otherwise. Ask God to change hearts and mindsets.

For further thought

If you have not already done so, read Nelson Mandela's autobiography, *Long Walk to Freedom* (Abacus, 1995) and learn more about South Africa during apartheid.

Wednesday 10 July
The rights of women

Read Galatians 3:23–29

There is neither Jew nor Gentile, neither slave nor free, nor is there male and female, for you are all one in Christ Jesus.

(verse 28)

In biblical days, women were seen as property in a similar way to cattle. They belonged to a father, a son or a husband. Jewish rabbis did not have female disciples. Women were not allowed to be witnesses in court, as they were considered irrational and untrustworthy. Yet when Jesus came, he ministered to women – to the disdain of many. Indeed, a woman was the first to meet the risen Jesus, and was commanded to go and tell the men. Then in his letter to the Galatians, Paul includes women as being one in Christ, equal and important to the Christian mission.

However, women in the twentieth century still had very little legal protection, and few rights to education and work. They were not allowed to have a bank account or to vote. They were expected to marry a man, have children and keep home!

The suffrage movement fought for the rights and freedoms of women, starting with the right to vote. The suffragists believed in peaceful protests, whereas the suffragettes' mantra was 'deeds, not words'. They chained themselves to railings, burning homes and churches, and ended up in prison and on hunger strike, some dying in the process. Eventually, women gained the right to vote, which also led to further rights being granted.

Many women still do not have freedom or rights today. They have no say in their lives or in the way they are treated. Can we really say in all honesty that there is neither male nor female when many women are still fighting for their basic rights?

† Pray for the women in countries that have no human rights who are being killed for protesting against their oppressors.

For further thought

In 1 Timothy, Paul speaks against women having authority over men and about them remaining silent in church. How do we reconcile this with the verse above?

Civil rights – 2 Justice

July

192

Thursday 11 July
A voice for the voiceless

> **Read 2 Samuel 13:1–22**
>
> *When King David heard all this, he was furious. And Absalom never said a word to Amnon, either good or bad; he hated Amnon because he had disgraced his sister Tamar.*
>
> (verse 21)

I have always read this story with dismay. Tamar, the dutiful sister abused by her brother, then dismissed and left to suffer. A lonely, broken, 'tainted' woman, never again to enjoy life.

As much as I am angry at Amnon for what he did, I also feel a deep anger for King David. David, being king and sovereign, was furious when he heard what had happened to Tamar. But my question is: what did David do with his fury? Nowhere does it say that he did anything once he heard the news. He did not call Amnon and ask him to explain himself. He did not call Tamar and try to work it out with her or give her somewhere to live. Being the king, he left her in her brother's house, a desolate woman. And yet she was *his* daughter. I feel Tamar was not only abused by Amnon, but also by King David's inaction. By contrast, when his sons were killed, David tore his robes and mourned for many days – even for Amnon.

Today, just like then, many people are groomed and abused (sometimes for many years) by family members or someone they know. Sometimes the people who should speak out do not believe them or do not take it seriously. It offends the very heart of God when a person who should be a protector does not act on behalf of the vulnerable or become the voice for the voiceless.

† Loving God, I pray for those who are suffering abuse today and cannot find a way out. Please help them to find someone who can, and will, help them.

For further thought

What are your thoughts about King David's actions/inactions?

Friday 12 July
Human trafficking

Read Genesis 37:17b–28

*'Come, let's sell him to the Ishmaelites and not lay our hands on him;
after all, he is our brother, our own flesh and blood.' His brothers
agreed … and sold him for twenty shekels of silver to the Ishmaelites,
who took him to Egypt.*

(verses 27–28)

In 2022, Olympian Mo Farah told his story of being trafficked into
the UK at the age of nine, using a false passport. He became a
domestic slave to the traffickers' family and was not properly cared
for. After years of involuntary servitude (the most prevalent form
of modern-day trafficking) he was eventually rescued with the help
of a good teacher and went on to win four Olympic gold medals.

Yet Mo Farah is not alone. According to the Salvation Army,
15,000 trafficked people have been rescued in the UK alone in a
ten-year period.[1] Although it is very difficult to provide an accurate
estimate, it is believed that some 27 million people in the world
have been subjected to trafficking.

Many people pay traffickers to take them to other countries with
the promise of jobs, whereas others are trafficked by family (often
unwittingly) in the hope of a better life.

In today's text we see Joseph sold into Egypt by his brothers, who
did not care what fate awaited him. Joseph served his masters for
many years in involuntary servitude, eventually ending up in prison
for a crime he did not commit. Many people who are trafficked
also end up in prison, sometimes through no fault of their own.

However, the story of Joseph (and others) shows that being
trafficked does not have to dictate where a person's life ends. Just
as Joseph became prime minister, others can shake off the shackles
of trafficking and flourish. However, this takes time and often
requires help from a discerning society.

† Compassionate God, there are many people experiencing human trafficking today.
Please help them to find a way out, and help us to be discerning as friends and
neighbours.

For further thought

Check out the Salvation Army's human trafficking project. Can you
help in any way?

[1] 'Supporting Survivors of Modern Slavery: Report on The Salvation Army's Modern
Slavery Victim Care Contract July 2020 to June 2021': https://www.salvationarmy.
org.uk/sites/default/files/resources/2021-10/684%20SA%20Modern%20Slavery%20
Report%202021%20FINAL%20NEW%20%281%29.pdf (accessed 28 April 2023).

Saturday 13 July
Leaders with integrity

Read Exodus 18:13–23

But select capable men from all the people – men who fear God, trustworthy men who hate dishonest gain – and appoint them as officials over thousands, hundreds, fifties and tens.

(verse 21)

It can be difficult to trust governments and leaders today. Too often it feels as if leaders are self-serving and not working for the people they lead. This can trickle down to church leaders, some of whom find themselves on the wrong side of the law due to false accounting or misuse of power.

Throughout the Bible, God speaks against corrupt leaders and encourages people to select leaders with integrity. A definition I really like for integrity is 'what you do when no one else is looking'. This means being true to yourself as well as others. When church leaders fail to use integrity, it not only denigrates themselves; it defames who God is.

In today's text, Moses' father-in-law, Jethro, encourages Moses to choose leaders with integrity, who are accountable. Today, some leaders start churches from scratch without any accountability. Other churches with so-called accountability use and abuse their power. Both end up answering to themselves. It is sad to see more and more leaders falling from the faith due to a lack of integrity and accountability. Some started well but fell by the way.

God calls us to choose leaders with integrity, whether secular or sacred; leaders who fear God and are not self-serving; who are servant leaders. We also need to continually pray for our leaders, knowing they are human beings and are tempted as much as anyone else, and that sadly they sometimes succumb and fall – also like everyone else!

† Pray for your leaders today. Ask God to help them lead with integrity and accountability.

For further thought

Many of the prophets prophesied against corrupt leadership. Can you find and reflect on five texts that encourage leadership with integrity?

Civil rights – 2 Justice

July

Arts in the Bible (2)

Dance

Notes by **Audrey Jose**

Audrey and her husband serve with Radstock Ministries and divide their time between Canada and Albania, where they mentor Albanian missionaries serving across the Balkans. An author and Bible teacher, Audrey speaks internationally and is passionate about people having a transforming relationship with Jesus. Her book, *Guard Your Heart* (WhiteFire, 2010) challenges believers to explore that kind of transforming relationship with Jesus. Audrey has used the NIVUK for these notes.

Sunday 14 July
Victory at the Red Sea

Read Exodus 15

Then Miriam the prophet, Aaron's sister, took a tambourine in her hand, and all the women followed her, with tambourines and dancing. Miriam sang to them: 'Sing to the Lᴏʀᴅ, for he is highly exalted. Both horse and driver he has hurled into the sea.'

(verses 20–21)

Throughout the Old Testament, worship and praise to God is often expressed through dance. Here, the Israelites had just seen God work on their behalf, leading the entire nation through the sea on dry ground as he rescued them from the hands of the Egyptians. In response to God's overwhelming victory, and in celebration of their newfound freedom from slavery, the people sang and danced.

Miriam led them in a song that tells of a God who is both incomprehensibly powerful and intensely personal. As the Israelites sang, their emotions engaged. They were filled with an irrepressible joy that could only be expressed with their whole body – so they danced! I have great cause for celebration in my heart as I praise God for his salvation and redeeming power in my life, without which I could easily have been jailed or even dead. While I seldom dance, my heart sings of the mercies of the Lord!

The Israelites were to head into the desert the next day – into an unknown future. But still they danced. They danced because they had just witnessed victory over evil. They danced because it expressed the joy that was in their heart.

† Lord, as we sing to you because you are highly exalted, move our spirits to dance at one with your Spirit, in praise and thanksgiving.

Monday 15 July
David danced before the ark

Read 2 Samuel 6:1–15

Wearing a linen ephod, David was dancing before the LORD with all his might, while he and all Israel were bringing up the ark of the LORD with shouts and the sound of trumpets.

(verses 14–15)

To understand David's exuberance, it's important to recognise the significance of the ark of the Lord. Constructed by Moses, according to God's instructions, the ark was a physical representation of the presence of God among his people. Inside the ark was a bowl of manna, the nourishment God had provided in the desert; Aaron's staff, which had budded overnight; and the two tablets on which God had written the ten commandments. These were tangible reminders of God's power, goodness and mercy, and of his involvement in the people's lives.

Having been neglected and forgotten for 300 years, and even captured by the Philistines for seven months, and hidden in the house of Abinadab for at least a further twenty years, it was time to bring the ark home to Jerusalem! David was about to fulfil a long-held desire for Israel to have a central place of worship, where God's presence and glory could dwell among his people. No wonder he was excited.

As the ark was carried up the long, steep, dusty road into the city, David danced before the Lord. He danced in celebration. With people shouting and trumpets blaring, he danced and rejoiced with all his heart, soul, mind and strength. He didn't care what anyone thought. The dance was between him and his God. His whole body responded with an intense love and pure joy because God was coming home. Emmanuel – God with us!

How wonderful it would be to feel the freedom to worship like this, without hesitation or embarrassment; with no other thought than to honour the One who is worthy of everything we have to give.

† Lord, may we also experience the joy that comes from knowing Emmanuel, God with us, and be able to dance as David danced.

For further thought

Read Psalm 145 or Psalm 62. Imagine David dancing before the God he's writing to and about. What can you dance about?

Arts in the Bible (2) – Dance

July

197

Tuesday 16 July
Mourning into dancing

Read Psalm 30:1–12

You turned my wailing into dancing; you removed my sackcloth and clothed me with joy, that my heart may sing your praises and not be silent. LORD my God, I will praise you for ever.

(verses 11–12)

In this psalm David focuses on God's deliverance, which he had experienced first-hand. As he reflected on the impact God's presence had made in his life – moulding, shaping and transforming every decision, choice, action and attitude – David danced with thanksgiving. I often look back over my life and feel regret, even despair. But as David looked at his life – despite having lived many regret-inducing and despairing years – he praised God.

A friend of mine who was battling cancer wrote: 'If I don't live in the moment with God, I miss the hope and security he gives. It means I would have to face the huge hurdles alone. I cannot imagine doing this. So I seek out God. I long after him. And he is faithful and ever-present.'

Knowing who God is, and what he says, is the antidote to despair and hopelessness. In the context of fear or in the panic of asking 'Is God here with me?' or 'Will God provide for me?', his answer, as Joshua 1:8–9 suggests, is: 'Read about me! Get to know me. Know what I've done, meditate on my word, memorise it!' We need to learn God's word and keep learning it. Our faith will grow to the degree that we remember God's words and acts.

Knowing God is present is always a cause for celebration. David actively looked for God's presence everywhere, and could write with conviction: 'You turned my wailing into dancing; you removed my sackcloth and clothed me with joy, that my heart may sing your praises and not be silent.' Don't miss God at work in your life!

† Lord God, thank you that you are the same yesterday, today and forever. May my heart sing your praises and not be silent.

For further thought

Ask God to show how he removed your sackcloth and clothed you with joy, turning your wailing into dancing.

Praise him in the dance

Read Psalm 150

Praise him with tambourine and dancing, praise him with the strings and pipe, praise him with the clash of cymbals, praise him with resounding cymbals. Let everything that has breath praise the LORD. Praise the LORD.

(verses 4–6)

Have you ever watched people as they listen to a band? Virtually no one can sit still, even if they just tap their feet. Our bodies were designed for movement, just as our hearts were designed for worship and our voices for praise. It was movement by God's Spirit that brought creation into life. It is movement that brings praise to life.

As the writer of this psalm passionately calls people to praise and worship, you can feel his enthusiasm rising. Get out those trumpets! Grab those lutes and harps. Clash those cymbals as loudly as you can! Praise him with tambourines. And dance with joy! How can you sit still when singing of the mercies of the Lord – when you give voice to his victories and mighty works?

Satan wants to rob *us* of the joy of praising him and rob *God* of the praises due to him. During worship time at a conference, I sang with enthusiasm. After the song, a woman in front of me turned around and said, 'I just wanted to see who has the loud voice.' I was mortified. What power we give to the opinions of others. (I confess, I have restrained my singing, which saddens me. I'm sure it saddens God as well.)

We should never let anyone keep us from praising the Lord with everything that is in us. On earth, in the heavens, in the sanctuary or in the streets, the psalmist's final words are: 'Let everything that has breath praise the LORD.' Let's join the chorus!

† Lord, I confess to putting what others think above what you deserve: all of me, all of my praise, with everything that's in me.

For further thought

What would your own praise psalm look like? What does God's greatness look like to you?

Arts in the Bible (2) – Dance

July

Time to mourn, time to dance

Read Ecclesiastes 3:1–4

There is a time for everything … a time to weep and a time to laugh, a time to mourn and a time to dance.

(verses 1a, 4)

Here we are presented with the gift of time. In a poetic series of comparisons, the writer of Ecclesiastes shows us a serious side of life along with the lighter side. Whether we have little or plenty, whether we are ill or healthy, we have God's gift of time. Time to grieve. Time to heal. Time to grow. Time for God to work in our hearts, lives and circumstances. We're even allotted a time to dance!

We have an instinctive desire to celebrate, to sing and dance, in celebration of birthdays, marriage and other happy occasions. Who hasn't done a little happy dance when something good happens? My calendar has a celebration marked for every day of the year. Today, somewhere, someone is celebrating National Cat Day. We also celebrate meeting friends or family we haven't seen in many months, or spring blooms after a long winter. Celebration is sometimes loud and sometimes soft and quiet.

There is a time for every season. Some seasons may last longer than others. A Canadian winter, for example, seems like it will never end. The important thing to remember is that there is a purpose for every season, for every time element. A freezing cold winter is good, because in the north plants and trees need the shorter days and cold temperatures to store energy for new growth.

As the seasons pass our circumstances change, but what does *not* change is God's love for you. He has a wonderful plan for your life – a plan to redeem what was lost; a plan that brings hope for your future.

† Father, thank you for your gift of time, and for the healing and growth it brings me.

For further thought

How can you see God in the time or season you are in right now? What would you like to tell him?

Friday 19 July
Hope for the Future

Read Jeremiah 31:1–13

The LORD appeared to us in the past, saying: 'I have loved you with an everlasting love; I have drawn you with unfailing kindness. I will build you up again, and you, Virgin Israel, will be rebuilt. Again you will take up your tambourines and go out to dance with the joyful.'

(verses 3–4)

In this passage we hear an echo of Exodus 15, when Miriam grabbed her tambourine and led the nation in a circle dance. I experienced many circle dances while living in Albania. What stands out to me is the inclusiveness of it. Little ones are swept up, the elderly are gathered in – no one is left out.

I once missed the wedding of an Albanian woman I was close to. My husband, who was able to attend, picked me up at the airport at 1:30 a.m. and we drove straight to the venue. The wedding was over and the musicians had packed up. As I walked in (at about 2:30 a.m.), the man carrying out the last piece of equipment paused and asked, 'Audrey, shall we set everything up again so you can dance?' The wedding guests had danced for hours, it was late, everyone was going home, yet they were willing to do it a bit longer so no one would be left out of 'dancing with the joyful'.

Jeremiah paints for Israel a picture God had given him: one of hope rooted in the truth of God's love for them. They were steeped in, immersed in, permeated by God's love: 'I have loved you with an everlasting love; I have drawn you with unfailing kindness.' He is more than willing to show his people grace and kindness, even though they consistently turn away from him. This is cause for rejoicing! Everyone is included – it's never too late for you to join the circle and rejoice in the dance.

† Thank you, Lord, for including me in your dance with the joyful.

For further thought

What kindness of God have you experienced and celebrated this week?

Arts in the Bible (2) – Dance

July

201

We played but no one danced

Read Luke 7:29–35

Jesus went on to say, 'To what, then, can I compare the people of this generation? What are they like? They are like children sitting in the market-place and calling out to each other: "We played the pipe for you, and you did not dance; we sang a dirge, and you did not cry."'

(verses 31–32)

Luke 7 is a busy chapter. Jesus healed a Roman soldier's servant from a terminal illness, raised a widow's son from the dead as the boy was being carried out to be buried, confirmed to John the Baptist that he is indeed the Messiah and was anointed with perfume by a woman who publicly acknowledged his authority to forgive sins.

Jesus was playing the song of the Messiah, yet so many people failed to respond. The Pharisees and other experts in the law of Moses refused to respond. They refused to dance, even though they knew the scriptures. Speaking directly to the Pharisees, Jesus lamented: 'We played … and you did not dance.'

We face the same question the Pharisees did: 'What am I going to do with Jesus?' My brother-in-law Tim asked me this question when I was at the lowest point in my life. My response was, 'I don't want to hear about God. I'm done with all that.' Tim's response was immediate and gentle: 'Audrey, I'm not talking about *God*. I'm asking what you are going to do with *Jesus*?' Jesus the Messiah (which means 'Saviour' or 'Deliverer') was playing a song to me. He was calling me into a saving relationship with him, into peace with God, into a life redeemed.

This chapter in Luke is Jesus' invitation to the great faith the centurion had; to the joyful thankfulness the widow had; the unshakeable belief in Jesus as Saviour John the Baptist had; and to the deep gratefulness the repentant sinner expressed.

† Jesus, please give me the courage I need to respond to your invitation to a deeper relationship with you.

For further thought

What song is Jesus playing to you? One calling you to greater faith? One calling you to thankfulness? One calling you to belief? One calling you to gratitude?

Philippians

Joy and unity in Christ

Notes by **John Proctor**

John Proctor is a minister of the United Reformed Church (URC). Now retired, he has served in a Glasgow parish, at a Cambridge college and at the URC's central office in London. John has written commentaries on Matthew (BRF, revised edition 2022) and the Corinthian letters (WJK, 2015), as well as several Grove booklets on New Testament themes. John is married to Elaine, and they live near Cambridge. John has used the NRSVA for these notes.

Sunday 21 July
Not forgotten

Read Philippians 1:1–11

I thank my God every time I remember you ... because of your sharing in the gospel ... I am confident of this, that the one who began a good work among you will bring it to completion by the day of Jesus Christ ... And this is my prayer, that your love may overflow more and more with knowledge and full insight.

(verses 3, 5a, 6, 9)

Philippi was a smallish and rather isolated town in northern Greece. Rather few in number, quite new in the faith, even their neighbours and friends thought the Christians there strange. Paul is keen to remind them that they are not forgotten.

He tells them he remembers them with regular, grateful prayers. The Philippians, despite their difficulties, have sent money to support Paul's mission. They have 'shared in the gospel'. Now Paul reaches out to them in warmth, friendship and joy. This is an intimate, emotional letter; hopeful and upbeat. The writer and his readers really care for one another.

God remembers the Philippians, too, says Paul. They may feel threatened and their circumstances may be uncertain, but God is nurturing their faith and Christian character. Only the 'day of Jesus Christ', his eventual coming in judgement and victory, will reveal the finished product. Yet even now Paul prays for them to grow in love and wisdom, as stepping stones on the path to glory.

Remembered by friends, remembered by God. This is quite an encouragement for a church that might have felt forgotten.

† Do you pray regularly for someone who would like to be reminded of your support and love? What would be the best way of telling them?

203

Monday 22 July
Paul in chains

Read Philippians 1:12–30

What has happened to me has actually helped to spread the gospel, so that it has become known throughout the whole imperial guard and to everyone else that my imprisonment is for Christ … It is my eager expectation and hope that I will not be put to shame in any way, but that by my speaking with all boldness, Christ will be exalted now as always in my body, whether by life or by death. For to me, living is Christ and dying is gain.

(verses 12–13, 20–21)

Philippians is a letter about relationship. It moves to and fro. Some passages talk about the situation in Philippi, while others focus on Paul's own circumstances. Most of today's reading tells of his imprisonment. We do not know the venue, except that the mention of 'imperial' personnel suggests a major city. Paul describes his captivity in stark and graphic terms, as 'chains' (verses 7, 13, 14, 17). His comfort and liberty had been taken away, and in human terms his prospects might have looked gloomy and grim.

So what matters to him, as he thinks about the future? Not the thought of dying. That would actually bring him closer to Christ. He is not afraid for himself, but three things do concern him greatly.

The first is the spread of the Christian message. He is glad to know that other people are sharing their faith, and grateful that his situation seems to have inspired some of them. The second is his own faithfulness. Whether in freedom or in chains, he wants to conduct himself in a way that honours Christ. The third is the thought of service to other people. He wants to live longer, because he recognises how much he can contribute to the wellbeing of his friends.

Even in captivity, Paul is not turned in on himself. He knows that Christ will stay close. He is grateful to hear about the spread of the gospel. He is glad that other people value him. He still wants to contribute all he can to the cause of the kingdom and the work of God.

† Pray for faithfulness in your living, especially in situations where decisions are out of your hands. Ask that Christ be honoured, however events turn out.

For further thought

Can you find anything out about places where Christians are persecuted and imprisoned today?

Putting Christ into practice

> **Read Philippians 2:1–18**
>
> *If then there is any encouragement in Christ … Do nothing from selfish ambition or conceit, but in humility regard others as better than yourselves. Let each of you look not to your own interests, but to the interests of others. Let the same mind be in you that was in Christ Jesus … Work out your own salvation with fear and trembling; for it is God who is at work in you, enabling you both to will and to work for his good pleasure.*
>
> (verses 1a, 3, 5, 12–13)

Nature loves repeating patterns. Sometimes a motif will appear again and again – in different sizes and pointing different ways, yet all bound together as a single reality. The branches, twigs and even leaves of a conifer tree can look like miniatures of the whole tree. Certain kinds of crystal, if fractured, break into shapes that copy the bigger one, with the same number of sides and the same angles at the corners – little clones of the great original. The pattern keeps finding ways to emerge, to express itself.

So it is with Christ. The template is his own story: his self-giving and sacrifice as he shared our life and suffered our death; his vindication and victory as risen and ascended Lord. The cloning, the copying, the breaking down of that great original into smaller pieces, comes in the daily life of Christian people. When we 'count others better than ourselves' we are following Christ the servant. When we set aside 'selfish ambition and conceit' we start to see the world with 'the mind of Christ'.

That is the sort of life God can work with. People like that build good relationships, strengthen community and give others the confidence to follow Jesus too.

Living this way is what Paul means by 'work out your salvation'. 'Put your salvation into practice' would be another way of saying this. Salvation is a gift. Jesus has won it, and he shares it with us. Now it is for us to follow, to live the life of our Lord amid the people and places of today.

† Lord, please help me to be a person in whom others can discover the life of Jesus Christ.

For further thought
Consider the words 'with fear and trembling'. If we are daunted by the call to follow Jesus, perhaps that is the way it ought to be.

Philippians – Joy and unity in Christ

July

205

Wednesday 24 July
Team players

Read Philippians 2:19–30

I have no one like him who will be genuinely concerned for your welfare ... But Timothy's worth you know, how like a son with a father he has served with me in the work of the gospel ... Welcome [Epaphroditus] then in the LORD with all joy, and honour such people, because he came close to death for the work of Christ, risking his life to make up for those services that you could not give me.

(verses 20, 22, 29–30)

Timothy and Epaphroditus are two of the team players in the New Testament. They are by no means unusual. Many such people figure in Paul's letters – friends who travelled with him, helpers who supported the new Christians, colleagues he trusted with tricky pastoral work, messengers who kept contact across a scattered network of churches. Here are just two who made important contributions.

Timothy appears often; in Acts and many of the letters. Paul had trained him and had come to trust him. If Paul could not get to Philippi himself, Timothy would be a faithful envoy – honest, caring and concerned. So as soon as Paul had firm news to report about his own prospects, he would send Timothy without delay, in the confidence that Timothy would do everything possible to strengthen and help the church.

Meanwhile, Epaphroditus would come immediately. He was from Philippi himself, and the church there had sent him with money for Paul (4:18). Now, after a serious spell of ill-health, he would be glad to get home. It seems likely that he was the carrier of this letter. Paul respects him as a 'co-worker and fellow-soldier' (2:25) in the gospel, and writes warmly of his commitment and courage (2:30).

Yesterday's reading showed us the pattern of Christ. Today we find two examples of that pattern being worked out. Timothy was more concerned for the Philippians than for himself. Epaphroditus put himself in danger to show care and support for Paul. These are team players indeed, whose captain is Jesus Christ.

† Lord Jesus, please help me to be a team player, even in busy days and among difficult people.

For further thought

Can you see anything of yourself in someone who worked with Paul? Barnabas, Lydia, Luke, Phoebe, perhaps? What can you learn from that person?

Thursday 25 July
Defined by discipleship

Read Philippians 3:1–11

If anyone else has reason to be confident in the flesh, I have more: circumcised on the eighth day, a member of the people of Israel, of the tribe of Benjamin, a Hebrew born of Hebrews; as to the law, a Pharisee; as to zeal, a persecutor of the church; as to righteousness under the law, blameless. Yet whatever gains I had, these I have come to regard as loss because of Christ.

(verses 4b–7)

The sharp words that begin this chapter reflect an ongoing struggle that surfaces in several places in the New Testament. Most people in Philippi were Gentiles, and Paul believed that Gentiles could become Christians without switching their racial identity. They did not need to take on the external customs of Judaism, such as circumcision (for men) or Jewish dietary laws. He urges the Philippian Christians to resist any suggestion or pressure to do this.

Paul's own testimony of setting aside former privilege in order 'to be found in Christ' (verse 9) might make us think that he himself had abandoned Judaism, but that was not the case. The very word 'Christ' – 'God's anointed one' – is Jewish in meaning, rooted deeply in the hopes of the Old Testament. Paul lived in, and by, that heritage, but now he felt differently about what it meant.

He realised that being born a good Jew didn't make him a better Christian. What mattered most was not where he came from, but where he was going, and how closely he could follow the crucified and risen Lord Jesus.

So Paul's message for the Philippians is, in essence: 'You follow, too. Don't let anyone criticise where you came from – roots, accent, family, race. Concentrate on where you are heading. Centre yourself and your hopes on Jesus. Embrace his risen life.' Neither the privileges nor the problems with which we began life can define us as Christians. What defines us is the future; the path of faith and discipleship that stretches ahead.

† Pray for anyone you know who might be re-evaluating something big in their life. May God give them wisdom, clarity and hope.

For further thought

Can you think of one thing from your background that has helped you follow Jesus, and one thing that might have made this harder?

Friday 26 July
Citizens of heaven

> **Read Philippians 3:12 – 4:1**
>
> *But our citizenship is in heaven, and it is from there that we are expecting a Saviour, the Lord Jesus Christ. He will transform the body of our humiliation so that it may be conformed to the body of his glory, by the power that also enables him to make all things subject to himself. Therefore, my brothers and sisters, whom I love and long for, my joy and crown, stand firm in the Lord in this way, my beloved.*
>
> (verses 3:20 – 4:1)

'Our citizenship is in heaven.' For a Christian, heaven is the centre of the community to which we belong. It gives us identity and status as we walk with God in the world. It is the power behind our living and the purpose we are aiming towards.

Philippi knew about this sort of citizenship. It was a colony, legally regarded as a little piece of Rome. Even though the capital of the empire was hundreds of miles away, Philippi counted as part of the mother city. It belonged. This arrangement brought status and pride, legal benefits and tax breaks. It also encouraged people to value and copy Roman standards and culture.

To belong to a fellowship of Christians is to be part of a little outpost of heaven. This gives us confidence and purpose, values and connections, a wide community and a deep identity in the life of God. It also gives us hope. One day heaven will envelop and transform earth. The life of the risen Lord Jesus will grasp and glorify his people. The Easter gospel we live by will fill our whole being.

With that thought in mind, Paul starts to round off his main message before the letter moves on to more personal matters. Stand firm, he urges, as a united fellowship. Stay steady under pressure and persecution. Be resolute if anyone tries to insist on Jewish customs and practices. Stand firm as a hopeful people that belongs to heaven and presses forward without fear.

† Pray for anyone you know who might be finding hope difficult at the moment. Ask for courage, calm and patience.

For further thought

Have you ever felt closely connected to another Christian, even though you are from two quite different earthly countries? What was important about that relationship?

Spring of joy

> **Read Philippians 4:2–23**
>
> *Rejoice in the Lord always; again I will say, Rejoice. Let your gentleness be known to everyone. The Lord is near. Do not worry about anything, but in everything by prayer and supplication with thanksgiving let your requests be made known to God. And the peace of God, which surpasses all understanding, will guard your hearts and your minds in Christ Jesus.*
>
> (verses 4–7)

The letter is finishing. As often happens, Paul's writing becomes more personal at this stage. He advises about a personal difficulty in Philippi and recalls the Philippians' gifts to him over a long period. He is glad and grateful, both for the money itself and for this sign of their commitment and generosity. Then there are greetings at the end.

In all of this, Paul emphasises the presence and provision of God. When Christians pray about their worries and concerns, he says 'the peace of God will guard your hearts'. When we focus our minds and lives on qualities that are good and true, 'the God of peace will be with you'. Paul has learned amid patches of sufficiency and periods of scarcity to 'do all things through him who strengthens me' (verse 13). So the Philippians may also be confident that 'God will satisfy every need according to his riches in Christ' (verse 19).

These are not easy or complacent words. Experience has given Paul the right to speak, so we should take him seriously when he talks about rejoicing. Joy is a steady heartbeat in Philippians (4:1–10, for example). This is not the sort of momentary light-heartedness triggered by a good joke or a lively tune, but a deep and steady delight in the goodness of God and the love of Christ.

Philippians is a happy letter. It speaks of sacrifice and struggle, but within and alongside these is the generous provision of God. The companionship of Jesus Christ is a spring of joy – satisfying, sufficient and sure.

† Lord Jesus Christ, please make my life a source of joy; of refreshment for the weary; of friendship for the lonely; of peace for the troubled.

For further thought

What experiences in life have helped you trust God through thick and thin?

Nahum and Obadiah

Notes by **Christopher Took**

Chris is an Anglican from an open evangelical tradition. Currently living near the top of a tower block in inner London, he has lived in the English Midlands, Durham Castle and County Dublin. Chris runs a website for Irish election results, has had some success in the Sermon of the Year competition, chairs a residents' group on fire and building safety for his local council, and is studying Biblical Hebrew with City Lit. Find more resources on his website (www.biball.org). Chris has used the NIVUK for these notes.

Sunday 28 July
Only one kingdom

Read Nahum 1:1–11

*The L*ORD *is slow to anger but great in power; the L*ORD *will not leave the guilty unpunished.*

(verse 3a)

This week we're looking at some of the most obscure passages of scripture. Obadiah and Nahum are the only books of the Bible not included in the Revised Common Lectionary (RCL), a three-year reading scheme used by many churches for their Sunday readings and sermon themes. That says something quite significant about these two books (and perhaps also the RCL!).

Even if Nahum is unfamiliar to us, Nineveh probably seems like an old friend from its starring role in another of the minor prophets, Jonah. Yet how times have changed! It seems God is no longer sending reluctant prophets to evangelise a lost city. Nineveh has had her chance – or undoubtedly several chances – as we are reminded that 'the Lord is slow to anger'.

Paul tells Timothy that 'all Scripture is God-breathed' (2 Timothy 3:16), whether it's a rarely read minor prophet or the most familiar passage from the Gospels (surely the Lord's Prayer). There are several ways to answer the question: 'What is the main theme of the Bible?' But one response could be: 'Your kingdom come, your will be done ...' (Matthew 6:10).

We see that this God who is slow to anger can still be roused to wrath. Ultimately, there is only room for one kingdom.

† Father God, help me to hear you speak in every part of your word; from the obscurest verse to my favourite passage. Amen

Monday 29 July
Proclaiming peace

Read Nahum 1:12–15

*Look, there on the mountains, the feet of one who brings good news,
who proclaims peace!*

(verse 15a)

Judah (the southern kingdom – the northern one being Israel) had been disciplined and punished by God for its unfaithfulness. It's easy to focus on this period of affliction being over and the fact that relief is coming, but this chapter reminds us that God's protection comes with obligations and responsibilities. Yesterday's reading stated that God 'cares for those who trust him' (1:7b). Taking someone for granted isn't the same as trusting them. Today, the people of Judah are told to 'celebrate your festivals and fulfil your vows'.

Festivals such as Passover reminded the Jews of the way God had acted in their history to save them. Another theme of the Bible is God saving his people from slavery – either in Egypt or to sin – and bringing them to a better place: the promised land of Canaan, the kingdom proclaimed by Jesus and eventually the new heavens and new earth (Isaiah 65:17; 2 Peter 3:13).

Nahum refers to 'one' person 'who brings good news, who proclaims peace'. Paul uses a similar quote in Romans 10:15 (from Isaiah 52:7) referring to those who bring good news. Whoever was in Nahum's mind, we can understand that Jesus is the source of good news and that he brings peace. The 'beautiful feet' belong to those who have shared the gospel with us, and we in turn should become these beautiful feet (metaphorically, at least!) as we share the good news of Jesus.

God promised Abraham that his descendants would be as numerous as the stars (Genesis 22:17), in contrast with the Ninevites, who would have 'no descendants to bear your name' (Nahum 1:14). We can add to Abraham's descendants ourselves as we share the good news!

† Lord, help me to bring good news and to proclaim peace to the people around me, especially those who are oppressed or marginalised. Amen

For further thought
How can you celebrate what God has done in your life? A mini festival, or even just lighting a candle, could remind you of his goodness.

Nahum and Obadiah

July

The Lord will vindicate his people

Read Nahum 2:1–13

The Lord will restore the splendour of Jacob like the splendour of Israel, though destroyers have laid them waste and have ruined their vines.

(verse 2)

As I write, the war is Ukraine is still raging. A successful counter-offensive is underway, and many are surprised by Russia's inability to defend the Ukrainian territory it had occupied. Russia is not in the situation of Nineveh (which stands as a symbol for the entire Assyrian Empire), and it would be very dangerous if it were. But there is something visceral in seeing the bully get its comeuppance.

During the Covid-19 pandemic, my church adopted 2 Chronicles 20:12 as its motto: 'We do not know what to do, but our eyes are on you.' We started every Sunday service with this verse for more than two years. It wasn't about us feeling useless and hopeless, but about renewing our faith and trust in a God who is bigger than the destruction wrought by a virus or by the military might of Nineveh.

Even in times of great upheaval and uncertainty, Christians have a clear call to action to 'go and make disciples of all nations' (Matthew 28:19), with an equally clear promise from God that if we are 'strong and courageous' he will never leave us nor forsake us (Deuteronomy 31:6).

Elsewhere in scripture it's made clear that all the events of history are in the hands of God: 'It is mine to avenge; I will repay ... The Lord will vindicate his people' (Deuteronomy 32:35–36). Whether we are faced by horrific war that threatens the sovereignty and security of nation states, or simply the daily trials and tribulations we suffer as individuals (which can seem just as oppressive and overwhelming), our *only* hope is in God.

† Help me, Lord, to keep my eyes fixed on you so I can say and do the right thing at the right time. Amen

For further thought

What does it mean to be 'strong and courageous' spiritually? Do you spend enough time in the spiritual gym to develop your muscles of faith?

Wednesday 31 July
Powers and authorities disarmed

> **Read Nahum 3:1–13**
>
> *'I am against you,' declares the LORD Almighty. 'I will lift your skirts over your face.*
> *I will show the nations your nakedness and the kingdoms your shame.'*
>
> (verse 5)

Assyrian propaganda portrayed its enemies as feminine, and those it captured were stripped as a sign of humiliation. It was common to personify cities as female and use (in)appropriate language about them. Nahum uses the metaphor of the prostitute as a contrast with Nineveh's treatment of her foes. This also reverses the image of Assyria seizing (raping) foreign lands and the way those lands were plundered (stripped).

Nineveh was never like a desperate woman forced into sex work due to dire circumstances. This city was all about the allure of power and promise of wealth in order to 'enslave nations by her prostitution and peoples by her witchcraft' (verse 4). This 'wanton lust' had to be exposed and Nineveh humiliated. Lifting the skirts revealed what was really underneath: pure evil.

We noted on Sunday that there is only room for one kingdom: the kingdom of God. Sooner or later, all those who oppose and challenge it will find themselves rendered impotent and humiliatingly exposed. Paul wrote: 'Having disarmed the powers and authorities, [God] made a public spectacle of them, triumphing over them by the cross' (Colossians 2:15).

Exodus 34:6–7 is frequently referred to in the Hebrew Bible (including Nahum 1:3), because it sums up the nature of God. He is 'slow to anger, abounding in love … yet he does not leave the guilty unpunished'. This conflict between God's love and justice is reconciled through the cross. Jesus bore our sins willingly so we would no longer be separated from God, and the likes of Nineveh would be disarmed so that they, and all evil, would no longer have any power over us.

† Lord, may I be alert to evil and injustice. Give me the courage to confront what is wrong and to do something about it. Amen.

For further thought

Where are you most susceptible to the allure of false promises and deceptive thinking? How can you identify and expose the enemy?

Two types of shepherd

> **Read Nahum 3:14–19**
>
> *King of Assyria, your shepherds slumber; your nobles lie down to rest. Your people are scattered on the mountains with no one to gather them.*
>
> (verse 18)

The tone from verse 12 onwards is less intense than the start of the chapter, and Nahum may even be having some fun at Nineveh's expense. The commands to improve the defences expose the futility of fighting against divine purposes. The innumerable merchants (perhaps recalling Abraham's equally uncountable but far more productive descendants) leave nothing of value. The guards aren't so much defeated as inexplicably vanished.

The last two verses taunt the King of Assyria, claiming he has failed in the most basic of sovereign duties: to protect his people. His shepherds are asleep while his people are scattered – surely a contrast with God, who is the perfect Shepherd (and King), gathering his people to him (Isaiah 40:11; John 10:11). There is the irony of the scattering to the mountains where peace was being proclaimed in Nahum 1:15. Good news comes to God's people on the mountains, but the same place spells disaster and the end for God's enemies.

The prophecy of Nahum brings comfort ('comfort' is the root meaning of the name 'Nahum') to God's people at times when it may seem as if God isn't in control or as if his anger is burning more slowly than we might like. The pride and ignorance of God's enemies will inevitably lead to their destruction and humiliation.

Jonah and Nahum are the only biblical books to end with a rhetorical question. In 3:19 we have both a promise and a warning. We will clap our hands and rejoice when our enemies fall, but we are not immune from experiencing their cruelty.

† Thank you, Lord, for providing hope and comfort in difficult and challenging times. Help me to discern your purposes and to be patient as you fulfil them. Amen

For further thought

How might you heed the warning and grasp the promise in Nahum 3:19? How could Nahum comfort you in times of trouble?

Friday 2 August
Ever mingled

Read Obadiah 1–9

'In that day,' declares the LORD, 'will I not destroy the wise men of Edom, those of understanding in the mountains of Esau?'

(verse 8)

Obadiah (which means 'servant' or 'worshipper of God') is the shortest book in the Hebrew Bible. It's a prophecy against Edom, a small country in the mountainous area to the southeast of the Dead Sea in modern-day Jordan. Edom's inhabitants were descendants of Esau (Genesis 25:30), so perhaps conflict was inevitable. The book is similar to Nahum in being an almost relentless invective against the enemy.

Edom was protected by her lofty position among inaccessible rocky heights. The destruction in the prophecy is total. Usually, thieves would grab the most valuable loot and scarper, but Edom is to be picked clean. We read that friends and allies will turn against and deceive her. Edom had a reputation for wisdom, but that will be of no use to her. Once again, we see that nothing can frustrate the purposes of God: not military might, not clever thinking, not hiding in the mountains.

Of course, it's good to see evil destroyed, injustice punished and deceit exposed; however saddened we might be that these things occurred in the first place. It's easy (and not wrong) to see ourselves on God's side, raising the banner of truth and cheering as justice is dispensed. We are happy to leave the focus on Edom as the enemy of God's people.

Yet, as the Church of England's twenty-sixth Article of Religion reminds us, 'the evil be ever mingled with the good'. We may not be in a position to inflict evil on those around us in the same way Edom and Nineveh were, but the allure, the lies and the sin are always there to mislead and tempt us.

† Father, give me the courage to examine myself and my motives. Help me to identify and root out everything that is not honouring to you. Amen

For further thought

Nothing we encounter, apart from God, is pure good. And very few things are pure evil. How could you think more critically about good and evil?

Nahum and Obadiah

August

Saturday 3 August
The kingdom will be the Lord's

Read Obadiah 10–21

Deliverers will go up on Mount Zion to govern the mountains of Esau. And the kingdom will be the LORD's.

(verse 21)

Edom is condemned both for joining in and for standing by as Jerusalem is attacked, as well as for gloating over the city's misfortune.

The golden rule about doing to others what we would have them do to us (Matthew 7:12) is referenced in verse 15, not to encourage lovingkindness towards others, but to proclaim judgement on those who have acted selfishly, cruelly and unjustly. This is in the context of 'the day of the Lord'; the final judgement at the end of time when God will put right all injustices. At this point his people will be vindicated and saved, and his enemies will be condemned and punished.

The focus then turns to Mount Zion (at the heart of Jerusalem). The fortunes of God's people (Jacob and Joseph) are contrasted vividly with her enemies (Esau). One will be fire and flame, the other stubble. Even the little that is left of Edom's former glory will be set alight and utterly destroyed. There's no doubt which side anyone would want to be on!

Nahum and Obadiah may be short and obscure, but they ring out, loud and clear, with the central themes of scripture: God rescuing and saving his people, the proclamation of good news to the nations and the triumph of God's kingdom.

We mustn't wait until the last judgement to take sides. God has already invited us to enter his kingdom through Jesus, and the powers and authorities are already defeated (see Wednesday's reflection and Colossians 2:15). Our prayer, 'your kingdom come, your will be done' will be answered fully and decisively. And the kingdom will be the Lord's.

† Father, as I pray 'your kingdom come, your will be done', help me to understand my part in your kingdom and your call on my life. Amen

For further thought

Do you spend enough time thinking about what the kingdom of God looks like now and in the future, and about how you live as part of it?

Fresh from The Word 2025

Thinking ahead, now is the right time to order *Fresh from The Word 2025*.

Order now:

- direct from IBRA web shop (see below)
- from your local IBRA rep
- from the SPCK website: www.spck.org.uk
- in selected Christian bookshops
- from online retailers such as Amazon, Eden and others

To order your copy from IBRA

- Website: **ibraglobal.org**
- Email: **sales@christianeducation.org.uk**
- Call: **0121 458 3313**
- Post: **using the order form at the back of this book**

E-versions of *Fresh from The Word* are available through online retailers such as Kindle, Kobo and Eden.

How are you finding this year?

Let us know how you are finding this year's daily Bible reading notes. If you are on Facebook or Twitter, we would love to hear your thoughts, as little or as often as you like! You never know, it may also encourage others to investigate The Word and form a deeper connection with our fellow readers.

www.facebook.com/freshfromtheword
www.twitter.com/IBRAbibleread

Would you consider leaving your own legacy to help spread the Good News?

IBRA and *Fresh from The Word* are only possible through you, the readers, and your donations. At this moment, when the world is changing rapidly, we need your help. A gift in your will to IBRA's International Fund will help continue its Bible reading legacy of 142 years. Every penny of your donation goes directly towards enabling hundreds of thousands of people around the world to access the living Word of God.

'Go into all the world and preach the Good News to everyone.'
Mark 16:15b (NLT)

It was the vision of Charles Waters to empower people in Britain and overseas to benefit from the Word of God through the experiences and insights of biblical scholars from around the world. The goal was to strengthen and encourage people in their homes and situations, wherever they were. His legacy lives on today, in you, as a reader, and in the IBRA team, across the globe.

Our work at IBRA is supported by sales of our books, and since 1882 we continue to ensure that 100% of donations to the IBRA International Fund go to benefit our local and international readers. We are blessed every year by those who leave a legacy in their will – ensuring that their hopes are carried on and fulfilled by IBRA, when they have risen into eternal life with our Lord. To continue this important work, would you consider leaving a legacy in your will?

To find out more please contact our CEO, Zoë Keens, on 0121 458 3313, email zoe.keens@christianeducation.org.uk or write to International Bible Reading Association, 5-6 Imperial Court, 12 Sovereign Road, Birmingham, B30 3FH.

To read more about the history of IBRA, see the website ibraglobal.org or go to the back pages of this book.

Creation

1 Choosing how we live within God's creation

Notes by **Jan Sutch Pickard**

 Jan is a poet, storyteller and liturgist living on the Isle of Mull, and a member of the dispersed Iona Community. She has been a teacher, a mission partner in Nigeria, an editor for the Methodist Church based in London and Manchester, and warden of the Abbey in Iona. Family life includes the joy of three children and five grandchildren. Using and writing for *Fresh from The Word* are, for her, ways of listening to others and sharing an evolving faith. Jan has used the NIVUK for these notes.

Sunday 4 August
Delight in diversity

Read Genesis 1:9–13

God called the dry ground 'land', and the gathered waters … 'seas'. And God saw that it was good. Then God said, 'Let the land produce vegetation: seed-bearing plants on the land that bear fruit with seed in it according to their various kinds.' And it was so … and God saw that it was good.

(verses 10–12)

Stand with me on the shore, between high-water mark and breaking waves. Here's the boundary between land and sea – one that is constantly changing with the tides. Sand shifting, seaweed and shells being brought in as flotsam. Here in the Hebrides we find that the Gulf Stream sometimes floats strange seeds, coconuts or even leatherback turtles all the way from the Caribbean; reminders of our connected world and signs of rich diversity.

Theologian John Bell is often quoted as saying that diversity is part of God's deal, pointing out that Genesis 1 is full of contrasts: darkness and light; sea and land; plants and then creatures of many kinds, including man and woman. This poem about creation has a refrain: 'And God saw that it was good.' Just as contrasts, uniqueness and diversity give delight to God, so we too can appreciate the rich variety of this world we share.

We should never take our world for granted. David Attenborough's *Living Planet* celebrates the 'web of life on earth',[1] and this strengthens my belief in a creative, continuous power at work in the universe. The limits of human language and dogma cannot contain such mystery.

† Wonder beyond words, Creator God. We give thanks for your presence within the living world – and in our hearts.

[1] D. Attenborough, *Living Planet: The web of life on earth* (William Collins, 2021).

Monday 5 August
Taking responsibility, taking care

Read Genesis 1:26–31

God blessed them and said to them, 'Be fruitful and increase in number; fill the earth and subdue it. Rule over the fish in the sea and the birds in the sky and over every living creature that moves on the ground ... I give you every seed-bearing plant on the face of the whole earth and every tree that has fruit with seed in it. They will be yours for food.'

(verses 28–29)

During Covid, a growing concern for our local community led to the setting up of the island's first food bank, but delivery of fresh food was a problem. More of us needed to grow our own food, so why not cooperate? The scrub and brambles were cleared, and raised beds were built, then filled with compost and seaweed. The fresh air prevented infection as folk gardened together. Two years have already shown many benefits for the health of old and young, and as we have grown crops that all can enjoy, companionably, we have also grown as a community.

The nursery beds hold seedling trees from berries the children collected. The saplings will be planted out on land bought by the local community, formerly a commercial forestry plantation. As these native-species trees grow tall, they will change the landscape. There are challenges, however. We share this island with many deer, so the garden and forest need high fences. Hazelnuts planted to grow trees are eaten by mice and voles, so for our next planting we'll need to find ways to deter tiny creatures. And how on earth do we subdue all the slugs?

When the Genesis story was told, human beings believed their God-given task was to 'fill the earth and subdue it'. Right now, on a much larger scale than in this island garden, humankind – just one species among many – subdues and exploits, pollutes and wastes the natural world. Do we see this as our right? Or is it our responsibility to live creatively with creation?

† God of growing things, the garden of the world reminds us of your generous love. May we share and value it, not seeking to subdue it. And help us see the good, even in slugs!

For further thought

Go into your garden or park, or look at a window box or front gardens along a street, or weeds on a piece of wasteland. Focus on one growing thing ... and enjoy it!

Tuesday 6 August
What have we done?

Read Genesis 6:11–22

God saw how corrupt the earth had become, for all people on earth had corrupted their ways. So God said to Noah, 'I am going to put an end to all people, for the earth is filled with violence because of them. I am surely going to destroy both them and the earth.'

(verses 12–13)

It's Hiroshima Day, so it feels appropriate to read this passage, where God reacts with horror and wrath to the way human beings have filled the earth with violence. The story imagines God's reaction – and his radical solution.

As a gardener, I can grasp this. Today I realised that my tomato plants, which had seemed to be flourishing, have developed some kind of blight – leaves brown, fruit rotting. To prevent it spreading to neighbouring plots, I uprooted all the plants and destroyed them.

And at the same time – in the same world as my garden – a dictator in Russia is threatening the world with nuclear annihilation. I hope that's an empty threat. But how have we come to this point? What have we done? More than one war is being waged in our world right now, amid a climate crisis increased by our greedy lifestyles. The earth is filled with violent change and social breakdown because of our choices. Floods, hurricanes and wildfires are often described as 'acts of God'. But while we glimpse God's power in the natural world – both creative and destructive – is it also cruel? Or are we judging God by our own corrupt standards?

We make choices. The first atomic bombs, dropped on Hiroshima and Nagasaki, killed tens of thousands of innocent people. Politicians justified this, claiming it was a way of ending a war. Yet the website of the Imperial War Museum describes the 'terrible cost'. Ever since then we have lived with a global nuclear arms race and the threat of 'mutual assured destruction'. What have we done?

† What have we done? Just and merciful God, forgive our wrong choices, as nations and as individuals. Teach us how to transform our lives.

For further thought

How much do you know about Hiroshima and Nagasaki? What would you have done?

221

Wednesday 7 August
Never again

Read Genesis 8:13–22

'Never again will I curse the ground because of … And never again will I destroy all living creatures … As long as the earth endures, seedtime and harvest, cold and heat, summer and winter, day and night will never cease.'

(verses 21–22)

Cataclysmic events happen. Some, like the meteorite that led to the extinction of the dinosaurs, are seemingly random. Others unambiguously point to human wickedness. Today, as I write, has been declared the UN International Day for the Total Elimination of Nuclear Weapons, which reminds us again of the bombing of Hiroshima and Nagasaki. When we read in today's passage that 'every inclination of the human heart is evil from childhood' and consider such wickedness, there is no wonder that we read the story of the flood and interpret it as an angry God punishing the world for its sin.

But we know that God does not act wickedly, as we sometimes do. The truth behind the mythology of the flood isn't that an angry God lashes out in punishment. It's that God creates fresh beginnings and, despite natural and man-made calamities, provides a means of salvation for all who respond.

In this case he does so through a righteous man (Noah), lifted high above the earth (on flood waters) on something made of wood (the ark). To show that God has compassion on all who are unable to choose for themselves, Noah is told to seek out at least one breeding pair of every animal and bird.

At the end of the story, Noah worships God in the only way he knows how. We can respond to Jesus having been 'lifted high above the earth' in other ways. On Hiroshima Day in 2022, peace activists built a cairn out of 140,000 paper cranes. They were placed outside a government military building while songs commemorated human suffering, with this commitment: 'Never again.'

† 'Jesus, confirm my heart's desire to work, and speak, and think for thee; still let me guard the holy fire, and still stir up thy gift in me.'[1]

For further thought

If possible, find instructions for making an origami peace crane and a story that goes with it. Make it, think about what it represents, then give it away.

[1] C. Wesley, 'O Thou Who Camest from Above' (public domain, 1762).

Thursday 8 August
Do something, Lord!

Read Jeremiah 14:1–7

They go to the cisterns but find no water. They return with their jars unfilled; dismayed and despairing, they cover their heads. The ground is cracked because there is no rain in the land ... Although our sins testify against us, do something, LORD ....

(verses 3–4,7a)

Watching the world news, we see many disturbing images. Grasslands dead and brown instead of green and full of goodness for grazing animals – we feel helpless. Leaves shrivelled and crops dead before they can be harvested – we feel confused. Men and women, their heads covered as they mourn dead children – we feel distressed. Land tinder-dry and wildfires breaking out – we feel afraid.

Over the years we've read of droughts, seen shocking pictures of famines, donated to emergency aid appeals and prayed, 'Do something, Lord.' And now we see drought on our doorsteps. Why? *Do something, Lord!* But while it is good to pray, we must also act, and quickly. This climate crisis is made worse every day by the way we choose to live in God's world.

Different translations of the passage above vary in one detail. Often, uncovering one's head was seen as a symbol of shame and the Revised English Bible uses 'uncover', yet most translations have 'covered their heads' in this passage. Not being a Hebrew scholar, I'm not sure which is more accurate. But I can see two strong emotions expressed in this symbolic action: grief at devastating changes in the world's weather, failed harvests and lives lost; and shame because we – particularly in the developed world – are largely responsible because of our carbon footprint, our polluting lifestyles and our waste of the resources we should share in the world for which we should care.

† We grieve for a suffering world in a climate crisis, shamed by our way of life, and by all that we carelessly take for granted. Forgive us.

For further thought

Find a picture of a drought-stricken landscape, with or without people. Reflect on what you see, and how people live in these conditions. Consider supporting a charity like WaterAid.

Friday 9 August
Do nothing, for a change!

Read Exodus 23:1–12

'For six years you are to sow your fields and harvest the crops, but during the seventh year let the land lie unploughed and unused. Then the poor among your people may get food from it, and the wild animals may eat what is left … Six days do your work, but on the seventh day do not work, so that your ox and your donkey may rest, and so that the slave … and the foreigner living among you may be refreshed.'

(verses 10–12)

This passage offers gentle wisdom about how we might live in the world, sharing it with other people and creatures. But it also provides hard advice for us to follow, driven by the desire to be in charge; dominating and defining ourselves by what we do.

In a passage about acting with integrity to build a just society, two verses focus on getting the balance between work and rest right – for the good of human beings, other creatures and the land itself. Greed and ignorance unbalance things, for instance how we treat what is literally down-to-earth: the soil; a resource for all growing things, for life itself.

The centuries-old practice was to let fields lie fallow between growing years. Nowadays they are ploughed up every year and dosed with commercial fertilisers to push the soil into producing more and more. By contrast, our community garden's plots are enriched with homemade compost and barrows of seaweed from the shore. Crops are rotated to rest and refresh the earth. Getting our hands dirty, we learn how to feed ourselves, help each other and respect creation.

Social reformers took many years to achieve better working hours for most, while low wages, the gig economy and stressful overtime still burden folk. Yet wise employers offer sabbaticals to enable reflection and refreshment – a gift of time, bringing health.

That same concept underlies the Sabbath. Sabbath laws are not about setting limits, but offering liberation. The seventh day, when God rested, can be a time for human beings to find the freedom and healing of a holy day.

† Thank you, God, for the daily work, paid or unpaid, that puts our feet on the ground, uses our gifts and serves others. And thank you for the blessing of 'Sabbath' times to rest and be refreshed.

For further thought

What might constitute a 'Sabbath' time for you? It could mean setting aside months, a day or even just an hour.

Saturday 10 August
For crying out loud!

Read Romans 8:18–25

The whole creation has been groaning as in the pains of childbirth right up to the present time … But hope that is seen is no hope at all. Who hopes for what they already have? But if we hope for what we do not yet have, we wait for it patiently.

(verses 22, 24b–25)

I'm not sure about the word 'patiently' here! In labour with my first child, I reached a stage many mothers will recognise. Amid waves of unfamiliar pain, my emotions were so confused that I shouted, 'This is a terrible idea! I've had enough – stop it!' But of course there was no stopping. And at last a child was born, alive and well – the fulfilment of hope.

Between my writing these notes and you reading them, irreversible changes may have taken place. In the natural events of the climate crisis, there is great human responsibility. Governments and big corporations destroy forests, relentlessly extract fossil fuels and overuse them, overfish the oceans and overwhelm the world with plastic waste. We want God to intervene in this 'uncreating' – in our destructive way of life. We see creation groaning under the burdens we have laid on it, and we want to say, 'This is terrible! We've had enough.'

We are part of the problem, but we may also be part of the solution. We don't know what the future will look like, but we can't wash our hands of it. We have a responsibility keep on labouring with God, to bring hope to birth.

'For Crying Out Loud', a climate crisis ceilidh, has just happened here on the island. In true Hebridean style, thirty-five local people met in a barn to share food and poetry, songs and great fiddle playing, laughter and tears, and to celebrate the beauty of the world around us, lamenting what may be lost, and speaking out for what we can do and where we see hope. Perhaps 'steadfast' and 'engaged' are better words for us than 'patient'!

† God of creation, community and hope, if we can't be patient, make us steadfast. Help us, through laughter and tears, to engage with your work in the world.

For further thought

How will you share what you have learned this week with others? Through words, song, pictures or action?

Creation

2 Climate justice

Notes by **Louise Jones**

Louise Jones lives and works in Winson Green, Birmingham, in an embedded, community-based organisation (Newbigin Community Trust), which aims to create a sense of family, purpose and social cohesion in a community that is often overlooked. Louise recently finished an MA in Theology (Social Justice and Humanitarian Development), and has a passion for empowering, resourcing and loving those who have slipped through the cracks of our systems to help people see their immense value and worth in Jesus. Louise has used the NIVUK for these notes.

Sunday 11 August
Enough for everyone

Read Genesis 26:17–22

He moved on from there and dug another well, and no one quarrelled over it. He named it Rehoboth, saying, 'Now the LORD has given us room and we will flourish in the land.'

(verse 22)

Isaac has arrived in a new area and makes a few attempts to find a water source for his family. However, his servants keep interfering with other people's land when trying to dig a well, causing friction as locals become concerned that their water source is being stolen.

This problem is as relevant today as it was all those years ago. Muynak in Uzbekistan was once a fishing port on the edge of the Aral Sea. Now it is famous as the 'ship's graveyard', with rusting boats many miles from the little that remains of the sea, the water having been diverted to irrigation schemes elsewhere. Self-interest has allowed the powerful in our world to acquire so much at the expense of the poor.

This week we will look at more stories highlighting issues of environmental injustice and, in considering that 'God so loved the *world*', explore ways in which we can echo that love.

Isaac had the wisdom to give back the water sources his servants had usurped, and in doing so loved the people around him, understanding that there is enough space for everyone if we share the resources God has provided.

† God, would you help us to reflect on where we have too much of something, and show us how we can bring justice by redistributing?

Monday 12 August
The world that God loves

Read John 3:11–21

For God so loved the world that he gave his one and only Son, that whoever believes in him shall not perish but have eternal life. For God did not send his Son into the world to condemn the world, but to save the world through him.

(verses 16–17)

It is hard to read this passage with fresh eyes, as it is one many of us learned to recite as children. However, my previous assumptions about this passage were recently challenged. It is important in a discussion about God's heart for the environment to note that Jesus says, 'for God so loved *the world*' and not 'for God so loved *humans*'. In fact, it goes further than that. The word used is *cosmos*, and Paul describes the whole cosmos as groaning – waiting for someone to intervene and save it. As we witness climate change and environmental injustice on a massive scale today, we can perhaps understand something of what he meant.

We all know people who seem to delight in announcing doom and gloom. They look at the work you are doing, then shake their heads and declare it won't work, that it will end in disaster, and they offer no help to create a better outcome. Thankfully, this famous passage tells us Jesus isn't like that. Even though he experienced first-hand on earth where sinful choices were leading the cosmos, instead of declaring us condemned he acted to save. Of course he warned us to watch the signs of the time, and of course he told us where things would head if nothing changed. But he didn't condemn us to those outcomes; he acted to provide a different ending.

God has given us significance. He gave us authority over 'the world'. But with that authority comes a responsibility to love the world as he does and to act for its salvation.

† Help us to love your world as much as you do, and in doing so inspire us to find ways to fight for environmental justice.

For further thought
Some scientists believe humans have quickened species extinction by a thousand times. How does this impact the heart of God, who loves diversity and created abundance?

Creation – 2 Climate justice

August

Tuesday 13 August
God's care for its creatures

Read Matthew 10:28–31

Are not two sparrows sold for a penny? Yet not one of them will fall to the ground outside your Father's care. And even the very hairs of your head are all numbered. So don't be afraid; you are worth more than many sparrows.

(verse 29)

Reading this verse reminds me of a story a teenager I work with shared a few months ago. Jamal (not his real name) is very observant, easily distracted and fascinated by nature. A few months ago, Jamal realised he was locked out his house, as he had forgotten his key. As he sat on the doorstep waiting for his mum to get home, he noticed a pigeon lying in the road, motionless with uneven breath. While most people would have ignored the bird, Jamal picked it up and wrapped it in his school jumper to keep it warm, in an attempt to nurse it back to health. Sadly, by the time his mother came home the pigeon had died and Jamal was distraught. He wanted to tell everyone at youth group what had happened.

Jamal's love and care for this pigeon remind me of the care described in this verse in Matthew. I notice two things: firstly, that God honours and loves what most of us would overlook, with great care and attention. Whether it is the unnoticed pigeon or the small detail in our lives, God sees, understands its real value and cares. Secondly, God's care does not make us immune from the consequences of living in an unjust, 'groaning' cosmos. The sparrow falls to the ground and the pigeon dies, despite Jamal's best efforts. It isn't immunity that comforts; it is his presence, his attention, his seeing that transforms.

In a world of overwhelming need, this is our part. To notice, and to be the ones who care for the overlooked.

† Lord, may I never be so busy that I don't notice the creature or person needing my care, needing to know that they are seen.

For further thought

When was the last time you let someone, or something, interrupt your busy day?

Wednesday 14 August
Fighting against exploitation

Read Deuteronomy 25:1–10

Do not muzzle an ox while it is treading out the grain.

(verse 4)

Today's passage begins with what seems like the obvious: in the case of a dispute, the innocent should be acquitted and the guilty punished. But this goes further and places limits on the extent of the punishment to prevent it destroying the value of the individual in other people's eyes. In other words, the purpose of the punishment is to correct, to encourage reform, to value the victim – not to destroy.

The part of the passage quoted sets similarly fair limits. Before windmills, an ox would turn the grindstones that crushed the grain into flour. The ox would stop from time to time to eat some of the grain, and, in order to maximise productivity and minimise losses, some were muzzling their animals. The Bible tells us not to be so focused on profit that we lose our connection with those who work for us. Allow the ox time to eat. Allow it some of the fruits of its labour.

The fast-fashion industry is a tragic modern-day example. We may be delighted to only have to spend pennies on a T-shirt, but cheap clothing can only be produced by 'muzzling' the workers – often young women and children who work in inhumane conditions for unsafe lengths of time, with little or no pay.

We can help to unmuzzle our brothers and sisters by refusing to take advantage of clothing and other products that we know must have been produced in ways that offend God, and which should offend us. We can advocate on their behalf by lobbying our politicians and giving a voice to the voiceless.

† God, would you free those who are oppressed in modern-day slavery and oppressive working conditions? And would you challenge us to be wise in how we spend our money?

For further thought

According to the International Labour Organization (ILO), around 250 million children between the ages of five and fourteen are forced to work in sweatshops for up to sixteen hours per day.[1]

[1] 'ILO Global Report on Child Labour cites 'alarming' extent of its worst forms': https://www.ilo.org/global/about-the-ilo/newsroom/news/WCMS_007784/lang--en/index.htm (accessed 8 May 2023).

Creation – 2 Climate justice

August

229

Thursday 15 August
There will be famines …

Read Matthew 24:1–8

Nation will rise against nation, and kingdom against kingdom. There will be famines and earthquakes in various places. All these are the beginning of birth-pains.

(verses 7–8)

In my work I have supported individuals who are trying to combat their addictions by entering rehabilitation programmes. It's a hard road for all. It often involves setbacks, sometimes appears to end hopelessly, and – wonderfully, on occasion – results in lasting freedom. While it can be demoralising to watch people drop out and re-enter numerous times, the potential for relapse is no reason to stop hoping or to stop supporting people as they try again.

As we read today's verse, we could see it as an excuse to do nothing. If Jesus predicted and prophesied natural disasters, then they are inevitable and there is nothing we can do to stop them. But as we have seen, while Jesus is clear with his warnings, he doesn't condemn us to that outcome. This verse reflects Jesus' grief over the consequences of human behaviour, but it doesn't excuse us from responding – any more than his statement that 'the poor you will always have with you' (Matthew 26:11) gives us permission to leave the homeless unhoused or the hungry unfed. Rather, Jesus is being realistic in acknowledging that while humans continue to be greedy and sin, there will always be poor people suffering the consequences of those choices, including as a result of famine.

In the same way that we continue to feed the hungry in famines, we should ask how we can reduce the root causes of those famines; whether they are caused by environmental issues such as deforestation, diverting water or climate change, or by the unfair distribution of resources. We need to reduce our carbon footprint and campaign for governmental policies that protect and conserve the environment.

† Lord, would you motivate us to reduce our environmental footprint and advocate for environmental justice, even when it feels hopeless and global deterioration seems inevitable.

For further thought

'You must take action. You must do the impossible. Because giving up can never be an option' (Greta Thunberg).[1]

[1] G. Thunberg in her speech at the UN Climate Action Summit.

Friday 16 August
A restored ecology

Read Isaiah 65:17–25

*'They will not labour in vain, nor will they bear children doomed to misfortune ... The wolf and the lamb will feed together, and the lion will eat straw like the ox, and dust will be the serpent's food. They will neither harm nor destroy on all my holy mountain,' says the L*ord.

(verses 23a, 25)

At the beginning of the story described in Genesis, we see God create an ecology that is in perfect balance – a 'cosmos' over which humanity is given the authority to nurture and extend. Tragically, far from nurturing, we have used our position of dominance to exploit and the consequences of this are beginning to be felt across the world.

But of course, those consequences are not felt equally by everyone. Those of us who have more than our fair share of resources can use them to insulate ourselves, to buy warmer clothing, to build stronger houses, to pay the rising energy costs. As ever, it is those who are already poor and powerless who suffer the most. Living and working in my community, I see the impact of this first-hand. Those who had little to begin with have less and less, while those with the power to make decisions that would bring change remain largely immune and deaf to our pleas.

This passage brings hope. It is a dream of justice and restoration, for a world as God intended, and it is a dream that we can help come true. The passage tells us that efforts made to bring it about will not be in vain. Future generations, our own children, will not be doomed. Those serpents who sought our harm through their deceptive words will ultimately eat dust and will no longer be able to harm anyone! Perhaps it is our job to turn the tables, as Jesus did with the corrupt market sellers, on the people in authority who are exploiting the natural world for the sake of increased wealth and power.

† Lord, would you give us wisdom to know how to challenge our corrupt systems and would you give those in positions of power insight to see beyond economic wealth and power.

For further thought

'The greatest impact of climate change is felt by those in the global south, who are least responsible for causing it. This is fundamentally a justice issue' (Ban Ki-moon).[1]

[1] B. Ki-moon cited in A. G. Reddie, 'The Monstrous Shadow, Race, Climate and Justice' in J. Williams (ed.) *Time to Act: A resource book by the Christians in extinction rebellion* (London: SPCK Publishing, 2020), p. 73.

Saturday 17 August
A new heaven and earth

> **Read Revelation 21:9–27**
>
> *I did not see a temple in the city, because the Lord God Almighty and the Lamb are its temple … On no day will its gates ever be shut … Nothing impure will ever enter it, nor will anyone who does what is shameful or deceitful …*
>
> (verses 22, 25, 27)

There is a paradox in this verse between the gates of a new earth never closing, and there not being anything 'impure', or anyone who brings 'deceit' and 'shame'. How does that work? And it sparks other similar questions: how do I live in this world but not be consumed by it? How do I keep my heart open, yet have healthy boundaries? How can I keep God's commands without becoming legalistic?

I wonder if there isn't a common answer to all of these. It isn't that God closes the gates to those who would spoil; it is that their spoilt-ness prevents them from entering. The purity of the new creation is simply incompatible with their impurity. It repels them like polarised magnets; they simply cannot coexist.

And while this is perfectly the case in this new ecology, this renewed cosmos, we can taste it now. Each day this week we have seen that we have a part to play and that, no matter how hopeless it seems, we can make a difference. I love the way this passage endorses this. Even though it is only through the work of Jesus that we are able to share his purity, human kings and human nations add splendour, glory and honour to the final scene. We, who so devastatingly empowered the destructive trajectory of the cosmos, get to be a part of the solution.

Together with God, we can reimagine a hope for the world we live in today.

† Lord, would you reveal to us areas where we are disrespecting your creation and help us to learn how to better care for your earth, which we are blessed to be a part of?

For further thought

How are you working with God to recreate the cosmos he entrusted to us?

Travelling

1 People on the move

Notes by **Joshua Taylor**

Joshua Taylor is an Anglican priest in New Zealand, currently working on his PhD in Theology through Otago University. He is married to Jo, with three daughters (Phoebe, Esther and Eve), and together they have been exploring what it means to follow the way of Jesus as a family. In his spare time, Joshua loves to run, read and play in his pottery studio. Joshua has used the NRSVA for these notes.

Sunday 18 August
Adam and Eve leave Eden

Read Genesis 3:22–24

Therefore the Lord God sent him forth from the garden of Eden, to till the ground from which he was taken. He drove out the man; and at the east of the garden of Eden he placed the cherubim, and a sword flaming and turning to guard the way to the tree of life.

(verses 23–24)

This passage captures the tragedy of the fall. In their desire to be like God, Adam and Eve have failed to bear the likeness of God. They have turned their faces from him, and the consequences ripple outward through the whole story of the Bible. They are sent eastward out of the garden, on a road of suffering and restless wandering.

This week we will be exploring the theme of being 'on the move'. In today's reading, Adam and Eve are on the move, away from God. Sadly, this is part of our stories, too. 'Sin' is the word we use to describe the impulse within every one of us to turn our faces from God. Thankfully, God is gracious. In this story, even though Adam and Eve are cast out of the garden, they are clothed by God and given a promise. This promise is fulfilled in the good news of Jesus Christ, who, in his life, death and resurrection, breaks the power of sin and death and invites us to come home. The Christian life can be thought about as a journey home to God. A journey Jesus leads us on.

† Lord, when we are tempted to turn from you and walk in our own way, draw our eyes to Jesus Christ, who calls us home to trust in and walk with you. Amen

Monday 19 August
Abram sets out for Canaan

Read Genesis 12:1–9

Now the LORD said to Abram, 'Go from your country and your kindred and your father's house to the land that I will show you. I will make of you a great nation, and I will bless you, and make your name great, so that you will be a blessing.'

(verses 1–2)

'Go!' This word has energy and vigour. It is a sending word. This word occurs many times in Scripture, often uttered by God to his people. In today's story we hear of God calling Abram to 'go'. God will bless Abram and his family, and through them he will bless the nations of the world. In Abram a gospel seed is planted as God gathers a people to bless, through whom he will bless and rescue the world. Likewise, in Mark 16:15, Jesus says: 'Go into all the world and proclaim the good news to the whole creation.'

As we reflect on God's 'go' to Abram, and to the first disciples of Jesus, we might reflect on God's 'go' to us, too. Where is God calling us to go? This theme of discerning the call of God in our lives is an important one for each of us as we follow Jesus. God calls each of us to participate in his mission to the world, being a blessing wherever we are. God will use our gifts, and wherever we are there will be opportunities to respond to God's call. This will work its way out in our everyday lives – our work, our lives at home and in our communities. Are we listening for God's 'go'?

We serve a sending God, who blesses his people and calls us to a life of faithfulness. That call is to each and every one of us. Will we hear it afresh today?

† Lord, like Abram, help us to be people who hear your call and who follow. Amen

For further thought
Where has God called you to be a blessing right now? How can you be faithful to this call this week?

Tuesday 20 August
Travelling to freedom

Read Exodus 14:10–29

But Moses said to the people, 'Do not be afraid, stand firm, and see the deliverance that the LORD will accomplish for you today; for the Egyptians whom you see today you shall never see again. The LORD will fight for you, and you have only to keep still.'

(verses 13–14)

The story of God delivering his people from slavery in Egypt helps us understand what is going on in the Bible. The Bible is full of lots of stories about amazing figures – Abraham, Moses, Jacob, Elijah, Esther, Ruth, Isaiah … the list could go on. But none of these people are the main characters of the story. The main character throughout is God – a God who rescues his people.

Here in Exodus, we see that the Lord is central. The Lord will deliver the people, the Lord will fight for them. Moses doesn't lead the people out of slavery, God does. Yes, God calls Moses to work with him – yet without him parting the sea, the people would have been back in Egypt where they started.

This perspective of God at the centre is an important one for us. It is God we put our hope in. It is God who delivers us and rescues us through Jesus Christ. If we have any hope for freedom from the bondage of sin and death, it is only through the Lord. When we are tempted to carve our own paths, to set out on our own journeys, we echo the grumbles of the Israelites who say: 'It would have been better for us to serve the Egyptians than to die in the wilderness' (Exodus 14:12b). This inclination to have things our way, even if it means suffering and misery, is sadly a pattern of sinful human behaviour we come back to all too easily. Yet God calls us to trust in his salvation rather than carving our own paths.

† Lord, let us put our trust in you. May we trust in you as our Saviour, who will lead us, guide us and provide for us. Amen

For further thought

Do you know God as your rescuer and redeemer? In which ways do you resist God's guidance and prefer to carve your own path in life?

Travelling – 1 People on the move

August

Wednesday 21 August
Into the promised land

Read Joshua 3:14–17

While all Israel were crossing over on dry ground, the priests who bore the ark of the covenant of the LORD stood on dry ground in the middle of the Jordan, until the entire nation finished crossing over the Jordan.

(verse 17)

I remember going on school camps as a teenager by the braided rivers of Canterbury in New Zealand. These powerful, flowing rivers can be dangerous to cross. We were taught how to link arms and work together to cross parts of the rivers safely. But there were certainly parts we would never attempt because they were simply too dangerous.

We read in today's story that the river waters are in flood, overflowing the banks. How will the people get across into the promised land? This is when God, yet again, steps in as the deliverer of his people. The miraculous nature of the story is highlighted as it is recounted here in Joshua. Just in case we don't get it, we hear the words of Joshua to the people reflecting on this event, saying that God did this 'so that all the peoples of the earth may know that the hand of the Lord is mighty, and so that you may fear the Lord your God for ever' (Joshua 4:24). In other words, this event leads to the praise and worship of our awesome God.

One of my favourite hymns is 'Guide Me, O Thou Great Redeemer'. I've sung it many times at church. It contains these beautiful words: 'When I tread the verge of Jordan, bid my anxious fears subside; death of death, and hell's destruction, land me safe on Canaan's side.'[1] This song draws directly on the imagery of today's reading. What an incredible picture we see in this story of the people crossing the Jordan. All we can do in response is worship in awe.

† Almighty God, you delivered your people across the Jordan, just as you have delivered us from the power of sin and death. We praise you for your faithfulness, in Jesus' name. Amen

For further thought

Can you recall what God has done in your life and in the lives of those around you? Let these stories prompt you to give him praise and worship.

[1] William Williams, translated by Peter Williams, 'Guide Me, O Thou Great Redeemer' (public domain, 1771).

Thursday 22 August
A risky journey

Read Ruth 1:1–19a

But Ruth said, 'Do not press me to leave you or to turn back from following you! Where you go, I will go; where you lodge, I will lodge; your people shall be my people, and your God my God. Where you die, I will die – there will I be buried. May the LORD do thus and so to me, and more as well, if even death parts me from you!'

(verses 16–17)

Relationships with in-laws can be difficult at times. For some families that might be an understatement! Naomi and her two daughters-in-law come from very different backgrounds. Naomi was an Israelite who had travelled to Moab to escape famine, and Orpah and Ruth – both Moabites – had married her sons.

There was enmity and disagreement between the Moabites and the Israelites. The Moabites worshipped various gods, but not Yahweh, the God of Israel. So when Naomi is widowed and her sons die, she seeks to return home. It makes sense for Orpah to remain in Moab with her family. Ruth's decision to go with Naomi is a departure from what would have been expected, and frankly it is an outrageous decision. Ruth leaves the gods of Moab behind and pledges to serve Naomi and her God, declaring to be a faithful friend to Naomi as long as she lives.

As I hear this story, I think of the new community that forms around Jesus. Among his earliest followers, many decide to make a break from previous allegiances and commitments – to family or friends, even – to be part of the community that follows Jesus. We might think of Jesus' words when he says: 'Everyone who has left houses or brothers or sisters or father or mother or children or fields, for my name's sake, will receive a hundredfold, and will inherit eternal life' (Matthew 19:29).

What we see modelled by Ruth is a risky journey; a commitment to place herself in the hands of the God of Israel as she journeys with, and serves, Naomi and her God.

† Father, we thank you for the inspiring commitment and courage of Ruth. Inspire us to love and serve you all the days of our lives, for the sake of your Son, Jesus Christ. Amen

For further thought
What risks has God called you to take in being faithful to Jesus?

Travelling – 1 People on the move

August

237

Friday 23 August
Into exile

Read Jeremiah 29:1–14

Build houses and live in them; plant gardens and eat what they produce. Take wives and have sons and daughters; take wives for your sons, and give your daughters in marriage, that they may bear sons and daughters; multiply there, and do not decrease. But seek the welfare of the city where I have sent you into exile, and pray to the LORD on its behalf.

(verses 5–7a)

Here Jeremiah writes to the exiles, the people of God who have been taken into captivity in Babylon. Just as the Lord had delivered the people, it was the Lord who carried them into exile, allowing them to experience the consequences of their disobedience and unfaithfulness.

This is a sobering thought; one that I believe Paul echoes in Romans 1 when he speaks of God giving the people over to their sinful ways. In turning away from God, the people have turned away from the very source of their life and hope. The exile was an incredibly painful moment for the people of God, because so many of their hopes were tied to the land they had been led into by the Lord.

So here they are in Babylon, in a foreign land. False prophets were proclaiming it would be over soon, but Jeremiah knows better. He tells the people to settle in, to build houses, to plant gardens and to marry. The immediate response might be one of disbelief. Yet, through Jeremiah, God calls the exiles to be a hopeful people; not just in thought, but also in deed. Building, planting, marrying and bearing children amid despair, homelessness and disarray are incredibly hopeful acts.

These are concrete and real ways of affirming hope in a God who will eventually deliver the people and bring them home. This is also true for the faithful today, wherever we are. We are called to be a people of hope, even in dark times – building, planting, praying and trusting in the future God has for each and every one of us.

† Lord, wherever we may be, help us to be a people of hope. Help us to build, not to tear down, and to trust in the good future you have planned for your world. Amen

For further thought

What concrete acts of hope is God calling you to where you are? What are you building that will last in God's good future?

Saturday 24 August
Return to Jerusalem

Read Ezra 1

In the first year of King Cyrus of Persia, in order that the word of the LORD by the mouth of Jeremiah might be accomplished, the LORD stirred up the spirit of King Cyrus of Persia so that he sent a herald throughout all his kingdom, and also in a written edict declared: 'Thus says King Cyrus of Persia: The LORD, the God of heaven, has given me all the kingdoms of the earth, and he has charged me to build him a house at Jerusalem in Judah.'

(verses 1–2)

Yesterday we looked at exile, and today we read of a wonderful returning home for God's people. As we have seen throughout this week, God is the prime mover, stirring the heart of King Cyrus of Persia to let the exiles return to Jerusalem. This shows how the God of Israel is not just any god. Yahweh is not a parochial deity. He is not just the God of Israel; rather, he is God of all the earth.

The theme for this week has been 'journeys'. We have seen people on the move, and we have seen God at the heart of this story – leading, rescuing and redeeming his people. In today's story the exiles return home. For Christians, this story of homecoming is at the heart of our journey; a journey that ends in a heavenly Jerusalem. Revelation 21:3b–4 speaks of the new heaven and new earth to come: 'See, the home of God is among mortals. He will dwell with them; they will be his peoples, and God himself will be with them; he will wipe every tear from their eyes. Death will be no more; mourning and crying and pain will be no more, for the first things have passed away.'

We started our journey this week in the garden of Eden, where Adam and Eve go their own way, away from God. We finish here, reflecting on the exiles returning home, and the hope we have for the future, when God will call us home to the heavenly Jerusalem through Jesus Christ.

† Lord, thank you that you journey with us. Thank you that even when we wander you don't reject us, but you call us home through Jesus Christ. Amen

For further thought
What difference does it make to live in light of the heavenly Jerusalem described by the book of Revelation?

Travelling – 1 People on the move

August

Travelling

2 God's travel directions

Notes by **Emma Wagner**

Emma spent thirteen years in missions, leading teams and initiatives to reach out and share God's love. Emma now lives in Scotland with her husband, three children and her sourdough starter, Doris. Under pen name Emma Browne, she co-authors books for nine- to twelve-year-olds (the Jack & Bea's Survival Guide to Church series) and writes contemporary Christian romance novels. Emma has used the NIVUK for these notes.

Sunday 25 August
Taking responsibility

Read Jonah 1:1–17

He answered, 'I am a Hebrew and I worship the Lord, the God of heaven, who made the sea and the dry land.'

(verse 9)

Jonah got on the ship and met the sailors, and for the rest of the chapter this story is about them. They were people who knew from experience to fear the seas – and they believed that a storm meant someone had upset some god somewhere. This storm was beyond their ability to safely navigate, reminding us perhaps of the storm on the lake that the disciples encountered.

So the sailors do what they can to appease every god they can think of, calling on any god that might be able to overpower the storm. When Jonah acknowledges that his God, 'who made the sea and the dry land', is responsible for this storm, they cry out to him and throw Jonah overboard. And when the sea calms down, they know the fear of the Lord. Though Jonah was in the wrong, these sailors meet God when he takes responsibility for his actions.

Sometimes we are in the wrong. We know we've made a mess of things and see how it affects the people around us, and we are ashamed. That's when we get to choose how to act. We can choose denial. Or, like Jonah, we can choose to take responsibility for our actions and thereby demonstrate the love of God.

† Lord, help me take responsibility for the consequences of my choices, and may my repentance honour you.

Monday 26 August
You are there

Read Jonah 2:1 – 3:3a

But you, LORD my God, brought my life up from the pit.

(2:6b)

Sometimes our choices take us to the depths of despair and, like Jonah, we're stuck in the chaos, seemingly with no way out. Most of us know what it's like to choose our own way instead of God's, and to suffer as a result. From Eden onwards, the consequence of choosing to go our own way is that something dies, and Jonah experiences this in a graphic way – by being thrown into the sea.

Was three days in the belly of a fish God's way of punishing Jonah for going to Tarshish instead of Nineveh? God isn't into punishing people, so what else might be going on here?

When Jonah is thrown overboard into the chaos of the sea – which the ancient world would have understood as a form of hell – God provides a fish to keep him safe. And when Jonah cries out to God from this awful place, he finds that God has not abandoned him, even there. Psalm 139:8b says: 'If I make my bed in the depths, you are there.' As Jonah calls on God, God answers him and gives him another chance. A chance to make a different choice.

When have our choices led us to the depths of despair? Where are we stuck in hell, feeling far away from God? Where has God, in his great kindness, provided a safe space for us, even as the terrible consequences of our wrong choices or the wrong choices of others rage around us?

† Lord, thank you that even when I am unfaithful, you are faithful. Even when I do wrong, you keep extending kindness towards me.

For further thought
In the darkest times of your life, how has God shown you his kindness?

Travelling – 2 God's travel directions

August

Tuesday 27 August
Follow that star

Read Matthew 2:1–12
'Where is the one who has been born king of the Jews? We saw his star when it rose and have come to worship him.'

(verse 2)

Are you into astrology? Probably not. You've probably been told to stay clear of such things – that it is ungodly. However, some of the first people to visit Jesus were the Magi. They are likely to have been astrologers from Persia who looked for signs about the future in the stars.

In Christian tradition, they have often been referred to as the three wise men. Three based on the number of gifts and wise because they sought out Jesus. Yet if we simply labelled them based on their background (non-Jewish astrologers), we probably would have dismissed or avoided them as ungodly.

Yet even if Mary and Joseph were surprised when these foreigners showed up with their strange gifts and ideas, they welcomed them. They probably weren't used to meeting Magi, or to seeing people worship God like that, but nevertheless they allowed them to meet with Jesus in their way.

When I married my husband, I wondered about his Christian faith. He never seemed to read his Bible, pray or sing worship songs like I expected. He didn't even particularly enjoy going to church (gasp!). But he loved connecting with God in nature or through mindfulness, and his life was full of the fruit of the Spirit. As time went on, I started to see that maybe God could be found in ways that I'm not used to. If Jesus could be found through astrology, what other ways (even ways that I might even consider 'ungodly') might people find him? Perhaps it is the seeking with all our heart that is more important than the ways we do the seeking.

† Lord, help me to welcome people who seek you, even when they worship you in a way I'm not used to.

For further thought

Who do I know that may be seeking Jesus in ways I might consider 'ungodly'? How can I welcome them, as Mary and Joseph welcomed the Magi?

Wednesday 28 August
Jesus the refugee

> **Read Matthew 2:13–15, 19–23**
> *So he got up, took the child and his mother during the night and left for Egypt.*
>
> (verse 14)

In recent years, migrants have been in the news a lot. We see people in dinghies trying to cross the sea to get to safety, walls being built to stop migrants from entering 'our' lands, newspaper headlines about how immigrants are 'stealing our jobs' and so on. Foreigners are seen as a threat.

Yet God cares about foreigners. Leviticus 19:34a says: 'The foreigner residing among you must be treated as your native-born. Love them as yourself.' He honours them (see the book of Ruth, where Ruth the foreigner shows God's faithful love to his people; or indeed the lineage of Jesus, where four out of the five women mentioned are foreigners).

And he chose to become one. Jesus was a refugee in Egypt for a time. Jesus was displaced, he couldn't go back to his home. He was a foreigner in a different region. Was Jesus a threat? Of course he was. He threatened the establishment and caused all sorts of chaos. And he was also the biggest gift the world has ever had. God decided that the gift of Jesus wouldn't be complete unless he came as a foreigner, as a refugee.

What if being called to follow Jesus is not just about *loving* the foreigner, but about *becoming* the foreigner? Being a citizen of the kingdom of God is, after all, rather different from being a citizen of a country in this world. The kingdom of God operates differently from any other country.

† Lord, help me to see you in the foreigners I meet. Help me to love the foreigners around me.

For further thought

How am I a foreigner in the country I'm living in? In what ways am I a gift in disguise to the people around me?

Thursday 29 August
Walking to Emmaus

Read Luke 24:13–35

They asked each other, 'Were not our hearts burning within us while he talked with us on the road and opened the Scriptures to us?'

(verse 32)

In my thirties, after years of journeying with Jesus, I found myself with questions. As my questions grew, I had to take them seriously. Some of the things I'd taken for granted about God didn't actually have any basis in the Bible, in truth or in my experience. This was distressing for me and for the people around me. Had I got it all wrong? Did I even believe in God any more?

In the account of the walk to Emmaus, there are two people, one of whom was Cleopas. The other we don't know much about. It wasn't one of the Eleven, because Cleopas and his friend later go to tell the Eleven what had happened. It could have been anyone. A woman, perhaps? I like that we don't know them – they were anonymous, like most of us. Somebody like you and me. Somebody who had loved Jesus and found his death upsetting on every level. Somebody who didn't understand how it all fitted together. Someone with all the questions.

Though my questions, thoughts and doubts were frustrating, they were also good. Looking back, I see how my heart was burning. I was determined not to settle for easy answers. I see how Jesus walked next to me, listening to my questions and gently discussing them with me. Just as he did with Cleopas and his friend.

Do you, like Cleopas and his friend, love Jesus but have all kinds of questions about him? Know that Jesus will walk (not run) next to you as you unpack your questions. None is too big for him.

† Lord, thank you for taking my questions seriously. Thank you that you want to reason with me and that you want to share truth with me.

For further thought

Taking our questions seriously often takes time, and that can feel frustrating. But Jesus isn't frustrated by our questions. He loves them.

Friday 30 August
The believers scattered

Read Acts 8:1a–8

So there was great joy in that city.

(verse 8)

I don't think persecution is ever God's idea, but something about the hardship and grief experienced by the believers in Jerusalem made them say, 'No. We will not sit idly in grief as people are being killed. We must get up and do something!' Instead of picking up swords and fighting back, the followers of Jesus scattered throughout Judea and Samaria, and fought back in the only way that made sense to them: by bringing joy. They preached the word, people were healed and there was joy.

Isaiah 61:3 says that God will give us 'the oil of joy instead of mourning, and a garment of praise instead of a spirit of despair'. This is the way the kingdom of heaven works. Though we may experience hardship and grief, God offers fullness of life for us and for the people around us.

I used to be a missionary. I worked with lots of different forms of evangelism. You name the type of outreach and there's a high likelihood I've done it. Still, the idea of 'preaching the word wherever they went' is not an idea I'm particularly comfortable with. I know very few people that are. But the early followers of Jesus in Jerusalem weren't just told to go and preach the word in Samaria and Judea. No! They felt the pressure of this world as it closed in on them, and would not settle for a world in which grief and hardship were acceptable. Fuelled by the knowledge that God's love makes a difference in this world, they went about sharing that love with other people.

† Jesus, help me not to accept the status quo, the injustices or the grief in this world, but instead to rise up and share your joy with the people around me.

For further thought
How can I share God's joy with the people around me today?

Travelling – 2 God's travel directions

August

245

Saturday 31 August
Spreading the word

Read Acts 16:6–10

After Paul had seen the vision, we got ready at once to leave for Macedonia, concluding that God had called us to preach the gospel to them.

(verse 10)

How do you react to a change of plans? I don't tend to handle it well. I get disappointed, annoyed and start feeling like everything sucks. I'm great at staying in that pit of defeat, where I'm frustrated and know that nothing is going to cheer me up. I almost revel in it. However, there's a rather obvious downside. By staying in my disappointment, I miss opportunities to throw myself into the next good thing God has for me.

Paul and his friends had already faced a few setbacks when they received a vision of the man in Macedonia calling for help. But they weren't going to let a few setbacks keep them from the new opportunities God had for them. 'At once', as soon as they received this vision, they prepared to take a new path. Imagine being that open to God. Imagine not letting your defeats prevent you from saying yes to the new thing God has for you. A friend of mine says followers of Jesus are called to be FAT: flexible, available and teachable. I think he's on to something.

When I'm stuck in disappointment, I'm not flexible or teachable, and I stop being available to God. I make up my own mind about what life is like (it sucks), instead of letting him show me new things. What are some of the defeats you're holding on to? How are they keeping you from responding to the next opportunity God has for you? What would help you let go of your disappointment?

† Lord, help me to let go of my disappointment. Show me where I can take part in what you're doing. Help me to help with a willing heart.

For further thought

What would it look like if you were to respond to God at once when he showed you a new opportunity?

The Gospel of Mark (4)

1 Not to be served, but to serve

Notes by **Eve Parker**

Eve is Lecturer of Modern Theology at Manchester University, UK. She is author of *Theologising with the Sacred 'Prostitutes' of South India* (Brill, 2021) and *Trust in Theological Education* (SCM, 2022). She previously worked at Durham University, the Council for World Mission and for the United Reformed Church. Eve is passionate about intercultural ministries and liberationist theologies. She is married to James, and they have three children. Eve has used the NRSVA for these notes.

Sunday 1 September
The wealthy man

Read Mark 10:17–34

Jesus said to them again, 'Children, how hard it is to enter the kingdom of God! It is easier for a camel to go through the eye of a needle than for someone who is rich to enter the kingdom of God.'

(verses 24b–25)

The unequal distribution of wealth across the world is staggering. The richest ten per cent of the world's population owns seventy-six per cent of the wealth. This means that the wealthy elites have their own kingdom on earth. They have access to the best healthcare, education, property, clothing, food and holidays. So why would they want to give it up?

The wealthy ten per cent are also the ones who run the world: the CEOs of multinational corporations, the owners of media networks, the politicians who can control the taxation system in favour of the rich. It would no doubt be exceptionally difficult for them to give up such privileges for the sake of others … or to enter the kingdom of God, where they cease to be gods themselves. A kingdom that Jesus tells us involves the wealthy man selling what he owns and giving the money to the poor (10:21).

This kingdom of wealthy demigods on earth has forced many of us to make choices between heating homes and having food on the table. Simply look around at the world we live in; where access to health care is limited; where children die of malnutrition. It is a kingdom of injustice.

† We pray for all who are struggling in earthly kingdoms of inequality and who long for God's eternal kingdom to be realised.

Monday 2 September
A leader who serves

Read Mark 10:35–45

Jesus called them and said to them, 'You know that among the Gentiles those whom they recognize as their rulers lord it over them, and their great ones are tyrants over them. But it is not so among you; but whoever wishes to become great among you must be your servant, and whoever wishes to be first among you must be slave of all. For the Son of Man came not to be served but to serve, and to give his life a ransom for many.'

(verses 42–45)

More than eighty years ago the English author, George Orwell, wrote his famous essay 'England Your England'. In it, he describes England as 'a land of snobbery and privilege, ruled largely by the old and silly'.[1] Orwell spoke of a context that is comparable to the one called out by Jesus in Mark's Gospel, where a culture of deference is displayed by the Gentile masses to the tyrants who lord it over the people. The rulers seem to be indifferent to the injustices of persecution.

When power is held by those who inhabit a world that serves only the elite, it operates through an ethos of entitlement. But who are the ordinary people that accept such models of leadership driven by greed over servitude? What interests me about Jesus' point on leadership here is the aspect of recognition: who we recognise as leaders and why. He polarises the leadership of the tyrant against that of a leadership of servanthood and solidarity, and by doing so he highlights that there is an alternative possibility.

In today's passage, James and John are called on to imitate Jesus' own selfless service and willingness to suffer on behalf of others. Jesus not only appears to challenge corrupt models of tyrannic leadership, but also calls into question the choice of the masses when it comes to choosing 'leaders'. He appears to suggest that the people must become conscious of the injustices of corrupt leadership in order to bring about change.

† We pray for those with power to be guided by a selfless love for the common good that encourages a leadership of integrity, compassion and justice.

For further thought

Which leadership attributes do we tend to recognise as being critical today?

[1] G. Orwell, 'England Your England' (public domain, 1941).

Bartimaeus witnesses the Messiah

Read Mark 10:46–52

When he heard that it was Jesus of Nazareth, he began to shout out and say, 'Jesus, Son of David, have mercy on me!' Many sternly ordered him to be quiet, but he cried out even more loudly, 'Son of David, have mercy on me!'

(verses 47–48)

Throughout the four Gospels we see instances of Jesus carrying out divine acts of healing. In this passage from Mark's Gospel we read of Jesus healing a blind man named Bartimaeus.

Bartimaeus, son of Timaeus, is sitting at the roadside and calls out, 'Jesus, Son of David.' In doing so, Bartimaeus adopts a title that is significant, as it is often used in the New Testament as a way of referring to Jesus as the Messiah or the anointed one, promised by God to come and save the people. It is a reference to the prophecies in the Hebrew Bible about the coming Messiah. According to these prophecies, the Messiah would be a descendant of King David, and would deliver the people from their enemies and establish God's kingdom on earth.

Bartimaeus recognises that Jesus is the promised Messiah prior to the act of the miracle of Jesus giving him sight. It is a significant moment in the story because it highlights the importance of faith. Bartimaeus also refers to Jesus as 'rabbi', highlighting Jesus' authority as a religious teacher and leader.

We also see Jesus living out the leadership he had promised (10:35–45), he is inclusive in his ministry, and he is known as a leader who represents wisdom, nurture and new life. Bartimaeus recognised these truths prior to the act of the miracle because he had faith in the teachings, leadership and salvation of Jesus.

† We pray today for the courage and strength to be truthful witnesses to your love and grace. May our words and actions reflect the love of Jesus.

For further thought

Consider the ways in which faith and persistence have given you strength in times of need.

Wednesday 4 September
Jesus curses the fig tree

Read Mark 11:12–14

On the following day, when they came from Bethany, he was hungry. Seeing in the distance a fig tree in leaf, he went to see whether perhaps he would find anything on it. When he came to it, he found nothing but leaves, for it was not the season for figs. He said to it, 'May no one ever eat fruit from you again.' And his disciples heard it.

(verses 12–14)

When reading the story of Jesus cursing the fig tree in the current context of the climate crisis, my concern and grief is for the tree. It implies the collapse of an ecosystem – especially after the curse of Jesus. This passage paints a potentially tragic scene when read from an ecological perspective – particularly when we take into consideration the destruction of the natural environment, including the loss of biodiversity as a result of human activity, such as the burning of fossil fuels and deforestation.

The fig tree, in its Jewish context, is symbolic of life, abundance and God's favour. Many scholars claim it was used by the Gospel writer in this passage as a prophetic curse to portray God's coming judgement against the corruption of the temple. Shortly after Jesus curses the fig tree, he enters the temple in Jerusalem, and begins to drive out the merchants and money changers doing business there.

How might an ecological reading of this text speak of God's judgement on humanity today, particularly if the fig tree is representative of the natural world or the environment? Could Jesus' curse be seen as a warning or a judgement on humanity for our failure to care for the earth and preserve its resources? In such a reading, the fig tree could be seen as a symbol of God's disappointment at humanity's disregard for the environment, and as a call to repent and change our ways.

† We pray for God's wisdom and guidance as we work to address the climate crisis. May we find ways to reduce our impact on the earth. We pray for just, equitable and sustainable solutions that protect the most vulnerable among us.

For further thought

We can no longer afford to do things the way we have always done them. The climate crisis demands leadership that will help bring about radical change in the way we live, work and relate to each other and to the natural world.

Thursday 5 September
The authority of Jesus is questioned

Read Mark 11:27–33

Jesus said to them, 'I will ask you one question; answer me, and I will tell you by what authority I do these things. Did the baptism of John come from heaven, or was it of human origin? Answer me.' They argued with one another, 'If we say, "From heaven," he will say, "Why then did you not believe him?" But shall we say, "Of human origin"?' – they were afraid of the crowd, for all regarded John as truly a prophet.

(verses 29–32)

Jesus is confronted by the chief priests, scribes and elders, who seek to challenge his authority and ask him in whose authority he is acting. Jesus responds with a question of his own, asking them about the baptism of John. They then discuss what they should say in response.

Those with power often appear confused about telling the truth. Their answers are sometimes swayed by popular opinion or ideology; rooted not in compassion, but in control. In this case in Mark, those who seek to maintain religious authority question the legitimacy of Jesus and refuse to state whether John's baptism came from heaven. They appear hesitant to deny this, but more through their fear of the crowd than their fear of God.

It is no surprise that the religious elite are concerned about Jesus, having witnessed him overturn tables in the temple. They know they must challenge him, as he represents a threat to their power and authority, as well as to their system of economic exploitation in Palestine.

Jesus' refusal to show deference to their questioning and authority served only to further antagonise them. He publicly humiliated them through his wisdom, faith and continued solidarity with John the Baptist. Jesus presents a leadership that is not afraid to engage in conflict, particularly if it is for the sake of the oppressed. This is a type of leadership that recognises the power dynamics at play in society, and works to challenge and dismantle systems of oppression and inequality.

† We see the suffering and injustice that exists in the world, and we long for a better way. We pray for solidarity, justice and the courage to resist those who oppress.

For further thought

Conflict is often inevitable in the face of resisting oppression. Think about how we can navigate conflicts with compassion while also seeking to bring about change.

The Gospel of Mark (4) – 1 Not to be served, but to serve

September

Friday 6 September
A landlord and his tenants

Read Mark 12:1–12

'A man planted a vineyard, put a fence around it, dug a pit for the wine press, and built a watch-tower; then he leased it to tenants and went to another country. When the season came, he sent a slave to the tenants to collect from them his share of the produce of the vineyard. But they seized him, and beat him, and sent him away empty-handed.'

(verses 1b–3)

I have always struggled with this passage. My instant reaction is to question the acts of the man who plants the vineyard, as for me Jesus' parable speaks of class conflict in Jerusalem. The upper-class landowner appropriates peasant land, planting a vineyard to profit from labouring tenants and creating a system of dependency. He builds a fence and a watchtower around it, signifying the boundaries of his claim. These boundaries later become battlegrounds where voiceless slaves, owned by the wealthy man, are caught in the crossfire of a rich man's demand for *his* capital and the tenants' demand for their rights.

Many scholars argue that the landowner in this parable is representative of God, and that the tenants are those who refuse to do God's work. Read this way, the story appears to validate a social and economic model that portrays the landlord as righteous and the tenants as violent (which of course they are). But this fails to acknowledge the role of the landlord in creating a system of inequality and brutality. This is not about siding with the tenants; it is about questioning the power dynamics and the system at play, where the life of the enslaved seems irrelevant to the wealthy man.

Too often we see how the systemic structures of inequality have determined that some lives don't matter. In the UK today, thousands of people sleep on the streets every night. More than 17.5 million people live in overcrowded, dangerous, unaffordable conditions. Meanwhile, the wealthy elite continue to disproportionately capitalise from such inequality.

† May God guide us in knowing what is righteous and what is just. May he enable us to be led in life by the logos of hope, love and justice.

For further thought

How can we advocate for the enslaved who have no voice, and who have become the victims of narratives or structures of inequality?

Saturday 7 September
Discussion about the resurrection

Read Mark 12:13–27

Jesus said to them, 'Is not this the reason you are wrong, that you know neither the scriptures nor the power of God? For when they rise from the dead, they neither marry nor are given in marriage, but are like angels in heaven.'

(verses 24–25)

The Sadducees don't believe in the resurrection, and they invent a story intended to make those who do believe look foolish. But it backfires, and instead they end up looking foolish. This is a common problem. When we come to scripture with our views already fixed, we interpret everything in that light, no matter what the actual words might say. And in so doing, we misrepresent God to others and miss out on truth that could set us free.

So many situations seem irreversibly dead: a broken relationship, a dead-end job, a serious health issue, a financial problem, an accumulation of 'little' things that threaten to overwhelm. And our experience combines with the evidence to create filters through which we see the future. A future that is hopeless, inevitable and dark. When we come to look at scripture, the same filters colour our interpretation, and, like the Sadducees, we risk missing the hope that is there all the time.

In Luke 24:13–35, two men walk away from Jerusalem, the city of peace, into the darkness of the night on their way to Emmaus, their hearts and minds trapped by what they have seen – and we often do the same. Seeing Jesus crucified had blinded them to the Jesus walking with them. 'But we had hoped ...' they say.

In the discussion recorded in today's reading, Jesus shows us how to overcome, how to break through the traps we have made. Use the whole of scripture to build your view, not just the bits that support what you already think. And where your conclusion from the whole of scripture seems impossible, bear in mind that God can do the impossible! Jesus is alive.

† Living Lord, help us to see where we have become trapped in unhelpful ways of seeing scripture. Help us, by your Holy Spirit, to allow the truth to set us free.

For further thought

Are there any views you hold about God that are based more on your tradition than on the fullness of scripture?

The Gospel of Mark (4) – 1 Not to be served, but to serve

September

253

The Gospel of Mark (4)

2 Approaching the kingdom

Notes by **Bruce Jenneker**

Bruce Jenneker is a retired Anglican priest who lives alternately in Cape Town and with his grandsons' family in Johannesburg. During his thirty-five years of ministry, Bruce's passion and primary occupation was worship, liturgy and Christian formation. He has chosen to be 'completely retired', taking no vocational, ministerial or professional commitments. Bruce remains actively engaged in academic study, provides short daily prayers with an image and a hymn for a sick list, and writes similar evening prayers for Sundays and feast days. Bruce has used the NRSVA for these notes.

Sunday 8 September
The gospel imperative

Read Mark 12:28–34

'"He is one, and besides him there is no other"; and "to love him with all the heart, and with all the understanding, and with all the strength", and "to love one's neighbour as oneself", – this is much more important than all whole burnt-offerings and sacrifices.'

(verses 32b–33)

In response to Jesus' question: 'But who do you say I am?', Peter answers, 'You are the Messiah' (Mark 8:29). With the question of Jesus' identity settled, the rest of Mark's Gospel is an account of Jesus' mission. As the faithful suffering Messiah, his objective is Calvary; to suffer on the cross and to give his life as a ransom for many (Mark 10:45).

Jesus predicts his passion, death and resurrection three times (Mark 8:31–33, 9:30–32, 10:32–34). Each prediction is followed by a clear statement relating to the cost of following Jesus, the pioneer and paragon of self-sacrificial faithfulness to God's purposes.

After the third Passion prediction, followed by Jesus' triumphal entry into Jerusalem, a scribe who was impressed by the answers Jesus gave in response to the testing questions of the religious leaders, asked him, 'Of all the commandments, which is the most important?' Jesus announces his two-fold summary of the law: to faithfully love God and earnestly to love one's neighbour.

† O God, ruler of the universe, open our eyes and hearts to understand the laws your love commands, and enable us to live by them.

Monday 9 September
Located in the truth

Read Mark 12:35–40

'Beware of the scribes, who like to walk around in long robes, and to be greeted with respect in the market-places … They devour widows' houses and for the sake of appearance say long prayers.'

(verses 38–40)

In Mark 7:5–8, Jesus reminds the Scribes and Pharisees that Isaiah prophesied rightly about them: 'These people come near to me with their mouth and honour me with their lips, but their hearts are far from me' (Isaiah 29:13). Pretending to believe and act a certain way, while in fact believing and acting in the opposite way, is Jesus' ultimate definition of unfaithfulness. He urgently cautions us five times in Mark to beware of these hypocrites:

1 'Be careful,' Jesus warned them. 'Watch out for the yeast of the Pharisees and that of Herod' (8:15).
2 'Watch out for the teachers of the law. They like to walk around in flowing robes and be greeted with respect in the market-places.' (12:38).
3 'Watch out that no one deceives you' (13:5).
4 'You must be on your guard. You will be handed over to the local councils and flogged in the synagogues' (13:9).
5 'Be on guard! Be alert! You do not know when that time will come' (13:33).

We are summoned to a pilgrimage. Our goal is reunion and reconciliation with God. The quest is fraught with besetting lies, undermining falsehood and assaulting meanness.

In *The Pilgrim's Progress*, John Bunyan writes: 'There stood a man with his sword drawn, and his face all over with blood. Then said Mr. Great-Heart, Who art thou? The man made answer, saying, I am one whose name is Valiant-for-truth. I am a pilgrim, and am going to the Celestial City.'[1]

After a three-hour battle with Wildhead, Inconsiderate and Pragmatic, Valiant-for-truth single-handedly drives them off.

† God of truth, our arrogance makes us consumers of lies, our greed makes us peddlers of deceit. Deliver us from every falsehood and make us eager to embrace the truth, whatever the cost.

For further thought

Consider the truth of the news you hear and the stories you pass on.

[1] J. Bunyan, *The Pilgrim's Progress* (public domain, 1678).

Tuesday 10 September
Costing no less than everything

Read Mark 12:41–44

'Truly I tell you, this poor widow has put in more than all those who are contributing to the treasury. For all of them have contributed out of their abundance; but she out of her poverty has put in everything she had, all she had to live on.'

(verses 43–44)

We are bombarded by countless realities that demand our attention; our commitment, even. When one of them – a thing or a person or a cause – lays hold of us and affirms deeply who we are, it calls us to a fuller realisation of the possibilities that our time and place hold for us. We realise that this reality, above all others, holds the truth of who we are and what we can become.

Nothing whatsoever can hold us back from surrendering ourselves to this invitation. All that we are, all that we have and all that we hope to be – everything comes into the orbit of this new and defining reality.

It happens every time we truly fall in love. It also happens when faith is given and hope is kindled.

In the final lines of T. S. Eliot's poem 'Little Gidding', time and eternity merge into an explosion of tranquil contentment. It features two ancient symbols: fire and the rose. Fire is a symbol of passion and purification, and the rose is a symbol of beauty, innocence and love. Together they speak of the peace we find on arriving at authenticity. It costs no less than everything, but it is worth more than all that we have and are.

This the widow knew.

† God of love, your embrace offers everything and your caress holds us in eternal security. Let us lose ourselves in your offer, giving all that we have and all that we are.

For further thought

Consider what you are willing to abandon to obtain lasting love and enduring security. To what extent are your primary relationships transactional and conditional?

Wednesday 11 September
A matter of extreme urgency

Read Mark 13:1–20

'Brother will betray brother to death, and a father his child, and children will rise against parents and have them put to death; and you will be hated by all because of my name. But the one who endures to the end will be saved.'

(verses 12–13)

Mark is a concise Gospel; the shortest of the four Gospels. It can be read aloud in ninety minutes. It is a fast-paced Gospel, and in it he uses a word translated as 'straightway' or 'immediately' more than forty times.

Mark is a vibrant Gospel, full of dramatic details. It is an evangelistic Gospel. It urges commitment and action. It starts with: 'The beginning of the good news of Jesus Christ' and ends with: 'Go into all the world and proclaim the good news to the whole creation.'

The mission of Jesus is urgent; a crucial choice between possibility and disaster, life and death. It is insistent. Urgency does not come easily to us, lost, as we are, in world-weariness and lethargy: the challenges too absorbing, the demands overwhelming. We choose apathy, indifference and insulation rather than engagement. The Jesus of Mark is too urgent for us.

'Late I have loved you: a beauty so ancient and so new, late I have loved you! Behold - you were within but I was outside and searching for you there ... You were with me, and I was not with you ... You called and cried aloud and broke through my deafness: you gleamed, you shone bright and chased away my blindness.'[1]

In words generally attributed to American theologian Carl F. H. Henry: 'The gospel is only good news if it gets there in time.'

† God of time and eternity, you set life and death before us; a critical and urgent choice. Enable us to see the crucial choices that confront us in all things, and to choose well.

For further thought

Consider how you make life-determining choices and how you resolve the crucial compromises that confront you. What are your life-defining values and priorities?

[1] St Augustine, *Confessions* X.xxvii(38), translation: IBRA 2023.

Thursday 12 September
A matter of unwavering resolve

Read Mark 13:21–37

'And if anyone says to you at that time, "Look! Here is the Messiah!" or "Look! There he is!" – do not believe it. False messiahs and false prophets will appear and produce signs and omens, to lead astray, if possible, the elect. But be alert; I have already told you everything.'

(verses 21–23)

At the beginning of the journey to his destiny in Jerusalem, Jesus says to the crowd: 'If any want to become my followers, let them deny themselves and take up their cross and follow me. For those who want to save their life will lose it, and those who lose their life for my sake, and for the sake of the gospel, will save it' (Mark 8:34b–35).

There is something profoundly counterintuitive about this invitation. We are programmed for self-preservation, to hold on for dear life. We are asked to throw our lives away, and for what? To be weighed down with a burdensome cross? Surely that is to waste oneself.

Consider for a moment what we are holding on to so desperately. Comfort, possessions, esteem, success? In the scales of meaning, how do these vanities weigh against the embrace of God's love, the security of his amazing grace, the lavish provision of his loving-kindness? And above all, what could ever match the blessing of authenticity; being graced to be what you truly are and to become what you genuinely can be?

As fifteenth-century priest Thomas à Kempis explained in *The Imitation of Christ* (Penguin Classics, 1952), many of us proclaim Jesus and claim to love his kingdom, few of us are willing to bear the cross or to suffer for him.

† O God, who defines every boundary, and whose reach encompasses everyone everywhere, make us alert to what demands our ultimate loyalty, and keep us aware of the commitments that define us and our reality.

For further thought

Consider the commitments you have made and the extent to which you are faithful to them. Do you honour them in thought, word and deed?

Friday 13 September
Can this allegiance hold?

Read Mark 14:27–31

And Jesus said to them, 'You will all become deserters; for it is written, "I will strike the shepherd, and the sheep will be scattered."'

(verse 27)

Eighteenth-century abolitionist and reformer William Wilberforce declared: 'I am disturbed when I see the majority of so-called Christians having such little understanding of the real nature of the faith they profess. Faith is a subject of such importance that we should not ignore it because of the distractions or the hectic pace of our lives.'[1]

What was true of Christians then remains true today. We are distracted. Like dragonflies, we dash off to perch on random lily pads haphazardly, arbitrarily, indiscriminately. Commitment grows impossible for us. We are allergic to promises. We shy away from duty. We refuse obligations. Nothing is allowed to intrude on our self-absorption, our egotism. Let's call it what it is: our selfishness.

Is fidelity still possible? Is there a thread of dependability in the tangled web of our shielded desires?

The love that holds the universe together comes gently to draw our gaze to a fullness of goodness, truth and beauty that may be irresistible – if we can break free for once … and gaze.

Turning and turning in the widening gyre
The falcon cannot hear the falconer;
Things fall apart; the centre cannot hold;
Mere anarchy is loosed upon the world,
The blood-dimmed tide is loosed, and everywhere
The ceremony of innocence is drowned;
The best lack all conviction, while the worst
Are full of passionate intensity.[2]

† God of steadfast love, your trust in me is unwavering, despite my unreliability. I often lose sight of your blessed assurance. Embolden my acceptance of your nearness, that I may be wholly yours.

For further thought

Consider what makes you unwilling or unable to be consistently dedicated to God. What makes you waver? What threatens your ability to stand firm?

[1] W. Wilberforce, *Real Christianity*, revised edn (Ada: Bethany House, 2006), pp. 17–18.
[2] Extract from W. B. Yeats's 'Second Coming' (public domain, 1920).

Saturday 14 September
Lord, is it I?

Read Mark 14:66–72

After a little while the bystanders again said to Peter, 'Certainly you are one of them; for you are a Galilean.' But he began to curse, and he swore an oath, 'I do not know this man you are talking about.'

(verses 70–71)

We are afraid. Essentially, profoundly afraid. That the worst will happen. That we will be revealed for what we are: wounded, broken, damaged. That we cannot bear the consequences. We are afraid.

This deep-seated fear is in our nature, and was also in the Twelve's. It should not surprise us that the disciples scattered when disaster struck. They were afraid. They took cover. They ran away.

'In the midst of our lives, of our freedom and our struggles, we have to make a radical, absolute decision. And we never know when lightning will strike us out of the blue. It may be when we least expect to be asked whether we have the absolute faith and trust to say yes.'[1]

We can grasp the situation, we can understand the consequences and even the results of our cowardly timidity, but can we find the courage to say 'Yes'?

Our fear is met with two powerful graces: the steadfast loving-kindness of God, and the brave witness that makes saints and martyrs out of the least of us. God knows who we are. 'For he knows how we were made; he remembers that we are dust' (Psalm 103:14).

I think this quote from Rainer Maria Rilke is very apt: 'Perhaps all the dragons in our lives are princesses who are only waiting to see us act, just once, with beauty and courage. Perhaps everything that frightens us is, in its deepest essence, something helpless that wants our love.'[2]

† God of forgiveness, your unconditional love seeks and finds us, loves and saves us when we stray from your embrace or rebel against your goodness. Shatter the barricades of our hearts and save us.

For further thought

Consider the source of your rejection of God's love and your rebellion against his goodness. What makes you turn against God?

[1] K. Rahner, *The Great Church Year: The best of Karl Rahner's homilies, sermons and meditations*, translated by Harvey D. Egan (Chestnut Ridge, NY: Crossroad, 1993), p. 133.
[2] R. M. Rilke, *Letters to a Young Poet* translated by Stephen Mitchell (New York: Random House, 1984), p. 92.

Eat of the bread and drink of the cup

1 Bread

Notes by **Stephen Willey**

 Stephen is a Methodist minister who has been involved in mission to the economic world through industrial chaplaincies and work against human trafficking. Much of his ministry has been in areas of multiple deprivation. He is currently based at a city-centre church in Coventry, England, where he has encouraged the use of the arts to develop community cohesion and spirituality, and to address mental health issues, especially for people who are young or vulnerable. Stephen has used the NRSVA for these notes.

Sunday 15 September
Bread in a hurry

Read Exodus 12:33–39

They baked unleavened cakes of the dough that they had brought out of Egypt; it was not leavened, because they were driven out of Egypt and could not wait, nor had they prepared any provisions for themselves.

(verse 39)

I've moved house several times and have been surprised each time how quickly the contents of our home have been put into a van and taken away, leaving us with next to nothing. At that point we usually become aware that we're hungry and that some crockery or food we meant to keep back has disappeared into the van.

The Israelites had urged the Egyptians to give them valuable objects, but when they finally left they were in a hurry; too late to sort out a few things to make life a little better. They didn't have any leavened dough and had to start their time in the wilderness with unleavened bread.

Centuries of residency in Egypt (Exodus 12:40) concluded in a terrible rush, and the Israelites were unprepared for the reality of their escape. Perhaps they felt nervous about the challenges that would come and became hesitant at the last minute. There were certainly occasions after leaving Egypt when they questioned whether they had done the right thing. They missed aspects of their former lives, even though they were finally free. Unleavened bread, as part of the Passover meal, became hugely significant, reminding them that God's action had freed them from captivity.

† Loving God, help us to accept the changes that bring us closer to you but leave us without the comforts we usually enjoy.

261

Monday 16 September
Bread from heaven

Read Exodus 16:2–8

*The Israelites complained against Moses and Aaron in the wilderness.
The Israelites said to them, 'If only we had died by the hand of the Lord
in the land of Egypt, when we sat by the fleshpots and ate our fill of
bread; for you have brought us out into this wilderness to kill this whole
assembly with hunger.' Then the Lord said to Moses, 'I am going to rain
bread from heaven for you, and each day the people shall go out and
gather enough for that day.'*

(verses 2–4a)

I once knew a woman called Ramona, who I had met though some
charitable housing work. She was a refugee, and one of the many
difficulties she was facing was a lack of income. I was giving her
a lift home after a meeting when she asked me to stop the car.
Going into an Iranian bakery I had never noticed before, she picked
up three flat loaves – still hot from the oven – and gave them to
me for my family to eat. As we ate the bread so generously offered
at supper we felt ourselves touched by a new reality. We had never
eaten the like of this bread before. The flavour and the consistency
were something new. It was delicious!

The Israelites had never eaten manna before, but Moses told
them that God would feed them in a new way. A gift from God,
raining down on them, that they could gather each day and be
nourished one day at a time. On the day of collection the food
would be fresh and good, but it was not for storing up. Bread
that comes in unexpected, even miraculous, ways can change our
experience of the world.

The Israelites' experience of manna transformed their
understanding of identity and their understanding of how God
cared for them. God does a new thing for the Israelites, which
gives them hope and a new understanding of his generous love.

† God of life, you open the windows of heaven to give us good things. Help us to
appreciate how your gifts sustain us.

For further thought

When someone gave you food you had never eaten before, did it
open your heart to something new?

Eat of the bread and drink of the cup – 1 Bread   September

262

Tuesday 17 September
Not by bread alone

Read Deuteronomy 8:1–3

[God] humbled you by letting you hunger, then by feeding you with manna, with which neither you nor your ancestors were acquainted, in order to make you understand that one does not live by bread alone, but by every word that comes from the mouth of the Lord.

(verse 3)

As part of a Mennonite family, Anna's great-grandparents moved from Germany to Ukraine in order to find a life where they were free to worship as they wished and live without fear. A few generations later, Anna and Jacob (my children's great-grandparents) moved to Canada from Ukraine for the same reason. The family was on the move again; crossing the Atlantic and looking for a place to stay where they would be safe to practise their faith.

Arriving with just a few cents, they eventually made it to the province of Saskatchewan, where they settled. Anna used to say, 'They can take everything you have from you, but they can't take away your education.' Her life also showed me that 'they' can't take away your faith. Anna remained a Mennonite in Canada, able to get on with her life there without the threats she had lived with previously.

'One does not live by bread alone,' says the writer of Deuteronomy. The things that nourish us throughout our lives – the things that give meaning and direction – are often invisible. On life's journey we may not discover wealth, familiar bread, a settled place to live or even an education, but we have a God whose word offers sustenance, hope and direction. Although invisible, God's word is ultimately the food we need most. Day by day, God gives manna to the Israelites, revealing the invisible truth that, even in the wilderness, God's children are precious and loved, and will never be abandoned.

† Generous God, through reading your word, which guides and protects us, may we discover more of your life in the world.

For further thought

How can I be part of God's response to those who are seeking sustenance and security in uncertain times?

Eat of the bread and drink of the cup – 1 Bread

September

Wednesday 18 September
Bread for the hungry

Read Matthew 15:32–38

Then Jesus called his disciples to him and said, 'I have compassion for the crowd, because they have been with me now for three days and have nothing to eat; and I do not want to send them away hungry, for they might faint on the way.'

(verse 32)

Once while we were on pilgrimage, we had been walking all day and had set up our tent on a wild moor surrounded by heather and soft, damp peat. Tired and hungry, we lit our primus stove and cooked a simple meal of pasta, adding cheese when it was cooked. In our hunger it was like a banquet. There was a moment of realisation as I ate the food, when I said out loud, 'This is what I needed!' In the act of eating, I discovered how hungry I had been, but I did not realise this until I started to revive. I had not known my hunger.

That night we went to bed in the tent and slept soundly on the soft ground, despite it being a wild and windy night. After breakfast in the pouring rain, we set off with renewed energy.

In Matthew's Gospel, Jesus' feeding miracle comes from a compassionate and generous heart. He doesn't want people to faint from hunger, so he makes sure all are fed and satisfied. He doesn't just feed them with enough bread for the journey (like the manna); he gives out much more than they can eat, so there is food left over. By the time Jesus has fed them, they are far from being faint on their way. They are replete and ready for the journey. After they have eaten, the people come to a realisation that Jesus has satisfied their hunger with words and bread, and they desire to be with Jesus even more … if only for the bread!

† Pray for someone who has a problem with eating food, whatever the reason may be. Pray that, by God's love, they may be nourished.

For further thought

When have you needed something without knowing it until you have received it? How will you know if you need something again?

Thursday 19 September
Food for eternal life

Read John 6:25–34

Then Jesus said to them, 'Very truly, I tell you, it was not Moses who gave you the bread from heaven, but it is my Father who gives you the true bread from heaven. For the bread of God is that which comes down from heaven and gives life to the world.' They said to him, 'Sir, give us this bread always.'

(verses 32–34)

Maureen's husband died when she was a young mum. Left alone with three children, at a time when most mothers stayed at home looking after their families, Maureen managed to find work and care for her children. But something else remarkable happened. With three hungry children to feed and care for, her example became a sign of hope in her local community, where many people were struggling to make ends meet. Other children came to eat at Maureen's house and she always found food for each hungry child.

She shared with me that, although she lived in a 'rough' area of town, she always knew where her own three children were and who they were spending time with because those children also ate at her house. She became to the children of that area a protector and a source of comfort; not just because of the food, but because of the love she shared with so many young people, several of whom had difficulties at home – her love rooted in Christ.

Jesus wants to take the disciples beyond their earthly hunger and reveal to them the steadfast love of God. They need to know that God loves them and all the world, and wants to give something more precious even than bread. God gives us life itself. The bread that can sustain us is present in Christ, who can feed us when we are empty, alone or facing difficulties.

† Generous God, have compassion on all who are hungry and thirsty for the life you offer. May your life enrich each one.

For further thought

How does Christ enable you to share your bread, your life, with those who are in need?

The bread of life

> ### Read John 6:35–40
>
> *Jesus said to them, 'I am the bread of life. Whoever comes to me will never be hungry, and whoever believes in me will never be thirsty. But I said to you that you have seen me and yet do not believe.'*
>
> (verses 35–36)

A few hundred yards from where we lived in the city of Bradford, we discovered an artisan bakery producing all sorts of bread. Once we had found this warm, simple place that smelled of freshly baked goods, we used to go whenever we wanted a treat for ourselves or others.

The bread that Jesus offers is given in a surprising way. It is bread that sustains a person for the whole of life: something a person may come across with surprise – 'I can't believe this!', 'How can this be?' Such phrases are often used in relation to Jesus and in the Gospels. And here Jesus says, 'You have seen me and yet do not believe.'

There are moments when the disciples taste the bread that Jesus gives them and see who Jesus is. They discover that he is the bread of life. At those points they think they will never leave him. Indeed, Peter says, when asked if he will leave Jesus, 'Lord, to whom can we go? You have the words of eternal life' (John 6:68).

I no longer live in Bradford and have not been back to the bakery since I left, but I still remember that bread. The disciples left Jesus before his death, but through his resurrection Jesus remained what he had been to the disciples before his death – though perhaps they had not entirely realised it. He was the source of a bread that sustained their lives. Physically, life may be over when our physical bread runs out, but Christ's bread sustains life even beyond death.

† Risen Christ, bread of life, you never abandon us but sustain us each day. Satisfy our hunger and thirst each day with your presence.

For further thought

How can Christ sustain my life and the life of my community?

Saturday 21 September
The breaking of bread

Read Acts 2:41–47

All who believed were together and had all things in common; they would sell their possessions and goods, and distribute the proceeds to all, as any had need. Day by day, as they spent much time together in the temple, they broke bread at home and ate their food with glad and generous hearts, praising God and having the goodwill of all the people. And day by day the Lord added to their number those who were being saved.

(verses 44–47)

I was once eating with a group of young adults who had come together from six countries and four continents. Some at our table were struggling with grief and loss. As we ate a mixture of foods from different countries, we could all find something we liked to eat. We came from different continents and enjoyed different foods, but something united and nourished us; not just our bodies, but also our spirits. In the kitchen afterwards I said to my wife how I happy I was to hear laughter welling up in the hearts of these young people, several of whom had known suffering at a young age.

On another occasion at the house of a member who had died, the community gathered as I led a short service. Afterwards I was served food and, looking at the community around me, including the young people serving me, I was reminded of the importance of sharing food in times of sorrow.

Jesus understood the need to eat together, even as he prepared to offer himself as a sacrifice. After his resurrection, in these first chapters of the Acts of the Apostles, Jesus' early followers broke bread together and recalled that Last Supper. As they ate, prayed and were in fellowship together, they remembered – brought together and embodied – a new reality. This breaking of the bread, the source of new life among the early believers, nourished the early church's rapid growth: a new community of faith, sustained by the One who feeds his followers even now.

† Jesus, bread of life, break down barriers in the human family so often caused by grief and sorrow. Nourish us on our journey towards reconciliation.

For further thought

Where can you go in your community to share bread with new people and discover new possibilities?

Eat of the bread and drink of the cup – 1 Bread

September

267

Eat of the bread and drink of the cup

2 Wine

Notes by **Dortje Brandes**

Born in Germany, Dortje is the second of four children whose loving parents taught her about God from a young age. After finishing a degree in International Business, Dortje's quest to travel the world and discover God's plan for her life led her to missionary organisation YWAM, with whom she worked for six years. These days she feels privileged to work for both a church and a business. Dorje has used the NIVUK version for these notes.

Sunday 22 September
Gladness

Read Psalm 104:14–30

He makes grass grow for the cattle … wine that gladdens human hearts, oil to make their faces shine, and bread that sustains their hearts.

(verses 14–15)

Have you ever been amazed at how each apple seed contains the potential to produce several new apple trees? The writer of Psalm 104 had that same sense of awe, marvelling at the abundance in God's creation to provide food and shelter for every living creature.

When it comes to providing for humans, however, God doesn't just meet our basic needs. He created grapes that we can turn into wine, which gladdens our hearts; a drink the Bible often uses to symbolise joy, celebration and God's blessing, but which we can also abuse. Why would God take that risk? After all, we could live without wine.

Perhaps the answer·lies in the last part of verse 15: 'bread that sustains or strengthens their hearts'. Why 'hearts'? Wouldn't it make more sense for it to read: 'bread to sustain their bodies?' But as Jesus said, life is about more than food (Luke 12:23). God does not simply want us to survive, to just get by. He wants us to flourish, to have glad hearts, to live life to the full.

Hand on heart, how are you doing today? Are you just getting by, just 'surviving' the day or week? Or are you enjoying life and living it fully, as God longs for you to do? Whatever your current circumstances, look at the apple again, consider the grapes and the wine, and allow the God of abundance to gladden your heart.

† Lord, thank you for your goodness and abundance. Thank you that you don't just want me to get by; that you want me to flourish and live life to the full.

Monday 23 September
The Nazirite

Read Judges 13:2–7

'Now see to it that you drink no wine or other fermented drink and that you do not eat anything unclean. You will become pregnant and have a son whose head is never to be touched by a razor because the boy is to be a Nazirite, dedicated to God from the womb. He will take the lead in delivering Israel from the hands of the Philistines.'

(verses 4–7)

When I was a teenager there were times when being 'godly' felt like missing out on all the fun stuff! Always having to be the good girl, doing the right thing, felt like strict rules designed to stop me having a good time. It took me years to understand that God's intention isn't to restrict my life, but to expand it.

In the passage we read the requirements for being a Nazirite and the strict rules Manoah would have to follow and the lifestyle his parents would have to model. Each served as physical symbols of his consecration; visible reminders to himself and to others that he was set apart for a specific purpose – to lead the people to freedom.

Have you ever given anything up during Lent? I've discovered the beauty of choosing not to watch TV shows and movies for a period. It's not easy – and it isn't wrong to watch them – but I've found that it helps me to focus more on God in my everyday life, to hear his voice more clearly and to be more sensitive to his presence.

The world is full of things that that can bring happiness and fun, and God longs for us to enjoy them in healthy ways. But there's something bigger on offer: not the temporary relief from boredom or anxiety, not a fleeting distraction from pain, but life in all its fullness – a life filled with meaning and purpose, long-term healing from the causes of pain, and the joy and strength that comes from his presence.

† Lord, please search my heart and show me which things in my life are distracting me from focusing on you.

For further thought

Jim Elliot famously said: 'He is no fool who gives up what he cannot keep in order to gain what he cannot lose.'[1]

---

[1] E. Elliot, *Through Gates of Splendor* (Wheaton: Tyndale, 1981), p. 172.

Eat of the bread and drink of the cup – 2 Wine

September

269

The wine of God's wrath

Read Revelation 14:8–20

'Take your sharp sickle and gather the clusters of grapes from the earth's vine, because its grapes are ripe.' The angel swung his sickle on the earth, gathered its grapes and threw them into the great winepress of God's wrath. They were trampled in the winepress outside the city, and blood flowed out of the press, rising as high as the horses' bridles for a distance of 1,600 stadia.

(verses 18b–20)

Have you ever felt angry about the injustice and suffering in the world? Ever felt furious that people who are corrupt or choose to do evil seem to get away with it? Have you ever asked: 'God, why aren't you doing anything?' Perhaps the answer can be found in at least two parts.

First, God patiently holds back the natural consequences of our sinful choices in order for us to have space to respond to his love in repentance and faith. An example of this can be seen when God passes in front of Moses and proclaims that he is 'slow to anger, abounding in love and faithfulness, maintaining love to thousands, and forgiving wickedness, rebellion and sin' (Exodus 34:6b–7a). The problem comes when people ignore the opportunity to change and carry on in their sin. We often mistake God's grace for a lack of interest, and it appears as if people can just get away with it.

Which leads to the second part of the answer: they will not! In Revelation 16:19b we find vivid picture language describing the day that 'God remembered Babylon the Great and gave her the cup filled with the wine of the fury of his wrath.' Ultimately, there is justice.

Wine often symbolises joy or blessing. Here, the joy and blessing are for those who have suffered, who have been robbed, who have been treated unjustly. As the wine of God's anger at wickedness is finally poured out, all that we have lost as a result of other people's sin is restored.

† Thank you, Father, for being faithful, long-suffering and righteous. Search my heart and show me where I need to change my ways to become more like you.

For further thought

Isn't it comforting to know that one day there will be true justice for every wrong and evil deed that has ever happened?

Wednesday 25 September
Be careful

Read Ecclesiastes 3:1-13

He has made everything beautiful in its time. He has also set eternity in the human heart; yet no one can fathom what God has done from beginning to end. I know that there is nothing better for people than to be happy and to do good while they live. That each of them may eat and drink, and find satisfaction in all their toil – this is the gift of God.

(verses 11–13)

Are you excited by the thought of eternity? As believers, we know we are supposed to be, but when I was younger the thought of living forever in a never-ending worship service sounded boring and exhausting! Later, like the writer and many others, I realised that I was already living as if I was going to live forever. Sure, I knew that my life could end at any time, but mostly I lived my life as if there were endless new days to come – and for many that can seem daunting, too.

The writer of Ecclesiastes poetically reflects on these things – the seemingly endless pursuit of happiness, the vanity of life and trying to extract meaning from the everyday. Yet he points to something more than this that he doesn't quite understand: 'He has also set eternity in the human heart; yet no one can fathom what God has done from beginning to end.' Today we are in a better place to understand what it means. Shortly before his death, Jesus prayed to the Father with his disciples: 'Now this is eternal life: that they know you, the only true God, and Jesus Christ, whom you have sent' (John 17:3).

While life has its different seasons, and our earthly bodies will undoubtedly age, we have been created for something bigger; for more than just waking up, going to work, eating, drinking and sleeping. We are created to know God and be known by him. Eternity isn't just about a length of existence. It is about depth and quality. It's about the growing adventure of living in love with those who love the God who is love.

† Jesus, in my day-to-day life, I sometimes forget that I was created for something bigger. Remind me that I'm created to know you and be known by you. I want to know you more.

For further thought

Revelation 4 pictures the elders repeatedly laying down their crowns to worship God. Perhaps this is less about a task they must perform and more about the fact that each time they look up they discover something new about God.

Eat of the bread and drink of the cup – 2 Wine

September

A wedding party

> **Read John 2:1–11**
>
> *The master of the banquet tasted the water that had been turned into wine. He did not realise where it had come from, though the servants who had drawn the water knew. Then he called the bridegroom aside and said, 'Everyone brings out the choice wine first and then the cheaper wine after the guests have had too much to drink; but you have saved the best till now.'*
>
> (verses 9–10)

Have you ever wondered if God has 'perfect' timing for things in our lives … and what happens if we miss that?

Jesus, Mary and the disciples are at a wedding when on the third day the wine runs out. This lack of hospitality will bring shame on the whole community. But when Mary alerts Jesus to the problem, it seems as if the timing isn't right. 'My hour has not yet come,' he says (verse 4b). Perhaps he knows that if he acts now it will make it more difficult to fulfil his bigger mission.

Yet Jesus acts anyway. Perhaps the look in Mary's eyes convinced him. She knew how shame felt; she could probably still hear the slamming doors from that night in Bethlehem when hospitality was refused her. Despite the cost to him of it not being 'the right time', Jesus, out of compassion, turns the water into wine.

In the last few years especially, I have wondered whether I missed the perfect timing to meet someone with whom I could spend the rest of my life. What if I messed up God's timing when I wasn't ready for marriage in my early twenties, even though my boyfriend back then was? What if I've missed out on 'the plan', 'the timing'?

This story fills me with hope. Even if I mess up the timings in my life, I can always trust God to give his very best when I let him. Not only did Jesus turn the water into wine, but miraculously, despite the poor timing, it was the very best wine.

† Thank you, Lord, that you care more about our hearts than your own convenience. Thank you that you always give your very best.

For further thought

On the third day of the wedding, Jesus turned despair into celebration. Meditate on the other third day: Easter Day. Which areas of your life need that same miracle? Ask him …

Friday 27 September
Be considerate of each other

Read Romans 14:13–21

Therefore do not let what you know is good be spoken of as evil. For the kingdom of God is not a matter of eating and drinking, but of righteousness, peace and joy in the Holy Spirit.

(verses 16–17)

I was at a conference recently where one member of the discussion panel was promoting a particular approach to Bible analysis that another was convinced that 'true' believers wouldn't use. It was painful to watch Christians judge each other in front of hundreds of people.

Does this mean we all have to agree with one another? Absolutely not. The problem comes when disagreement turns into a judgement of the person with whom we disagree: 'I am right, you are wrong. I am better than you, holier than you.' God loves diversity! It is unity he longs for, not conformity. I have found that when I judge people it causes my heart to become hard towards them. It sets me against them and creates division – the opposite of love.

In the same way, the disagreement in our passage risked disunity, and Paul highlights a way back to love. It isn't about what they should eat; it's about why they are choosing to eat or not. Is the person abstaining from eating out of fear of what others might think? Are they eating as an act of rebellion against tradition? Or are they acting in line with their conscience and the leading of the Spirit?

The same behaviour can be either sinful or righteous, depending on what motivates it, and we cannot safely judge which it is. What we can do is be fully convinced in our own minds about what we should do. And whatever we decide, we should do it in love.

† Jesus, search my heart and show me where I am judging others. Teach me to love and respect, despite any disagreement.

For further thought

Have you ever judged someone for not living their faith the same way you do? Have you ever thought of another believer as a 'lesser' Christian?

Eat of the bread and drink of the cup – 2 Wine

September

Saturday 28 September
Bread and wine

Read Matthew 26:26–29

'I tell you, I will not drink from this fruit of the vine from now on until that day when I drink it new with you in my Father's kingdom.'

(verse 29)

As we've seen throughout this week, wine is so often symbolic of good things, yet in this passage Jesus says he will not drink it again until he is able to do so with his friends. Because ultimately it isn't the wine that brings joy; it is the celebration of drinking it with those we love that is truly joy-filled. And even though Jesus was going to return to the Father and have all the wonders of heaven, his joy would not be complete until the day we were there with him.

But there's more. As he speaks these words, his disciples still haven't realised he is about to die. Soon, they will know a loss of joy. Grief, persecution and, for many, martyrdom would soon follow. In telling them that he would not drink something that symbolises joy, Jesus is saying that he will share in our experiences of lack in this life.

And finally, his words bring hope that one day all will be put right. Hope is incredibly powerful, and while life isn't a fairy tale for any of us in a fallen world, Jesus' words mean that, as believers, we can be confident that the happily-ever-after is to come one day.

What an incredible, loving and relational God! It amazes me that one who could be fully content and fully satisfied without us chooses to withhold from himself in order to share in our suffering. That, in the face of his own suffering, he was concerned about bringing us hope.

† Lord, thank you for the proclamation of hope that the elements of bread and wine bring.

For further thought

Meditate on what an incredible day of celebration it will be when we finally get to share bread and wine with Jesus.

Questions

Notes by **Shirlyn Toppin**

Shirlyn is a presbyter in the Methodist Church. She believes passionately in the preaching of the word of God without compromise, and in exercising a pastoral ministry of grace. She enjoys various forms of leisure, reading and shopping. Shirlyn has used the NRSVA for these notes.

Sunday 29 September
Who is my neighbour?

Read Luke 10:33–37

'Which of these three, do you think, was a neighbour to the man who fell into the hands of the robbers?'

(verse 36)

Jesus redefined the interpretation of a neighbour and shattered the lawyer's preconceived notion when he addressed the question 'Who is my neighbour?' By using the art of storytelling, the language engages the reader and hints at the possibility of a role in the narrative.

Is it the role of the priest, who believed that touching an injured or dead person would make him unclean, therefore choosing ceremonial rite over charity? Or perhaps the Levite, clearly too busy to stop and putting his own safety above someone else's need. Or maybe it is the victim who needs someone to exemplify neighbourly kindness like that of the Samaritan?

Irrespective of whether the personification of a role is adopted or not, the story acts as a reminder that religious beliefs are meaningless if not accompanied by realism. Disciples of Christ cannot choose to pull down shutters and ignore uncomfortable issues, but should seek to follow the example of the Samaritan and actually risk something to be a good neighbour.

Who is our neighbour? The narrative suggests that there can be no limitations on the definition of a neighbour, but that we must demonstrate a willingness to reach out to those who are in need. Many questions will be posed in this week's readings. Some will be contemplative, others emotive. What will your response be?

† 'Search me, O God, and know my heart; test me and know my thoughts' (Psalm 139:23). Amen

September Questions

Monday 30 September
Whom shall I send?

Read Isaiah 6:6–10

Then I heard the voice of the Lord saying, 'Whom shall I send, and who will go for us?' And I said, 'Here am I; send me!'

(verse 8)

This direct and penetrating question posed to every would-be disciple of Jesus requires Isaiah to step out in faith, laying down his fear, feelings of unworthiness and pride. Willing discipleship and courageous faithfulness resonate in Isaiah's confident offer. Was he confident in himself? Far from it. His assurance was in the One who had revealed a glimpse of his holiness, and whose commissioning question implied that it was not a spur-of-the-moment decision but an intentional mission.

Though familiar to us, Isaiah's response is interesting. By replying, 'Here am I', he indicates that he was keenly committed. But then he goes on to intensify his conviction with 'Send me!', which highlights his sacrificial dedication. His approach did not stem from a place of duty, but was a reaction to God's heartfelt anguish for his people, which created a stirring that resulted in an empathetic, faithful self-offering. A sense of obligation can never be the basis for serving God if the heart is not engaged.

'Whom shall I send?' This question remains imperative for God's ongoing missional activity. Can we truly ignore it when God's mission to the world is unfinished? Can we say that it is a question for him or her, but not for me? Are we able to hear God's voice for compassion amid our own hurt? Isaiah clearly had the same choice as us to willingly sign up or remain indifferent. He chose the path of service without question. What will you choose?

† Loving Father, the desire to fulfil your purpose is still relevant today. Remove the spirit of rigidity within me and help me to respond, 'Here am I; send me!' Amen

For further thought

Every believer has something to offer in relation to God's mission. What might yours be?

Tuesday 1 October
What do you want me to do for you?

Read Matthew 20:29–34

Jesus stood still and called them, saying, 'What do you want me to do for you?' They said to him, 'Lord, let our eyes be opened.'

(verses 32–33)

'Lord, let our eyes be opened.' There is something remarkable, but also delightful, in the direct reply to Jesus' question. There is no beating around the bush, no hesitancy and apparently no fear. The intense desire and willpower of the blind men show that if the need for change or a miracle is greater than the present situation, giving in to other people's pessimism is not an option. Personal conviction matters when it comes to voicing our response.

Have your passionate longings dissipated, your desires waned or your purposes been buried because of other people's opinions or the waiting period? The decisiveness of the blind beggars should dispel negativity and herald hope for anyone who believes they have lost focus in fulfilling an aspiration. The intimidating and unrelenting crowd could not inhibit Jesus from stopping and enquiring. It is probable that no one had ever asked before, and in doing so he saw them. They were not treated as irrelevant, overlooked members of society, but as people with a profound need for something other than momentary gratification.

'What do you want me to do for you?' Perhaps you have allowed the crowds to dull your sense of hearing. The crowd of doubt that says you are unworthy or not spiritual enough. The crowd of unbelief, pointing out that there is no God or that he is not listening. The blind men did not allow the crowd to determine their outcome, and neither should you.

† Lord, help me not to ignore the needy, to see the poor as less than myself or to listen to voices of cynicism. Amen

For further thought
Jesus said, 'You will always have the poor with you.' Does this mean that we should disregard those in need?

Wednesday 2 October
What have you done?

Read Genesis 4:1–12

Then the LORD said to Cain, 'Where is your brother Abel?' He said, 'I do not know; am I my brother's keeper?' And the LORD said, 'What have you done?'

(verses 9–10a)

We continue our reflection on this week's 'questions' theme with another searching query: 'What have you done?' This question has undoubtedly been asked by most parents whose child is inclined to be a bit mischievous. However, the incident between the two brothers in today's reading is not just a bit of harmless fun; it is the culmination of a growing discord in their human relationship, followed by the consequences of sin. Cain's iniquity includes envy, arrogance, rebellion and murder, and the punishment includes separation from family and from God.

The tone of God's enquiry indicates that he is already aware of the situation. Yet by demanding 'What have you done?' he introduces an element of doubt. This prompts a pang of guilty conscience not only for Cain, but for anyone who would like to forget any acts that require contrition. Cain may feel that his defensive denial about Abel's whereabouts ought to be sufficient to stave off further questioning, but God wants him to face up to the reality of his actions. This explains his continual probing to see if the conversation will become a confessional moment.

Most human beings would probably admit to feelings of guilt, either through their actions or their thoughts. We feel guilty for not giving money to a rough sleeper; for making an excuse not to help a friend; for spending too much money; for making unfair judgements; for not spending enough time reading the Bible and praying. The list goes on and on. Even when nobody knows our inner musings, the conscience, or the voice of reasoning, may cause us to question what we have done.

† Forgive me, Lord, for not always doing your will, for giving little or no thought to others and for acting selfishly. Amen

For further thought

Can you recall the last time you acted as your brother or sister's keeper?

Thursday 3 October
Is it right for you to be angry?

Read Jonah 4:4–11

'And now, O LORD, please take my life from me, for it is better for me to die than to live.' And the LORD said, 'Is it right for you to be angry?'

(verses 3–4)

The word is preached, lives are changed dramatically; and the evangelist witnesses an entire city turning to God in repentance. Surely this calls for jubilant rejoicing at the fulfilment of the great commission and on witnessing an extraordinary conversion. Sadly, this is not the case for Jonah.

Jonah is aware of God's compassion and forgiveness because he has experienced it fully, yet he cannot reconcile himself to God's grace towards the Ninevites. He wants them to be destroyed and deems them unworthy of salvation.

Regret is displayed instead of celebration because the people have turned to God, and Jonah feels he has a right to be angry with God. He has lost sight of God's nature; therefore, death is preferable to the forgiveness offered. Jonah's reaction, though dramatically unbelievable, may create feelings of dismay in us, and possibly even empathy. Maybe because he daringly expresses his emotion like the psalmist who ranted in a similar way: 'How long will you judge unjustly and show partiality to the wicked?' (Psalm 82:2). This level of honesty is rarely encouraged, yet it is so necessary to express the confusion and raw emotions that life in a fallen world engenders.

Like others in the Bible, we may need to express our anger when God shows mercy to our enemies; when he does not answer our prayers the way we think he should; when he remains silent at times of chaos. And in that place, like Jonah, we may discover that God's compassion is not for a select few, but that he is with us in the storm of our responses and can lead us to a fuller understanding of who he is.

† Father, thank you for your compassion and mercy, for your forgiveness and grace, even when I fail to reveal it to others. Amen

For further thought
Do you feel expressing anger the way Jonah does is contrary to your Christian belief and practice?

What do you think?

> ### Read Matthew 18:10–14
>
> *'What do you think? If a shepherd has a hundred sheep, and one of them has gone astray, does he not leave the ninety-nine on the mountains and go in search of the one that went astray?'*
>
> (verse 12)

God's merciful compassion witnessed in yesterday's reflection is also manifested in today's reading. Instead of a prophet revealing his mercy and love, he personally goes in search of, and finds, the one who has strayed. God is as concerned for the one as he is for the many, and he does not dismiss the one who went missing in favour of the remaining ninety-nine.

We are informed of how well the shepherd knows his flock (John 10:1–18). Therefore, it would not take him long to realise that one of the sheep was missing. He instantly starts searching for it. If the shepherd knows his sheep so well, don't you think we are also known by God? He knows each person intimately, and it does not matter which one goes astray; he is equally distressed, for all belong to him. Status, wealth, power or lack of these things make us no more or less valuable to God. The key point to note here is the possibility of restoration.

Perhaps there have been times when someone you care deeply about has continued in a pattern of behaviour that is deemed harmful, and your impulse was to shake your head in frustration and walk away. What do you think God does in this situation? How grateful are we that God does not shake his head in disgust; that he does not abandon or dismiss us? He comes after us, despite our immaturity and frailty. He leaves the others in order to bring us safely back to his fold.

† Jesus, my Good Shepherd, thank you for knowing me. Thank you that you went in search of me and laid down your life for me. Amen

For further thought
Meditate on these words from John 10:3 'He calls his own sheep by name.'

Saturday 5 October
Which of you by worrying ...?

Read Luke 12:22–26

*'And can any of you by worrying add a single hour to your span of life?
If then you are not able to do so small a thing as that, why do you
worry about the rest?'*

(verses 25–26)

A member of a congregation once said to me, 'I like to worry.' My
immediate response was, 'Has anything changed as a result?' Of
course, nothing had shifted dramatically or otherwise in her life,
but somehow, she felt compelled not only to share what she likely
considered a virtue, but the possibility of seeing it as a God-given
purpose to fulfil.

This woman is not alone. Despite knowing that worrying is an
exercise in futility, many people seem unable to stop. There is a
clear distinction between legitimate concern and worry, however.
While concern may lead to action, worry does not change anything.
It can be a debilitating factor, in fact, because we are consumed by
thoughts of what could possibly go wrong in the future.

The mind becomes preoccupied with contingencies, emotions
are wrapped up in fear and aspirations die because we engage
in what Jesus describes as folly. 'Can any of you by worrying
add a single hour to your span of life?' The simple answer is no!
Worrying cannot help us live longer. More likely it will shorten our
lives because it can affect our health.

An old proverb says: 'Worry is the interest you pay on trouble
before it arrives.' If you are a worrier, do you know what sort of
interest you might be paying?

† Generous God, help me to trust in you instead of worrying. Remove any spirit of
anxiety from my life. Amen

For further thought

What is your response to Philippians 4:6, a well-known verse that
tells us not to be anxious?

Questions

October

Readings from Song of Solomon

1 A Passion for God

Notes by **Catherine Williams**

Catherine Williams is an Anglican priest who works as a freelance spiritual director, retreat conductor and writer. She writes biblical reflections for a variety of publications and is the lead voice on the Church of England's Daily Prayer app. Catherine lives on the Sandringham Estate in Norfolk, where her husband Paul is Domestic Chaplain to the royal household. Catherine enjoys reading, singing, theatre, cinema and poetry for leisure. She keeps chickens and is passionate about butterfly conservation. Catherine has used the NRSVA for these notes.

Sunday 6 October
A passionate start

Read Song of Solomon 1:1–8

Let him kiss me with the kisses of his mouth! For your love is better than wine.

(verse 2)

Today we begin a journey through the Song of Solomon, the great love song at the heart of the Wisdom literature in the Hebrew Bible. This little book has been interpreted in various ways down the centuries. On one level it can be taken literally as a celebration of mutual human love and intimacy. On another it can be seen as various allegories, including the covenant between God and Israel, the marriage of Christ and his bride (the church) and the loving union between God and each individual soul. It could also be seen as a vision of the return to Eden; a new heaven and a new earth restored, filled with delight and fruitfulness.

Opening on a passionate note, the beloved voices her desire for the consummating kiss of her lover. In the medieval church in Europe, the kiss was a symbol of the presence of Christ and an indication of God's favour. As we begin this week, let's open ourselves up to exploring our relationship with the living God, whose desire for each of us knows no bounds. As you read this passionate love poetry, believe yourself to be utterly loved by God. How do you respond to this intimate invitation?

† Loving God, reveal your love to me through your passionate, life-giving word. Encourage me to express the deep longing and desire I have for you.

Mutual affection

Read Song of Solomon 1:9–17

Ah, you are beautiful, my love, ah, you are beautiful; your eyes are doves.

(verse 15)

The lovers in our passage today share their mutual affection. They are not shy in telling each other what draws them together or sharing their responses to each other's physical characteristics.

The male lover uses images of his beloved that emphasise strength and power. This is no submissive or passive partner, but one that is willing and free to take the initiative and be independent. He considers her very beautiful, likening her eyes to doves – an ancient symbol of love. In response, the female lover mirrors the word 'beautiful' and imagines them lying together in a forest full of fragrant trees, similar to those used to build the temple. She is perhaps imagining them together in a holy place in which she longs to draw her lover close. All her senses are engaged as she describes her desires.

Imagine now that the male lover is God and the female lover is your soul. How do you respond to God when he offers you great riches and calls you beautiful over and again? How does this loving attention from God make you feel? How do you want to respond to God? Which words are bubbling up inside you as gaze on God? Use your senses to imagine the smell, sound, taste, sight and feel of the living God. Is this a sensuous experience? Does anything surprise you about engaging with God in this way?

What would you most like to say to God? Whisper it now. Then listen for God's response.

† Lord, thank you for reminding me that I am beautiful in your sight. Help me to express the desire for your ongoing presence in my life.

For further thought

Continue to imagine God, using all your senses. What new things are you experiencing as you do this?

Tuesday 8 October
Sustained with goodness

Read Song of Solomon 2:1–7

Sustain me with raisins, refresh me with apples; for I am faint with love.

(verse 5)

In chapter 2, the lovers continue to praise one another using imagery from the natural world. Flowers and fruit – symbols of abundant life and fertility – predominate. The love experienced sustains and refreshes the lovers, leaving them giddy and faint. They adore being with each other.

This is a powerful and potent relationship, and the woman is not shy in expressing her desire and longing. Passionate mutual love requires a level of maturity in order to be sustainable, otherwise it will burn itself out once the initial fireworks are over. The woman is keen to stress to her female companions not to enter into such a passionate partnership until they are ready!

St Augustine is often quoted as saying that: 'God loves each of us, as though there was only one of us.' Sometimes our human relationships are far from loving, and it is hard for us to believe that God loves us perfectly and eternally, with no strings attached. There is nothing we can do that would stop God loving us.

Keeping that love at the forefront of our minds and hearts can sometimes be challenging, so it's good to fuel our faith. What sustains and refreshes you in your relationship with the living God? Is it prayer, the reading of scripture, Holy Communion, contemplation or something else? What are the raisins, apples, lilies and roses of your faith; the things that keep your relationship with God blooming and fruitful? Allow yourself to experience and enjoy God gazing on you with deep, unconditional love and affection.

† Lord, thank you for your perfect, eternal love that promises never to let me go. Please help me to embrace and enjoy this truth.

For further thought

If you can, use raisins and apples in a recipe or as part of one of your meals today. Give thanks for the many ways in which God's love sustains and refreshes you.

Readings from Song of Solomon – 1 A Passion for God

October

Wednesday 9 October
Springtime

Read Song of Solomon 2:8–17

Arise, my love, my fair one, and come away; for now the winter is past, the rain is over and gone. The flowers appear on the earth; the time of singing has come.

(verses 10b–12a)

Where I live, spring is a beautiful season. It is full of blossom, new growth, birdsong and the promise of fruitfulness after a dark and dreary winter. The lovers in our passage today revel in this season, enjoying its current abundance and future potential. They continue to seek each other, each yearning for a glimpse of the other through a window, behind a wall and on the mountaintop.

This is reminiscent of an elaborate and playful game of hide-and-seek. The male lover encourages his partner to move out of her ordered domestic life to join him in the wide outdoors and celebrate the beauty of the natural world. It's like a return to the original Eden before the fall, and a fulfilment of Isaiah's prophecy of the desert blossoming and bursting into song (Isaiah 35:1–7).

What season are you in when it comes to your relationship with the living God? Do you recognise these elements of spring in your faith – vitality, energy, potential and joy – which will eventually lead to the fruitfulness of high summer? Or is your relationship more autumnal or wintry right now? Seeking God in new ways, listening for his call with eager anticipation, and responding with excitement and commitment to his surprises and adventures are all part of being a faithful disciple, regardless of our age or situation. Throughout, we need to be mindful of those 'little foxes' that cause havoc in the vineyard (verse 15), undermining our relationship with God, and uprooting and damaging our love and faithfulness.

'My beloved is mine and I am his' (verse 16a) is the song we need to keep in our minds and hearts.

† Lord God, call me to adventure and new growth. Fill me with your Spirit and lead me into joy.

For further thought

Spend some time outdoors. Be attentive to the signs of God in the natural world around you. What can you see? How does the created order bear witness to its Creator?

Readings from Song of Solomon – 1 A Passion for God

October

285

Thursday 10 October
Soul love

Read Song of Solomon 3:1–5

I will rise now and go about the city, in the streets and in the squares; I will seek him whom my soul loves …

(verse 2)

Here is the woman yearning for her lover in the night. Perhaps she is dreaming of him, or awake, missing and longing for him. His absence makes her frustrated and anxious. She gets up in the dead of night to search for him throughout the city, asking others if they have seen him. When she eventually finds him, she holds on to him tightly and leads him home. Again, she stresses to her companions not to enter into a passionate relationship before the time is right. Love hurts!

Occasionally, God seems to withdraw from us, and we have to search hard to be reunited. He is not always easy to catch, but our searching and longing for him can lead us into a deeper, more mature relationship as our faith is tested and strengthened. On finding God again we hold on more tightly, knowing we have come home.

Several times in this passage the phrase 'him whom my soul loves' is used. It's a reminder of the Shema (the daily Jewish prayer): 'Hear, O Israel: The Lord is our God, the Lord alone. You shall love the Lord your God with all your heart, and with all your soul, and with all your might' (Deuteronomy 6:4–5).

Loving God is a 'soul love'; a love that is wholehearted and comes from our very core. Jesus calls the Shema the first great commandment. The second is: 'You shall love your neighbour as yourself' (Mark 12:31). Seeking God – the one our soul loves – naturally leads us to care and be concerned for those around us, whom he also loves.

† Lord God, strengthen me to love you with all my heart, all my soul and all my might. Then lead me to love my neighbour as myself.

For further thought

Do something today that shows your care and concern for those who live near you. Let the Holy Spirit guide your words and actions as you show God's love to your neighbours.

Friday 11 October
Perfumed and fragrant

Read Song of Solomon 3:6–11
What is that coming up from the wilderness, like a column of smoke, perfumed with myrrh and frankincense, with all the fragrant powders of the merchant?

(verse 6)

A misty and romantic vision of the beloved coming in from the desert heralds today's meeting of the lovers. We're not sure who is speaking here, or who is being longed for, but whoever it is seems to be fragrant and perfumed, beautiful and irresistible.

Frankincense is very precious and was often connected with sacrifices in the temple, so it is often used as a reference to holiness. The vision goes on to imagine a rich, exotic and expensive display; the sort that might have been seen at one of Solomon's weddings. The lovers are like royalty – rich and rare, and crowned with love.

The wilderness or desert is an important motif in our faith. The Israelites entered the promised land after spending years in the desert. Isaiah looked towards the desert for the promised Messiah. Jesus returned from temptation in the desert to enter into his ministry. We, too, are called from dry, dusty places to enter into a loving relationship with the living God.

Worshipping the three-in-one God, the One who creates, redeems and sanctifies us, fills us with a divine fragrance. This makes us beautiful – irresistible, even – to God, whose desire continues to draw us ever closer to his heart of love. When we are close to him, those around us will catch the perfume of the divine that emanates from our lives and want to know more. God's royal presence enables us all to flourish as citizens of the kingdom, both now and in the renewed heaven and earth to come.

† Lord God, fill me with your divine fragrance so that others may be drawn to you through my witness.

For further thought

In 2 Corinthians 2:15, Christians are called the 'aroma of Christ'. What do you think this means? How is your life perfumed with Jesus?

Readings from Song of Solomon – 1 A Passion for God

October

287

Flawless

As this first week of readings from Song of Solomon ends, we reach the middle of the book and a high point in the lover's praise and admiration of his beloved, whom he calls 'my bride'. The imagery used to describe the beloved may seem strange, and if we were to take it literally she would look very odd indeed – with hair like a goat, teeth like a sheep, a neck like a tower and breasts like fawns! But notice how the images are full of life, vitality and energy.

The images of beauty are taken from the natural world, while the references to strength are taken from human constructions. The beloved is utterly beautiful and flawless, scented with the spices of the temple and flowing with living water. Sensuous and holy, she is a beautiful garden: open, ready and waiting to be united with her lover.

This week we have considered what it means to be in a passionate and intimate relationship with the living God, who loves us utterly and sees us as flawlessly beautiful. Created by God, we are made flawless by Jesus' gift of himself to us. Filled with the Holy Spirit, we are open to the wild beauty of a life lived to the full, overflowing with God's goodness and grace. The ongoing positive regard and unconditional love of God gives us confidence to be fully ourselves. Such confidence enables us to look beyond ourselves to others, and to desire for them all that God offers. This desire naturally leads us into acts of compassion and justice on behalf of the whole created order.

† Lord Jesus, thank you for opening the way for the entire cosmos to be perfected and redeemed. Encourage me to enjoy intimacy with God.

For further thought

Look back through this week's reflections. Has anything changed or deepened in your relationship with God this week? Do something creative to express your love for him, and for those around you.

Readings from Song of Solomon

2 Intimacy with God

Notes by **Catherine Williams**

You can read Catherine's biography on Sunday 6 October.

Sunday 13 October
Love's highs and lows

Read Song of Solomon 5:1–8

I sought him, but did not find him; I called him, but he gave no answer.

(verse 6b)

This week we continue our journey through the Song of Solomon, experiencing the highs and lows of intimate love, and considering our relationship with God through the allegory of the lover and the beloved. Last week we left the beloved open and ready. Today the lover enters the garden of his beloved and enjoys the good things therein. We are encouraged to be intoxicated with the sweetness, urgency and mystery of love. Here we read of the full consummation of the lovers' relationship.

However, the lovers lose each other after this. The beloved is slow to respond to her lover, who disappears into the night. Although she seeks and calls for her lover she cannot find him, and those who should be protecting her in the night turn hostile, violating her. A period of frustration, loss and vulnerability follows. Her heart is broken and her soul fails. Something that had been so successful seems to be falling apart.

There are similar highs and lows in the life of faith. At times we experience deep, joy-filled communion with God, and are fully aware and responsive to his beauty and holiness. Conversely, we can also be fearful of his advances and slow to respond. At such times God may appear to slip through our fingers, and no amount of searching or calling brings him close. At such moments we need to place our trust in the God who loves us and works all things for good, even when we seem not to connect.

† Lord God, however demanding or urgent your call may be, help me to respond with faith, trust and love.

For further thought

Have there been times when you struggled to find, hear or connect with God? Who, where or what has helped you to revive your relationship with God?

Lovers and friends

Read Song of Solomon 5:9–16

His speech is most sweet, and he is altogether desirable. This is my beloved and this is my friend.

(verse 16)

While waiting to reconnect with her lover, the beloved extols him to her friends, who are wondering what all the fuss is about. Why is he so special? She describes him from top to toe, using imagery from both the natural world and human creativity. Her memory conjures him as energetic and statuesque. She describes him using the most beautiful words and images she knows. He is fragrant, golden, bejewelled and radiant – rich and rare. Everything about him is desirable. He is her lover and her friend.

Which words and images do you use when you tell others about the God you love and worship? Can others tell how much you love him from your language and enthusiasm? What is it about God that most catches your attention and sparks your desire? In these past days we have been exploring the idea of God as our 'lover'. This may be a new concept for you, or perhaps it is a familiar one. How are you responding to this idea of intimacy with God? For the woman, this is not just her lover but also her friend.

Just before his death, Jesus encourages his disciples into a friendship with him and with each other (John 15). He suggests that friends are equals. They are loving, reliable, trustworthy and a delight to be with. They are also prepared to sacrifice themselves for others. Jesus gives the ultimate example of this on the cross. In this intense, beautiful and sacrificial relationship, God is both our divine lover and our friend. God loves us *and* likes us.

† Dear God, thank you that you are both my lover and my friend. Help me to tell many others of your love and friendship.

For further thought

Use the most beautiful words and images you know to describe God, who is both your lover and friend. What sort of picture are you conjuring up? Who might you share it with?

Belonging together

Read Song of Solomon 6:1–13

I am my beloved's and my beloved is mine.

(verse 3a)

Despite seeming to have lost her lover, the beloved shows her companions that she knows exactly where he is. He is in the gardens, gathering flowers and feeding his flock. This may be a veiled reference to love-making, which the lovers enjoy in the garden among the spices and lilies. An exotic, heady and sensuous scene is set. The beloved declares that the lovers belong to each other. The relationship is mutual and wholehearted.

Following this declaration, the lover praises his beloved again, using similar imagery to that of chapter 4 but drawing in more of the cosmos this time. She is as beautiful and constant as the moon and the sun. Caught up in the light of this intense beauty and love, everything is blossoming and fruitful.

The declaration of mutuality, 'I am my beloved's and my beloved is mine' reminds us of the covenantal love God has for Israel: 'I will take you as my people, and I will be your God' (Exodus 6:7). The love is reciprocal: given and received. The lovers belong to each other. God and Israel belong to each other. Jesus and his bride, the church, belong to each other.

Each soul shares in that relationship of mutual love with God the Trinity; both as an individual and as part of the body of Christ. The love given and received is continuous and unending, flowing through creation. God, in Jesus, promises to never let any of us go. This commitment is passionate, strong, sacrificial and true. No wonder it has been imagined as the best and most beautiful of human love-making.

† Lord, thank you for drawing me into your covenant of love. Keep me faithful to you, and to all those to whom you send me.

For further thought

Play or sing your favourite love song. Imagine yourself and God singing this song together. Now imagine God singing similar love songs to the whole of creation.

Readings from Song of Solomon – 2 Intimacy with God

October

Wednesday 16 October
Loving the body

Read Song of Solomon 7:1–9

Your eyes are pools in Heshbon, by the gate of Bath-rabbim.

(verse 4a)

Today in Song of Solomon we have arrived at the book's most sensuous and erotic writing. The lover describes his beloved's body from her feet to her head, using images drawn from the natural world and from the surrounding towns and cities. In the eyes of her lover, the woman is graceful, beautiful, strong, supple, regal and utterly desirable. Her body arouses her lover, and he is not ashamed to articulate his desire. Under her lover's gaze, the woman is calm, relaxed and tranquil. Her eyes are like deep, serene pools of water in the middle of a noisy, bustling city.

It's refreshing to read of such love and respect given to the body. So often we are uncomfortable or embarrassed about our bodies. We wish we looked different, and we try to hide or change our appearance, longing to be a different shape or size. In this passage we hear an echo of life in the Garden of Eden, where the first people were relaxed and unashamed about their bodies. It's good to be reminded that God created us, loves us just as we are and longs to walk with us.

In Jesus, God knows exactly what it is like to inhabit human flesh with all its joys, sorrows and complexities. Through baptism, we are part of the body of Christ, and together we embody a way of being that links us both to the Garden of Eden and to our future resurrected body, when all will be made new. So let's love our bodies, treating them with respect and honour.

† Lord God, you created and love me just as I am. May I love, honour and respect my body and the bodies of others.

For further thought

How do you feel about your body? What is it that God sees when he looks at you? How might God describe your physical attributes? Speak with God about this.

Courage and confidence

Following her lover's high praise and affirmation, the woman is confident that she belongs to her lover and is desired by him. This assurance enables her to initiate and lead plans for their relationship. She encourages her lover into the countryside, where all is blooming and fruitful. There, the promise of love-making is offered and accepted. We sense freedom, adventure and closeness to the created order. The lovers are attentive to the fragrant new life around them and are glad to be within its flourishing fruitfulness.

Knowing that God loves us deeply and desires us intimately can give us the courage and confidence to step out in faith and go on adventures with God, guided by the Spirit. Fuelled by his love and desire, we are enabled to let go of old patterns of being so we can embrace the wildness and freedom of becoming who God is calling us to be.

Following in the footsteps of Jesus will lead us to seek and serve those on the margins of society, enabling us to be attentive to where God is already at work and eager to join in. He may call us away from the work we are already doing. Or he may encourage us to stay where we are and engage more deeply in our current context, finding new life within. All of this is underpinned by the mutual deep love and desire between God and us, given and received. This is essential if we are to flourish. Joining God in the dance of creation is a joy and a delight.

† Lord God, call me to join you on new adventures. Together, may we delight in your creation, as you seek to restore and renew everything.

For further thought

Be attentive to where God is at work in your context. How are you joining with and celebrating this new life? Ask the Holy Spirit to indicate who else could be drawn into God's service.

Readings from Song of Solomon – 2 Intimacy with God

October

Private and public

Readings from Song of Solomon – 2 Intimacy with God

Read Song of Solomon 8:1–4

O that his left hand were under my head, and that his right hand embraced me!

(verse 3)

In today's passage, the woman is struggling with the tension between the public and private aspects of her relationship with her lover. This intimately involved couple seems not to have publicly declared their love. The woman wishes they were siblings rather than lovers, so that they might be seen together in public without fear of reprisal. She is longing to be held and embraced again, and to bring her lover home.

Over the past fortnight we have been exploring intimacy with God. At times during the church's history, and especially in the medieval church, Christians have been very open and unabashed about their intense desire for God and their passionate relationship with the divine. Song of Solomon has been a rich source of metaphor and allegory for the soul's romance, union and consummation with God. Drawing on this, poetry, sermons and spiritual works regularly referred to the soul's ecstatic union or mystical marriage with God.

Today's Christians are more reticent to tell others about this aspect of faith, for fear perhaps of being misunderstood or ridiculed. There can be a gap between what we believe and experience privately in prayer and the way we portray God in public. We are more likely to describe God as a parent and Jesus as a brother than we are to use the word 'lover' when we talk about our relationship with the living God. And yet, as we have seen over the past fortnight, intimately loving God and knowing ourselves to be intimately loved in return leads to joy, fulfilment and abundant flourishing.

† Lord God, your deep love for me knows no bounds. Help me to open myself fully to your embrace.

For further thought

Read some of the writings of Bernard of Clairvaux, Catherine of Siena, Teresa of Ávila or St John of the Cross. What can you learn about desire for God from these Christians?

October

Sealed with love

Read Song of Solomon 8:5–14

Set me as a seal upon your heart, as a seal upon your arm; for love is strong as death, passion fierce as the grave.

(verse 6)

We end this fortnight with one of the best-loved verses in Song of Solomon. It's often read at weddings – both Jewish and Christian. The private–public tension we explored yesterday is resolved as the beloved calls out to her lover to accept her as a permanent fixture. She chooses to be sealed in relationship with him privately – on his heart – and publicly – on his arm. This love, so strong, can stand against threats of chaos and annihilation. No amount of money in the world can buy a love this precious.

The relationship we each have with the living God can be intimate – deep within – and public – for all the world to see. To be sealed to God is to respond with our whole being to him calling. It means holding nothing back, giving everything to God, and believing that such a relationship will last forever. When we were baptised we received the sign of the cross on our foreheads. This is the seal of God's identity. It shows that we belong to Jesus, and it indicates to the world that we are a part of Christ's body on earth: the church. Death will only enhance this commitment as we give ourselves wholly to God and are drawn into his deep embrace and promise of new life.

We see this supremely in the death and resurrection of Jesus, who goes before us on this journey of discovery. Through the passion of Jesus, we need not fear the grave. Nothing can break the seal of God's love for us. It is eternal.

† Thank you, Lord, that nothing can separate me from your love. Help me to love you with trust, passion and commitment.

For further thought

Write a love letter to God expressing your deepest desires, hopes and dreams for your relationship with him. Think of ways to express God's love within your community.

Readings from Song of Solomon – 2 Intimacy with God

October

Parts of the body

1 Gifts from God

Notes by **Angharad Davies**

Angharad has served with Youth With A Mission (YWAM) in England, China, France, Romania, Argentina and South Africa. She lived in Cape Town for seven years, where she helped set up The Dignity Campaign (www.dignity.org.za). She recently completed a book based on her personal experience of overcoming eating disorders and depression; believed to be the first of its kind in the Welsh language. Angharad has a BA in Welsh Literature and currently home-educates her two lovely kids while studying for an MA. Angharad has used the NRSVA and NLT for these notes.

Sunday 20 October
Shaped by God

Read Job 10:8–12

Your hands fashioned and made me; and now you turn and destroy me. Remember that you fashioned me like clay; and will you turn me to dust again?

(verses 8–9)

It seems that Job is wrestling with what he thought he knew about God and what his lived experience is right now. His suffering seems to conflict with the fact that his God, the Creator of heaven and earth, carefully made him. By raising questions with God, Job is reminding himself of his own origin. He is trying to make sense of his own existence, in the context of being delicately formed by God but simultaneously enduring hardship.

Why does a good God allow suffering? I once found myself driving through rural Wales in torrential rain in the dark of winter. I was driving home to an empty house and my life was falling apart around me. I remember tears streaming down onto the car steering wheel. I cried out to God, declaring that even if he didn't take away the grief, the pain, the sorrow or the loneliness – even if he didn't help me stop my destructive, life-controlling issues, I still wanted him! At that moment I began to mature, and this memory is etched onto my heart. No matter how bad it gets, I have him … and I never want to turn my back on him.

† God, you know me. However bad things are or become, let me keep seeking you. You are who I need.

Monday 21 October
Flesh and blood

> **Read Genesis 29:13–14**
> *When Laban heard the news about his sister's son Jacob, he ran to meet him; he embraced him and kissed him, and brought him to his house.*
>
> (verse 13)

Running to meet and greet relatives is a cultural practice that outwardly displays unconditional welcome to the one who is arriving at the family home, and Laban does just that for Jacob. But is his action really motivated by love? It seems Laban was hoping for a blessing of wealth and prosperity to accompany his sister's son, but once he discovered Jacob's true position in the world, he made up his mind to use him for his own advantage. I guess the story shows that we don't always receive the response we should from 'flesh and blood', or indeed anyone in a position of power.

At the age of twenty-five I went off on my own, on a Saturday night, with a bottle of wine in each pocket of the black duffel coat I had worn to my mother's funeral a few years previously. I had recently joined a discipleship community, YWAM, in York, England, and my leaders and new buddies came looking for me. I was puzzled as to why. Where I came from, you did what you wanted – no concern was ever shown, no boundaries set. I was shocked that my new friends and leaders were genuinely concerned for me. Unlike Laban, they acted like flesh and blood, even though they weren't. They helped me find a grief counsellor and supported me when I took four months out to go to a rehab for people with eating disorders. On my wedding day, these guys were my family.

† Lord, lead us to the good shepherds, and train us to become them.

For further thought

When we are in desperate need of help, can we find people we trust and who have our best interests at heart?

Head: held high and low

Read Luke 18:9–14

But the tax-collector, standing far off, would not even look up to heaven, but was beating his breast and saying, 'God, be merciful to me, a sinner!'

(verse 13)

We seem to live in a world in which outward appearance is everything and inner character counts for very little. The pressure to appear flawless, to avoid any hint of imperfection, stretches from politics to celebrities, and has an influence on us all. Acknowledging error and admitting fault is so threatening to our image that it is a surprise when someone has the courage to be like the tax collector.

In reality, of course, we will never be able to hide our true hearts from God and those closest to us. Deep down we all know that there is something wrong with us and that something needs to compensate for that brokenness. We may try to succeed at work, lose weight, get fit, be perfect … the list is endless. We can all be guilty of trying to run away from our own brokenness.

Being fully honest with ourselves and with God requires humility. But it is only when we humbly confess our helplessness that he can come and meet our deepest needs.

I am a home-educating parent. This gives me plenty of opportunity to see the sin in my own heart. What's on the inside expresses itself externally. Do I put myself or the children first? Do I have a gracious tone of voice when I speak to them? We all have 'mirrors' – spouses, children, jobs, relatives, church acquaintances – that can expose the true heart condition of our hearts. The only solution is to admit the obvious and receive a cleansing of our sins so that we can start afresh. Regularly.

† Lord, please help me to understand that being honest with you is a healthy and healing process, and is not one to be afraid of.

For further thought

When we acknowledge that we are sinners, we can be open to receiving an abundance of much-needed mercy.

Wednesday 23 October
Face: it says so much

Read Job 29:21–24

When they were discouraged, I smiled at them. My look of approval was precious to them.

(verse 24)

Have you ever been unsure of what to say or do? The anxiety of not getting it right or of disappointing others can be paralysing. The challenges of life are made a hundred times easier when the smile of a loved one oozes warmth and encouragement towards us.

I remember the beginning of my 'career' as a missionary when I had to speak in front of an unfamiliar congregation. I looked out into the audience with trepidation, but then I saw my leaders. Their smiles communicated their confidence in me. The light in their eyes said that they approved of me. I knew then that even if the talk itself went badly, they would still love and value me. And this knowledge encouraged me. It literally poured courage into my being.

These days I have the privilege of being a leader, coach and mentor to my own children. When they're taking part in a group activity and are feeling a bit unsure, they search for me and want eye contact. They need to be reassured that they are loved unconditionally. It's what makes them feel safe, secure, confident and brave.

Job had known times when people thirsted after what he was about to say, and when God's favour was clearly on him. But all that has changed. He has no answers to the questions his circumstances are raising, and the empty words of others do not boost his confidence or bring a smile of peace to his face.

But when he sees God's face he is put at ease by the supremacy of his lord, and by the love that his king has for him.

† Lord, I want to look into your face today and see your love shining right back at me.

For further thought

God's acceptance of us only sinks in as we meditate, contemplate, accept, believe and experience it to be absolutely, unequivocally true.

Ears: for listening

Read Zechariah 7:8–12

But they refused to listen, and turned a stubborn shoulder, and stopped their ears in order not to hear.

(verse 11)

My second son was born in a big old bathtub at a midwife-led unit in Wrexham. Although the birth itself was fine, it seems I received water damage to my ear during the labour! For years I frustrated my family with all the words I missed or misunderstood. I became quite sad that I couldn't correctly interpret the excited words of awe and wonder my children so desperately wanted to share with me. I finally decided to get a hearing aid. The minute this tiny device was inside my ear I cried. I could finally hear all the things I had been missing out on!

But sometimes we hear the words being spoken and choose not to listen. Has there ever been a situation in which something happened in a relationship and you just chose to shut down the lines of communication because it was too hard or too painful?

I once had to leave the best work team I had ever been part of to live overseas. This devastated me, and for a while it made me shut God out. I was hurting and I blamed him as the source of my pain. I was angry with him. Needless to say, this silent treatment towards God did not make the relationship flourish.

I came to a point where being intentionally deaf was causing me more pain than if I had continued a dialogue with him. I still question his leading, but I had to let go of the pain and choose to turn my ear towards the living God.

† Lord, help me to choose to turn towards you, even when I'm angry or in pain.

For further thought

Miscommunication will be an ongoing theme in our relationship with God. He is God and we are human! We need soft hearts that do their best to trust him.

Eyes: lamps of the body

Read Matthew 6:22–23

'The eye is the lamp of the body. So, if your eye is healthy, your whole body will be full of light.'

(verse 22)

Every morning, come rain or shine, winter or summer, I must take our dear little dog for a walk. He is my daughter's 'baby', but it is usually my son who is awake early enough to accompany me on our dark morning walks in this autumnal season.

Today I strapped him onto my back, put the headtorch on over my curly morning hair and headed out for our urban stroll around the red-terraced houses of this old mining town. My son delighted in playing the 'reflective game'. I would show him how workmen's clothes, road signs and traffic cones looked when no light shone on them. Then I would shine my headlamp at those very same objects. He was mesmerised by the partnership between light and reflective material.

The experiment would not have worked so well if the reflective items had been damaged or soiled. When a car's licence plate is blackened by exhaust fumes we can't make out the letters, so we can't identify it. If a 'sharp corner' road sign has been spattered with mud, we have no way of knowing how to accurately navigate the turn.

But sometimes the problem isn't with the light, but with our eyes. Sometimes they have become damaged, so that we cannot see. At other times we choose to close them to the light.

God is the light. He is our light and the light of the world. In him there is no darkness. He wants to shine the light of his life into us so that we reflect him to the rest of humanity. When other people watch our lives, they see the brilliantly clear light of day shining back at them.

† Help us to keep our hearts pure so that you can pour your light into us and reflect it into a world in need.

For further thought

The way to stay healthy is to fill our lives with all that is good, excellent and worthy of praise. Let's intentionally seek out these wholesome things.

Parts of the body – 1 Gifts from God

October

Saturday 26 October
Nose: a pleasing aroma

Read 2 Corinthians 2:14–17

For we are the aroma of Christ to God among those who are being saved and among those who are perishing: to the one a fragrance from death to death, to the other a fragrance from life to life.

(verses 15–16a)

When the Romans had a victory parade they would burn incense to celebrate. To the Romans, this was the sweet smell of victory. For anyone captured by the Romans, the smell would create fear and dread as they were taken away to be imprisoned or executed.

It is always so encouraging when I meet fellow believers. We swap stories and testimonies, and form a bond that goes beyond nationality, personality, age or economic status. When I choose to place myself in non-Christian settings I often experience pushback. Many of the people I encounter are truly wonderful humans, but we don't see eye to eye about the most foundational One in the history of humankind.

What we believe, and who we are in Christ, becomes a threat to others. Some are drawn to us and want to know more. Others are repulsed and cannot connect with us. Christ in me can trigger people to reject my friendship.

Before I became a believer I was both drawn to and repulsed by other Christians, especially if they were in groups. Their purity exposed my sin, yet their holiness attracted the part of me that desperately wanted to know that there was hope for a better future. The 'fragrance' they gave off made me feel dirty, but it also offered me the hope of salvation. It was up to me to follow the aroma and enter the 'house of God', where he was cooking up an expensive feast of forgiveness, grace and mercy. All I had to do was accept and partake.

† God, lead us to the people who need to get close enough to you in us, so that they may be enticed to draw near to you.

For further thought

How can we become secure enough to accept the fact that some people will reject us purely because of our allegiance with God?

Parts of the body

2 What to do with them

Notes by **Mark Mitchell**

Mark manages emergency logistics for relief organisations. He has been engaged in the aid and development sector over the last twenty-five years, and is inspired to demonstrate God's love through a practical application of his reading of scripture and an understanding of God's love for the poor. Mark is based in New Zealand and lives with his wife and two daughters, who are in their late teens. Mark has used the NIVUK for these notes.

Sunday 27 October
Mouth: for sharing God's word

Read Ezekiel 3:1–4

And he said to me, 'Son of man, eat what is before you, eat this scroll; then go and speak to the people of Israel.' … So I ate it, and it tasted as sweet as honey in my mouth. He then said to me: 'Son of man, go now to the people of Israel and speak my words to them.'

(verses 1–4)

This week we're looking at the way God uses parts of the body as pictures to describe spiritual truths: the mouth, tongue, arms, hands … and we start with the mouth. In this passage Ezekiel is called to open his mouth and eat a scroll. This seems very strange. Parents of toddlers spend most of their time trying to stop them eating random bits of paper!

But the reason becomes clear. God is telling Ezekiel to first feed on the word, then speak the word. Ezekiel would be given challenging messages to share, but before he could effectively share God's message, he needed to know the God who was speaking. He needed to know and trust his character, his plan for humanity, his justice. And it wasn't just a quick snack before bed; he ate his fill, chewed on it, digested it.

I love that it tasted 'as sweet as honey'. We can all empathise with Mary Poppins when she sang 'A Spoonful of Sugar' – we all find unpalatable things easier to swallow if there is something to sweeten them! Many of the messages Ezekiel was to be given were unpalatable. He needed the sweetness that comes from knowing God to give him the courage to deliver them.

Is your mouth open for all that God wants to reveal this week?

† Holy Spirit, reveal more of your character as I read your word today, that I might be able to speak that word to others.

Tongue: sometimes better held

Read Proverbs 10:19–20

Sin is not ended by multiplying words, but the prudent hold their tongues. The tongue of the righteous is choice silver, but the heart of the wicked is of little value.

(verses 19–20)

We have a phrase we use when someone has said something wrong or foolish, and rather than stop they try to make it better by continuing to speak. We tell them to 'stop digging'! The hole is big enough, so don't make it any worse … Perhaps the writer of this proverb had that same idea in mind. Sin doesn't become any less by our adding words of explanation or excuse!

And similarly, have you ever known anyone stop doing something they enjoy, sinful though it may be, just because of nagging? In fact, don't we see the exact opposite – that the more people nag, the more people tend to dig their heels in. Perhaps they feel judged and condemned, irrespective of the good intentions of the one speaking. Or perhaps I'm just stubborn!

So how can we use our tongues wisely and effectively? Perhaps we should ask first if it is our place to speak. Have we earned the right to speak into a person's life by a history of loving them unconditionally? Do we have credibility in this area of our life or is there a 'plank' in our eye that might stop us seeing the piece of dust in theirs? And are we motivated by a genuine love for them, or by more selfish reasons – to make our life easier by having them stop that annoying habit, for example.

In John 1:17 we read that Jesus came with truth and grace. Perhaps we need to learn that the truth is not ours to use as a big stick, but rather that it should be tempered with grace and spoken in loving humility.

† Lord, teach me to hold my tongue and to demonstrate your unmerited favour while addressing the truth.

For further thought

Reflect on times when good people have spoken truth lovingly into your life. How did it feel? How much easier was it to respond well than if they had come with condemnation in their voices?

Arms: the arm of God

Read Hosea 11:1–4

When Israel was a child, I loved him, and out of Egypt I called my son. But the more they were called, the more they went away from me. They sacrificed to the Baals and they burned incense to images. It was I who taught Ephraim to walk, taking them by the arms; but they did not realise it was I who healed them. I led them with cords of human kindness, with ties of love. To them I was like one who lifts a little child to the cheek, and I bent down to feed them.

(verses 1–4)

We saw yesterday how often we stubbornly resist the well-intentioned words of those trying to save us from ourselves. This is a theme picked up by Hosea as he describes the yearning in God's heart; the frustration of a loving parent whose child fights against healing, resists their kind leading and wriggles free from their loving embrace.

It's a picture we can all relate to, either from our own childhood or as parents. Walking comes with bruised knees and leading comes with stumbles as the child refuses to hold the hand that is there to guide and keep it safe. We read of the Israelites' behaviour with the recurring theme of turning their back on God, of rebellion, and it reminds us of the toddler – and perhaps we wonder why.

Yet when I look at my own life (and I don't need to look back very far!) I find the same pattern of turning away from God when, metaphorically, my own knees get bruised or the way seems harder than I would like. And in response I turn away, become lost and try to do things in my own strength. And yes, I look to my own 'idols' to make my way through.

In those times, let's let Hosea remind us of this most intimate, tender love of a parent. We stumble and graze our knees; we're hurting and confused. Why did Dad let me fall? Then we feel those strong arms swoop down, gather us up and hold us close. We feel his warm breath on our cheek as he kisses away our tears. And moments later, the graze forgotten, we're running off on new adventures.

† Lord, help me to remember that in your love you continue to guide and protect us.

For further thought

When do you need to hold tight to God's hand, and when is it OK to run free? How can you know the difference?

Parts of the body – 2 What to do with them

October

Wednesday 30 October
Hands: for blessing

> **Read Matthew 19:13–15**
>
> *Then people brought little children to Jesus for him to place his hands on them and pray for them. But the disciples rebuked them. Jesus said, 'Let the little children come to me, and do not hinder them, for the kingdom of heaven belongs to such as these.' When he had placed his hands on them, he went on from there.*
>
> (verses 13–15)

A touch. It's a simple thing, but it makes all the difference. A touch says, 'I see you.' Or, 'You're safe, I've got you.'

A touch can change attitudes. Who can forget when, at the height of the AIDS epidemic, when many were looking away and ignoring what was happening to people in hospital beds, Princess Diana touched (hugged, even) a person with the disease. Or the pictures of Mother Theresa touching the 'untouchables'. These loving touches transformed not just the individuals on the receiving end, but the attitudes and approaches that had isolated them.

And of course, it's what we see in Jesus. Touching the leper, hugging Mary and, as we see here, welcoming the children. Loving the ostracised of society, the feared, the misunderstood, the marginalised. Making space, spending time, taking the risk to reputation and personal health.

In my work I have constantly met people who have been displaced, refused access to those who could make a difference and made homeless through war or famine. The very ones who should have been most protected, like the children in this story, were let down and excluded by those in power. Perhaps in the disciples' eyes there were other more important, more deserving, people – adults – who could be trusted with the message. But Jesus has a different set of values, and he laid hands of blessing on the children, saying to all who were watching, 'I see you. You're important to me.'

He says the same to you today.

† Lord Jesus, help us to see those who are marginalised and to reach out in a way that changes attitudes.

For further thought

Children are still often marginalised and pushed aside. Even if you cannot be physically there, how could you ensure that they receive the touch they need?

Thursday 31 October
Legs: for walking

Read 3 John 1:1–4

The elder, to my dear friend Gaius, whom I love in the truth. Dear friend, I pray that you may enjoy good health and that all may go well with you, just as you are progressing spiritually. It gave me great joy when some believers came and testified about your faithfulness to the truth, telling how you continue to walk in it. I have no greater joy than to hear that my children are walking in the truth.

(verses 1–4)

I recently tore a muscle in my calf playing squash. For a few days it was painful to walk, but after a short period, and some exercises from the physio, I was able to walk without pain. However, even though I persisted with the exercises and gave the muscle time to recover, it still took several additional weeks of exercise and treatment before I could play again.

I think that walking in the truth may be like this. Although God promises to walk with us, being a Christian doesn't mean that we won't face injuries and challenges that can affect our walk with Jesus. In fact, along with the promise to be with us, we are promised that we will face trials of many kinds (James 1:2). This is a promise I have yet to see a meme about!

And when those trials come, when we tear that spiritual muscle, I have found that the exercise required to recover is to speak out and rely on the promises of God. At times I have spoken them through gritted teeth as I endured the pain of injustice on behalf of those I have served. But as with any exercise it becomes easier over time. The 'belief muscle' becomes stronger and the healing of the human spirit is able to take place.

Paul praises Gaius for his persistence in walking the road of truth, but it was mutual friends who brought him the news. Who can you speak encouraging words to? And which promises are you exercising to strengthen your walk with Jesus?

† Lord, help me to stand on the truth of your promises, so that my walk with you might be strong.

For further thought

'Religion' literally means 'to re-ligament'. Reflect on how your faith can join things together that have been torn apart, whether it be relationships between friends or between nations.

Parts of the body – 2 What to do with them

October

Friday 1 November
Knees: for praying

Read Acts 9:39–42

Peter sent them all out of the room; then he got down on his knees and prayed. Turning toward the dead woman, he said, 'Tabitha, get up.' She opened her eyes, and seeing Peter she sat up. He took her by the hand and helped her to her feet. Then he called for the believers, especially the widows, and presented her to them alive.

(verses 40–41)

What is it about praying on our knees that makes a difference? Today's reading does not elaborate about why Peter got down on his knees. It doesn't even say how long he was on his knees for, but I can imagine why he was down there. With heightened expectations from the crowd, he had been taken into a house and asked to perform a miracle on Tabitha, now a dead body. I'm sure there was more than a touch of doubt and uncertainty as to what he could do. So he sank to his knees and prayed.

Obviously, we can pray in any position. We can stand, we can sit, we can lie. However, there are times when we are literally brought to our knees in desperation. It means we have nothing and there is not a single thing we can do to bring about a change in the situation. So many times I have surveyed a situation in my work and been brought to my knees with the enormity of the suffering I see and the smallness of *my* – and *our* – ability to bring real change.

Kneeling, then, is a physical demonstration of our surrender and humility before God. As Paul describes in Ephesians 3:12–14, kneeling before the Father is an act of faith and surrender to him, recognising that it is only through faith, and in his strength, that the situation can change. Peter knew there was nothing he could do, but he knew where his strength truly lay. His response was to trust in the sovereign, majestic and all-powerful Father of all creation.

† Heavenly Father, help me to surrender all to you and to trust in the power of your love to guide me through whatever I am facing today.

For further thought

Where is your strength? Is it time to surrender?

Saturday 2 November
Feet: be careful where you tread

Read Proverbs 4:26–27

Give careful thought to the paths for your feet and be steadfast in all your ways. Do not turn to the right or the left; keep your foot from evil.

(verses 26–27)

If you've ever been hiking or walked a difficult path with loose rock or exposed roots, you will know how important it is to be careful when choosing your steps. A misplaced step can result in a twisted ankle or send loose rocks flying down the side of a mountain, potentially causing a hazard for others below. Instead, each step needs to be tested and planted firmly to ensure confidence as you move forward.

This reminds me of Psalm 23, where David describes the role of a shepherd: to go ahead of the sheep, to test the way, to lead safely, and to take the risk of the hidden pothole or the fragile foothold themselves. Only having walked the way first does the shepherd call the sheep to follow. Of course, even then each sheep must watch where it is stepping to make sure it is keeping to the safe footsteps the shepherd has left.

I can only imagine this is what the writer of this proverb was thinking about. As we journey through life, there are many obstacles that can trip us up, divert our attention or create a hazard for others. We need to trust the shepherd that it is the right way, and then we must be diligent to walk in it, being deliberate about focusing on our path.

In truth, there are many distractions that can lead us away from that path, but as we are reminded in Psalm 119:105, his word is a lamp to our feet and a light to our path.

† Holy Spirit, help me to keep in step with you today. Help me to walk with confidence, even if the path is rough.

For further thought

By continuing to apply the word of God to every situation, we can test each step and know that we are in step with his Spirit (Galatians 5:25).

Parts of the body – 2 What to do with them

November

False gods

Notes by **Dafne Plou**

Dafne is a retired social communicator and a women's rights activist who participates in the women's movement in her country, Argentina, where she is a member of the Methodist Church. At her local church, in the suburbs of Buenos Aires, she works in the area of community building and fellowship in liturgy. She has a big family and loves spending time with her ten grandchildren. Dafne has used the NIVUK for these notes.

Sunday 3 November
What is a false god?

Read Deuteronomy 4:6–20

What other nation is so great as to have their gods near them the way the LORD our God is near us whenever we pray to him?

(verse 7)

When I read that Moses warned the people of Israel about being persuaded or tempted to adore any kind of idol, be they humans, creatures or even 'the heavenly array', I wonder if he would add 'the cyberspace array' today? An array of bloggers, influencers, YouTubers and popular TikTokers seek to capture our minds and emotions for their own profit. Moses points out that God has 'no form of any kind'. Is it possible to remain faithful to someone we can never see? Can we avoid becoming attracted to fancy characters and their deceitful commitments?

During the pandemic, there were no services at my local church and its doors remained closed for many months. We decided to open a WhatsApp chat, which included everyone from the church who accepted the invitation. Seventy people of various ages and backgrounds signed up, all willing to share, pray and rely on each other during those dark times. A deep bond was built among these participants. We couldn't physically see each other, but we trusted that everyone was paying attention whenever we shared our prayers in need, in fear, in hope, in adoration. We could feel God's presence in that network, shaping our hearts and minds in love, support and understanding, and beating false certainties.

† In times of despair and need, help us, God, to confidently share worries and anxieties in our faith circles and find peace. Amen

Rebuild covenant relationships: false gods in the Old Testament

Read Jeremiah 19:1–11

They have forsaken me and made this a place of foreign gods; they have burned incense in it to gods that neither they nor their ancestors nor the kings of Judah ever knew.

(verse 4)

The people of Israel have lost track and are walking towards disaster. They have offered their souls and hopes to the altars of gods who find satisfaction in bloody sacrifices and dark ceremonies. The Canaanite god, Baal, had attracted the Israelites' worship, as they longed to secure fertility and an abundant harvest in their land. But it seems they didn't mind the harsh consequences of a decision that was dumping them into a stormy ditch, wild and thundery, while they rejected the true God who had liberated them from slavery in Egypt. 'They have forsaken me,' says God, and he sounds revengeful.

Modern humanity seems to have lost track, too. No Baal this time, but endless prosperity, market rules, growing profit, success and economic power seem to have taken his place on new altars, where gruesome sacrifices also happen. Massive fires, huge floods and long droughts are the consequences of a global warming we don't seem to want to stop. It is not only plant and animal life that is suffering, but also the individuals who, like Jeremiah, have warned us of the perils and implications of our behaviour. Quite a few environmental activists around the world have been threatened, beaten up, persecuted and even killed. Have we forsaken God?

Jeremiah rebukes the Israelites because they have broken the ground rules of their relationship with God. Every day God calls us to organise our collective life within the covenant, the decalogue, the jubilee. Are we willing to rebuild our covenant relationship with God?

† Lift up our hearts, God, so that we may follow you in truth and confidence, having regard for your creation, loving our neighbours and thus obeying your rules. Amen

For further thought

Are we willing to talk in our church groups about the ground rules we so often break in our relationships with God? Let's do it now!

False gods

November

Turning to the living God: false gods in the New Testament

Read Acts 14:8–18

'Friends, why are you doing this? We too are only human, like you. We are bringing you good news, telling you to turn from these worthless things to the living God.'

(verse 15)

Paul and Barnabas' consistent faith always led them to move forward with great courage and determination. Many Bible scholars consider that Paul's short speech in Lystra is an example of pre-evangelisation. He wanted to announce Jesus' gospel, but first of all he had to announce God: the only One, the Almighty, the Creator. A living God and a loving God.

It is interesting that in his brief address to this noisy and excited crowd, Paul highlights monotheism, underlying that this one true God surpasses their motionless, lifeless gods because, through the ages, 'he has shown kindness by giving you rain from heaven and crops in their seasons; he provides you with plenty of food and fills your hearts with joy' (verse 17).

'Kindness', 'plenty' and 'joy' are key concepts that describe a living God who is truly present in the world he has created, and who cares affectionately for all. Human beings and all of creation need to be treated with kindness, benignity and even tenderness so they can live a happy, plentiful life. The same happiness and plenty the lame man surely felt when he was healed. Paul had looked directly at this man and perceived his deep certainty in a healing God.

When Paul preaches about God's generosity and big-hearted actions, he assures people, animals and nature that God the Creator offers a plentiful and joyful life for us all. He is a God to follow and accept as supreme ruler of our lives.

† In times of confusion and hardship, when we see people and nature suffering, help us, Lord, to share the good news with action and determination. Guide us to change minds and behaviours, so that we may all fulfil your will. Amen

For further thought

Some people believe that God is an angry, vengeful god, and that they are worthless sinners. Is it possible to challenge that mindset?

False gods

November

Wednesday 6 November
A modern example: celebrity

Read 1 Corinthians 1:18–31

It is because of him that you are in Christ Jesus, who has become for us wisdom from God – that is, our righteousness, holiness and redemption.

(verse 30)

In ancient Corinth the Isthmian Games – a festival of athletic and musical competition – took place during the second and fourth year of each Olympiad, in honour of the Greek god Poseidon. During the Games, dozens of philosophers and teachers came to the city and organised open lectures and debates that attracted many listeners and fans. Some were truly famous and would attract massive audiences. People loved their witty rhetoric and persuasive talents. For these 'wise' men and their followers, Paul's preaching sounded unpolished, coarse, unenlightened and foolish. It seemed that the Christian message would achieve little success in that environment.

What challenges do we face today in declaring the gospel? In a society absorbed by a diversity of media, social networks and virtual settings, where all sorts of images and voices spread convincing messages, Christian teachings can also sound foolish. Paul did not draw back at his time, and Christians should not do so today. We should testify, as Paul did, that Christ Jesus has spoken, and that by his wisdom and doings we will hear his call, know his purpose and feel ready to let him rule and guide our personal and public lives.

As Lesslie Newbigin asserts in his book, *Foolishness to the Greeks*,[1] the church needs to be 'bold' and 'unembarrassed' in its testimony, understanding that conversion is not only a matter of the heart but also of the mind.

† Help us to bear witness to Jesus' truth and love in our society today, dear God, with firm voice, knowing that your wisdom is guiding us. Amen

For further thought

We often avoid sterile debates on religion and beliefs, but we cannot keep silent. How can we help to lead fruitful exchanges?

False gods

November

[1] L. Newbigin, *Foolishness to the Greeks* (Michigan: William B Eerdmans Publishing Co, 1986).

The blessing of worshipping a true God

Read Psalm 40:1–5

He lifted me out of the slimy pit, out of the mud and mire; he set my feet on a rock and gave me a firm place to stand. He put a new song in my mouth, a hymn of praise to our God.

(verses 2–3a)

It is hard to live in a country with an almost one hundred per cent annual inflation rate. It is not only about the country's economy, but also each person's economy. Prices go up almost every day, and workers and employees find it hard to make ends meet. People's standard of living crashes, and people are becoming stressed and living in anguish. How do we tell people that we can stand on Jesus' firm rock in the midst of turmoil?

When pandemic limitations were relaxed, our local congregation decided to hold short coffee gatherings after services so people would be able to meet again, for a brief moment, in a friendly environment. That sickness feels like a distant memory now, but we are facing economic misfortune. The coffee gatherings have been extended and now last longer than the service sometimes!

Why is this? Is it simply a place socialise? Or is it that each of us needs a community of faith that is ready to listen to our worries and dreams; a space where we can share emotions and doubts, even our distress, and always find support, hope, courage and solidarity to overcome difficulties? We don't look to the 'proud' or to false gods, but to our sisters and brothers, who give witness of Jesus' love and care.

As the psalmist proclaims, we are called to sing new songs of praise and to trust in our unmatchable God, who plans wonders for us all.

† Even when we think we have fallen into a profound deepness, your affectionate hand, God, is always ready to assure us that you are by our side, granting us a firm place to stand. Amen

For further thought
Let's read the gospel deeply and nourish our spirituality, so that we may share with others God's saving help.

False gods

November

Dealing with false gods (1)

Read Judges 6:25–32

'If Baal really is a god, he can defend himself when someone breaks down his altar.'

(verse 31b)

It takes courage to defy your father's beliefs and authority, and your townspeople's beliefs and rules, but Gideon did so, knowing that God was by his side. In a time of war, rivalry for the land, and multiple gods and deities struggling to dominate culture and minds, it was imperative to show that his was the only God, the only one who could lead his people with strength and care. Breaking down Baal's altar, and building a stronger and higher one to God, was a sign of moral fortitude and might.

Gideon had already built an altar to God, calling it 'The Lord Is Peace' (verse 24), affirming his great faith and trust in the Lord. In this new position of power, he was set to fight for his people and achieve that peace. He was ready to transform power into energy, and to challenge his people's fragility and fear of the Midianites, to ensure a new and safe land for them, and to lead them to reaffirm their commitment to the one true God.

Are you ready to contend with Baal today? It seems we have easily accepted the domination of the market economy and its moral norms: competitiveness that leads to exclusion, individualism that lacks solidarity, and an unjust concentration of resources and possessions in only a few hands. Christians and faith communities need to challenge these with boldness. We need to build a solid and higher standard that proclaims justice and inclusion, the reconstruction of life in all its dimensions and God's transforming grace.

† Lead us, God, when dealing with injustice, inequalities and discrimination in our society today. Let your Holy Spirit inspire us and renew our commitment to build solidarity, fellowship and life. Amen

For further thought

Is it possible to build a culture of solidarity and renew life values in our society? How? Open this discussion in your church group.

False gods

November

Dealing with false gods (2)

Read 1 Kings 18:20–40
'Answer me, LORD, answer me, so these people will know that you, LORD, are God, and that you are turning their hearts back again.'

(verse 37)

Nowadays it would sound odd to compete with gods and deities, as Elijah did. The impact of a wondrous performance shown live on TV or social networks would only last for a few hours. Even if people loved it, it would soon be replaced by other images – as we have seen with the images of refugees sinking in the Mediterranean, or of once-beautiful and industrious cities destroyed by bombs in current wars, or of woods and nature ruined by fires that could have been prevented. If the proclamation of the gospel is to have a transforming impact on our world today, it has to address the issues of justice and equity with compassion and true concern.

What struck me in this reading is that, in the middle of such a stressful situation, Elijah has time to pray wholeheartedly for the people around him, and for a conversion in their hearts and minds. His action inspires us to consider that we need to proclaim Jesus' teachings in such a way that justice and solidarity grow, prompting decisions for consistent change in the situation of our world today. Violence and domination must not prevail. We need just decisions that become entry points to understanding and peace for all, including God's creation.

Emilio Castro, a Latin American missiologist, once wrote: 'We do not love our neighbour to save ourselves.'[1] As Christians, we are called to be a community that proclaims God's transforming justice and all-embracing love in all situations and places.

† Be with us, dear Jesus, as we get ready to declare your gospel with boldness and commitment in difficult situations. Let our prayers be sustained by your love. Amen

For further thought

Do you pay attention to the many ways people are working for a better world? Spot them today and support them in prayer and solidarity.

[1] E. Castro, *Sent Free* (Geneva: WCC, 1985). p. 43.

Remembering and remembrance

*The following readings are by **John Birch**. You can read his biography on Sunday 3 March. John has used the NIVUK for these notes.*

Sunday 10 November
How God remembers

Read Psalm 103:1–14

As a father has compassion on his children, so the LORD has compassion on those who fear him; for he knows how we are formed, he remembers that we are dust.

(verses 13–14)

I love a good cathedral! It is not the splendour of the building, with the sunlight shining through stained-glass windows, celebrating the people and stories in our Bibles, or even the scale of such an immense building project in its day. It is how its creators aspired to build something worthy of the God they served and worshipped, and to lift to its very steeple each echoing note of praise to be played and sung by choir and congregation.

The cathedral, and this psalm, speak to me of the grandeur of a God who created all things and placed us at the very heart of his plans. A God who walked alongside Adam and Eve. A God who led his people through a wilderness and, despite the frequent stumbling and complaints on such an arduous journey, always remembered his promise to care for them as a loving father would.

My somewhat humbler place of worship speaks to me of a God who is among us as we meet for worship next to a pharmacy and department store, alongside social housing, a car park and the bustle of everyday life. A God who knows us intimately and loves us simply for who we are: his children.

† Loving God, we thank you for accepting and loving us for who we are, and that all are welcome in your family.

I will not forget you

> **Read Isaiah 49:8–18**
>
> *'Can a mother forget the baby at her breast and have no compassion on the child she has borne? Though she may forget, I will not forget you! See, I have engraved you on the palms of my hands.'*
>
> (verses 15–16a)

This poetic prophecy speaks of God's exiled people returning from Babylonia to their home, Zion, but also to a Jerusalem that is now in ruins, its walls reduced to rubble. Fortunately, God's love for this city and its people has not dwindled in their absence. It is as strong as a mother with a child at her breast, and will remain so throughout the process of restoration, which is as much about relationships as walls. The picture Isaiah presents is of the city of Zion proudly wearing her citizens, as a bride might adorn herself with jewels. This is not a God who has forgotten, but a God whose commitment to care and love is never-ending.

As a family, we have known many places as 'home', and the people we lived, worked and worshipped with were an important part of our lives. Moving around the country with careers, we lost touch with many of these friends, other than through the annual Christmas cards and catch-up letters.

But that's not the remembering Isaiah talks about when describing God's enduring and motherly love. Despite the behaviour of the people, God describes them not just as friends, but as family. Their names are not just scribbled into an address book, but engraved on the palms of his hands. God's commitment to remembering goes well beyond ours, and as a people who are just as prone to stumbling on faith's journey as the people we read about in our Bibles, that is something to be treasured in our hearts.

† Thank you, gracious God, that despite our regular stumbling on this journey of faith, you are always there for us, and your love is our strength each day.

For further thought

Remember and pray for all those who have had a positive influence on your life and faith.

Remembering life

Read Ecclesiastes 12:1–7

Remember your Creator in the days of your youth, before the days of trouble come and the years approach when you will say, 'I find no pleasure in them.'

(verse 1)

I confess to having favourite Bible passages committed to memory, which are called to mind when life becomes a struggle. These words are important to my faith because they are affirming, uplifting and healing. I also include familiar hymns and worship songs in my arsenal of defences when life is more of a burden than a joy. Ecclesiastes brings us a familiar phrase, 'There is a time for everything …' (chapter 3), and I know there is much truth in those words as we pass from childhood into adulthood, gaining experiences we can learn from and share with others.

In this passage, the writer takes us back to our early years and to what is often called 'the innocence of youth'. I grew up in a churchgoing family, although faith was never a topic of conversation at home. As a young choirboy I sang hymns, anthems and psalms, and many decades later I can still recall them. But it was as a teenager that those sung words became part of the faith I still have, thanks to a youth fellowship I belonged to. That experience of God's love and grace in my life helped me through tough years of bullying and became the bedrock of a faith that has guided me through the highs and lows of life ever since. So yes, it is good, as the writer says, to remember the early days of our youth, and within them to find the strength to cope with all that has happened since.

† We give thanks for the strength and wisdom to be found within scripture's words.

For further thought

Pray for all those whose mission focus is with children, that they might sow the seeds of faith in young and enquiring minds.

Remembering and remembrance

November

Wednesday 13 November
Remembering God

Read 1 Chronicles 16:8–27

*Give praise to the L*ORD*, proclaim his name; make known among the nations what he has done. Sing to him, sing praise to him; tell of all his wonderful acts.*

(verses 8–9)

Music is a big part of my life, be it singing at the local folk club, leading worship or singing with the small choir I belong to, where each year at Lent we bring out a particular set of choral pieces focusing on Jesus' journey to the cross. The beauty of their words and musical settings is something we look forward to each year, and it certainly focuses thoughts in the weeks leading up to Easter.

Today's passage stresses the importance of remembering all that God has done. For the writer that meant the bigger picture of God being with his people during 'a thousand generations' – from the time of Abraham, through exile and exodus from Egypt, and during the time spent wandering as a nation. But also in the detail of the everyday miracles; that inner strength and healing every day; that love that sees beyond an individual's disobedience to forgive. Remember, rejoice and tell others this good news, the writer tells his readers.

We might not have a thousand generations to look back on, but we do have around eighty generations from the time of Jesus Christ up to today to consider. We can give praise to God that the good news found its way to us through a handful of apostles going out, despite lots of opposition, and by the power of God's Spirit within them sharing what God had done, and through Jesus' death and resurrection, to draw all people back into his family. Good news indeed, and worth proclaiming to every generation and nation!

† We give thanks for all who proclaim your word and share their faith with others.

For further thought

Looking back on your life, can you see God's guiding hand at work in the paths you have taken?

Remembering and remembrance

November

320

Thursday 14 November
Remembered by God

Read Luke 23:32–43

Then he said, 'Jesus, remember me when you come into your kingdom.' Jesus answered him, 'Truly I tell you, today you will be with me in paradise.'

(verses 42–43)

Jesus had many conversations about faith, healing and other matters with people he met on his travels, and we have a selection of them in our Bibles. This one, with a convicted criminal on a nearby cross, stands out because it is so close to the death of Jesus and because of its brevity. Here is a man who knows he is guilty of a crime punishable by death, talking to Jesus, who he knows is innocent and possibly even the longed-for Messiah.

While thinking about that brief conversation, in which Jesus sees a spark of faith in this man's heart large enough to welcome him into fellowship 'in paradise', I'm drawn to think about other encounters Jesus had. Some seem rather challenging, such as the wealthy young man wanting to know what he might physically do to inherit eternal life and, having not received the reply he wanted, going away sad. And others, such as the woman who knew in her heart that if she could just touch Jesus' cloak she might find the healing she desired, who discovered that her mustard seed of faith was sufficient.

What I see in these conversations, however brief, is that Jesus sees through spoken words and actions to the hearts and souls of those he comes across. He recognises where there is enough humility, need and faith to be embraced and welcomed into God's kingdom and family. Some church denominations have boxes to tick before people can be accepted into membership. Jesus looked at hearts and souls, and in them he saw all that he needed to see.

† Gracious God, take our mustard seeds of faith and help them to grow and blossom.

For further thought

Are we sometimes too judgemental in our opinions of others?

Friday 15 November
Peter remembered

Read Matthew 26:69–75

Then Peter remembered the word Jesus had spoken: 'Before the cock crows, you will disown me three times.' And he went outside and wept bitterly.

(verse 75)

It's fair to say that Peter is a disciple many can relate to because he seems similar to the majority of us: often enthusiastic, sometimes fragile, speaking without thinking first, and loyal but occasionally prone to letting down his friends. We can empathise with Peter because, by putting ourselves in his place in facing persecution or worse, we would probably all do the same and let Jesus down. Every denial he utters is a hole Peter digs deeper and eventually falls into, as the cock crows and he remembers those prophetic words of Jesus.

We forget at that moment that Peter had been the bravest of all the disciples, following Jesus as they took him into custody rather than deserting him and running away, as all the others did. Peter's denials, his acknowledgement of what he had done and his subsequent weeping are indeed tragic. This could have meant the end of his calling to become the apostle, the rock on which the church would be built. But Jesus knew this would happen. He knew that within Peter was the courageous heart of someone who would learn through this experience and become the person Jesus knew he could be.

And that's why I can relate to Peter, having been like him and known lots of others who would admit the same. And in our remembrance of Peter we can take comfort from the knowledge of who he became and how God used him. We need to think about ourselves in the same way, for Jesus loves us just as deeply.

† Loving God, grant us the courage to be the people you know we can be.

For further thought
Which individual's stories in the Bible can you best relate to?

Saturday 16 November
In remembrance of me

Read 1 Corinthians 11:23–26

In the same way, after supper he took the cup, saying, 'This cup is the new covenant in my blood; do this, whenever you drink it, in remembrance of me.' For whenever you eat this bread and drink this cup, you proclaim the LORD's death until he comes.

(verses 25–26)

After many decades of receiving the bread and wine at Holy Communion, I now find myself on the other side of the altar rail offering the sacraments, a role I willingly accepted. In doing so, I considered perhaps more deeply than before the importance of this tradition of our faith, handed down to us from the very people who were closest to Jesus – gathered together for one last Passover meal with him before the arrest, trial and crucifixion that would soon follow.

Remembering Jesus, whom they had followed for around three years, would have been relatively straightforward for the disciples considering the impact he'd had on their lives, but what about those who would follow, such as Paul and indeed ourselves, some 2,000 years later?

Paul was concerned that the believers in Corinth were not properly observing Jesus' instruction. Their meetings ended in drunkenness and the divisions among them left some feeling unworthy or ignored. This contrasted with what he had been told of Jesus' request to his disciples, words that were engrained in his heart.

The established Passover meal was designed to remember the exodus and the old covenant, and included the sacrificial slaughter of a lamb. The Lord's Supper is a remembrance of Jesus' once-for-all sacrificial death as our Passover lamb, heralding in a new covenant. Our participation in it is a constant reminder of Jesus' spiritual presence in this act, our daily lives and fellowship, and a way of proclaiming the gospel message until Jesus returns.

† Precious Jesus, may we always be aware of your presence in our lives, and of all that you have done for us.

For further thought
How important is participation in the fellowship of the Lord's Supper to you?

Remembering and remembrance

November

Arts in the Bible (3)

Handicraft

Notes by **Karen Sawrey**

A designer, speaker and award-winning author, Karen has a passion to help an emerging generation discover new ways to connect with God and his life-giving word. For more than twenty-eight years she has engaged people creatively to see and digest information. In 2018 *The Infographic Bible*, published with HarperCollins, became her first book. More recently Karen has worked in the Christian speaking and teaching world with the YouVersion Bible App and RightNow Media. Her heart is to communicate and create products that celebrate diversity, making God's story more accessible for everyone. Karen has used the NLT for these notes.

Sunday 17 November
Master Creator

Read Genesis 1:1–8

In the beginning God created the heavens and the earth. The earth was formless and empty, and darkness covered the deep waters. ... Then God said, 'Let there be light,' and there was light. And God saw that the light was good. Then he separated the light from the darkness. God called the light 'day' and the darkness 'night.' And evening passed and morning came, marking the first day.

(verses 1–3)

I love to savour the first words of a book, as they so often evoke wonder and curiosity. In these first words we are introduced to God as Elohim: supreme, mighty and strong. And the first thing Elohim does with all that power is create!

Like an artist putting the first brushstrokes on a canvas, or an author writing the first words on a blank page, God speaks the world into being. He creates order from the chaos, a world in which life can flourish. And as the pinnacle of his creation, God made us in his creative image.

But he didn't just create us and then observe from a distance. The Bible tells us we were created for intimate connection with God. It is a relationship that invites us to be creative, too; a relationship that gives us a significant role to play in cocreating with him. May that precious invitation flood your whole being today.

† Creator God, may I again hear your invitation to cocreate in making all things new with you today. Elohim, may your order speak to the chaos surrounding us today and bring peace.

Designing clothing for the priests

Read Exodus 28:1–14

'Call for your brother, Aaron, and his sons, Nadab, Abihu, Eleazar, and Ithamar. Set them apart from the rest of the people of Israel so they may minister to me and be my priests. Make sacred garments for Aaron that are glorious and beautiful. Instruct all the skilled craftsmen whom I have filled with the spirit of wisdom. Have them make garments for Aaron that will distinguish him as a priest set apart for my service.'

(verses 1–3)

We saw yesterday how God created order out of chaos and called us into a creative collaboration with him. Tragically, we rejected that invitation. Instead of bringing order out of chaos, as we can see all around us, we have returned that beauty to chaos, including the loving relationship with God he so longed for.

The narrative of Exodus is where God establishes beautiful new places and rhythms in which to reconnect with him. As we see in these verses, this will involve setting apart priests: ambassadors chosen to represent God to the people and the people to God. They will wear garments that are 'beautiful and glorious' – not because the priests are these things, but because they represent a God who is, and who calls us to the same. The amazing thing is that God chooses to cocreate these clothes. He fills the skilled craftsmen with divine wisdom to make bespoke clothes of fine linen with gold, blue, purple and scarlet.

As a designer, colours are important to me, and the choice of this stunning palette is significant. It is a complete contrast to the colour palette of the desert around them and, I imagine, to the clothes the people had previously worn as slaves in Egypt. There's a beautiful exchange – from the clothes they had worn to make bricks into new garments designed to make a relationship with God. And as if to echo that, each priest's robe is embedded with the name of every tribe – a visual call to unity; a continual invitation for community, collaboration and connection between God and one another.

† God, help me to notice your call for connection and community in beautiful ways around me today.

For further thought
Do you feel there are collaborations God is inviting you into today, with him and with others?

Arts in the Bible (3) – Handicraft

November

A special gifting

> **Read Exodus 31:1–11**
>
> *Then the Lord said to Moses, 'Look, I have specifically chosen Bezalel son of Uri, grandson of Hur, of the tribe of Judah. I have filled him with the Spirit of God, giving him great wisdom, ability, and expertise in all kinds of crafts. He is a master craftsman, expert in working with gold, silver, and bronze. He is skilled in engraving and mounting gemstones and in carving wood. He is a master at every craft!'*
>
> (verses 1–5)

As someone who delights in intentional details of design, God spoke powerfully to me through this story during the creation of *The Infographic Bible*. As a team, we were creating a book that was full of intentional design choices and painstaking detail. Reading this story revealed to me more of God's creativity, the intricacies of his design – and it poured courage into my heart and gave me the permission I needed to be attentive to detail. I saw that God didn't just tell them to get any old tent, but instead he directed, with meticulous detail, a stunning place in which to meet. He stipulated colours and materials for the meeting place that reflected the priests' clothes, as a divine colour pallet began to emerge.

I love that in order to create something of excellence it required a collaboration between the wisdom of the Spirit and the human experience and dedication of Bezalel. Cocreating with God is always like that; human gifts and experience magnified by the wisdom and character of God; human tenacity and determination empowered by the Spirit. The result was that even in the wilderness, where hope was deferred and promises were delayed, even in the place where relationship was tumultuous and difficult, where the people had no permanent place to dwell, God cocreates a beautiful place to meet.

Sometimes our lives can seem a bit like a desert. Our relationships with God and others can be a bit tumultuous, with promises yet to be fulfilled. In those places, look out for opportunities to cocreate places of beauty in which to reconnect with God.

† God, may I see your beauty in areas of my life that feel like wilderness today.

For further thought

Are there collaborations God has invited you into that now require endurance to finish? What might it look like to invite Elohim, mighty and strong, to renew your strength today, releasing freshness and wisdom?

A master craftsman

Read 2 Chronicles 2:11–16

'I am sending you a master craftsman named Huram-abi, who is extremely talented. His mother is from the tribe of Dan in Israel, and his father is from Tyre. He is skillful at making things from gold, silver, bronze, and iron, and he also works with stone and wood. He can work with purple, blue, and scarlet cloth and fine linen. He is also an engraver and can follow any design given to him. He will work with your craftsmen and those appointed by my lord David, your father.'

(verses 13–14)

The capital city in the promised land is Jerusalem, 'city of shalom' (a name that means 'wholeness'), and at its heart they plan to build a permanent place in which to meet with God. It was a desire that began with David but had been delayed until Solomon – whose name also derives from 'shalom' – finished the job. Solomon had asked God for wisdom, which, as we remember from yesterday, was key to God's collaboration with people when creating the tabernacle. Spurred on by Solomon's great wealth, the work begins.

In the passage we see a collaboration between God, existing craftsmen and an artisan whose father was not an Israelite. How wonderful that God chose to name Huram-abi, highlighting his family line while honouring his contribution to the most spectacular design project. This is a wonderful example of the way God invites all nations to cocreate and meet with him.

Far surpassing the wilderness meeting tent, the temple's size and opulence really must have been breathtaking, the inside literally lined with gold! And yet I love the echoes of the tabernacle and the priests' clothes – the purple, blue and scarlet cloth, the fine linen. Our God of detail begins to establish the colour palette and choice of material.

This is a secure and magnificent meeting place with God that I still marvel at today. I suspect the people couldn't imagine any better place to connect with God … as we can today.

† Thank you that you are a God of continuity, weaving together different parts of my story with beautiful threads.

For further thought

Are there people outside your community who God may be inviting you to honour or to collaborate with?

Arts in the Bible (3) – Handicraft

November

Thursday 21 November

Opposition when rebuilding the walls of Jerusalem

Read Nehemiah 4:1–23

Then as I looked over the situation, I called together the nobles and the rest of the people and said to them, 'Don't be afraid of the enemy! Remember the LORD, who is great and glorious, and fight for your brothers, your sons, your daughters, your wives, and your homes!'

(verse 14)

Things look bleak in this part of the story. Solomon's glorious, seemingly permanent, temple has been destroyed and the people are in captivity again. And although some people have been allowed back to rebuild, those who had known the original temple wept when they saw its replacement. Adding to that sense of disappointment, the city walls are in ruins, leaving everything vulnerable, and Nehemiah has asked the king for permission and provision to rebuild it.

In our other readings, people with specific skills have been invited to collaborate with God, using their gifts and expertise to create beautiful things to God's design specifications. But building walls of protection is different. Everyone is called on to contribute: goldsmiths, silversmiths, tailors, singers… This is a divine invitation for the people to work together to protect their meeting place with God and their community. They laid down their specific skills for a season to collectively build walls and protect each other. Nehemiah tells us they took turns to build and be on guard.

As the wall grew in height, so the opposition increased. From a few individuals shouting taunts to whole armies threatening violence, it ended with assassination attempts against Nehemiah. But despite all that, with the Spirit-inspired wisdom of Nehemiah, the tenacity of the people and God's design, the wall was finished.

Our identity, the image of God in us and our unity are things that will always be opposed. In Philippians, the apostle Paul says we need 'walls of peace' to protect our hearts in this continual battle.

† God, thank you that we were not created for isolation but for connection with you and each other. We never have to stand and fight alone.

For further thought

What might it look like to invite God and others into your places of opposition? Ask God if there are others who need protective walls and community today.

Arts in the Bible (3) – Handicraft

November

Friday 22 November
Fearfully and wonderfully made: God's handiwork

Read Psalm 139:1–18

You made all the delicate, inner parts of my body and knit me together in my mother's womb. Thank you for making me so wonderfully complex! Your workmanship is marvellous – how well I know it. You watched me as I was being formed in utter seclusion, as I was woven together in the dark of the womb.

(verses 13–15)

In this well-known piece of poetry, David gives us a glimpse of God's part in creating human life. As we might expect from our other readings, his design is detailed, meticulous, and full of intent and wonder. Each person is utterly unique, utterly loved. David himself, a shepherd, king and worshipper, rejoiced in his uniqueness and in the love of the God who had formed him. Far from perfect as a result of his choices, he pioneered creative and authentic ways of connecting with God. A man after God's own heart.

Each of us is wonderfully and intricately designed by Elohim. God, the Master Artisan who wove the complex parts of our being together, producing a person who is completely marvellous. Each and every one of us is a bespoke design, created to uniquely reflect our diverse God and have a relationship with him. This relationship is intended to be eternal. His presence with us began in the womb and, as Jesus dwells in us, as we are filled with the Holy Spirit, that presence continues.

This is the most stunning part: we no longer need a tent or temple in which to meet with God. He has woven an even more wonderful, more glorious place than those: you! And having created the essence of who you are, filled you with the extraordinary potential needed to reflect his glory, you get to cocreate your future with him. Each and every one of us gets to contribute to making all things new around us today.

† God, thank you for sending the Helper. May I know an increase of your presence in me and continually with me today.

For further thought

At which moments in your story have you been aware of God's presence? What could it look like to celebrate those, as David did in this psalm?

Arts in the Bible (3) – Handicraft

November

Lydia the merchant

Read Acts 16:11–15

On the Sabbath we went a little way outside the city to a riverbank, where we thought people would be meeting for prayer, and we sat down to speak with some women who had gathered there. One of them was Lydia from Thyatira, a merchant of expensive purple cloth, who worshiped God. As she listened to us, the LORD opened her heart, and she accepted what Paul was saying. She and her household were baptized, and she asked us to be her guests. 'If you agree that I am a true believer in the LORD,' she said, 'come and stay at my home.' And she urged us until we agreed.

(verses 13–15)

We've seen artisans in our readings who created extraordinary beauty, inspired by God's design. Here we meet Lydia, someone who takes their produce and uses her entrepreneurial gifts as a merchant. However, while we rightly admire people's gifts, the thing that leaves a lasting impression is their love. Lydia worships God without fully knowing him, making her heart soft and responsive. And when she hears the message about Jesus from Paul, she receives the good news and responds lovingly. A non-Jewish woman bravely invites the male disciples into her home, breaking down social barriers to be inclusive, just as Jesus modelled.

We have seen that purple is a common thread (pun intended!); that it is part of God's intentional colour palette. Often signifying royalty, maybe because it was more expensive to produce than gold or maybe because of the rich depth of colour. From priests to tabernacle to temple, and ultimately to the cloak Jesus was mocked with before the cross, purple represents royalty, and Lydia had the privilege of clothing royalty.

Research suggests that purple and blue soothe pain and promote healing, while red stimulates circulation. The Master Designer uses a palette that not only points to him, but also restores our wellbeing.

I wonder what it would look like for me to be more like Lydia – someone who uses my and other people's gifts to reflect Jesus and to work tirelessly to create the most precious thing we can: a soft heart towards God.

† May I see your intentional threading together of my story, God, connecting me to you and others.

For further thought

Which ways of connecting with God bring you life? In which collaborations have you noticed yourself flourishing?

Arts in the Bible (3) – Handicraft

November

A God of surprises

Notes by **Kate Hughes**

Kate worked for the church in Southern Africa for fourteen years. Since her return to the UK she has worked as a freelance book editor, mainly specialising in theology. She lives on a small council estate in Coventry, is involved in her local community and regularly preaches at her local Anglican church. Kate has used the NRSVA for these notes.

Sunday 24 November
A surprise for Sarah

Read Genesis 18:9–15; 21:1–8

The LORD said to Abraham, 'Why did Sarah laugh, and say, "Shall I indeed bear a child, now that I am old?" Is anything too wonderful for the LORD?'

(18:13–14a)

We don't know how old Sarah was, but she obviously considered herself well beyond childbearing age. She played no direct part in entertaining their visitors, but busied herself making bread for them. Afterwards she hovered in the tent, peeping out to see what was going on, near enough to hear what the visitors were saying to her husband. What she heard gave her the giggles. She and Abraham weren't even having sex any more, so how was she going to have a baby? That'll be the day!

Earlier, Abraham's visitors had been referred to as three men, but now one of them takes the lead (verse 10), and in verse 13 he is revealed as 'the Lord'. This baby is going to be so important for the people of Israel that God himself comes to tell them about it and pledges to make it happen. I don't suppose Sarah was ever again surprised by what the Lord came up with. Truly nothing was too wonderful for him.

This week we are looking at how God intervenes in the lives of his people –often in unexpected and surprising ways.

† God of surprises, keep us alert to your unexpected activity in our lives.

A God of surprises

November

331

David: the least likely son

Read 1 Samuel 16:1–13

The Lord does not see as mortals see.

(verse 7)

Samuel knows that the Lord has sent him to anoint one of Jesse's boys and presumes that it will be the eldest. When Eliab is brought before him, he indeed looks every inch the king. But God isn't impressed. One by one, Jesse parades his other sons in front of Samuel in turn, but Samuel keeps shaking his head. 'No, it's not that one... or that one.'

None of Jesse's sons is right, but Samuel trusts the Lord. If God says he is going to anoint a king here today, then the problem is that he is not seeing what the Lord is seeing. Jesse must have another son. It had clearly not even occurred to Jesse that Samuel would be interested in David, who was still young enough to be keeping an eye on the sheep while his father and older brothers went to the sacrifice.

On this occasion, the Lord surprised not only Samuel but also Jesse and all his other sons. God does not see things the way we see them. He has infinitely more knowledge than us; both in terms of what he needs in order to fulfil his plans and of who will be right for the role. So we will repeatedly be surprised by what he does. Like Samuel, we have to trust him.

† God of surprises, help us to expect the unexpected, especially in your choice of leaders for your people.

For further thought

What examples can you think of when God has called unexpected people to lead his church?

A God of surprises

November

332

Tuesday 26 November
Wind, fire and strange languages

Read Acts 2:1–13

And suddenly from heaven there came a sound like the rush of a violent wind, and it filled the entire house where they were sitting.

(verse 2)

Well, that came out of the blue. Jesus had told them to stay in Jerusalem, so that's what they did. They prayed together and did some admin by electing a twelfth man to replace Judas. On the Day of Pentecost they got together as usual and then … A howling gale, flames all over the place, and all of them talking their heads off in languages they never knew they could speak. What on earth was happening? Spending three years with Jesus had been full of surprises, but this topped the lot!

It was a new beginning, a new way of living, and I doubt any of them felt prepared. And then Peter stood up and made a long speech. Peter the fisherman, who was better with a fishing net than with words, and quite often managed to say the wrong thing. But this time they all had the Spirit of God to enable them to do amazing things. Did they ever stop being surprised by God?

We are so familiar with this passage being read on Pentecost Sunday every year that it's easy to forget just how life-changing these events were. The church was a new creation, a new people, a revolutionary group. It is easy to get bogged down in the problems and shortcomings of our denominations and local congregations, and to forget the bigger picture of God's world-changing surprise that was Pentecost.

† God of surprises, help me to experience the power of your Spirit at work in your church and – surprisingly – in me.

For further thought
Where can you see the Spirit at work in your local church and in your own life?

A God of surprises

Nobody was expecting Peter

Read Acts 12:1–17

When he knocked at the outer gate, a maid named Rhoda came to answer. On recognizing Peter's voice, she was so overjoyed that, instead of opening the gate, she ran in and announced that Peter was standing at the gate.

(verses 13–14)

It must have been a terrifying time for the newborn church. The bloodthirsty King Herod had decided that the Christians were a threat – or perhaps that they were upsetting the Jewish authorities by their preaching. He beheaded James Zebedee, then moved against Peter. He couldn't risk upsetting the Jews by executing Peter over Passover, so he put him in prison under a close guard. All the church could do was pray.

And God answered their prayers. He sent a messenger to get Peter out of prison: chains fell off, gates opened and he was invisible to the guards. It was so unexpected – such a surprise – that Peter thought it was all a dream. But standing on his own in a lane outside the prison, he realised he was awake. It wasn't a dream. God had acted. He had answered his people's prayers in a way that went far beyond what they could have expected.

When Peter appeared at the gate of Mary's house, the maid was so surprised to see him that she forgot to do her job and let him in. She left him standing on the doorstep and ran off to tell everybody else he was there. At first they didn't believe her. They couldn't take in the fact that their prayers had been answered by the amazing action of God. All – Peter, Rhoda and the praying church – were dumbfounded by God's great surprise.

† God of surprises, help me to pray for your help in a way that anticipates being surprised by your love, care and generosity.

For further thought

Can you remember a time when you were surprised by the way God answered your prayers? How did you react to his response?

A God of surprises

Thursday 28 November
A sudden lightning flash

Read Acts 9:1–9

Now as he was going along and approaching Damascus, suddenly a light from heaven flashed around him. He fell to the ground and heard a voice saying to him, 'Saul, Saul, why do you persecute me?'

(verses 3–4)

Nobody could have been as surprised by God as Saul was. By his own account in his letter to the Christians in Philippi, he was 'a Hebrew born of Hebrews', a Pharisee of the tribe of Benjamin (Philippians 3:5), a Jew to the core. He hated the Christians, who claimed that the Messiah had come and had been crucified. He hated them so much that he had obtained permission from the high priest to travel to Damascus, arrest them and take them back to Jerusalem to face the Jewish authorities. And then he was totally taken by surprise by God.

God didn't just surprise Saul by throwing him off his horse, striking him blind and making him completely change the direction of his life. Saul, who became Paul, remained surprised for the rest of his life. Surprised that God changed him in spite of the way he had treated his people. Surprised that God called him to spread the good news of Jesus. Surprised that God cared for him, guided him, loved him, rescued him and gave him his Spirit.

Paul lived in a constant state of surprise, and we need to do the same. We need to be constantly surprised that God never stops loving us, in spite of the times we fail him. Surprised that if we are honest about our failures God will always forgive us and guide us to do better. Surprised that God sends people to help us, teach us and journey with us. Surprised that we never need to earn God's love; only to accept it with gratitude and joy.

† God of surprises, help me to never stop being surprised by your love for me and for all your people.

For further thought

Spend time today simply being surprised – amazed, even – by the depth and constancy of God's love for you.

A God of surprises

November

Friday 29 November
In the twinkling of an eye

Read 1 Corinthians 15:51–57

Thanks be to God, who gives us the victory through our LORD Jesus Christ.

(verse 57)

We can be surprised by God's love for us and by his leading, which can give us confidence and peace. Yet we are still surrounded by a world that seems to reject God. A world of wickedness and evil. A world that human beings are destroying through their exploitation and selfishness. We recognise our own selfishness and sin, our own share in the corruption and climate change. It is easy to become overwhelmed by the darkness, to feel helpless and useless.

And yet, in Jesus, God's love faced the darkness and sin of the world and was not deterred by it. The love of God in Jesus never wavered. 'The light shines in the darkness, and the darkness did not overcome it' (John 1:5). Not even death can resist God's love. The disciples did not expect the resurrection; it came as a complete surprise. But Paul, writing to the Christians in Corinth, tells them that God is a God of surprises. His pattern is death and resurrection, darkness and light, rejection and love, sin and victory.

Even though the present state of the world may last many more centuries, we are actually in the last phase of God's plan for his world, when he will spring his final surprise. We have a foretaste of that final victory because Jesus lived, died and rose – and, through it all, loved with the constancy of God. Look forward to God's final surprise, when death and all that is evil will be swallowed up in the victory of love.

† God of surprises, help me to remain steadfast amid the pain and wickedness of the world, trusting in your love and looking forward to your day of victory.

For further thought

How can you display the love of God in the darkness of the world and live in confidence of the final victory?

Saturday 30 November
Terror and amazement

Read Mark 16:1–8

So they went out and fled from the tomb, for terror and amazement had seized them; and they said nothing to anyone, for they were afraid.

(verse 8)

The followers of Jesus were not expecting the resurrection. The women were exhausted by grief; by the trauma of seeing their beloved teacher and friend betrayed, humiliated and murdered; by the guilt and helplessness of the men; by the fact that they were all crowded inside the house, doing nothing on the Sabbath. It was probably a relief to get out of the house and into the fresh early morning air with a job to do. The women's job was to tend to a dead body, giving the final acts of care to someone they loved.

It was only as they came closer to the tomb that they discussed the problem. The tomb was closed by a heavy stone – too heavy for the three of them to roll away. How would they get in? But God's first surprise was that the tomb was already open when they arrived, and the stone had been rolled away. The next surprise was that there was someone in the tomb. Yes, they were expecting a body, but not a shadowy figure in a white robe. What was he doing there. Was he a friend or a foe? His words – 'He has been raised; he is not here' (verse 6) merely added to their confusion.

When something beyond our expectations happens, it often takes time for the truth of it to penetrate our preconceptions. For the three women on that Sunday morning, the last thing they expected was the thing they had most hoped for, and the surprise of it was so shocking that they couldn't quite believe it. Jesus is alive!

† God of surprises, help me to contemplate the glorious surprise of your resurrection and to be surprised by joy at your pattern of death and resurrection in my own life.

For further thought

Can you recognise the pattern of death and resurrection with which God has surprised you in your own life?

Hope at Advent

1 Watching and waiting

Notes by **Liz Carter**

An author and poet living with long-term illness, Liz writes about finding God's treasure in the midst of brokenness. She lives in Shropshire, UK, with her husband Tim, a church leader, and their two children. Liz's first book, *Catching Contentment* (IVP, 2018) explores finding peace when life doesn't work out as we would hope. Her new book, *Valuable* (Good Book Company, 2023), reframes our worth within God's abundant, upside-down love. Liz has used the NIVUK for these notes.

Sunday 1 December
Prepare the way of the Lord

Read Isaiah 40:1–5

A voice of one calling: 'In the wilderness prepare the way for the LORD; make straight in the desert a highway for our God. Every valley shall be raised up, every mountain and hill made low; the rough ground shall become level, the rugged places a plain.'

(verses 3–4)

I'm a last-minute person when it comes to Christmas. I love the lights and the carols, but I'm not very good at preparing. This week we will explore what it means to watch, wait and prepare together, and what it means to wait for God when the waiting time is tough. Today, I invite you to reflect on preparing the way for Jesus as much as on preparing decorations, presents and food. Let's take some time out to sit within the compassion of a God who speaks tender words of comfort to us.

Today's passage paints a vivid picture of an eager longing for God to come among us; a calling out to make smooth the path ahead. It speaks clearly of God dwelling with us in the hard places: the wilderness, the rough ground, the rugged places.

As we make room in our hearts this Advent to prepare for Christ, let us reflect on the staggering truth that he will come, just as he did, just as he always will. He is Emmanuel, God with us. So, as you wrap presents and decorate your tree, think about the rugged places, too, and find him there with you.

† Lord Jesus, I praise you for meeting me in my wilderness. Help me to prepare your way and run forward to encounter you here.

Monday 2 December
Wait in hope

Read Psalm 130:1–8

*I wait for the LORD, my whole being waits, and in his word I put my
hope. I wait for the LORD
more than watchmen wait for the morning, more than watchmen wait
for the morning.
Israel, put your hope in the LORD, for with the LORD is unfailing love.*

(verses 5–7a)

Living with long-term lung disease, I spend a lot of time in hospital
waiting rooms. I try to break up the waiting with my phone, with
magazines, with planning work, but waiting rooms somehow have
a habit of making the waiting seem even starker and longer.

In our world, we do not like waiting. We are taught that we
should have everything as soon as we want it. It's there, at the
click of a button. Waiting is seen as a drain; something to endure,
to wish away. But the kind of waiting the psalmist describes here
is nothing like this. This is a waiting that is bursting at the seams
with yearning and expectancy. His 'whole being' waits with a great
sense of both an immediacy in his longing and a longevity in his
preparedness to wait.

In repeating the line 'more than watchmen wait for the morning',
the poet plaintively expresses his raw need for the presence of
God. City watchmen would wait with great purpose and strength
of will. He knows that God has forgotten his sins, and he longs to
feel the whisper of unfailing love once again.

What about you today? Is your waiting painful? This psalmist
has discovered that God is with him in the waiting; that it is within
the very act of yearning and desire for God that he is reminded of
God's love. As the psalmist reminds you to put your hope in God,
may you take hold of it in this Advent period – even in your desert
of waiting.

† Father, thank you for your unfailing love. Thank you that I can stand before you
    because of what Jesus has done. Help me to yearn for you in my waiting, and to
    find you there with me.

For further thought

What does your waiting room look like? Ask God to meet you there
and to lead you into a new place of peace within your waiting.

Tuesday 3 December
A celebration worth waiting for

Read Isaiah 25:6–9

On this mountain the LORD Almighty will prepare a feast of rich food for all peoples, a banquet of aged wine—the best of meats and the finest of wines … He will swallow up death for ever. The Sovereign LORD will wipe away the tears from all faces.

(verses 6, 8a)

What are you waiting for?

Sometimes it feels as though life is one long wait. We are waiting for better health, a better job, for relationships, for children, for a home. We are waiting for God to come and sort out the difficult things in our lives, and when it feels as though nothing is happening, the wait can be loaded with anxiety and disappointment.

In today's reading we are reminded of what we are ultimately waiting for. This poet writes with rich language of a feast to which we are all invited. It's a feast where we will experience the best of everything, and it's a feast God is preparing for us even now. In John 2, Jesus begins his earthly ministry with a vibrant foretelling of this feast by turning water into the best wine. God loves to turn things upside-down, so instead of giving the guests the mediocre wine that is standard at the end of a party, Jesus brings out the choice stuff in an example of God's extravagant generosity.

This is what we are waiting for: a banquet of such lavish richness, a place where the norms of the world are upended, a place where our tears will be wiped away. It will be the celebration of all the ages, worth all our long waits, consuming all our misery as God takes us to the place of freedom where we will, at last, be home.

Today, as you ponder what you are waiting for, look wider. Look at the bigger picture of what God has in store for you.

† Thank you, Father, that you are a God of lavish generosity. Thank you that you have a banquet in store for me, and that as I wait you wait with me, drying my tears.

For further thought

Read the account of the wedding at Cana in John 2 and ask God to speak into your heart with a reminder of his upside-down generosity.

Wednesday 4 December
Wait for the Lord!

Read Isaiah 40:25–31

*He gives strength to the weary and increases the power of the weak …
But those who hope in the LORD will renew their strength. They will soar
on wings like eagles; they will run and not grow weary, they will walk
and not be faint.*

(verses 29, 31)

I looked at the advert that told me all my problems would be solved if I just joined this fitness programme. I could get strong, and then I would be living my best life at last.

Weakness is seen as something to be avoided in our world. You just have to look at social media or TV to see how strength is exalted. When you are weak – in mind, body or spirit – these messages can become a burden and drag you into a feeling of uselessness.

Scripture turns weakness on its head, though, as with so many other things the world exalts. In 2 Corinthians 12:7–8, Paul talks about his weakness in very relatable terms as a thorn in the flesh, then expresses the upside-down truth that God's power is made perfect in weakness. Paul, of course, lived within the confines of great weakness and suffering.

In our reading today, the prophet Isaiah reminds us that even the youngest and strongest people get worn down, but God never grows weak or weary, and is always working in us to renew our strength. I wonder if the strength Isaiah is referring to here is not so much physical strength as the fortitude and vitality that comes from a place of being rooted and grounded in God – in other words, hoping and waiting on the Lord (verse 31). It is in the very act of waiting on God that we discover this unlikely energy, this reverse power. It's a holy overflowing that causes us to soar with eagles and run forward, contained in God's great and perfect strength.

† Father, thank you that you are the creator of all, and that you never grow weak. As I wait on you today, please speak to me within my weakness and exhaustion.

For further thought

Reflect on whether you have subconsciously taken in unhelpful health and wealth teaching. How can you break out of this narrative?

Hope at Advent – 1 Watching and waiting

December

Thursday 5 December
Wake up! The day is near

Read Romans 13:11–13

And do this, understanding the present time: the hour has already come for you to wake up from your slumber, because our salvation is nearer now than when we first believed. The night is nearly over; the day is almost here.

(verses 11–12a)

Not long ago, my children were at an age when getting out of bed in the morning seemed far too arduous, let alone tidying their rooms. I would knock on their doors, telling them to wake up and sort themselves out. Eventually I remembered what I was like at that age and stopped trying so hard. In our passage today we are reminded to wake up from our slumber. I wonder if God is knocking on our doors, inviting us to tidy our rooms and get ourselves in order.

Paul's letter to the Romans is a theology of salvation, laying out all that Jesus has done for us and urging us to respond to him. This section reminds us that while we are waiting for Jesus to return, we are not called to be passive. We are called to live in the light of God's promises and leave behind the things that cause us to stumble.

As someone who sometimes finds waking and getting up difficult due to disability, I don't always find this analogy an easy one, as sometimes my days are spent in slumber. But in the verse before, Paul reminds us in verse 10 that love is the fulfilment of the law. So it is love we are called to, whatever our situation.

What does it mean, then, to be awake in Christ? How can we tidy our soul rooms? Perhaps it's less about productivity and more about an attitude of heart. As we wait this Advent, let's keep reminding ourselves of the heart of the gospel: the love of God.

† Father, wake me from my slumber and my lethargy. Urge me on towards your light, challenge me to leave behind the things of darkness, and surround me with your love as I wait for you.

For further thought

Read Ephesians 6:10–18 and pray for the Spirit's help as you take up the armour of God to live in the light of Jesus' return.

Friday 6 December
Waiting expectantly

Read 1 Corinthians 1:4–9

Therefore you do not lack any spiritual gift as you eagerly wait for our
LORD Jesus Christ to be revealed. He will also keep you firm to the end,
so that you will be blameless on the day of our LORD Jesus Christ.

(verses 7–8)

It's Christmas Eve, and the little girl is hopping with excitement as she waits by her bedroom window, gazing wide-eyed at the star-studded night sky. Today's passage draws us into this eager, expectant kind of waiting. Paul reminds us that we have been enriched in every way, so we don't have to wait until the end of our waiting period to receive from God. It's in the very act of waiting that we are given spiritual gifts.

American pastor and author Max Lucado refers to this kind of waiting as 'waiting forwardly'.[1] It's the kind of waiting that is heavy with yearning and even moments of joy, just like the little girl on Christmas Eve. It is the kind of waiting where our eyes are lifted from our own situations. Sometimes we find it difficult to wait forwardly because the moment we are in is too painful and we want it to come to an end. At other times we find it difficult to wait forwardly because we are so content in the moment we forget to gaze up at wide-open skies.

Paul knows what it means to wait with pain. Even as he writes this letter he is being persecuted. He has been in jail, he has been shipwrecked and he is suffering with an ailment that keeps him caged in. Yet he knows that the secret to joy and contentment is to look up and look forwards, while digging for the riches God gives in the present moment.

I encourage you to take a moment today to contemplate the skies. Wait both forwardly and eagerly for your King to come.

† Father, thank you for the riches you have given me in Christ. Thank you that you meet me in the waiting. As I look up and away from myself today, open my eyes to a new, joy-filled anticipation.

For further thought

Read Luke 2:36–38 and reflect on Anna's long wait. What could it mean for you to wait with this kind of worshipful expectancy?

[1] M. Lucado, *When Christ Comes* (Nashville: Word Publishing, 1999).

Hope at Advent – 1 Watching and waiting

December

Saturday 7 December
Keep awake! Be ready

Read Matthew 25:1–13

'Later the others also came. "LORD, LORD," they said, "open the door for us!" 'But he replied, "Truly I tell you, I don't know you." 'Therefore keep watch, because you do not know the day or the hour.'

(verses 11–13)

What do you think about last thing at night? I often think about the work I need to do, or about my worries for family and friends. Sometimes I think about a series I'm watching or a video game I'm playing. I don't always give much time to thinking about the most important thing in my life.

The things we give most attention to point to our priorities. In Jesus' words today we are reminded of what it means to prepare ourselves for his coming, and how easy it is to allow the things of this world to become so all-consuming that we forget to prepare. The season of Advent is all about looking forward to Christ's return, but we don't always live as though we believe he will return.

The five young women who had their oil ready were the ones who went on to experience the joy of the feast. It's not that we are excluded from the feast if we are not always perfect Christians – God's grace is much too big for that – but we are called to be ready *within* the constraints of our brokenness.

We are called to wait with purpose as well as with expectancy. When we are waiting for beloved friends to arrive, we prepare a meal and we prepare our homes. We want to welcome them in and make them comfortable. As we are waiting for our beloved Saviour to arrive, then, let's reflect on this: are we preparing that meal? Are we plumping those cushions? Are we flinging wide those doors?

† Lord Jesus, thank you that you are coming back. Help me to prepare my home for you, to spend my thoughts on you, to wait for you with expectant purpose and joyful yearning.

For further thought

Make a list of the things you think about before you go to sleep. How can you make room on your list for Jesus?

Hope at Advent – 1 Watching and waiting

December

344

Hope at Advent

2 Prophets looking ahead

Notes by **Immaculée Hedden**

Immaculée Hedden is from Rwanda. She worked as National Intercession Co-ordinator at African Revival Ministries, then served with YWAM Rwanda before relocating to the UK to work with YWAM England. There she served in reconciliation ministries, on the prayer team and in counselling. It was in England that Immaculée met her husband, Richard, and together they wrote *Under His Mighty Hand*, the story of how she survived the 1994 Genocide. They are currently based in Rwanda with YWAM, serving in its healing and counselling support ministry. Immaculée has used the NIVUK for these notes.

Sunday 8 December
He shall be the one of peace

Read Micah 5:2–5

He will stand and shepherd his flock in the strength of the LORD, in the majesty of the name of the LORD his God. And they will live securely, for then his greatness will reach to the ends of the earth. And he will be our peace.

(verses 4–5a)

Bethlehem means 'house of bread', and Jesus is the bread of life. Can our lives have true meaning without this bread of life? Can a nation have true meaning without Christ? I am grateful that those who brought the gospel brought the Good Shepherd to my country, especially during the days of the East African Revival of the 1930s, which began in Rwanda and spread to Uganda and Kenya. Jesus gives us a peace that the world cannot understand. He has become my peace, even during times of darkness. He is the one to restore my country so it can arise and shine out to the whole world.

In 1946, King Mutara III Rudahigwa dedicated Rwanda to Christ. In the spiritual realms something happened. When a leader performs such an action, the country is opened to the gospel.

Like Israel, a nation may have a good leader, but Jesus is the only solution to bringing God's kingdom into nations. Without godly leadership, no nations will prosper. Christ, the Lion of Judah, is the one who has the word to lead wisely. He is the Good Shepherd who will lose no sheep.

† Pray that every nation will see Jesus as Messiah, the Prince of Peace, and make him their king.

A little child shall lead them

Read Isaiah 11:1–9

The wolf will live with the lamb, the leopard will lie down with the goat, the calf and the lion and the yearling together; and a little child will lead them.

(verse 6)

Symbolically, when we are able to live peacefully with our enemies, this is what Jesus can do in this current age. Prophetically, this is how things will be in the eternal age. There will be no fear of anything in the kingdom of the Messiah, as everyone will live in peace.

In a time of great peril during the 1994 genocide in Rwanda, I was confronted by one of the killers, who told me to get out of my cousin's house. He said he was going to end my life immediately. Placing my faith in Jesus, I said to him, 'Peace be with you.' Outside, I fixed my eyes on him and prayed silently, 'Lord, if this is my time to come to you, receive my spirit. But if not, I pray against the evil at work in this man, that he will not touch my body. In Jesus' name.'

After looking me up and down, he gave my ID card back in a respectful way and left. He said he would be back in an hour, but he never returned. The Prince of Peace was in our midst. The wolf was living with the lamb and a child was leading them. The way things will be in the eternal age was experienced then and there.

The beautiful words from this passage in Isaiah create a yearning in me for the fullness of this place of complete security and peace. Until that day, I proclaim the good news and believe in Jesus' rule to manifest. I love Jesus and all that he has done for me.

† Pray this biblical vision into being in your community and nation, even as you wait for its complete fulfilment on the return of Jesus.

For further thought

What 'wolf' do you need to confront today with the authority of a believer in Christ?

Tuesday 10 December
Joy and gladness

> **Read Isaiah 35:1–10**
>
> *A highway will be there; it will be called the Way of Holiness ... only the redeemed will walk there... They will enter Zion with singing; everlasting joy will crown their heads. Gladness and joy will overtake them, and sorrow and sighing will flee away.*
>
> (verses 8–10)

If we trust in God rather than in people and nations, God will turn the 'desert' into a garden. This is not some eternal-age hope, but a hope for the transformation of the world today. The restoration of our planet's wellbeing is a spiritual one, not a management of climate, environment and economies alone. It may be argued that a spiritual restoration to a trust in God holds the key.

We also read that God promises to those who trust him that he will make a way through the most difficult circumstances. This highway called 'the Way of Holiness' is a highway of purity, obedience and safety. We get to walk this way today with hope in our hearts that we will come to the city of God, where joy and gladness will displace sorrow and suffering forever. Faith in Christ really is a win-win situation.

As we prepare to celebrate the birth of Christ in this season, let us know that Christ has come to us in order that we might come to him. God has come to us, and day by day he makes it possible for us to walk with him until that last day when we arrive in the heavenly city, when gladness will displace sorrow forever.

† Pray for people to turn to the Lord in reverence and repentance during these days of global challenge, so that our trust in Jesus will make a way through the difficult circumstances our generation faces.

For further thought
What will it take for you to become more joyful in every circumstance you face? List three points of action you can implement this week.

Hope at Advent – 2 Prophets looking ahead

December

Wednesday 11 December
To bring good news

Read Isaiah 61:1–3

The Spirit of the Sovereign Lᴏʀᴅ is on me, because the Lᴏʀᴅ has anointed me to proclaim good news to the poor. He has sent me to bind up the broken-hearted, to proclaim freedom for the captives and release from darkness for the prisoners, to proclaim the year of the Lᴏʀᴅ's favour.

(verses 1–2a)

The means by which we, as God's people, live righteous lives is the Anointed One, the Messiah. But what about our broken hearts, our captivity to the powers of darkness, our grief and loss, our sense of despair? Embodied in the good news that Jesus proclaimed is the solution. The result is that we become oaks of righteousness (verse 3). Jesus not only delivers us from the brokenness and captivity; he also transforms.

Mama Lambert lost her family members during the 1994 genocide in Rwanda. Understandably, she suffered deep trauma from her loss and from the appalling violence and cruelty she witnessed. After the country was liberated from the genocidaires, she went to a meeting held by an organisation called Solace Ministries. Jean Gakwandi, the leader of that organisation, prayed for her.

In *For Those Who Do Not Believe in Miracles*, she writes: 'I'd been unable to sleep since the genocide. The stifling fear of the murderers held me tightly in its grip. I constantly saw the images of my children before me, while the terrible screaming and desperate voices of murdered victims penetrated deep into my being. Jean laid his hands on my head and prayed passionately for me.'[1]

That night she slept through until morning. For Mama Lambert this was a miracle. She continued to recover, and later went on to lead the counselling department of Solace. She has helped hundreds of women who experienced sexual abuse and rape during the genocide. She is an oak of righteousness, planted for the display of the Lord's splendour in her generation.

† Pray for the hearts of the broken-hearted around the world to be bound up through the proclaiming of the good news, through the anointed ministry of his people today.

For further thought

How can you be used by the Lord to minister this good news to those around you during this season of your life?

[1] Mama Lambert, *For Those Who Do Not Believe in Miracles* (Oisterwijk: Wolf Legal Publishers, 2015) p. 134.

Hope at Advent – 2 Prophets looking ahead

December

Thursday 12 December
The Lord is in your midst

Read Zephaniah 3:14–20

The LORD, the King of Israel, is with you; never again will you fear any harm.

(verse 15b)

Zephaniah prophesied in the final decades of the kingdom of Judah, during the reign of King Josiah. His great-great-grandfather was King Hezekiah, which means he is not only a prophet but could also have been a king.

Today's scripture, from the third section of Zephaniah, focuses on the hope that remains on the other side of judgement for Judah and Jerusalem. God's justice becomes a fire that consumes all evil in the land. This burning fire of divine judgement is not aimed at destroying people; rather its purpose is to purify. The prophet looks ahead to a time when the people of God will no longer fear any harm (verse 15) and will restore their fortune before their very eyes (verse 20).

As human beings, we are wired to remember. But *how* do we remember? Do we remember with bitterness, anger or revenge? Or do we allow the Holy Spirit to transform us, so that, with a heart of forgiveness, we remember without revenge? To no longer fear any harm means that trust has been restored. We trust wholeheartedly in the goodness of the Lord, but trust between human beings when trust was shattered is another, often complex matter. My beautiful people of Rwanda know this all too well. The people of Rwanda, as elsewhere, need to know that the Lord is with them; that he takes great delight in them and rejoices over them with singing.

† Pray for those whose trust has been shattered in these fragile days, so they can trust in the Lord and perhaps even rebuild trust with the people who hurt them.

For further thought
If trust is like a bridge, what will help to build a bridge with those who have hurt you?

A new covenant

> **Read Jeremiah 31:31–34**
>
> *'This is the covenant that I will make with the people of Israel after that time,' declares the LORD. 'I will put my law in their minds and write it on their hearts. I will be their God, and they will be my people.'*
>
> (verse 33)

The prophet Jeremiah looks ahead to the shift of God's covenant with his people from externals to internals. Through our confession that Jesus is Lord, and that God raised him from the dead, we enter the salvation that was prepared for us from the beginning of time. Through the power of the Holy Spirit, God's law is placed in our heart and minds. This is how we know the way to live as God intends.

For many of us, this presents a big challenge. When we cry out, 'Create in me a clean heart, O God, that I might serve you,' he does not disappoint. This relationship with Jesus leads to the regeneration of our inner beings. Rules and laws are there, but we are being led by the Spirit, and thereby becoming mature sons and daughters of God in our generation.

The Old Covenant was a demanding covenant. The Israelites responded, 'Yes, we do,' but then they were unable to fulfil the law. The same is true for every human being, including us, when we don't have Christ. Only the Lord Jesus was perfect and without sin. That is why, in the New Covenant, we have received the one who will help us to fulfil it, by his grace. What an amazing God. We have Christ in us, who is the hope of glory. We have as a teacher the one who forgives our sins and remembers them no more.

† Pray that the new covenant written on the hearts of God's people will flourish around the world.

For further thought

Are you living in the reality of the salvation Jesus brings internally, or are you still allowing laws and externals to govern your life?

Saturday 14 December
Salvation is at hand

Read Psalm 85:8–13

Surely his salvation is near those who fear him, that his glory may dwell in our land. Love and faithfulness meet together; righteousness and peace kiss each other.

(verses 9–10)

Where else can you find the reality of this scripture, except in the love of Christ? Jesus is the only one who is able to reconcile people so that former enemies can meet each other and be friends. The old is gone. Where there was hatred, there is love and compassion. Forgiveness freely received from God is freely given. What an amazing God we serve. What is stopping us from freely releasing forgiveness to someone who has offended us?

The ministry of Christian Action for Reconciliation and Social Assistance (CARSA) in Rwanda brings together perpetrators and victims, especially in rural areas where they must continue to live in close proximity. I have heard incredible testimonies from CARSA. One man had killed a neighbour's family member and spent time in prison for the crime. After he was released, he was filled with fear that a Tutsi would take revenge on him. He didn't want to live. He stopped believing that he could ever flourish or contribute something good to society.

When he came to understand the cleansing power of the blood of Jesus and the heart regeneration involved in being born again, he realised this was a lie. Through the mediation of CARSA, there has even been reconciliation with the neighbour. The victim was given a cow through a government scheme, and when the first calf was born she gave it to the perpetrator. They now help to farm each other's land. They support each other as friends and good neighbours.

That is the power of forgiveness and a shining example of the application of this scripture. Salvation is truly at hand.

† Pray for true reconciliation to happen in places affected by war and conflict.

For further thought

How can your divided relationships with family members, neighbours or enemies be reconciled?

Hope at Advent – 2 Prophets looking ahead

December

Hope at Advent

3 John the Baptist

Notes by **Ellie Hart**

Ellie Hart is a Bible teacher, writer, artist and the author of *Postcards of Hope* (BRF, 2018). She is passionate about reading the Bible in community, understanding it well and allowing it to change hearts and lives. She is especially enthusiastic about helping people read and reflect on narrative in scripture. After ten years in overseas missions she now lives in Derby, England, with her husband, Andrew, three children and a disobedient but loveable brown dog. Ellie has used the NRSVA for these notes.

Sunday 15 December
God invades the ordinary

Read Luke 1:5–17

Then there appeared to him an angel of the Lord … When Zechariah saw him, he was terrified; and fear overwhelmed him. But the angel said to him, 'Do not be afraid, Zechariah, for your prayer has been heard. Your wife Elizabeth will bear you a son, and you will name him John. You will have joy and gladness, and many will rejoice at his birth.'

(verses 11–14)

It was just another day at the office. Zechariah was in the temple, as his family's turn had come up on the rota. He was feeling the honour, but maybe not expecting much. Things had been pretty quiet for the last 400 years and perhaps God had forgotten his people. Holding on to God's promise – that one day he would remember them and send someone who would change everything – Zechariah (whose name means 'God remembers') continued to watch, wait and hope.

Old, righteous and childless, Zechariah chose to burn the incense while others waited outside. He carefully and prayerfully followed the plan … and was interrupted! God invaded Zechariah's act of doing what was in front of him with an extraordinary message of good news. Good news for the couple desperate for a child, and good news for a world desperate for a saviour. The silence had ended!

As we get caught up in the busyness of our preparations to celebrate – as children write lists and Christmas lights twinkle out their defiant protest against the darkness – let's leave space for God to invade our ordinary.

† Lord, thank you that you remember us. Help us, in the middle of this season, to remember you.

Monday 16 December
Zechariah asks for a sign

Read Luke 1:18–24

Zechariah said to the angel, 'How will I know that this is so? For I am an old man, and my wife is getting on in years.' The angel replied, 'I am Gabriel. I stand in the presence of God, and I have been sent to speak to you and to bring you this good news. But now, because you did not believe my words, which will be fulfilled in their time, you will become mute, unable to speak, until the day these things occur.'

(verses 18–20)

There is something terribly comical about this scene, isn't there? The only thing we know about Gabriel from Luke's account is that the angel is terrifying, because Zechariah was 'overwhelmed' (verse 12) with fear. The last time we hear of Gabriel showing up was with Daniel (Daniel 8) – and he was terrified too! So we can be clear that his appearance is not small and unassuming.

The incense altar was just in front of the curtain to the Holy of Holies, and I imagine the space to the side of it was pretty much filled with the presence of this creature. And then when he spoke, it's clear that he knew exactly who Zechariah was. He went straight for the heart when he told him that his years of prayer had been heard, and that Elizabeth would have a son. So when Zechariah asks, 'How will I know?' it's not entirely surprising that Gabriel seems a bit put out. If a terrifying angel who knows your name, your wife's name and your greatest need isn't quite enough of a sign for you, then you have to wonder what it would take!

Although I do smile a little at Zechariah's request for further proof, I wonder if we too fail to see the miraculous in front of our noses at times. Maybe we're so focused on our own problems and concerns that we forget what our God is capable of doing.

And isn't it beautiful that even though his faith fail leads to nine months of charades and writing things down, Zechariah and Elizabeth still get their miracle: a baby on the way?

† Lord, help us to see your hand at work in our lives today and to be aware of the miraculous under our noses.

For further thought

This is a story of prayer that was answered; not at the last minute, but several years after the last minute had passed. So keep praying!

What's in a name?

> **Read Luke 1:57–66**
>
> *Now the time came for Elizabeth to give birth, and she bore a son. Her neighbours and relatives heard that the Lord had shown his great mercy to her, and they rejoiced with her. On the eighth day they came to circumcise the child, and they were going to name him Zechariah after his father. But his mother said, 'No; he is to be called John.'*
>
> (verses 57–60)

It's a bit of a puzzle isn't it, how Elizabeth knew the name? Zechariah ('God remembers') had been unable to speak since his entertaining encounter with Gabriel, and was still mute when the time came to name the child.

In the months since Zechariah was struck dumb, an amazing miracle had taken place. Elizabeth the old and barren had become pregnant and given birth to a boy. God had taken away her shame at being childless and replaced it with joy.

I suspect that Elizabeth was used to being quiet while her husband did all the talking. At that time, the world was not a friendly place for women who couldn't conceive. Limited scientific understanding laid all the blame for infertility at the door of the woman, and gossip nearly always assumed that 'barrenness' was some sort of judgement from God.

We have no way of knowing how much of the angel's message Zechariah had been able to explain through hand signals and drawings in the dust. I suspect there was a lot that Elizabeth still didn't know. But after years and years of childlessness, she was holding a baby in her arms. And what she knew, without a doubt, was that God was the one who had done this.

So when the moment came, Elizabeth was ready to bear witness to what God had done in her life. The woman who didn't usually speak spoke up. The joyful village wanted to call the baby Zechariah after his father, but this baby was a gift from God – and that would be his name: John.

† Lord, thank you for hearing our prayers. Grant us the courage to stand up among our families and neighbours, to bear witness to what you have done in our lives.

For further thought

When God moves, it can be obvious to us but hidden to others. Sometimes, as Elizabeth does here, we need to speak up and bear witness.

Wednesday 18 December
Preparing the way

Read Luke 1:67–80

'And you, child, will be called the prophet of the Most High; for you will go before the Lord to prepare his ways, to give knowledge of salvation to his people by the forgiveness of their sins. By the tender mercy of our God, the dawn from on high will break upon us, to give light to those who sit in darkness and in the shadow of death, to guide our feet into the way of peace.'

(verses 76–79)

It's only a week until Christmas day! I suspect that most of you reading this will already be making preparations. Some of us are readying our homes to receive guests, with friends and family visiting or even staying over. There will be rooms to clean, food to cook, gifts to wrap, airbeds to inflate and spare towels to unearth from the back of the cupboard. In our house someone will be giving up their bed for grandparents, extra chairs will be found, and we'll be hunting out the lever that makes the table bigger. We will all be cleaning up and making room.

John was sent to prepare the way for Jesus. Not to roll out a red carpet, book hotel rooms or plan an itinerary, but to prepare the hearts of the people of Israel to receive their King.

In today's reading, Zechariah (finally released from his nine months of silence) suddenly and exuberantly prophesies. His message? That this baby would prepare the way for a King. How? By calling the people to repent and by breaking open a well of forgiveness that would be like a stream in a desert.

So it seems that, as part of these preparations, John was sent to do some cleaning. Israel needed to get its house in order. The King they had been waiting for was on his way.

As we anticipate the birth of Jesus, perhaps it's a good time to wash our hands and feet again in his forgiveness … and to make some room.

† Lord, we bring our hearts to you today. Help us to make room for you, even in the busyness of this week.

For further thought

As the nights become longer in the northern hemisphere, let's remember to pray for those who remain in spiritual darkness, that light would dawn in their lives.

Hope at Advent – 3 John the Baptist

December

Thursday 19 December
A sense of urgency

Read Luke 3:9–14

'Even now the axe is lying at the root of the trees; every tree therefore that does not bear good fruit is cut down and thrown into the fire.' And the crowds asked him, 'What then should we do?' In reply he said to them, 'Whoever has two coats must share with anyone who has none; and whoever has food must do likewise.'

(verses 9–11)

John's message may seem a bit dramatic, harsh even, to our ears. It shouts out like the red light at the crossroads or a screaming fire alarm: *This is important! It needs your attention right now!* Like the prophets of old, John has a message that is right up to date and requires not just thought but action on the part of the listeners.

I wonder how many people wrote John off as being overexcited. I wonder how many were too busy with family life or with the demands of work to stop and pay attention. I wonder how many simply failed to notice this world-changing moment because they were caught up with other things.

I think we all yearn to be fruitful. The point of an apple tree is to produce apples, and I desperately want to do whatever it is I am designed to do; to fulfil my purpose. But we all have different ideas about what fruitfulness looks like. Is it earning enough to feed our families, leading enough people to the Lord or preaching sermons that are remembered forever?

As far as John is concerned, fruitfulness is simply about sharing with those in need. Like many of the prophets who went before him (take a look at Amos or Micah), the gauge John uses to measure the spiritual health of the nation is the way they treat the poor. His answer is very simple: if you have more than you need, share it with someone who has nothing.

† Lord, help us to notice those who don't have what they need. Thank you for the generosity of your provision. Help us to be ready to share that blessing with those in need.

For further thought

Can you give something to someone who has less than you today?

Friday 20 December
A crisis of faith

Read Matthew 11:2–15

When John heard in prison what the Messiah was doing, he sent word by his disciples and said to him, 'Are you the one who is to come, or are we to wait for another?' Jesus answered them, 'Go and tell John what you hear and see: the blind receive their sight, the lame walk, the lepers are cleansed, the deaf hear, the dead are raised, and the poor have good news brought to them. And blessed is anyone who takes no offence at me.'

(verses 2–6)

In the last few chapters we have read about healing after healing. And it seems that John – now in prison for speaking out against Herod Antipas – has heard rumours about what is going on. Word has got around.

And then something strange happens. John, who has spent his whole life pleading with people to prepare themselves for the 'one who will come after me', has a crisis of faith. Is Jesus really the one?

John was there in that incredible moment when the heavens opened and the Holy Spirit descended. He witnessed the Father's 'This is my son' declaration. But in this moment of darkness, the wilderness man's faith gives way, and he asks, 'Are you the one?' Jesus answers; not with a theological statement or a rebuke, but by sending John's followers back to him with instructions to bear witness to what they have seen.

Jesus' message rings with the words of Isaiah 35:5–6: 'Then the eyes of the blind shall be opened, and the ears of the deaf unstopped; then the lame man shall leap like a deer.' And then, as we're supposed to, we hear the echo of other words from that chapter: 'Be strong, do not fear! Here is your God … He will come and save you … For waters shall break forth in the wilderness, and streams in the desert.' There is no doubt at all that Jesus is the one who was promised in Isaiah; the one who was sent to save the people; the one who John announced in the desert. Jesus really is the One!

† Jesus, thank you that you are the One sent to save us. Thank you that you have the power to make water break out, even in desert places. We welcome you into our lives.

For further thought

It's easy to have a faith collapse when things go wrong. I draw so much comfort from Jesus' reaction here. He doesn't rebuke John for his doubts, but instead pierces his darkness with hope.

Hope at Advent – 3 John the Baptist

December

357

Saturday 21 December
On moving the sofa

Read Acts 19:1–7

[Paul] came to Ephesus, where he found some disciples. He said to them, 'Did you receive the Holy Spirit when you became believers?' They replied, 'No, we have not even heard that there is a Holy Spirit.' Then he said, 'Into what then were you baptised?' They answered, 'Into John's baptism.' Paul said, 'John baptised with the baptism of repentance, telling the people to believe in the one who was to come after him, that is, in Jesus.' On hearing this, they were baptised in the name of the LORD Jesus.

(verses 1–5)

Good news spreads! Ephesus is about 1,100 miles from Galilee. On foot that's about a two-month journey. It's a long way. And in a time when people mostly walked (rather than getting in a car or writing an email), it makes this story a bit more surprising. Years and years after John's death, the apostle Paul arrives in Ephesus on his third missionary journey. To his surprise, he finds believers there who tell him they have been baptised according to the teaching of John.

Last week I decided to rearrange our living room. We wanted to live a bit differently, so I moved a few chairs around and all was looking good. Then I tried to move the sofa. Could I move it? Not even an inch! The thing is clearly made of rocks! However hard I tried, I simply couldn't budge it! In the end I had to enlist the help of three other members of my family. Together, we managed to shift it.

These faithful believers have repented. They have chosen to live a different life and their hearts are ready for the kingdom. But there's still a problem. They're trying to live that life by themselves.

When Jesus died, he earned our forgiveness. When he rose, he brought us new life. And when he ascended to the right hand of the Father, he sent the Spirit to help us. Living with only part of that – the repent-and-try-hard-to-be-better bit – is impossible. We need the power of the Spirit to make it possible.

† Lord, thank you for your power to move the immovable. Please send your Holy Spirit to empower us to live as you have called us to live.

For further thought

Is there a 'sofa' in your life that needs moving? Perhaps you have tried in your own strength to get rid of it. We cannot shift strongholds by ourselves, so ask the Holy Spirit for some help today.

Christmas with Luke

1 Mary's gift to the world

Notes by **Lucy Rycroft**

Lucy is founder of The Hope-Filled Family (thehopefilledfamily.com), a blog that supports Christian parents and adopters. You can also find her on Instagram (@thehopefilledfamily), where she offers regular encouragement. A former teacher and lecturer, Lucy now focuses on full-time blogging and writing, and is the author of *Redeeming Advent* (Gilead, 2019) and *Deborah and Jael* (Onwards and Upwards, 2020) for children. Lucy lives in York, England, with her husband, four children and a crazy cockapoo called Monty. Lucy has used the NIVUK for these notes.

Sunday 22 December
Here I am

Read Luke 1:26–38

'I am the Lord's servant,' Mary answered. 'May your word to me be fulfilled.'

(verse 38a)

This is a passage so familiar that every Christmas I find myself scrunching my face up in contemplation, trying to imagine how Mary might have felt during this extraordinary encounter.

It is easy to gloss over such well-worn words – but here is a meeting, quite literally, of heaven and earth. A heavenly angel descending to earth. The heavenly Holy Spirit entering an earthly womb. The promise of a Messiah whose origins are both heaven and earth, making him the only one who is able to bridge heaven and earth's gap for good.

Most of us will never have such an experience here on earth. God tends to get our attention not through angels but through quiet whispers, written words and the prompts of others. It is easy to ignore these less-dramatic communications, yet Mary's story demonstrates that a response is always needed, whichever way the call comes. We can ignore God today, but we cannot run away from him forever.

Just as Mary said 'yes' to that life-changing call, we can say 'yes' to the Son she was invited to bear. Just as Mary trusted that God's plans were greater than hers, we can lay aside our own goals and say 'yes' to God's.

† Lord, please give me more of Mary's humility and the faith to trust in your sovereign plan, so that I'll say 'yes' more often. Amen

Monday 23 December
Mary and Elizabeth

Read Luke 1:39–45

The baby leaped in her womb, and Elizabeth was filled with the Holy Spirit.

(verse 41)

When Mary visits Elizabeth, two key things happen. Firstly, Elizabeth's baby (John the Baptist) leaps in her womb as he recognises Jesus. John has already been filled with the Holy Spirit (verse 15), so perhaps it should come as no surprise that the Spirit recognises the Son! John will spend his adult life pointing people to Jesus and baptising those who join him in recognising Christ's deity.

Secondly, Elizabeth is filled with the Holy Spirit (verse 41). It is easy to overlook this as a common occurrence for modern-day Christians. But we must remember that, until the day of Pentecost, the Holy Spirit was only given to selected individuals at particular moments.

So notice this: John is filled with the Holy Spirit from birth and his mother is filled with the Holy Spirit during pregnancy, but his father Zechariah isn't filled with the Holy Spirit until several days after John's birth (verse 67). God chooses a tiny baby and an elderly woman to receive the Holy Spirit before a priest. He truly does use the weak things of the world to shame the strong (1 Corinthians 1:27).

What impact does the Holy Spirit have on Elizabeth? First, she is filled with faith. When others might have poured ridicule or shame on Mary, Elizabeth immediately recognises this strange turn of events as God's blessing (verse 42). Next, she is filled with humility and joy (verses 43–44), equally humbled and delighted by Mary's visit. Finally, Elizabeth is filled with a spirit of encouragement as she blesses Mary for answering God's call.

† Holy Spirit, fill me with faith, humility, joy and encouragement, just as you filled Elizabeth. May I be the blessing to others that she was to Mary. Amen

For further thought

Which of these four areas (faith, humility, joy or encouragement) do you need most from the Holy Spirit right now?

Christmas with Luke – 1 Mary's gift to the world

December

360

Tuesday 24 December
My spirit rejoices

Read Luke 1:46–56

'From now on all generations will call me blessed, for the Mighty One has done great things for me – holy is his name.'

(verses 48b–49)

If I had received the call Mary did, I don't know that I would have responded likewise. I'm fairly certain I would have allowed pride to take root, relying more on my own perceived holiness than on God's actual holiness. But God did not choose just anyone to bear his Son. Mary has already declared her state as a servant, and her hymn of praise in today's passage confirms her humble attitude.

Notice how she returns all the glory to God. Elizabeth has just honoured Mary, and now Mary shifts that honour back to where it belongs: 'holy is his name' (verse 49). Second, Mary demonstrates a remarkable sense of perspective in her song of praise. Given that she would soon be returning to her hometown to face scrutiny, shame and gossip, Mary is somehow able to find peace through an eternal perspective. She understands that this child she is carrying will change the whole of human history.

Finally, Mary connects history with the future, in her beautiful words that echo Hannah's song of praise (1 Samuel 2:1–10) and several psalms, and also pre-empt the Beatitudes that her unborn son will one day preach.

Mary's hymn is not only a literary masterpiece, but a wonderful showcase of her relationship with God. In it, we see her humility, her awareness of God's plan throughout history and her solid understanding of the scriptures. Oh, that we might elevate God the way Mary does!

† Sovereign Lord, you are indeed holy. You are awesome in power and there is no one above you. Train my heart and mind to honour you in everything I think, say and do. Amen

For further thought

Mary's humble submission is a far cry from the 'me first' culture of the twenty-first century. How does her example challenge you personally?

Christmas with Luke – 1 Mary's gift to the world

Wednesday 25 December
And Mary gave birth

Read Luke 2:1–7

While they were there, the time came for the baby to be born, and she gave birth to her firstborn, a son. She wrapped him in cloths and placed him in a manger, because there was no guest room available for them.

(verses 6–7)

If reading this today has involved sneaking off to a solitary room during the celebrations, waking early for a moment of quiet before the chaos descends, or staying up late to read when others have gone to bed, know that Jesus, too, was born in the margins of other people's celebrations. While Bethlehem was a heaving, noisy mass of families reunited for the census, Jesus was born quietly in basic surroundings.

Right from the start, our Messiah was living on the fringes of society. As a baby and toddler he was a refugee. As a child he was a humble carpenter's son. As an adult he had nowhere to call home, and no possessions other than the clothes he wore.

Jesus' birth also points towards what he would eventually do in bringing Jews and Gentiles to know God. After all, Jesus was only born in Bethlehem because a Roman census ordered his Jewish family to return to their ancestral home. Both the Romans (Gentiles) and Joseph's Davidic ancestry (Jews) were key to providing the location of Jesus' birth.

As we read this familiar passage, we are reminded of how the modest circumstances and geographical location of Jesus' birth point towards his later ministry. We can celebrate Christmas enthusiastically and generously because we know that the story didn't end there. Jesus came to bring us all, Jews and Gentiles, back to God – and as Christians we can bring this celebratory meaning of Christmas into every day of our lives.

† Lord Jesus, thank you for the example you set in birth, life, death and resurrection: to be concerned most of all with God's plan of salvation. Please give us that same focus. Amen

For further thought
Intentionally pause before one of your celebrations today, or over the coming days, to thank God for sending Jesus.

Thursday 26 December
Good news of great joy

> **Read Luke 2:8–14**
>
> *But the angel said to them, 'Do not be afraid. I bring you good news that will cause great joy for all the people. Today in the town of David a Saviour has been born to you; he is the Messiah, the Lord.'*
>
> (verses 10–11)

There are many grand and glorious ways that God could have announced the sending of his Son, the long-awaited Messiah. But he chose a deliberately humble start, as we saw yesterday, then a deliberately humble group of people to be the first to hear this good news.

Shepherds were very much on the margins of Jewish society. Their unsociable working hours, night shifts and many months spent working away in distant fields meant that they could not easily attend Jewish festivals or rituals; nor would their witness be accepted in a legal court. They were simply not around enough to be reliable.

Yet God seems to place a high value on shepherds. It's how Moses and David began their lives, after all, and Psalm 23 makes a very clear statement about the Lord being our shepherd. Jesus told many parables about shepherds, ultimately declaring that he was 'the good shepherd' (John 10:11), hinting at his deity.

It is fitting, therefore, that a group of shepherds were the first to hear this 'good news' of 'great joy'. Standing starkly in contrast to the arrogant claims of their earthly leader, Caesar Augustus, who placed himself in a god-like role without the ability to truly save his people, the news delivered by the angels is one hundred per cent true, evidenced by a vulnerable baby in a manger. This promised joy is not simply circumstantial happiness, but the everlasting peace of an untainted relationship with God. It is highly personal ('born to *you*'), available to each one of us, and will last forever – far beyond any earthly empire.

† Awesome God, thank you for valuing each one of us, regardless of how others see us. Thank you for loving us so much that you sent Jesus to bring us peace with you. Amen

For further thought

Where are you finding peace and security right now? Be honest before God. Recommit your life into his hands and perfect plans.

Christmas with Luke – 1 Mary's gift to the world

Friday 27 December
Glory to God!

Read Luke 2:15–21
When they had seen him, they spread the word concerning what had been told them about this child, and all who heard it were amazed at what the shepherds said to them. But Mary treasured up all these things and pondered them in her heart.

(verses 17–19)

The shepherds obediently hurry off to Bethlehem to find the Messiah the angels have told them about. And once they have seen him, several things happen.

First, they 'spread the word'. Essentially, they evangelise, telling others what they have seen. Second, those who hear are 'amazed'. This does not necessarily constitute a confession of faith, but it could well be the first step to these others exploring more. Third, Mary is *not* amazed – her shock having come nine been months earlier. But she carefully ponders the shepherds' response to her baby boy, piecing together God's plan in her heart. Finally, the shepherds return to work, 'glorifying and praising God'.

What is happening? The first community of believers has begun. Perhaps we imagine Christianity beginning at Pentecost, at the resurrection or when Jesus chose his disciples, but actually it starts right here. The simple response of the shepherds, Mary and others who have either seen or heard about the Messiah begins a movement that will grow and thrive over the next two millennia and beyond.

This is the start of a new community, a new covenant, a new kingdom. Rising up from within the vast, secular Roman Empire, this new heavenly empire is characterised by humility, service and sacrifice. It offers hope and freedom for those living under an oppressive pagan regime. It models servant leadership in Jesus, as opposed to the self-important leadership of Caesar. And without using military force, persuasion or bribery, this new kingdom will bring God's people back to him.

† Jesus, you came in humility, grace and love, and I praise you as my King. Fill me with these attributes, that I might point others to you as the shepherds did so powerfully. Amen

For further thought

How do you share Jesus with your family, friends, neighbours, colleagues, school run parents or whoever else you encounter during a typical week?

Saturday 28 December
A light to the Gentiles

Read Luke 2:22–35

For my eyes have seen your salvation, which you have prepared in the sight of all nations: a light for revelation to the Gentiles, and the glory of your people Israel.

(verses 30–32)

I think it's fair to say that the patience of the people of God had been tested. A Messiah had been promised, but after several centuries of apparent silence from God, many Israelites had abandoned hope that he would ever come. Instead, they had turned their energies to supporting or opposing the Roman regime, or to fulfilling their own ambitions.

Simeon, however, had not lost his patience. Luke introduces him to us as 'righteous and devout … waiting for the consolation of Israel' (verse 25). Although Simeon's story takes place in the temple, he probably wasn't a priest. (Some contemporary manuscripts suggest that he was, but their reliability is doubtful – and if he'd had priestly credentials Luke would likely have mentioned them here.) Simeon's opportunity to meet the Christ child does not come because of his position, but because of his faith.

The Bible consistently points to a God who prizes internal character over external appearance. Patient, devout Simeon not only receives Jesus into his arms (a physical sign of Israel receiving its Messiah), but also the Holy Spirit, making him the sixth person in the opening chapters of Luke to be filled (after John, Mary, Jesus, Elizabeth and Zechariah) – following centuries of very few anointings.

The propensity of key people being filled with the Holy Spirit around this time is just another sign pointing to the significance of Jesus' birth. Here is Israel's Messiah, no doubt about it. But even more momentous than that, here is 'a light … to the Gentiles'. Jesus has come not just for the Israelites, but for the whole world.

† Father God, thank you that you sent Jesus for us all, regardless of our status here on earth. And thank you that the Holy Spirit is available to all who call on your name. Amen

For further thought

God used an 'outsider' (Simeon) to give us an important prophecy. Do you ever feel like an outsider? Remember that God has important plans for you.

Christmas with Luke – 1 Mary's gift to the world

December

Christmas with Luke

2 Luke continues the Christmas story

The following readings are by **Jan Sutch Pickard**. *You can read her biography on Sunday 4 August. Jan has used the NIVUK for these notes.*

Sunday 29 December
Anna's blessing

Read Luke 2:36–40

There was also a prophet, Anna … She was very old … a widow until she was eighty-four. She never left the temple but worshipped night and day, fasting and praying. Coming up to them at that very moment, she gave thanks to God and spoke about the child to all who were looking forward to the redemption of Jerusalem.

(verses 36–38)

Into the echoing spaces of the temple a woman steps: the sort of 'little old lady' who could easily be overlooked. But we know her name, and Luke's Gospel calls her a prophet. She is someone with a lively awareness of God at work, called to speak truth to power and encouragement to the powerless. Fasting and praying in the temple, Anna has been preparing a long time for this meeting.

I recall many older women like Anna. Each offered a point of stillness in a busy world; a wise, welcoming presence. Jane, a volunteer cathedral guide; Inez, leading a Bible study in her inner-city flat; Jean, reaching beyond a conventional congregation to welcome incomers from different cultures. Runa sat in the pews of her parish church on Sundays, but on Saturdays she stood with an international group called Women in Black in the city centre, protesting against injustice. Freena's cheerful kitchen was a place of good food and good listening. Sally, housebound after living a full life, embraced new ways of 'being the church' and never stopped campaigning for peace with justice.

Having shared her message, Anna disappears into the shadows. The little family leaves the temple and returns to Galilee for a time of learning and growing. They go with Anna's blessing.

† We bless you, God, for those whose quiet presence has helped us to meet you and know your way. We name them in our hearts.

For further thought
How might you be an Anna to those who look lost and bewildered?

Monday 30 December
A child in the temple

Read Luke 2:41–52

After three days they found him in the temple courts, sitting among the teachers, listening to them and asking them questions. Everyone who heard him was amazed at his understanding and his answers. When his parents saw him, they were astonished. His mother said to him, 'Son, why have you treated us like this? Your father and I have been anxiously searching for you.' 'Why were you searching for me?' he asked. 'Didn't you know I had to be in my Father's house?'

(verses 46–49)

For folk in Nazareth, the temple was always there in the background. While religious observance went on year-round in the local synagogue and in each home, their prayers and psalms reminded them of its significance; a looming presence. Every year, many went on pilgrimage to Jerusalem to celebrate Passover there. The family of Joseph and Mary joined in this days-long journey, a community festival full of enjoyment and singing. There, children could be safely lost in the crowd of friends and neighbours.

But the temple wasn't just a focus for celebration once a year. Day by day, served by a hereditary caste of priests, it was a place for sacrifice, reading the scriptures and prayer. It was also a place where the Jewish tradition of studying and teaching the law, and deepening an understanding of faith, went on, with gatherings of theologians and teachers in animated debate. It was probably as noisy, in its own way, as the pilgrim crowds outside.

I know a twelve-year-old who is caught up in the constructive game of *Minecraft* – learning computer skills and different ways of communicating while building virtual cities online with her peers. To her parents it is another world! Likewise, Joseph and Mary, having lost Jesus and found him again in the temple, must have felt excluded by their boy's total engagement in the debate. But he knew that he belonged there and needed what this gathering of scholars offered. Like the Shabbat table at home, like the school in the local synagogue, this was yet another way of learning – of growing up as God's child, growing in grace.

† God, our loving parent, teacher and challenger, we thank you for the many places and ways we can learn about you. The whole world is your house.

For further thought

Jesus asked questions! What questions would you like to ask of God?

Tuesday 31 December
Jesus made fully human

Read Hebrews 2:5–11

'What is mankind that you are mindful of them, a son of man that you care for him? You made them a little lower than the angels; you crowned them with glory and honour and put everything under their feet' … Both the one who makes people holy and those who are made holy are of the same family. So Jesus is not ashamed to call them brothers and sisters.

(verses 6b–8, 11)

The writer of the letter to the Hebrews celebrates that God created human beings 'a little lower than the angels' and also that God, in Jesus, came to share our human lives, our human nature. I won't attempt, in such a small space, to unpack what this passage puts so powerfully. Instead, I'll reflect on the way God's grace was shown in both the child in the temple and in the old woman, Anna.

With Nativity plays fresh in the memory, on this last day of the year – and with angels in the air – here's a question:

How old were the angels?
About five years old, appearing on stage, blinking in bright lights, with
  tinsel halos askew. But how old were those in the story the children
  were telling, the angels that appeared to Mary, to Joseph, then to
  shepherds in the fields? As old as the hills, and as here-and-now as
  human hopes and fears: warriors with flaming swords, not mixed infants
  with mums looking on: so their first words were 'Do not be afraid!'
But how old where they? Who can tell? Angels exist in God's time, not
  according to our clocks and calendars, see eternity in the blink of an eye.
More to the point, how old were hands that held the newborn child, faces
  on which those wide-open eyes focused, voices speaking a blessing?
  Simeon and Anna, having waited so long to see their Lord, sang praises
  and announced salvation. How old were these angels? About the age of
  many who sit in our pews: as old as wisdom, as young as hope.[1]

† Old and young, we are God's children. Alleluia! Jesus is not ashamed to call us sisters and brothers. Alleluia! Now and forever, God is with us. Alleluia!

For further thought

Reflect on a new year about to begin. Are you facing it with fear? Hear again the angel's declaration, God is with you, so do not be afraid.

[1] J. S. Pickard, 'How Old Were The Angels?' from ed. R. Burgess *Hay and Stardust* (Glasgow: Wild Goose Publications (www.ionabooks.com), 2005), p. 21.

IBRA scheme of readings 2025

Promises and resolutions
1 Bad promises
2 Good promises

Letter to the Colossians

Sheep and shepherds

The Gospel of Luke (1)

Living with the Romans
1 At the time of Jesus
2 In the early Church
3 Pilate and his soldiers

Walking with Jesus: Christian life
1 Our example
2 Following the Way
3 Walking through the world with Jesus
4 Opposition
5 The One who goes with us

The Gospel of Luke (2)
1 The events of Holy Week (Luke 22—23)
2 Resurrection (Luke 24)

Trees
1 Rooted close to the source
2 Like a tree

Readings in Joshua
1 Into the Promised Land
2 Living in the land

The Gospel of Luke (3)

Pentecost

Prayer in the letters of the New Testament

Comfort and hope
Readings from Isaiah chapters 40—55

Abundance and want
1 Times of plenty
2 Times of scarcity

The letter to the Hebrews

Professions of faith
2025 will mark the 1700th anniversary of the Council of Nicaea, which produced the Nicene Creed.
1 Recognising Jesus
2 Jesus is Lord

The Gospel of Luke (4)

Encouragement

Without a name
Characters from the Bible who are mentioned but not named

Readings from 1 Samuel

Balance

New settings, new challenges
1 A travelling, wandering race called the People of God
2 A changing Church?

Samaria and the Samaritans

Persistence

Letters to Titus and Jude

Searching for Shalom

Gold
1 The value of gold
2 Better than gold

The character of God: the God who comes

Emmanuel: God with us

IBRA International Fund

IBRA brings together readers from across the globe, and it is your donations and support that make it possible for our international partners to translate, print, publish and distribute the notes to over a hundred thousand people. Thank you.

Are you able to make a donation today?

How your donations make a difference:

£5 can send an English copy of *Fresh from The Word* to any of our international partners

£10 can print 12 copies of *Fresh from The Word* in India

£25 provides 20 copies of *Fresh from The Word* in Nigeria

£50 could fund 1,000 IBRA reading lists for a country that does not currently receive IBRA materials

Our partners are based in ten countries, but the benefit flows over borders to at least thirty-two countries all over the world. Partners work tirelessly to organise the translation, printing and distribution of IBRA Bible study notes and lists in many different languages, from Ewe, Yoruba and Twi to Portuguese, Samoan and Telugu!

Did you know that we print and sell over 5,000 copies of *Fresh from The Word* here in the UK, but our overseas partners produce another 42,000 copies in English and then translate the book you are reading to produce a further 31,000 copies in various local languages? With the reading list also being translated into French and Spanish, then distributed, IBRA currently reaches over 700,000 Christians globally.

Faithfully following the same principles developed in 1882, we continue to guarantee that your donations to the International Fund will support our international brothers and sisters in Christ.

If you would like to make a donation, please use the envelope inserted in this book to send a cheque to International Bible Reading Association, 5–6 Imperial Court, 12 Sovereign Road, Birmingham, B30 3FH or go online to ibraglobal.org and click the 'Donate' button at the top of the page.

A global community following God's Word

Our overseas distribution and international partners enable IBRA readings to be enjoyed all over the world from Spain to Samoa, New Zealand to Cameroon. Each day when you read your copy of *Fresh from The Word* you are joining a global community of people who are also reading the same passages.

Fresh from The Word is read by Nigerians in many states including Lagos, Ogun, Abuja, Kano, Oyum Kaduna, Eno, Ondu Osun and Taraba. IBRA Nigeria's National President Segun Okubadejo observes:

'It makes the Bible become more relevant to their everyday situation and is aiding the development of their spiritual stamina.'

The Fellowship of Professional Workers in India values the shared experience of following *Fresh from The Word*'s daily readings with a world community:

'The uniqueness of the Bible reading is that the entire readership is focusing on a common theme for each day, which is an expression of oneness of the faithful, irrespective of countries and cultures.'

International Bible Reading Association partners and distributors

A worldwide service of Christian Education at work in five continents

HEADQUARTERS
IBRA
5–6 Imperial Court
12 Sovereign Road
Birmingham
B30 3FH
United Kingdom

www.ibraglobal.org

ibra@christianeducation.org.uk

SAMOA
Congregational Christian Church in Samoa
CCCS
PO Box 468
Tamaligi
Apia
Samoa

asst.gsec@cccs.org.ws / lina@cccs.org.ws

Congregational Christian Church in Tokelau
c/o EFKT
Atafu
Tokelau Island

hepuutua@gmail.com

Congregational Christian Church in American Samoa
P.O. BOX 1537
Pago Pago, AS 96799
American Samoa

gensec@efkasonline.org /
nfalealii@efkasonline.org

FIJI
Methodist Bookstore
11 Stewart street
PO Box 354
Suva
Fiji

mbookstorefiji@yahoo.com

Ekalesia Kelisiano Tuvalu Church
Congregations in Suva, Kioa, Lautoka and Labasa
31 Ratu Sukuna Road
Nasese
Suva
Fiji

GHANA
Asempa Publishers
Christian Council of Ghana
PO Box GP 919
Accra
Ghana

gm@asempapublishers.com /
info@asempapublishers.com

NIGERIA
IBRA Nigeria
David Hinderer House
Cathedral Church of St David
Kudeti
PMB 5298 Dugbe
Ibadan
Oyo State
Nigeria

ibndiocese@yahoo.com

SOUTH AFRICA
Faith for Daily Living Foundation
PO Box 3737
Durban 4000
South Africa

ffdl@saol.com

IBRA South Africa
The Rectory
Christchurch
c/o Constantia Main and Parish Roads
Constantia 7806
Western Cape
South Africa

Terry@cchconst.org.za

DEMOCRATIC REPUBLIC OF THE CONGO
Baptist Community of the Congo River
8 Avenue Kalemie
Kinshasa Gombe
B.P. 205 & 397
Kinshasa 1
DR Congo

ecc_cbfc@yahoo.fr

CAMEROON
Redemptive Baptist Church
PO Box 65
Limbe
Fako Division
South West Region
Cameroon

evande777@yahoo.com

INDIA
All India Sunday School Association
House No. 9-131/1, Street No.5
HMT Nagar, Nacharam
Hyderabad
500076
Telangana
India

sundayschoolindia@yahoo.co.in

Fellowship of Professional Workers
Samanvay
Deepthi Chambers, Opp. Nin.
Tarnaka, Vijayapuri
Hyderabad 500 017
Telengana State
India

fellowship2w@gmail.com